DATE DUE

OCT '98			
DEC 8 98			
FEB 1 1 '10			

DEMCO 38-296

Essays in Understanding

1930–1954

Essays in Understanding

1930–1954

HANNAH ARENDT

EDITED BY JEROME KOHN

Harcourt Brace & Company

NEW YORK   SAN DIEGO   LONDON

Contents

Introduction

What is important for me is to understand.

For me, writing is a matter of seeking this

understanding, part of the process of understanding.

    — " 'What Remains? The Language Remains' "

I T IS A curse to live in interesting times." So runs an ancient Chinese saying that Hannah Arendt, during the last eight years of her too short life, would cite as an aside in the midst of discussing the latest domestic disaster or international crisis. She did so wryly or pensively, as if its ironic meaning were transparently clear, neither requiring nor receiving any explanation. Nevertheless, it was difficult not to be struck by something paradoxical, not only in the saying itself but in hearing it from her, for her commitment to human affairs was uncompromisingly serious. She sought to understand the events of "this terrible century" with a passion that for many years has inspired scholars, artists, writers, intellectuals, public figures, and many others who read her work to confront unsentimentally, and without equivocation, the sufferings of "this none too beautiful world," even in "the darkest of times." The quoted words are hers, and it is on account of them that today, in retrospect, the Chinese proverb appears strangely evocative and even emblematic of this intensely thoughtful and private woman.

Hannah Arendt (1906–1975) is known throughout much of the world as a political philosopher, in spite of the fact that, for the most part, she repudiated that title, along with the claims and foundations of political philosophy. It is difficult to say *what* she was. Whereas some commentators have emphasized the sociological and historical aspects of her work, and others its literary and indeed poetic quality, still more have written of her as a political scientist (a label she applied to herself for many years). Later, when fame had come to her and she was asked to describe what she did, she reluctantly, but commodiously referred to it as political "theory" or "thought." She has been hailed, justifiably, as both a liberal wanting change and a conservative desiring stability, and been criticized for harboring an unrealistic yearning for the past or for being a utopian revolutionary. These various characterizations (and far more subtle ones might be adduced) reflect the diverse interests of those who make them, yet they also indicate the genuine perplexity encountered by any impartial reader who attempts to form a judgment of Arendt in terms of traditional academic disciplines or traditional political categories. It may be disconcerting to realize that by nature Arendt was not personally attracted to the political realm, not initially and perhaps not ever: even her striking and mature understanding of political action was due, she said, to the fact that she "looked at it from the outside."

What is beyond doubt, however, is that from first to last she was irresistibly drawn to the activity of understanding, an endless and circular mental activity whose principal significance for her lay in itself rather than in its results. She had plenty of ideas and opinions, to be sure; she made new distinctions, contributed new concepts, and altered old categories of traditional political thought. Those are results, and they have proved to be useful ones. But, although it is unexpected to find a political thinker who is not primarily concerned with solving problems, Arendt's ceaseless ventures in understanding were for her no more "instrumental" than life itself. What is more difficult to grasp is that the activity of understanding afforded her a measure of reconciliation to the world in which she lived. If others came to understand, in her sense of understanding, then she was gratified and made to feel "at home." This does not mean she wanted or thought it possible to hand over her own understanding to anyone else. That would have been sheer nonsense to Arendt, for whom thinking—understanding, endowing an event with meaning—was an engagement with oneself, solitary and private. She led an exemplary life, a life that has been told and will be retold, but ultimately the light shed on the world by her understanding of it is the only way to catch a glimpse of *who* Hannah Arendt was.

Born into a well-established nonreligious German Jewish family near the beginning of the century, she was prodigiously intelligent, bountifully educated, and heir to an old and rich culture which in many ways she embodied. In the 1920s two events, of fundamentally opposed nature, played a crucial role in the development of her thought and character. The first was her initial contact as a student, which was to develop into lifelong attachment, with two great thinkers in the vanguard of existential philosophy: Martin Heidegger and Karl Jaspers. The second event was the consolidation of the National Socialist movement in Germany.

For Arendt, the revolution in philosophy was a turning inward, not in the introspective, psychological sense, but as if her faculty of thinking had been liberated from the systematic rationalizations of the natural and historical worlds inherited from the previous century. She experienced what she called a "philosophic shock": the sheer *wonder* at existence, which is sharply to be distinguished from mere curiosity. From that shock sprang intense self-reflection, or thinking with oneself, which for her would be the hallmark of all genuine philosophizing. Thus, in addition to the content of the thought of Heidegger and Jaspers, there was opened to the youthful Arendt an inner spiritual realm, invisible and immaterial, which she could literally inhabit in solitude.

The opposed movement took place in the outward, apparent world, its radical intention being not to modify but to destroy the structures and institutions of civil association that had devolved through the centuries. She referred to the growth of this politically revolutionary movement as the "shock of reality."

It is not as if Arendt experienced separately the mind's withdrawal from the world in self-reflection and the approach of National Socialism. She was young and not one of the "professional" intellectuals who could leave Germany and in a freer country continue to work much as before in their fields of scholarship. Yet she was appalled by the ease with which some members of the intellectual community chose to swim with, and not against, the swelling tide of Nazism, or chose not to get out of that current altogether. A certain distrust of the tendency of intellectuals to let themselves be swept along by political currents in whatever direction was to remain with her throughout her life.

Arendt once remarked that she was not a "born" writer, meaning that she was not one of "those who from the very beginning of their

lives, from early youth, knew that this was what they wanted to do—
to be a writer or to become an artist." She had become a writer, she
said, by "accident," by the accident of the "extraordinary events of this
century."* She meant that, far from being a matter of choice, she could
not help but attempt to understand and judge totalitarianism. In other
words, it was upon her mind, the activity of which was conditioned by
withdrawal from the world, that, in the late 1920s and early 1930s, a
world in upheaval ineluctably impinged.

It was a world in which, she later said, even before Hitler actually
came to power she "had an awareness of the doom of German Judaism,"
of the end of that "unique phenomenon," the history and culture that
were her own (cf. *Rahel Varnhagen*, xvii). She was thus made aware of
something distinct from the forms of anti-Semitism which for centuries
had afflicted the Jewish people and which they had somehow weathered
and survived. (Later Arendt realized that it was not only the enormity
of the destruction of European Jewry that distinguished Nazi totalitarianism from older forms of persecution, but also that anti-Semitism was
but one aspect of an overall racist ideology.)

The originality of her political thought stems from the fact that what
was phenomenally revealed to her as new, without precedent, and extraordinary was actually going on *now*, in that ordinary world which
previously had been of such little significance in her reflective life. Thus
the political became a reality for her, not only as the arena of "politics"
in which politicians get on with the business of governing, harnessing
power, determining goals, and formulating and implementing the means
to achieve them, but also as the realm in which novelty, for better or
worse, can arise, and the conditions of human freedom, including the
freedom to think, and of human unfreedom are cast. In one way or
another political reality would henceforth orient all her attempts at
understanding—not least when, at the end of her life, her attention
turned to reflective mental activities as the conditions of that understanding.

Arendt once wrote that "the essay as a literary form has a natural affinity
to . . . exercises in political thought as it arises out of the actuality of

* Arendt said this on the occasion of her induction into the National Institute of
Arts and Letters, May 20, 1964.

political incidents." She went on to say, in the preface to *Between Past and Future*, that the unity of those essays "is not the unity of a whole but of a sequence of movements which, as in a musical suite, are written in the same or related keys." Those words partially describe other books of Arendt's as well; *The Origins of Totalitarianism*, *Men in Dark Times*, *Crises of the Republic*, and to a lesser extent *The Human Condition*, *On Revolution*, and *The Life of the Mind*, are works composed—woven and shaped—from essays and lectures that in earlier versions had been printed in journals or delivered in public.

The contents of the present volume have been culled from the scores of her unpublished and uncollected essays and lectures. This is not a book that she ever expressed an interest in seeing published. Its words, but not its structure, are hers. Its organization is for the most part chronological, as will be that of projected volumes drawn from later writings and writings on specifically Jewish themes.

Hannah Arendt left the bulk of her literary estate to the Library of Congress, where it occupies 33.6 linear feet of shelf space, fills more than 90 containers, and consists of approximately 28,000 items. These items include family papers and personal documents; extensive general correspondence with individuals, organizations, universities, publishers; notes, background information, transcripts, reports, and court rulings pertaining to the Eichmann trial; reviews of her book about Eichmann, and newspaper articles and letters relating to the bitter, emotional controversy that book generated; reviews of her other books; manuscript drafts; and, in approximately forty of the containers, handwritten, typewritten, and printed notes, poems, articles, book reviews, speeches, lectures, and essays. The earliest of these writings dates from 1925, the year Arendt was nineteen; the latest, from 1975, the year of her death. The greater part of them are from the period after her emigration to the United States in 1941.

With Arendt's worldwide stature today, virtually everything she wrote can be of interest to the general public as well as to scholars. Moreover, publication of her uncollected and unpublished writings may shed light in the controversy that today continues to be an element in the reception and evaluation of her thought. That element may have been most apparent in the disputes that raged over her account of the trial of the Nazi bureaucrat Adolf Eichmann. The idea that "evil" could be realized in the world through banality or thoughtlessness, the sheer conventionality, of such a man as Eichmann was perceived by many who read *Eichmann in Jerusalem* (and many more who never bothered to) as an assault on their propriety. In some cases the hurt from thirty years ago still smarts.

But the problematic aspect of Arendt's thought did not begin with her report on the banality of evil; nor did it end there. For more than a decade she has been increasingly the focus of scholarly attention, and the critical commentary on her work is striking for the sharp disagreement it contains—not only on the accuracy of her distinctions and judgments (which is to be expected), but also over what she meant by them and how, if at all, they fit together. To take a single but important example: What, exactly, does she mean by political *action*? What in today's world does it refer to? If it is, as she says, the "field of experience" of "freedom," does it follow that social and economic matters are distinct from politics? Is that feasible or even meaningful in the world in which we now live?

Despite the variety and incompatibility of the answers scholars have given to such questions, interest in her work remains undiminished. That Arendt is difficult to interpret is mainly due to her originality as a thinker, and, to a lesser extent, to the fact that she was nourished by classical and European sources often unfamiliar to contemporary readers. Nevertheless, the passionate, independent, poetic quality of her writing and, especially, her recognition that the political events of our times have no historical precedent have added to her reputation as one of the twentieth century's most fecund and compelling thinkers.

The English political theorist Margaret Canovan in *Hannah Arendt: A Reinterpretation of Her Political Thought*, has written a keen and discriminating work, one that is not at all polemical. She states her aim with deceptive simplicity: "to discover and explain what Arendt's political thought is about." Of particular interest is her thesis that, when a full appreciation of what Arendt meant by the "elements of totalitarianism"—the entire array of phenomena so specified—is seen as its ground, Arendt's political thought comes into focus as a whole. She does not mean that Arendt's distinctions and judgments necessarily demand assent, but that they cohere when seen in relation to her fundamental analyses of the conditions from which totalitarianism as a form of government arose. Those conditions, however, were not the *cause* of totalitarian regimes and did not disappear with their fall, and *that*, in a nutshell (as Arendt used to put it), is the crisis of our times. It is *our* crisis, composed of *our* predicaments, and makes Arendt's thought at least as relevant today as during the recent hot and cold global conflicts that threatened us externally.

In Canovan's felicitous words, Arendt's major works "rise like islands out of a partly submerged continent of thought, some of it recorded in obscure articles, some of it only in unpublished writings," and in no case is this of greater consequence than in *The Origins of Totalitarianism*. That strange masterwork—historical, political, philosophical, and full of literary allusions; its tripartite structure and even the meaning of its title often debated; its clear lack of balance in its treatment of Nazism and Bolshevism—has prompted its misapprehension. Canovan claims that when the "submerged" context of totalitarianism is brought to light, the grounds for misunderstanding the book are eliminated, and a new perspective is opened on Arendt's subsequent thought. Perhaps the most important of the several "trajectories" traced by the present volume stretches from the mid-1940s, when the vast project of *The Origins of Totalitarianism* was forming in Arendt's mind, to the years following its publication in 1951. The latter period was one of intense reflection on the book, in part explaining it, in part righting its imbalance as more information on Stalin and the Soviet Union became available, and in part deepening and securing its theoretical foundations.

In addition to casting light on obscure areas of Arendt's thought, publication of her uncollected and unpublished writings should contribute to the interest in her life and character stimulated by Elisabeth Young-Bruehl's richly detailed biography, *Hannah Arendt: For Love of the World*, and by *Correspondence: Hannah Arendt–Karl Jaspers, 1926–1969*. As do those publications, the writings collected here will contribute to an overall judgment of Arendt's work, for, as Wittgenstein once wrote, "the greatness of what someone writes depends on everything else he writes and does."

The chronological order of these ancillary writings should encourage readers to construct in their imaginations an exemplary person, a traveler through crucial events of the twentieth century, thereby to gain perspective on those events, as well as a sense of their unfolding. The acuity of Arendt's vision and the probity—even what at times may seem the rashness—of her judgment can generate an awareness of the immediacy of politics. She used to teach courses called "Twentieth Century Political Experience"—the emphasis always on *experience*—the point of which in part was to stem the tide of political apathy that tends to follow disillusion with political ideals and convictions.

This project was conceived from the first as a selection, rather than a complete edition, of Arendt's uncollected and unpublished writings. Book reviews, for instance, were never her favorite genre of writing and she stopped doing them on a regular basis as soon as she no longer needed the income. But during her early years in this country, she needed every commission she was offered, and some of the reviews she wrote then were extraordinary exercises—sometimes profound, sometimes sardonic—in thinking with or against (and therefore also with) the book's author. Three of the essays Arendt collected in *Men in Dark Times* were originally book reviews, and more of the many she wrote are included here.

Not included in this volume are lecture materials that are repetitive or less precise or forceful statements of similar points made elsewhere. In a few cases the subjects of essays—Adam Müller, Adalbert Stifter, Robert Gilbert—seemed too little known for inclusion. An essay on Hermann Broch's *The Death of Virgil*, a masterpiece of immense importance to Arendt, is included, but a review of his *Sleepwalkers* is not. Two essays on Bertolt Brecht are excluded because they appear to be preliminary studies for Arendt's wonderful 1966 essay "Bertolt Brecht, 1898–1956," published in her *Men in Dark Times*. A difficult decision was not to publish a long essay on Rilke's *Duino Elegies*, written in 1930 in collaboration with Arendt's first husband, Günther Stern (Anders). Its historical importance notwithstanding (at the time, just four years after his death, Rilke was hardly known in Germany), the essay's close analysis of the prosody and diction of the *Elegies* would be inaccessible to non-German readers; moreoever, it is not clear how much of it Arendt actually wrote. But the essay's emphasis on inner life and on the alienation of the lover from the transitory world; its reading of the poems as a "conscious renunciation of being heard," thereby transforming "elegy" into the essential "voice of being lost, rather than a mourning for what has been lost"—all that is in the spirit of other Arendt essays of the same period, in particular the one on Kierkegaard. The "despair" of the *Elegies* is, indeed, seen as "the last religious vestige."

The most important of the unpublished writings from the period covered by this volume and not included in it is the 1953 lecture series entitled "Karl Marx and the Tradition of Western Political Thought." These lectures initiated investigation into a field of inquiry that falls within a later period, an immensely fruitful one in Arendt's mental life. The mid-1950s burgeoned with so many diverse ideas that a strictly chronological order is difficult to maintain. Some of the later essays in this volume clearly indicate a fundamental change in her attitude toward the Bolshevik version of totalitarianism, a growing awareness that it was more completely realized than that of Hitler's Germany, in spite of the fact that its origins seemed "noble" in comparison to those of Nazism. Since the Soviet Union emerged from a Marxist revolutionary movement, and since Marx's thought purported to set straight the whole of Western political philosophy by realizing justice and freedom in the here-and-now, a huge project opened before her. What, exactly, was the tradition of political thought that started with Plato and Aristotle in ancient Greece and culminated in Marx? What relation did it bear to a form of government so terrible that it could not be likened even to tyranny? If the tradition was revealed as bankrupt, what did that imply for the foundations of morality and the meaning of evil? Or for human freedom, spontaneous action, and political association? What did it say about philosophy as such, about the relationship of solitude to plurality, and hence about the possibility of *political* philosophy? These were among Arendt's principal concerns from the mid-1950s until her death, the period to be covered by a subsequent volume.

Many references to Jews as victims of the Nazis inevitably figure in discussions of totalitarianism in this volume, but a separate collection of unpublished and uncollected essays will contain Arendt's writings on such topics as the Jewish question vis-à-vis German education and Enlightenment, modern Jewish history and culture, anti-Semitism, Zionism, the Jewish experience in World War II, Jewish politics and the formation of the State of Israel, Jewish-Arab relations, and the Eichmann controversy. They show that for Arendt Jewish existence, being Jewish and being a Jew in "this none too beautiful world," has both a "subjective" and an "objective" meaning.

In editing these writings certain general principles have been followed. It is apparent in the uncollected essays that some magazines and journals edited Arendt's originally quite ackward English with more care than others (on arrival in New York her knowledge of the language consisted of "one sonnet by Shakespeare," yet a year later she was publishing articles written in English). An effort has been made to attain clarity and some uniformity. The unpublished writings presented a different situation. In the Gaus interview Arendt says she frequently wrote as fast as she could type, and the manuscripts bear witness to that. They were for the most part prepared for lectures, with a plenitude of repetitions and ellipses, German rather than English grammatical constructions, including page-long sentences, and difficult and sometimes impossible to decipher handwritten corrections and additions in at least five languages. Moreover, the manuscripts are frequently in poor condition. Because Arendt used the "cut and Scotch tape" method of composition, and the tape long ago came loose, marks left on the primary pages had to be matched with marks on pieces sometimes far removed in the manuscript, or even in other manuscripts. Where editing has been needed, the overriding concern has been to keep intact Arendt's "voice" as well as her meaning.

Editorial comment and textual notes have been added only when clarification of references or obscure but interesting matters seemed called for. Arendt thought politics too serious a matter by far to be left to either experts or scholars. She wrote swiftly and surely (if not always grammatically) for a general audience, not a specialized one, and therefore it would have been neither in her spirit nor in the interest of her readership to add excessively academic appendages.

A number of essays in this volume exist in both German and English versions. There is, for instance, a German text of the Kafka essay that in some respects is more finished and refined than the English one. "When I came to this country I wrote in my very halting English a Kafka article . . . when I came to talk to them about the Englishing [Arendt's word for correcting her English usage] I read this article and there, of all things, the word 'progress' appeared! I said: 'What do you mean by this?' " ("Hannah Arendt on Hannah Arendt," *Hannah Arendt: The Recovery of the Public World*, M. Hill, ed., 334). So we know that Arendt, who had used "progress" ironically, wrote the English version—it was the first of many articles she published in *Partisan Review*—and therefore, in keeping with the principle of maintaining her "voice," it has been edited by consulting the German version but resisting the temptation to translate it. "Organized Guilt and Universal Responsibility" and "The Ex-Communists" also exist in German versions and were handled in the same way. It should be noted that Arendt never *translated* her own work, but sometimes—though she didn't much like doing it— *rewrote* in English what existed in German, and vice versa.

The version of the deeply reflective essay "What Is Existential Philosophy?" that was published in *Partisan Review* is an incomplete version of her original German manuscript. Parts of it seem less rewritten than mistranslated. It is not known who was responsible for the English version, but it seems unlikely that it was Arendt, though she may well have collaborated on it. Because it is a tightly argued and complex philosophical essay, one of critical importance to Arendt's development as a thinker—an essay she was shy of showing to Jaspers, and shyness is not a characteristic often associated with her—it was decided to make a new translation from the German for this volume. The process described above was thus reversed, the earlier *Partisan Review* text being consulted for hints of Arendt's "voice" while preparing the final version. Among much else, the essay is remarkable as an early indication of the fundamental influence of Kant on Arendt.

"Foreign Affairs in the Foreign-Language Press" presented a different problem. The title belongs to a manuscript, part of which had been extracted, cut up, added to, and published as "Our Foreign-Language Groups." What was added dealt with Jewish Americans, whose case, as Arendt says, is "different from all the others." What was left out were references to individuals who were "politically" controversial at the time (wartime America). The whole presented here has been woven together from its pieces. The focus of the essay is in some ways unusual for Arendt, but it clearly shows her growing interest in the socio-political makeup of her adopted country—an interest born out in a number of other essays in this collection, as well as her respect for journalism as a calling and for at least *some* reporters, who were, for her, along with *some* historians and poets, the only reliable guardians of factual truth. The news from the foreign-language press (in so many languages!) was filtered and made available to Arendt by *Aufbau*, the German Jewish newspaper for which she wrote.

In the Library of Congress two manuscripts are clipped together: one is called "On the Nature of Totalitarianism: An Essay in Understanding"; the other, untitled but separately paginated, continues from the first, but about three-quarters of the way through veers off on a not unconnected but nevertheless new tack. It ultimately breaks off in mid-sentence, coming to no conclusion (a relatively uncommon occurrence in Arendt's papers). Virtually every sentence and paragraph of "Understanding and Politics," which shows Arendt first grappling with the concept of judgment, is included in the first of these two manuscripts, but not in the same order. It is evident that the manuscripts were lecture materials, and it seems clear that Arendt did not extract from but consulted the first manuscript when she wrote "Understanding and Politics," which was published in *Partisan Review*. To add to the confusion, there is another manuscript in the Library of Congress that is the original of "Understanding and Politics," called "The Difficulties of Understanding." It is an educated guess that the magazine opted to change that title which has here been reinstated. Two sections of "The Difficulties of Understanding" that did not appear in "Understanding and Politics," probably due to what was thought in one case controversial and in the other obscure, have also been reinstated. With those additions, "Understanding and Politics" is presented here in the form in which it was published. Sections of the manuscript in which it was originally embedded, which genuinely complement the essay, were extracted and are now in the notes at the end of the essay.

"On the Nature of Totalitarianism" picks up where "Understanding and Politics" leaves off and continues into the second, "clipped" manuscript, of which the last, incomplete pages, embarking on a new tack, are not included here. A few paragraphs from an earlier manuscript in the Library of Congress, "Ideology and Propaganda" (most of which is repetitive of or used in previously published work), have been incorporated into the text of "On the Nature of Totalitarianism"; they round out Arendt's thoughts on the topic of ideology.

Toward its end, "On the Nature of Totalitarianism" distinguishes between loneliness and solitude. That, in a highly imaginative form, is the subject of the little fable about Heidegger, "Heidegger the Fox." In one sentence from the unused—and otherwise disconnected—part of the second, "clipped" manuscript it is difficult not to hear an ironic commentary on Heidegger's own reflection (which Arendt greatly appreciated) on the "distant nearness" of philosophy and poetry: "Philosopher and tyrant are as far removed from each other and as close together as solitude and loneliness."

There are exceptions to the chronological order of Arendt's writings presented here. (Exceptions, one finds, while not proving rules, do make them practical.) The first piece, " 'What Remains? The Language Remains,' " is from 1964, considerably beyond the dates of this collection. The reason for beginning with it is that Arendt rarely spoke personally about herself, and almost never for publication. Here she does speak about her life, and in particular about her youth, about her political awakening, and about discovering the evil of totalitarianism—all of which are directly relevant to many of the writings that follow. She also speaks poignantly about the German language, and about Karl Jaspers, who was always her friend and counsellor, whether or not they saw eye to eye on any given issue.

The following six essays date from 1930, when Arendt was twenty-four years old, to 1933, the year she fled her homeland. The first three are characterized by inwardness and spirituality, an emphasis on subjective life that some readers may find surprising in Arendt, while the following three give evidence of a burgeoning social and political awareness. Two of the first group deal with Christian thinkers, Augustine (the subject of her doctoral dissertation) and Kierkegaard, both greatly significant figures for Arendt. There is no question of theology here—Augustine is not treated as a Father of the Roman Catholic Church, and the piece commemorating the 1500th anniversary of his death is addressed to Protestants rather than Catholics—but, rather, of the two entirely different ways that these men, widely separated by time and circumstance, thought and lived their deep, inner relationship to God. Augustine was "exemplary" in his individual confession, and Kierkegaard "exceptional" in his experience of what Arnedt explains as the "paradox" of Christian existence.

Between these two pieces, the long reflective review of Karl Mannheim's *Ideology and Utopia* deals with a somewhat different relationship, that which mind or spirit (*Geist*) bears to the world and to time, a topic of fundamental importance to Arendt and on which she rang many changes until the end of her life. The essay takes in earnest Mannheim's notion of the "existential boundness" of all thought, not excluding philosophic or contemplative thought, seeking to disclose its origin in the "homelessness" of modern man. Such homelessness is seen by Arendt as a condition of socioeconomic "reality" and in contrast to reflective thought's own "solitude" which is "a genuine possibility of human life."

Heidegger and Jaspers appear here (as they do frequently in this volume) as pre-eminent representatives of contemporary philosophy, and in particular Jaspers's notion of transcendence *in* human existence (and not an ideological or utopian escape *from* reality) is vividly evoked in the example of St. Francis of Assisi. This essay also gives the first clear statement of the reasons for Arendt's rejection of psychoanalysis, as a practice and as a theory, from which she never wavered.

The next two essays from this period were abstracted from Arendt's work on the biography of Rahel Varnhagen. They have been translated and reprinted to call attention to that singular study of an astonishing woman, which has been unduly neglected by many of Arendt's critics and readers alike. (Exceptional in this respect is Dagmar Barnouw's *Visible Spaces: Hannah Arendt and the German Jewish Experience*; the chapter "Society, Parvenu, and Pariah: The Life Story of a German Jewess" offers an extremely knowledgeable and insightful account of Arendt's life of Rahel.) Taken together, they reveal Arendt's first and virtually palpable encounter with what was to become for her the crucial distinction between *public* and *private* realms of experience, a distinction that was to characterize and inform, if not determine, her mature political thought; and also with what later became for her the disastrous confusion of public and private matters in the realm of the *social*.

The essay published on the 100th anniversary of the death of the writer and statesman Friedrich von Gentz brings that most worldly of men—vain, hedonistic, unprincipled, recognizing only power, and seeking only "reality"—to the foreground, whereas in the biography one tends to regard him as only a player, though a major one, in Rahel's life. When Arendt wrote this piece, Gentz was, as she says, pretty much "forgotten" (the biographies by Paul R. Sweet and Golo Mann were not published until the 1940s). Arendt's attitude toward Gentz, a figure who bridges the Enlightenment and Romantic periods (which are not nearly as distinct in Germany, culturally or historically, as they are, for instance, in France) is ambivalent, just as Gentz's career was "ambiguous." In some respects he was conservative and in others liberal; he was an absolutist who believed that the very principle of legitimacy was historically relative; and he was a Romantic who above all wanted the world not to change. Yet he knew and could accept that the world *was* changing and that everything he had intervened to preserve would be lost. It was neither principle nor cause but knowledge of the affairs and course of the world that afforded him his place in it. It was from such a spectator's view, his "participatory knowledge" of his age's spirit and its secrets— in his own much more worldly way he shared the *Mitwisserschaft* ideal of the old Friedrich Schlegel—that he found his political credo in the Roman poet Lucan, *Victrix causa deis placuit, sed victa Catoni* ("The victorious cause pleased the gods, but the defeated one pleased Cato"), with which Arendt closes her essay. But just as she presumably did not at this time share Gentz's equivocal political position,* so she gives no hint, in citing this verse, of the meaning it will hold for her later. On the contrary, here it almost seems to mean that Gentz preferred the defeated cause because it was defeated. But on July 24, 1954, she referred to it in a letter to Jaspers as "the spirit of republicanism," and still later it encapsulated for her the very essence of political judgment.

It is noteworthy that just ten years after this early essay was published, in a short, favorable review (not included here) of Sweet's biography, *Friedrich von Gentz: Defender of the Old Order*, Arendt singles Gentz out from the company of Talleyrand, Castelreagh, Canning, and Metternich, all of whom served their respective "national" interests, as the defender of "the interest of Europe." She characterizes him as primarily a figure of the Enlightenment, who resisted its "decay . . . into chauvinism" and "based a completely independent and disinterested policy on the non-existence of a German nation." In 1942, while World War II raged, she praised the "strange and exciting timeliness" of Sweet's book, and found "the question of European unity" to be among "the most important political tasks" of the time. Moreover, the "tradition of political thinking" stretching back to Gentz (who had been Kant's student), after having been "almost lost in the nationalism of the 19th century," was then seen to be "our particular concern."†

---

* Certainly in 1933, after the Reichstag fire, she did not consider it possible to remain a "bystander," a spectator of events. But much later, in 1972, in reply to a question about whether she was a liberal or a conservative, she replied: "I don't know . . . You know the left think I am conservative, and the conservatives sometimes think I am left or I am a maverick or God knows what. And I must say I couldn't care less. I don't think that the real questions of this century will get any kind of illumination by this kind of thing" ("Hannah Arendt on Hannah Arendt," 333–34).

† Today, more than fifty years later, neither the "task" nor the "concern" seem less timely. Arendt's review, entitled "A Believer in European Unity" (*Review of Politics* 4 (1942), 2, 245–47), was her first published writing in English.

As far as Gentz and Rahel Varnhagen are concerned, she alone, among his many loves, understood him, and they both knew that. What she understood was that his attitude toward the world only seemed hypocritical to others, whereas in fact he had opened himself to the world naïvely, like a child. Arendt speaks of the possibility—had their love been consummated (which it was not)—of another "world" coming into existence, one held "up against the real world," a world that would "isolate" Gentz from the reality he craved. In "his private life he was dependent upon her understanding," but he was unwilling to sacrifice "his naïveté, his clear conscience, his position in the world—in short, everything" to it.* The distinction between private understanding and public participation could hardly be more sharply, or more concretely, drawn.

It is the power of Arendt's imagination that accounts for the uncanny originality of her portrait of Rahel, so utterly unlike the conventional one first contrived after her death by her gentile husband, Karl August Varnhagen, and then perpetuated by others (cf. Barnouw, *Visible Spaces*, 48). Arendt's ambivalence toward Rahel exists on an even deeper level than toward Gentz. Of course this has something to do with the fact that Arendt was a Jew and a woman, like Rahel, but she was not trying to understand her own *political* situation in the 1930s in terms of Rahel's life or experience in "society" more than a hundred years before; she was attempting, rather, to gain understanding of the "Jewish question," as it was embedded in German history and culture, by seeing it from the perspective of a unique Jewish woman.

"Berlin Salon" deals with an extraordinary but short-lived social phenomenon that grew out of German Enlightenment ideals, emerged in full Romantic flower in Rahel's attic, and came to an abrupt end when its "social neutrality" was overwhelmed by events in the real world. It "went under like a ship," as Rahel said, as if exploded by the cannons of Napoleon. Between the League of Virtue (with its notion of equality based on goodness) that preceded it, and the highly discriminatory, bourgeois Table Society that succeeded it, Rahel's salon was the epitome of Romantic "indiscretion." It was this indiscretion, a sort of bohemianism, unconventional and anything but bourgeois, that collapsed the distinction

---

* The quotations are from the completed biography, *Rahel Varnhagen: The Life of a Jewish Woman*, 86–87.

between public and private by taking seriously the interesting human being as such—whether woman, prince, statesman, Jew or whatever—the interest being life itself (happiness or unhappiness, for instance) and not the person, not the bearer of the life. Thus it was not at all a person's place in the world that recommended him to Rahel, but, instead, such a thing as a capacity to suffer "more than anyone I have ever known." Rahel herself epitomized the lack of discretion insofar as her life was ruled by the passion to escape the "misfortune" of her birth—of being a Jewess—by becoming "similar" (assimilated) to every other "cultivated personality." Her salon may have granted her the illusion of such assimilation, but it was a false dream of equality; the time "when we were all together" had vanished like a mirage when she wrote of it to Pauline Wiesel in 1818. In the intimacy of love, Rahel's understanding of Gentz might have shut out, even replaced reality, but it could never reconcile her to a world in which she was discriminated as a Jew. It was the same privacy of love for which Gentz refused to sacrifice the allure of the world that so delighted him in all its circumstances.

Arendt was struck by Rahel's brilliant mind, her great capacity to love and her understanding of others arising from that capacity, as much as by her wonderful, undiscriminating openness to life. But what Arendt discovered, in her own experience of political anti-Semitism—as distinguished from social discrimination—was that being a Jew was indeed a political, a public, *fact*. It did not matter whether, personally, she held religious beliefs or had Jewish "characteristics," or if under other circumstances her own brilliant mind and other gifts would have made her an "exception" in the eyes of society. Politically, the fact that she appeared in the eyes of the world as a Jew counted for more than "questions of personal identity," and to have claimed otherwise would have been "a grotesque and dangerous evasion of reality." Through that discovery she understood that the only real, nonillusory equality is political freedom; that the condition of political freedom is having a place, not in a salon, but in the world; and that the only way to obtain a place in her world was to claim it by saying: Yes, I am what I appear to be, a Jew. In 1933 Arendt went to work for the German Zionist Organization, although personally she was not a Zionist; that work led to her arrest. This is a hard and risky business, requiring courage (among much else it accounts for her calling out loud and clear for the formation of a Jewish army during World War II), and it is probably not too much to say that without such an experience of freedom she never would have been able to develop her concept of action.

"On the Emancipation of Women" is the only text Arendt devoted to women's issues (perhaps reason enough to include it here), although she alluded to contemporary debates within the German women's movement in her biography of Rahel Varnhagen. Arendt argues that the confusion of social with political aims can never unravel the specific complexity of a woman's life-situation, the first hint of a kind of criticism that later informed her approach to Marxist thought. Alice Gerstel, the author of the book that is the subject of Arendt's review, and her husband, Otto Rühle, were prominent figures in radical German political movements. Gerstel was also close to Milena Jesenská, Kafka's friend and correspondent, which makes a nice (if fortuitous) connection to the essay that follows, "Franz Kafka: A Revaluaton."

The hiatus of eleven years that separates the last piece Arendt wrote in Germany in 1933 from the 1944 essay on Kafka may seem surprising. From the Gaus interview it is clear that Arendt, on leaving Germany, was disgusted with intellectuals and intellectual life, and it is also clear that as a stateless refugee she had pressing practical concerns. In Paris she worked for Youth Aliyah, preparing Jewish children for emigration to Palestine, to which, in 1935, she accompanied a group of them. Yet she did not divorce herself entirely from the intellectual life of Paris. She attended some of Alexandre Kojève's famous seminars on Hegel, where she first encountered the philosophers Jean-Paul Sartre and Alexandre Koyré (she considered Koyré a far more subtle interpreter of Hegel than Kojève); she was also friendly with Raymond Aron and Walter Benjamin.* In view of the fact that she was so prolific a writer in all other periods of her life, it is certainly possible that some writings from the Paris years have been lost.

By far the greater part of the essays following the one on Kafka deal in one way or another with World War II and the multiple phenomena of totalitarianism. Even apparent exceptions—such as the pieces on Dilthey, Dewey, Broch, Jaspers, and Heidegger; the essays that consider philosophical issues, in particular German and French existential thought and political philosophy in general; and those on a variety of

---

* For a full account of this period of Arendt's life, see Young-Bruehl's *Hannah Arendt: For Love of the World*, chap. 4, "Stateless Persons."

matters relating to religion—are written from a perspective that is unmistakably informed by Arendt's understanding of what were, for her,
the unprecedented political events of the twentieth century. The reval-
uation of Kafka is itself made from precisely such a perspective: he is
not viewed as a "prophet" of things to come, but, rather, as the sober
analyst of the "underlying structures" of "unfreedom" in his own time,
issuing in "blueprints" of socialized mankind, of a bureaucratic society
and a society ruled by superhuman as opposed to human laws. For
Arendt, a mark of Kafka's genius was his ability to grasp the structures
of "the subterranean stream of Western history"* while they were still
hidden from general view. Moreover, his "image . . . of man as a model
of good will," of "anybody and everybody" wanting to be free, is redolent
of that "trust in people" of which Arendt speaks at the end of the Gaus
interview, a trust "in what is human in all people."

Arendt believed that political thought in the twentieth century had
to break with its own tradition in as radical a sense as the systematic
mass murder enacted by totalitarian regimes broke with the tradition of
political action. An early and clear example of her thinking can be seen
in the distinction she makes between "organized guilt" and "universal
responsibility." Moreover, it was Arendt, a Jew, who in the last days of
the war spoke out against Vansittartism; she saw that the German people
had no "monopoly of guilt" for the inhuman crimes of a racist ideology.
She felt that the defeat of the Nazis ought not to be greeted with euphoria;
her response was not victorious exultation, but a profound lament over
the destruction of German culture. Her anticipation of evil as "the
fundamental question" to be faced in the postwar world explains her
recognition of the need for peoples to be reconciled, for a new beginning,
for a European federation of states. Evil had become manifest as the
inversion of the age-old foundation of Western morality—Thou shalt
not kill—and was less abstractly understood as the "monstrousness,"
the "inhumanity," of the creation of "absolutely innocent" victims to
demonstrate the natural or historical movement of the world. The linking
of "monstrousness" and "inhumanity" with "innocence" seems strange
indeed until the utter novelty of totalitarianism as a form of government
is understood. That understanding is difficult, and it was a considerable

---

* This is Arendt's phrase in the preface to the first edition of *The Origins of
Totalitarianism.*

theoretical achievement for Arendt, drawing on Kant and, especially, Montesquieu, to have justified the addition of a new form of government to the list begun by Plato and Aristotle and hardly altered since antiquity.

By no means only a matter of theory, totalitarianism—its threat to humanity—is such a danger that Arendt tirelessly alerts us to the political conditions and mental attitudes from which it rises. Thus, it is not just Stalin's smashing of "eggs," terrible as that may have been, but the notion of action as fabrication—in the sense of making history—lying behind his violence to which she directs our attention. What distinguishes "ex-Communists" from "former Communists" is a fundamentally totalitarian way of thinking, an impatience with the "basic uncertainties" of action, and an ideological belief in an "end" of history. She is uncompromisingly critical of secular bourgeois society, of its deadly conventionality, and alert to its tendency to rob man of his spontaneity and change him into a "function of society." Typically attracted to neo-Catholic critics of bourgeois "morals and standards," such as G. K. Chesterton and Charles Péguy, she is impatient with Catholics, or anyone else, who seek to escape reality by hiding within the "certainty" of bygone truths.

If there is no escape in either the "not yet" or the "no longer," if the thread of traditional Western thought is definitively cut, then not even the greatest philosophy of history can effect reconciliation between mind and world. Hegel's notion of History, his explication of human affairs and the course of events as a "dialectical movement towards freedom," has become unreal—not philosophically unreal (whatever that may mean) but lacking "a sense of reality" when weighed in the balance with the political events of the twentieth century. It is not those events conceived abstractly—not, for instance, as signs of doom—that matters, but their actual weight and gravity in human experience. As this volume ends, Arendt views political philosophy, in full contrast to the philosophy of history, as having become possible in a way that it never had before. For decades thinkers had thought, as writers had written, that "the crisis of Western civilization" was imminent, and finally that crisis had emerged for everyone to see—in totalitarian regimes, in huge factories manufacturing corpses—on the earth men share with one another. It was not *another* political philosophy that was needed to account for this, but a new understanding of politics as such. Even though her serious researches into the thought of Heidegger, Jaspers, and others proved inconclusive, in

1954 Arendt seems convinced that it might, for the first time, be possible to "directly grasp the realm of human affairs and human deeds." To do that would require an act akin to the "speechless wonder of gratitude" even if it were now "speechless horror at what man may do and what the world may become." These words do not anticipate a return to traditional philosophy; they are, instead, the appeal of one who, while never entirely at home in it, ventured to understand and judge the world as long as her sojourn lasted. In four strong, beautiful lines from a poem written the same year as this collection's final essay, Arendt put it this way:

> Ich lieb die Erde
> so wie auf der Reise
> den fremden Ort
> und anders nicht.

> (I love the earth
> as a traveler loves
> a foreign place,
> and otherwise not.)

Shortly after Hannah Arendt's sudden death in December of 1975, her close friend and co-executor of her estate Lotte Kohler asked Larry May and me (both of us had worked for Arendt for some years as research and teaching assistants) to help her prepare the vast number of papers in Arendt's apartment on Riverside Drive for delivery to the Library of Congress. It was strange to be there day after day in her absence, the weeks stretching into months (the task was not completed until the summer of 1977). To the sadness of that time there was added a sense of discovery. Almost daily we came upon often wholly unexpected documents and discussed them over the excellent German lunches Lotte Kohler prepared.

Whenever she was in town, Mary McCarthy, Arendt's literary executor, would join us. Although the cast of that remarkable woman's mind was in many ways different from Arendt's, the acuity of their insight was similarly startling. During that time I also talked and corresponded at length with the American philosopher J. Glenn Gray. He had a profound understanding of Arendt's late thought, which he considered to be many generations, perhaps a century, ahead of its time. Until his untimely death in 1977, he was the best of guides through the intellectual maze of Arendt's papers.

It was apparent to all of us that a large number of those papers should be made public. Now, after many delays, that is finally happening with the publication of this volume, the first of several planned. Lotte Kohler and Mary McCarthy (until her own death in 1989) encouraged this project from the beginning, and for that, and much else, I owe them a debt of gratitude.

Elisabeth Young-Bruehl was among the first to make use of Arendt's papers. She studied them intently while writing *Hannah Arendt: For Love of the World*, still the major source for the story of Arendt's life. Since its publication in 1982, her biography has been widely read by the general public as well as scholars. Elisabeth and I have been friends for twenty-five years, since the day we met in Arendt's seminar. During that time many hours have been passed talking about Arendt; those ongoing conversations have meant more to me than I can say, not least in connection with the task of selecting and editing these writings.

Larry May and I continued to work with Mary McCarthy, who had undertaken the job of readying for publication Arendt's last lectures, *The Life of the Mind*. McCarthy's editorial standards were high indeed, and it was then, especially in answering her many long letters, filled with queries, that I came to realize something of what editing Arendt's work entailed. At that time, too, I became acquainted with people at Harcourt Brace Jovanovich, both Arendt's and McCarthy's principal publisher. At a memorable meeting with William Jovanovich, Lotte Kohler, and Mary McCarthy, the extent and order of publication of the papers were first determined. Drenka Willen and Julian Muller have been generous with advice. Roberta Leighton—drawing on long experience with Arendt's work—and my own editor, Alane Salierno Mason, and her assistant, Celia Wren, have shown great dedication to this project and contributed materially to its final form.

In addition, over the years many students, friends, and scholars have, perhaps unknowingly, helped inform the selection of the pieces here included. Three scholars must be singled out: Richard J. Bernstein, with whom I have had the pleasure and benefit of teaching Arendt's work; Margaret Canovan, whose acquaintance I made through correspondence, thanks to Mary McCarthy, and whose recent work has raised the understanding of Arendt's political thought to a level it did not previously enjoy; and Ursula Ludz, whose thorough (though as yet unpublished) bibliography and excellent German editions of Arendt's works, and whose kindness, have aided and encouraged me throughout. April Flakne must also be singled out. While still a graduate student, she prepared successive drafts of the two related essays, "Understanding and Politics" and "On the Nature of Totalitarianism," which together presented the most demanding and, in some respects, most problematic editing task in this collection. She is not, of course, responsible for any inadequacies that may remain in the final versions. Other scholars whose insights have taught me much are Jeffrey Andrew Barash, Seyla Benhabib, Françoise Collin, Melvyn Hill, Suzanne Jacobitti, George Kateb, Giuseppina Moneta, Hans-Joachim Schrimpf, Peter Stern, Ernst Vollrath, and Jean Yarbrough. John B. Black, Keith David, Iris Pilling, Patricia Ross, Fred Rowley (who gave up a summer's surfing in California to work with me in New York), and Christoph Schönberger have filled some of the many gaps in my knowledge.

The translators of Arendt's German writings included here, principally Robert and Rita Kimber, but also Joan Stambaugh and Elisabeth Young-Bruehl, are hereby thanked for the difficult work they have done. Lotte Kohler painstakingly went over almost every word of translation. I want to thank the staff of the Manuscript Division of the Library of Congress both for their unfailing courtesy and also for their efforts to maintain in as good condition as possible the Arendt collection placed in their safekeeping, which through continuous and ever increasing use has become quite fragile. My thanks go to Gerard Richard Hoolahan and to Mary and Robert Lazarus for their practical and moral support over many years, and to the Graduate Faculty of Political and Social Science at the New School for Social Research, which permitted me to take time off from teaching to complete this collection.

Although Hannah Arendt was decidedly impatient with any suggestion that she was a "genius," maintaining that her road to accomplishment was one of sheer hard work, no one who knew her could doubt her genius for friendship. Encouraging neither disciples nor epigones, she brought together in the bond of her friendship an extraordinary assortment of diverse individuals. It is to two of her greatest friends that this volume is dedicated: To Lotte Kohler and to the memory of Mary McCarthy.

Jerome Kohn
New York City
December, 1993

"What Remains?
The Language Remains":
A Conversation with Günter Gaus

[On October 28, 1964, the following conversation between Hannah Arendt and Günter Gaus, at the time a well-known journalist and later a high official in Willy Brandt's government, was broadcast on West German television. The interview was awarded the Adolf Grimme Prize and was published the following year under the title "Was bleibt? Es bleibt die Muttersprache" in Günter Gaus, *Zur Person*, Munich, 1965. This English translation is by Joan Stambaugh.

Gaus begins the conversation by saying that Arendt is the first woman to take part in the series of interviews he is conducting; then he immediately qualifies that statement by noting that she has a "very masculine occupation," namely, that of philosopher. This leads him to his first question: In spite of the recognition and respect she has received, does she perceive "her role in the circle of philosophers" as unusual or peculiar because she is a woman? Arendt replies:]

I AM AFRAID I have to protest. I do not belong to the circle of philosophers. My profession, if one can even speak of it at all, is political theory. I neither feel like a philosopher, nor do I believe that I have been accepted in the circle of philosophers, as you so kindly suppose. But to speak of the other question that you raised in your opening remarks: you say that philosophy is generally thought to be a masculine occupation. It does not have to remain a masculine occupation! It is entirely possible that a woman will one day be a philosopher. . . .*

GAUS: I consider you to be a philosopher. . . .

ARENDT: Well, I can't help that, but in my opinion I am not. In my opinion I have said good-bye to philosophy once and for all. As you know, I studied philosophy, but that does not mean that I stayed with it.

GAUS: I should like to hear from you more precisely what the difference is between political philosophy and your work as a professor of political theory.

ARENDT: The expression "political philosophy," which I avoid, is extremely burdened by tradition. When I talk about these things, academically or nonacademically, I always mention that there is a vital tension between philosophy and politics. That is, between man as a thinking being and man as an acting being, there is a tension that does not exist in natural philosophy, for example. Like everyone else, the philosopher can be objective with regard to nature, and when he says what he thinks about it he speaks in the name of all mankind. But he cannot be objective or neutral with regard to politics. Not since Plato!

GAUS: I understand what you mean.

ARENDT: There is a kind of enmity against all politics in most philosophers, with very few exceptions. Kant *is* an exception. This enmity is extremely important for the whole problem, because it is not a personal question. It lies in the nature of the subject itself.

GAUS: You want no part in this enmity against politics because you believe that it would interfere with your work?

ARENDT: "I want no part in this enmity," that's it exactly! I want to look at politics, so to speak, with eyes unclouded by philosophy.

GAUS: I understand. Now, let us turn to the question of woman's emancipation. Has this been a problem for you?

ARENDT: Yes, of course; there is always the problem as such. I have actually been rather old-fashioned. I always thought that there are certain occupations that are improper for women, that do not become

*The ellipses here and elsewhere are in the original; they do not indicate omission of material. —Ed.

them, if I may put it that way. It just doesn't look good when a woman gives orders. She should try not to get into such a situation if she wants to remain feminine. Whether I am right about this or not I do not know. I myself have always lived in accordance with this more or less unconsciously—or let us rather say, more or less consciously. The problem itself played no role for me personally. To put it very simply, I have always done what I liked to do.

GAUS: Your work—we will surely go into details later—is to a significant degree concerned with the knowledge of the conditions under which political action and behavior come about. Do you want to achieve extensive influence with these works, or do you believe that such influence is no longer possible in these times, or is it simply not important to you?

ARENDT: You know, that is not a simple question. If I am to speak very honestly I would have to say: When I am working, I am not interested in how my work might affect people.

GAUS: And when you are finished?

ARENDT: Then I am finished. What is important for me is to understand. For me, writing is a matter of seeking this understanding, part of the process of understanding. . . . Certain things get formulated. If I had a good enough memory to really retain everything that I think, I doubt very much that I would have written anything—I know my own laziness. What is important to me is the thought process itself. As long as I have succeeded in thinking something through, I am personally quite satisfied. If I then succeed in expressing my thought process adequately in writing, that satisfies me also.

You ask about the effects of my work on others. If I may wax ironical, that is a masculine question. Men always want to be terribly influential, but I see that as somewhat external. Do I imagine myself being influential? No. I want to understand. And if others understand—in the same sense that I have understood—that gives me a sense of satisfaction, like feeling at home.

GAUS: Do you write easily? Do you formulate ideas easily?

ARENDT: Sometimes I do; sometimes I don't. But in general I can tell you that I never write until I can, so to speak, take dictation from myself.

GAUS: Until you have already thought it out.

ARENDT: Yes. I know exactly what I want to write. I do not write until I do. Usually I write it all down only once. And that goes relatively quickly, since it really depends only on how fast I type.

GAUS: Your interest in political theory, in political action and be-havior, is at the center of your work today. In this light, what I found in your correspondence with Professor Scholem* seems particularly in-teresting. There you wrote, if I may quote you, that you "were interested in [your] youth neither in politics nor in history." Miss Arendt, as a Jew you emigrated from Germany in 1933. You were then twenty-six years old. Is your interest in politics—the cessation of your indifference to politics and history—connected to these events?

ARENDT: Yes, of course. Indifference was no longer possible in 1933. It was no longer possible even before that.

GAUS: For you as well?

ARENDT: Yes, of course. I read the newspapers intently. I had opinions. I did not belong to a party, nor did I have need to. By 1931 I was firmly convinced that the Nazis would take the helm. I was always arguing with other people about it but I did not really concern myself systematically with these things until I emigrated.

GAUS: I have another question about what you just said. If you were convinced that the Nazis could not be stopped from taking power, didn't you feel impelled actively to do something to prevent this—for example, join a party—or did you no longer think that made sense?

ARENDT: I personally did not think it made sense. If I had thought so—it is very difficult to say all this in retrospect—perhaps I would have done something. I thought it was hopeless.

GAUS: Is there a definite event in your memory that dates your turn to the political?

ARENDT: I would say February 27, 1933, the burning of the Reichstag, and the illegal arrests that followed during the same night. The so-called protective custody. As you know, people were taken to

---

*Gershom Scholem (1897–1982), German-born Zionist, historian, and eminent scholar of Jewish mysticism, was an old acquaintance of Hannah Arendt's. On June 23, 1963, he wrote a highly critical letter to her about her book *Eichmann in Jerusalem*; see "*Eichmann in Jerusalem*: An Exchange of Letters," *Encounter*, 22, 1964. The quotation given here is from Arendt's reply, dated July 24, 1963. —Ed.

Gestapo cellars or to concentration camps. What happened then was monstrous, but it has now been overshadowed by things that happened later. This was an immediate shock for me, and from that moment on I felt responsible. That is, I was no longer of the opinion that one can simply be a bystander. I tried to help in many ways. But what actually took me out of Germany—if I should speak of that; I've never told it because it is of no consequence—

GAUS: Please tell us.

ARENDT: I intended to emigrate anyhow. I thought immediately that Jews could not stay. I did not intend to run around Germany as a second-class citizen, so to speak, in whatever form. In addition, I thought that things would just get worse and worse. Nevertheless, in the end I did not leave in such a peaceful way. And I must say that gives me a certain satisfaction. I was arrested, and had to leave the country illegally—I will tell you how in a minute—and that was instant gratification for me. I thought at least I had done something! At least I am not "innocent." No one could say that of me!

The Zionist organization gave me the chance. I was close friends with some of the leading people, above all with the then president, Kurt Blumenfeld. But I was not a Zionist. Nor did the Zionists try to convert me. Yet in a certain sense I was influenced by them: especially by the criticism, the self-criticism that the Zionists spread among the Jewish people. I was influenced and impressed by it, but politically I had nothing to do with Zionism. Now, in 1933 Blumenfeld and someone whom you do not know approached me and said: We want to put together a collection of all anti-Semitic statements made in ordinary circumstances. For example, statements in clubs, all kinds of professional clubs, all kinds of professional journals—in short, the sort of thing that doesn't become known in foreign countries. To organize such a collection at that time was to engage in what the Nazis called "horror propaganda." No Zionist could do this, because if he were found out, the whole organization would be exposed. . . . They asked me, "Will you do it?" I said, "Of course." I was very happy. First of all, it seemed a very intelligent idea to me, and second, it gave me the feeling that something could be done after all.

GAUS: Were you arrested in connection with this work?

ARENDT: Yes. I was found out. I was very lucky. I got out after eight days because I made friends with the official who arrested me. He was a charming fellow! He'd been promoted from the criminal police to a political division. He had no idea what to do. What was he supposed to do? He kept saying to me, "Ordinarily I have someone there in front of me, and I just check the file, and I know what's going on. But what shall I do with you?"

GAUS: That was in Berlin?

ARENDT: That was in Berlin. Unfortunately, I had to lie to him. I couldn't let the organization be exposed. I told him tall tales, and he kept saying, "I got you in here. I shall get you out again. Don't get a lawyer! Jews don't have any money now. Save your money!" Meanwhile the organization had gotten me a lawyer. Through members, of course. And I sent this lawyer away. Because this man who arrested me had such an open, decent face. I relied on him and thought that here was a much better chance than with some lawyer who himself was afraid.

GAUS: And you got out and could leave Germany?

ARENDT: I got out, but had to cross the border illegally . . . my name had not been cleared.

GAUS: In the correspondence we mentioned, Miss Arendt, you clearly rejected as superfluous Scholem's warning that you should always be mindful of your solidarity with the Jewish people. You wrote—I quote again: "To be a Jew belongs for me to the indubitable facts of my life, and I never wanted to change anything about such facts, not even in my childhood." I'd like to ask a few questions about this. You were born in 1906 in Hannover as the daughter of an engineer, and grew up in Königsberg. Do you remember what it was like for a child in prewar Germany to come from a Jewish family?

ARENDT: I couldn't answer that question truthfully for everyone. As for my personal recollection, I did not know from my family that I was Jewish. My mother was completely a-religious.

GAUS: Your father died young.

ARENDT: My father had died young. It all sounds very odd. My grandfather was the president of the liberal Jewish community and a civil official of Königsberg. I come from an old Königsberg family. Nevertheless, the word "Jew" never came up when I was a small child. I first met up with it through anti-Semitic remarks—they are not worth repeating—from children on the street. After that I was, so to speak, "enlightened."

GAUS: Was that a shock for you?

ARENDT: No.

GAUS: Did you have the feeling, now I am something special?

ARENDT: That is a different matter. It wasn't a shock for me at all. I thought to myself: That is how it is. Did I have the feeling that I was something special? Yes! But I could no longer unravel that for you today.

GAUS: In what way did you feel special?

ARENDT: Objectively, I am of the opinion that it was related to being Jewish. For example, as a child—a somewhat older child then— I knew that I looked Jewish. I looked different from other children. I was very conscious of that. But not in a way that made me feel inferior, that was just how it was. Then too, my mother, my family home, so to speak, was a bit different from the usual. There was so much that was special about it, even in comparison with the homes of other Jewish children or even of other children who were related to us, that it was hard for a child to figure out just what was special.

GAUS: I would like some elucidation as to what was special about your family home. You said that your mother never deemed it necessary to explain your solidarity with Jewishness to you until you met up with it on the street. Had your mother lost the sense of being Jewish which you claim for yourself in your letter to Scholem? Didn't it play a role for her any more at all? Was she successfully assimilated, or did she at least believe so?

ARENDT: My mother was not a very theoretical person. I do not believe that she had any special ideas about this. She herself came out of the Social Democratic movement, out of the circle of the *Sozialistische Monatshefte,** as did my father. The question did not play a role for her. Of course she was a Jew. She would never have baptized me! I think she would have boxed my ears right and left if she had ever found out that I had denied being a Jew. It was unthinkable, so to speak. Out of the question! But the question was naturally much more important in the twenties, when I was young, than it was for my mother. And when I was grown up it was much more important for my mother than in her earlier life. But that was due to external circumstances.

**Sozialistische Monatshefte* (Socialist Monthly) was a well-known German journal of the time. —Ed.

I myself, for example, don't believe that I have ever considered myself a German—in the sense of belonging to the people as opposed to being a citizen, if I may make that distinction. I remember discussing this with Jaspers around 1930. He said, "Of course you are German!" I said, "One can see that I am not!" But that didn't bother me. I didn't feel that it was something inferior. That wasn't the case at all. And to come back once again to what was special about my family home: all Jewish children encountered anti-Semitism. And it poisoned the souls of many children. The difference with us was that my mother was always convinced that you mustn't let it get to you. You have to defend yourself! When my teachers made anti-Semitic remarks—mostly not about me, but about other Jewish girls, eastern Jewish students in particular—I was told to get up immediately, leave the classroom, come home, and report everything exactly. Then my mother wrote one of her many registered letters; and for me the matter was completely settled. I had a day off from school, and that was marvelous! But when it came from children, I was not permitted to tell about it at home. That didn't count. You defended yourself against what came from children. Thus these matters never were a problem for me. There were rules of conduct by which I retained my dignity, so to speak, and I was protected, absolutely protected, at home.

GAUS: You studied in Marburg, Heidelberg, and Freiberg with professors Heidegger, Bultmann, and Jaspers; with a major in philosophy and minors in theology and Greek. How did you come to choose these subjects?

ARENDT: You know, I have often thought about that. I can only say that I always knew I would study philosophy. Ever since I was fourteen years old.

GAUS: Why?

ARENDT: I read Kant. You can ask, Why did you read Kant? For me the question was somehow: I can either study philosophy or I can drown myself, so to speak. But not because I didn't love life! No! As I said before—I had this need to understand. . . . The need to understand was there very early. You see, all the books were in the library at home; one simply took them from the shelves.

GAUS: Besides Kant, do you remember special experiences in reading?

ARENDT: Yes. First of all, Jaspers's *Psychologie der Weltanschauungen* [Psychology of World Views], published, I believe, in 1920.* I was fourteen. Then I read Kierkegaard, and that fit together.

GAUS: Is this where theology came in?

ARENDT: Yes. They fit together in such a way that for me they both belonged together. I had some misgivings only as to how one deals with this if one is Jewish . . . how one proceeds. I had no idea, you know. I had difficult problems that were then resolved by themselves. Greek is another matter. I have always loved Greek poetry. And poetry has played a large role in my life. So I chose Greek in addition. It was the easiest thing to do, since I read it anyway!

GAUS: I am impressed!

ARENDT: No, you exaggerate.

GAUS: Your intellectual gifts were tested so early, Miss Arendt. Did it sometimes separate you as a schoolgirl and as a young student from the usual day-to-day relationships, painfully perhaps?

ARENDT: That would have been the case had I known about it. I thought everybody was like that.

GAUS: When did you realize you were wrong?

ARENDT: Rather late. I don't want to say how late. I am embarrassed. I was indescribably naive. That was partly due to my upbringing at home. Grades were never discussed. That was taken to be inferior. Any ambition was taken to be inferior. In any case, the situation wasn't at all clear to me. I experienced it sometimes as a sort of strangeness among people.

GAUS: A strangeness which you believed came from you?

ARENDT: Yes, exclusively. But that has nothing to do with talent. I never connected it with talent.

GAUS: Was the result sometimes disdain for others in your youth?

ARENDT: Yes, that happened. Very early. And I have often suffered because I felt such disdain, that is, knowing one really shouldn't, and one really must not, and so forth.

---

*Karl Jaspers, *Psychologie der Weltanschauungen*, was first published in Berlin in 1919. —Ed.

GAUS: When you left Germany in 1933, you went to Paris, where you worked in an organization that tried to provide for Jewish youngsters in Palestine. Can you tell me something about that?

ARENDT: This organization brought Jewish youngsters between thirteen and seventeen from Germany to Palestine and housed them there in kibbutzim. For this reason, I really know these settlements pretty well.

GAUS: And from a very early period.

ARENDT: From a very early period; at that time I had a lot of respect for them. The children received vocational training and retraining. Sometimes I also smuggled in Polish children. It was regular social work, educational work. There were large camps in the country where the children were prepared for Palestine, where they also had lessons, where they learned farming, where they above all had to gain weight. We had to clothe them from head to foot. We had to cook for them. Above all, we had to get papers for them, we had to deal with the parents—and before everything else we had to get money for them. That was also largely my job. I worked together with French women. That is more or less what we did. Do you want to hear how I decided to take on this work?

GAUS: Please.

ARENDT: You see, I came out of a purely academic background. In this respect the year 1933 made a very lasting impression on me. First a positive one and then a negative one. Perhaps I had better say first a negative one and then a positive one. People often think today that German Jews were shocked in 1933 because Hitler assumed power. As far as I and people of my generation are concerned, I can say that that is a curious misunderstanding. Naturally Hitler's rise was very bad. But it was political. It wasn't personal. We didn't need Hitler's assumption of power to know that the Nazis were our enemies! That had been completely evident for at least four years to everyone who wasn't feebleminded. We also knew that a large number of the German people were behind them. That could not shock us or surprise us in 1933.

GAUS: You mean that the shock in 1933 came from the fact that events went from the generally political to the personal?

ARENDT: Not even that. Or, that too. First of all, the generally political became a personal fate when one emigrated. Second . . . friends "co-ordinated" or got in line. The problem, the personal problem, was

not what our enemies did but what our friends did. In the wave of
Gleichschaltung (co-ordination),* which was relatively voluntary—in any
case, not yet under the pressure of terror—it was as if an empty space
formed around one. I lived in an intellectual milieu, but I also knew
other people. And among intellectuals *Gleichschaltung* was the rule, so
to speak. But not among the others. And I never forgot that. I left
Germany dominated by the idea—of course somewhat exaggerated:
Never again! I shall never again get involved in any kind of intellectual
business. I want nothing to do with that lot. Also I didn't believe then
that Jews and German Jewish intellectuals would have acted any differently had their own circumstances been different. That was not my
opinion. I thought that it had to do with this profession, with being an
intellectual. I am speaking in the past tense. Today I know more about
it. . . .

GAUS: I was just about to ask you if you still believe that.

ARENDT: No longer to the same degree. But I still think that it
belongs to the essence of being an intellectual that one fabricates ideas
about everything. No one ever blamed someone if he "co-ordinated"
because he had to take care of his wife or child. The worst thing was
that some people really believed in Nazism! For a short time, many for
a very short time. But that means that they made up ideas about Hitler,
in part terrifically interesting things! Completely fantastic and interesting
and complicated things! Things far above the ordinary level!† I found
that grotesque. Today I would say that they were trapped by their own
ideas. That is what happened. But then, at that time, I didn't see it so
clearly.

GAUS: And that was the reason that it was particularly important
for you to get out of intellectual circles and start to do work of a practical
nature?

ARENDT: Yes. The positive side is the following. I realized what

---

Gleichschaltung, or political co-ordination, refers to the widespread giving in, at the
outset of the Nazi era, to the changed political climate in order either to secure
one's position or to get employment. In addition, it describes the Nazi policy of
converting traditional organizations—youth groups and all sorts of clubs and associations—into specifically Nazi organizations. —Ed.

†More than one German intellectual attempted to "rationalize" Nazism after 1933.
For a fuller discussion of this issue, see Arendt's essay "The Image of Hell" in this
volume. —Ed.

I then expressed time and again in the sentence: If one is attacked as a Jew, one must defend oneself as a Jew. Not as a German, not as a world-citizen, not as an upholder of the Rights of Man, or whatever. But: What can I specifically do as a Jew? Second, it was now my clear intention to work with an organization. For the first time. To work with the Zionists. They were the only ones who were ready. It would have been pointless to join those who had assimilated. Besides, I never really had anything to do with them. Even before this time I had concerned myself with the Jewish question. The book on Rahel Varnhagen was finished when I left Germany.* The problem of the Jews plays a role in it. I wrote it with the idea, "I want to understand." I wasn't discussing my personal problems as a Jew. But now, belonging to Judaism had become my own problem, and my own problem was political. Purely political! I wanted to go into practical work, exclusively and only Jewish work. With this in mind I then looked for work in France.

GAUS: Until 1940.

ARENDT: Yes.

GAUS: Then during the Second World War you went to the United States of America, where you are now a professor of political theory, not philosophy . . .

ARENDT: Thank you.

GAUS: . . . in Chicago. You live in New York. Your husband, whom you married in 1940, is also a professor, of philosophy, in America. The academic community, of which you are again a member—after the disillusionment of 1933—is international. Yet I should like to ask you whether you miss the Europe of the pre-Hitler period, which will never exist again. When you come to Europe, what, in your impression, remains and what is irretrievably lost?

ARENDT: The Europe of the pre-Hitler period? I do not long for that, I can tell you. What remains? The language remains.

GAUS: And that means a great deal to you?

ARENDT: A great deal. I have always consciously refused to lose my mother tongue. I have always maintained a certain distance from

---

*Except for the last two chapters, which were written sometime between 1933 and 1936 in France. Cf. *Rahel Varnhagen: The Life of a Jewish Woman*, rev. ed., New York: Harcourt Brace Jovanovich, 1974, xiii. —Ed.

French, which I then spoke very well, as well as from English, which I write today.

GAUS: I wanted to ask you that. You write in English now?

ARENDT: I write in English, but I have never lost a feeling of distance from it. There is a tremendous difference between your mother tongue and another language. For myself I can put it extremely simply: In German I know a rather large part of German poetry by heart; the poems are always somehow in the back of my mind. I can never do that again. I do things in German that I would not permit myself to do in English. That is, sometimes I do them in English too, because I have become bold, but in general I have maintained a certain distance. The German language is the essential thing that has remained and that I have always consciously preserved.

GAUS: Even in the most bitter time?

ARENDT: Always. I thought to myself, What is one to do? It wasn't the German language that went crazy. And, second, there is no substitution for the mother tongue. People can forget their mother tongue. That's true—I have seen it. There are people who speak the new language better than I do. I still speak with a very heavy accent, and I often speak unidiomatically. They can all do these things correctly. But they do them in a language in which one cliché chases another because the productivity that one has in one's own language is cut off when one forgets that language.

GAUS: The cases in which the mother tongue was forgotten: Is it your impression that this was the result of repression?

ARENDT: Yes, very frequently. I have seen it in people as a result of shock. You know, what was decisive was not the year 1933, at least not for me. What was decisive was the day we learned about Auschwitz.

GAUS: When was that?

ARENDT: That was in 1943. And at first we didn't believe it— although my husband and I always said that we expected anything from that bunch. But we didn't believe this because militarily it was unnecessary and uncalled for. My husband is a former military historian, he understands something about these matters. He said don't be gullible, don't take these stories at face value. They can't go that far! And then a half-year later we believed it after all, because we had the proof. That was the real shock. Before that we said: Well, one has enemies. That is entirely natural. Why shouldn't a people have enemies? But this was different. It was really as if an abyss had opened. Because we had the idea that amends could somehow be made for everything else, as amends can be made for just about everything at some point in politics. But not for this. *This ought not to have happened.* And I don't mean just the number of victims. I mean the method, the fabrication of corpses and so on—I don't need to go into that. This should not have happened. Something happened there to which we cannot reconcile ourselves. None of us ever can. About everything else that happened I have to say that it was sometimes rather difficult: we were very poor, we were hunted down, we had to flee, by hook or by crook we somehow had to get through, and whatever. That's how it was. But we were young. I even had a little fun with it—I can't deny it. But not this. This was something completely different. Personally I could accept everything else.

GAUS: I should like to hear from you, Miss Arendt, how your opinions about postwar Germany, which you have often visited, and in which your most important works have been published, have changed since 1945.

ARENDT: I returned to Germany for the first time in 1949, in the service of a Jewish organization for the recovery of Jewish cultural treasures, mostly books. I came with very good will. My thoughts after 1945 were as follows: Whatever happened in 1933 is really unimportant in light of what happened after that. Certainly, the disloyalty of friends, to put it bluntly for once . . .

GAUS: . . . which you experienced personally . . .

ARENDT: Of course. But if someone really became a Nazi and wrote articles about it, he did not have to be loyal to me personally. I did not speak to him again anyhow. He didn't have to get in touch with me anymore, because as far as I was concerned he had ceased to exist. That much is clear. But they were not all murderers. There were people who fell into their own trap, as I would say today. Nor did they desire what came later. Thus it seemed to me that there should be a basis for communication precisely in the abyss of Auschwitz. And that was true in many personal relations. I argued with people; I am not particularly agreeable, nor am I very polite; I say what I think. But somehow things were set straight again with a lot of people. As I said, all these were only people who were committed to Nazism for a few months, at the worst for a few years; neither murderers nor informers. People, as I said, who "made up ideas" about Hitler. But the general, and the greatest experience when one returns to Germany—apart from the experience of recognition, which is always the crux of the action in Greek tragedy—is one of violent emotion. And then there was the experience of hearing German spoken in the streets. For me that was an indescribable joy.

GAUS: This was your reaction when you came in 1949?

ARENDT: More or less. And today, now that things are back on track, the distance I feel has become greater than it was before, when I experienced things in that highly emotional state.

GAUS: Because conditions here got back on track too quickly in your opinion?

ARENDT: Yes. And often on a track to which I do not assent. But I don't feel responsible for that. I see it from the outside now. And that means that I am far less involved than I was at that time. That could be because of the lapse of time. Listen, fifteen years are not nothing!

GAUS: You have become much more indifferent?

ARENDT: Distant . . . indifferent is too strong. But there is distance.

GAUS: Miss Arendt, your book on the trial of Eichmann in Jerusalem was published this fall in the Federal Republic. Since its publication in America, your book has been very heatedly discussed. From the Jewish side, especially, objections have been raised which you say are partly based on misunderstandings and partly on an intentional political campaign. Above all, people were offended by the question you raised of the extent to which Jews are to blame for their passive acceptance of the German mass murders, or to what extent the collaboration of certain Jewish councils almost constitutes a kind of guilt of their own. In any case, for a portrait of Hannah Arendt, so to speak, a number of questions come out of this book. If I may begin with them: Is the criticism that your book is lacking in love for the Jewish people painful to you?

ARENDT: First of all, I must, in all friendliness, state that you yourself have become a victim of this campaign. Nowhere in my book did I reproach the Jewish people with nonresistance. Someone else did that in the Eichmann trial, namely, Mr. Haussner of the Israeli public prosecutor's office. I called such questions directed to the witnesses in Jerusalem both foolish and cruel.

GAUS: I have read the book. I know that. But some of the criticisms made of you are based on the tone in which many passages are written.

ARENDT: Well, that is another matter. What can I say? Besides, I don't want to say anything. If people think that one can only write about these things in a solemn tone of voice . . . Look, there are people who take it amiss—and I can understand that in a sense—that, for instance, I can still laugh. But I was really of the opinion that Eichmann was a buffoon. I'll tell you this: I read the transcript of his police investigation, thirty-six hundred pages, read it, and read it very carefully, and I do not know how many times I laughed—laughed out loud! People took this reaction in a bad way. I cannot do anything about that. But I know one thing: Three minutes before certain death, I probably still would laugh. And that, they say, is the tone of voice. That the tone of voice is predominantly ironic is completely true. The tone of voice in this case is really the person. When people reproach me with accusing the Jewish people, that is a malignant lie and propaganda and nothing else. The tone of voice, however, is an objection against me personally. And I cannot do anything about that.

GAUS: You are prepared to bear that?

ARENDT: Yes, willingly. What is one to do? I cannot say to people: You misunderstand me, and in truth this or that is going on in my heart. That's ridiculous.

GAUS: In this connection I should like to go back to a personal statement of yours. You said: "I have never in my life 'loved' any people or collective group, neither the German people, the French, the Americans, nor the working class or anything of that sort. I indeed love only my friends, and the only kind of love I know of and believe in is the love of persons. Moreover, this 'love of the Jews' would appear to me, since I am myself Jewish, as something rather suspect."* May I ask something? As a politically active being, doesn't man need commitment to a group, a commitment that can then to a certain extent be called love? Are you not afraid that your attitude could be politically sterile?

ARENDT: No. I would say it is the other attitude that is politically

---

*Arendt to Scholem, July 24, 1963. —Ed.

sterile. In the first place, belonging to a group is a natural condition. You belong to some sort of group when you are born, always. But to belong to a group in the way you mean, in a second sense, that is, to join or form an organized group, is something completely different. This kind of organization has to do with a relation to the world. People who become organized have in common what are ordinarily called interests. The directly personal relationship, where one can speak of love, exists of course foremost in real love, and it also exists in a certain sense in friendship. There a person is addressed directly, independent of his relation to the world. Thus, people of the most divergent organizations can still be personal friends. But if you confuse these things, if you bring love to the negotiating table, to put it bluntly, I find that fatal.

GAUS: You find it apolitical?

ARENDT: I find it apolitical. I find it worldless. And I really find it to be a great disaster. I admit that the Jewish people are a classic example of a worldless people maintaining themselves throughout thousands of years . . .

GAUS: "World" in the sense of your terminology as space for politics.

ARENDT: As space for politics.

GAUS: Thus the Jewish people were an apolitical people?

ARENDT: I shouldn't say that exactly, for the communities were, of course, to a certain extent, also political. The Jewish religion is a national religion. But the concept of the political was valid only with great reservations. This worldlessness which the Jewish people suffered in being dispersed, and which—as with all people who are pariahs— generated a special warmth among those who belonged, changed when the state of Israel was founded.

GAUS: Did something get lost, then, something the loss of which you regret?

ARENDT: Yes, one pays dearly for freedom. The specifically Jewish humanity signified by their worldlessness was something very beautiful. You are too young to have ever experienced that. But it was something very beautiful, this standing outside of all social connections, the complete open-mindedness and absence of prejudice that I experienced, especially with my mother, who also exercised it in relation to the whole Jewish community. Of course, a great deal was lost with the passing of all that. One pays for liberation. I once said in my Lessing speech . . .

GAUS: Hamburg in 1959 . . .*

ARENDT: Yes, there I said that "this humanity . . . has never yet survived the hour of liberation, of freedom, by so much as a minute." You see, that has also happened to us.

GAUS: You wouldn't like to undo it?

ARENDT: No. I know that one has to pay a price for freedom. But I cannot say that I like to pay it.

GAUS: Miss Arendt, do you feel that it is your duty to publish what you learn through political-philosophical speculation or sociological analysis? Or are there reasons to be silent about something you know?

ARENDT: Yes, that is a very difficult problem. It is at bottom the sole question that interested me in the whole controversy over the Eichmann book. But it is a question that never arose unless I broached it. It is the only serious question—everything else is pure propaganda soup. So, *fiat veritas, et pereat mundus* [let truth be told though the world may perish]?† But the Eichmann book did not *de facto* touch upon such things. The book really does not jeopardize anybody's legitimate interests. It was only thought to do so.

GAUS: You must leave the question of what is legitimate open to discussion.

ARENDT: Yes, that is true. You are right. The question of what is legitimate is still open to discussion. I probably mean by "legitimate" something different from what the Jewish organizations mean. But let us assume that real interests, which even I recognize, were at stake.

GAUS: Might one then be silent about the truth?

ARENDT: Might I have been? Yes! To be sure, I might have written it. . . . But look here, someone asked me, if I had anticipated one thing or another, wouldn't I have written the Eichmann book differently? I

---

*Arendt's address on accepting the Lessing Prize of the Free City of Hamburg is reprinted as "On Humanity in Dark Times: Thoughts about Lessing," in *Men in Dark Times*, New York: Harcourt, Brace & World, 1968. —Ed.

†Arendt plays with the old Latin adage *Fiat iustitia, et periat mundus* (Let justice be done, though the world may perish). Cf. *Between Past and Future*, New York: The Viking Press, 1968, 228. —Ed.

answered: No. I would have confronted the alternative: to write or not to write. Because one can also hold one's tongue.

GAUS: Yes.

ARENDT: One doesn't always have to speak. But now we come to the question of what, in the eighteenth century, were called "truths of fact." This is really a matter of truths of fact. It is not a matter of opinions. The historical sciences in the universities are the guardians of truths of fact.

GAUS: They have not always been the best ones.

ARENDT: No. They collapse. They are controlled by the state. I have been told that a historian remarked of some book about the origin of the First World War: "I won't let this spoil the memory of such an uplifting time!" That is a man who does not know who he is. But that is uninteresting. *De facto* he is the guardian of historical truth, the truth of facts. And we know how important these guardians are from Bolshevik history, for example, where history is rewritten every five years and the facts remain unknown: for instance, that there was a Mr. Trotsky. Is this what we want? Is that what governments are interested in?

GAUS: They might have that interest. But do they have that right?

ARENDT: Do they have that right? They do not appear to believe it themselves—otherwise they would not tolerate universities at all. Thus, even states are interested in the truth. I don't mean military secrets; that's something else. But these events go back approximately twenty years. Why shouldn't one speak the truth?

GAUS: Perhaps because twenty years are still too little?

ARENDT: Many people say that; others say that after twenty years one can no longer figure out the truth. In any case, there is an interest in whitewashing. That, however, is not a legitimate interest.

GAUS: In case of doubt, you would prefer the truth.

ARENDT: I would rather say that impartiality—which came into the world when Homer . . .

GAUS: For the conquered as well . . .

ARENDT: Right!

> *Wenn des Liedes Stimmen schweigen*
> *Von dem überwundnen Mann,*
> *So will ich für Hectorn zeugen. . . .*

[If the voices of song are silent
For him who has been vanquished,
I myself will testify for Hector. . . .]*

Isn't that right? That's what Homer did. Then came Herodotus, who spoke of "the great deeds of the Greeks *and* the barbarians." All of science comes from this spirit, even modern science, and the science of history too. If someone is not capable of this impartiality because he pretends to love his people so much that he pays flattering homage to them all the time—well, then there's nothing to be done. I do not believe that people like that are patriots.

GAUS: In one of your most important works, *The Human Condition*, you come to the conclusion, Miss Arendt, that the modern period has dethroned the sense of what concerns everyone, that is, the sense of the prime importance of the political. You designate as modern social phenomena the uprooting and loneliness of the masses and the triumph of a type of human being who finds satisfaction in the process of mere labor and consumption. I have two questions about this. First, to what extent is this kind of philosophical knowledge dependent upon a personal experience which first gets the process of thinking going?

ARENDT: I do not believe that there is any thought process possible without personal experience. Every thought is an afterthought, that is, a reflection on some matter or event. Isn't that so? I live in the modern world, and obviously my experience is in and of the modern world. This, after all, is not controversial. But the matter of merely laboring and consuming is of crucial importance for the reason that a kind of worldlessness defines itself there too. Nobody cares any longer what the world looks like.

GAUS: "World" understood always as the space in which politics can originate.

ARENDT: I comprehend it now in a much larger sense, as the space in which things become public, as the space in which one lives and which must look presentable. In which art appears, of course. In which all kinds of things appear. You remember that Kennedy tried to expand the public space quite decisively by inviting poets and other ne'er-

*From Schiller's *Das Siegesfest.* —Ed.

do-wells to the White House. So that it all could belong to this space. However, in labor and consumption man is utterly thrown back on himself.

GAUS: On the biological.

ARENDT: On the biological, and on himself. And there you have the connection with loneliness. A peculiar loneliness arises in the process of labor. I cannot go into that right now, because it would lead us too far afield. But this loneliness consists in being thrown back upon oneself; a state of affairs in which, so to speak, consumption takes the place of all the truly relating activities.

GAUS: A second question in this connection: in *The Human Condition* you come to the conclusion that "truly world oriented experiences"—you mean insights and experiences of the highest political significance—"withdraw more and more from the experiential horizon of the average human life." You say that today "the ability to act is restricted to a few people." What does this mean in terms of practical politics, Miss Arendt? To what extent does a form of government based, at least theoretically, on the co-operative responsibility of all citizens become a fiction under these circumstances?

ARENDT: I want to qualify that a bit. Look, this inability to be realistically oriented applies not only to the masses, but also to every other stratum of society. I would say even to the statesman. The statesman is surrounded, encircled by an army of experts. So that now the question of action lies between the statesman and the experts. The statesman has to make the final decision. He can hardly do that realistically, since he can't know everything himself. He must take the advice of experts, indeed of experts who in principle always have to contradict each other. Isn't that so? Every reasonable statesman summons experts with opposing points of view. Because he has to see the matter from all sides. That's true, isn't it? He has to judge between them. And this judging is a highly mysterious process—in which, then, common sense* is made manifest. As far as the masses are concerned, I would say the

*By common sense (*Gemeinsinn*), Arendt does not mean the unreflective prudence that every sane adult exercises continuously (*gesunder Menschenverstand*), but, rather, as Kant put it, "a sense *common to all* . . . a faculty of judgment which, in its reflection, takes account . . . of the mode of representation of all other men," Immanuel Kant, *Critique of Judgment*, §40, cited in Arendt's *Lectures on Kant's Political Philosophy*, edited by R. Beiner, Chicago, 1982, 70–72. —Ed.

following: Wherever men come together, in whatever numbers, public interests come into play.

GAUS: Always.

ARENDT: And the public realm is formed. In America where there are still spontaneous associations, which then disband again—the kind of associations already described by Tocqueville—you can see this very clearly. Some public interest concerns a specific group of people, those in a neighborhood or even in just one house or in a city or in some other sort of group. Then these people will convene, and they are very capable of acting publicly in these matters—for they have an overview of them. What you were aiming at with your question applies only to the greatest decisions on the highest level. And, believe me, the difference between the statesman and the man in the street is in principle not very great.

GAUS: Miss Arendt, you have been in close contact with Karl Jaspers, your former teacher, in an ongoing dialogue. What do you think is the greatest influence that Professor Jaspers has had on you?

ARENDT: Well, where Jaspers comes forward and speaks, all becomes luminous. He has an unreservedness, a trust, an unconditionality of speech that I have never known in anyone else. This impressed me even when I was very young. Besides, he has a conception of freedom linked to reason which was completely foreign to me when I came to Heidelberg. I knew nothing about it, although I had read Kant. I saw this reason in action, so to speak. And if I may say so—I grew up without a father—I was educated by it. I don't want to make him responsible for me, for God's sake, but if anyone succeeded in instilling some sense in me, it was he. And this dialogue is, of course, quite different today. That was really my most powerful postwar experience. That there can be such conversations! That one can speak in such a way!

GAUS: Permit me a last question. In a tribute to Jaspers you said: "Humanity is never acquired in solitude, and never by giving one's work to the public. It can be achieved only by one who has thrown his life and his person into the 'venture into the public realm.' "* This "venture into the public realm"—which is a quotation from Jaspers—what does it mean for Hannah Arendt?

ARENDT: The venture into the public realm seems clear to me.

*"Karl Jaspers: A Laudatio," in *Men in Dark Times*, 73–74. —Ed.

One exposes oneself to the light of the public, as a person. Although I am of the opinion that one must not appear and act in public self-consciously, still I know that in every action the person is expressed as in no other human activity. Speaking is also a form of action. That is one venture. The other is: we start something. We weave our strand into a network of relations. What comes of it we never know. We've all been taught to say: Lord forgive them, for they know not what they do. That is true of all action. Quite simply and concretely true, because one *cannot* know. That is what is meant by a venture. And now I would say that this venture is only possible when there is trust in people. A trust—which is difficult to formulate but fundamental—in what is human in all people. Otherwise such a venture could not be made.

Augustine and Protestantism

T HE FIFTEEN HUNDREDTH anniversary of Augustine's death is being celebrated throughout the Catholic world this year. In Italy, France, and Germany, innumerable articles in Catholic newspapers reflect this event, and, at gatherings devoted to Augustine's memory, clergy and scholars assess the significance of his work, his person, and his influence. But in the Protestant world he is largely forgotten. In calling him *Saint* Augustine, the Catholics have so exclusively confiscated him as their own that the Protestants seem to shy away from laying any claim to him at all on their own behalf.

That was not always the case. In the Middle Ages, until Luther, the name Augustine carried the same weight for both the orthodox and the heretic, for reformers and counter-reformers. Luther himself appealed to Augustine's authority and felt himself to be following in Augustine's footsteps as strongly as he rejected Thomas Aquinas and, along with him, the Aristotelian tradition, which Luther regarded as the school of the "foolish philosopher." And indeed, neither the Protestant conscience, Protestant individuality, nor Protestant biblical exegesis, which

Published in German under the title "Augustin und der Protestantismus," *Frankfurter Zeitung*, 902, December 4, 1930. English translation by Robert and Rita Kimber.

began with young Luther's commentaries on the letters to the Galatians and the Romans, would be conceivable without Augustine's *Confessions*, on the one hand, or, on the other, without his great commentaries on the Gospel and letters of St. John, on Genesis, and on the Psalms. Because he was a citizen of the Roman Empire, a man of late antiquity when he abandoned the cultural world of his youth and became a Christian, Augustine was a forebear in two respects. In his youth, he gave himself up to all the cultural and intellectual currents of his time; he had been a Manichean, a Skeptic, then a Neo-Platonist. Indeed, he never abandoned his Neo-Platonism, the legacy of Plotinus, the last Greek. He never stopped trying to understand and interpret the world in philosophical-cosmological terms, and he introduced into the incipient Catholic Church all those elements—the hierarchical order, the rhetorical eloquence, and the claim to universality—in whose light we can still today regard the Church as the heir of the Roman Empire. In his *De civitate Dei*, Augustine gave legitimacy to this legacy by providing the Church with its own history as a secular institution. He knew that the Church could base its universality only on the universality of the declining Roman Empire, and he granted it the right to do so. We can understand the breadth and richness of the Christian Augustine only if we take into account the ambiguity of his existence as both a Roman and a Christian, only if we fully realize that he stood on the very border between declining antiquity and the rise of the Middle Ages.

The *Confessions* bear witness to that other, Christian empire that Augustine, at the close of antiquity, opened up for the centuries to come: the empire of the inner life. "Soul" for the Greeks did not in any way mean the inner life. Soul represented man's essence but not the mysterious and unknown realms of his inner world that were no less hidden to him than the distant realms of the outer world. The Greeks did not regard those inner realms as histories of their own lives, as biographies. There are of course in Greek literature *bioi*, lives of great men, which are written by others (but even they are not found before the Hellenistic period). They glorify famous men. But Augustine does not look back on his life to glorify himself, but for the glory of God. One's own life has meaning not only because it is earthly but also because in it we decide to be near or far from God, we decide for sin or redemption. At the moment of conversion, Augustine was redeemed by God; the whole world was not redeemed, but only Augustine, the individual, who stood before

God. He was redeemed from his sinful life, and that he confesses to this redemption redounds to the glory of God and is a human testimony to the power of God. In this confession, he is forced to recall his earlier life, indeed, every bit of his earlier life, because every moment of that life was sinful and therefore every moment of it magnifies the power and the miracle of redemption. Through such confession one's own life acquires a unified, meaningful continuity; it becomes the path to redemption. Memory opens up this life for us; only in memory does the past take on everlasting meaning; only in memory is the past both canceled out and preserved for all time.

Many doubts have been expressed about the veracity of the *Confessions*: Augustine exaggerated his sins, intentionally or unintentionally; he misrepresented his life, made it appear different from what it had really been; he forgot everything good; in short, people have said, his memory had falsified things. But without this memory, without this "representation," which is always something essentially different from naively experienced reality itself, this past would not have been preserved for us at all; it would have remained lost. It was "falsifying" memory that saved the reality for us. The search for the "real" reality, a reality apart from the one rescued for us in the *Confessions*, is pointless. The *Confessions* close, logically enough, with a long philosophical discourse on memory in which memory is shown to be the essence of the inner life, that is, of the life of the Christian human being.

The discovery of one's own inner life and the broad and thorough exploration of that life are in no way related to psychology or modern reflection, despite the innumerable and striking psychological details Augustine reveals. For the inner life in this context is not valuable because it is one's own and therefore interesting, but because it was bad and has become good. The individual life is not deserving of attention because it is individual and unique in the modern sense, or because it is capable of a unique development and full realization of its personal potential. It is of value not because it is unique, but because it is exemplary. As my life has been, so can all lives be. The individual confession carries a generally applicable meaning: God's grace can enter any and every individual life in this same way. Lives do not have their own autonomous histories; the basic principle of change is conversion, which divides a life into two separate parts. What makes a life worthy of being remembered, what makes it a monument for the Christian, is not any principle immanent in that life itself, but what is wholly other: the grace of God.

In the Christian tradition of Europe this kind of remembering has taken two separate paths in its later evolution: one is the Catholic confessional; the other, the Protestant conscience. By its very nature, the confessional altered the original meaning of confession. In Augustine, the individual who confesses is thrown back into the loneliness of his own inner life and stands with that inner life revealed before God. That this lonely being-revealed-before-God can be a warning and a testimony for others in no way changes its fundamental nature. Augustine confesses to God alone, not to other human beings, though we might possibly say he confesses for them. The confessional, however, places the authority of the Church between the soul and God, and this is precisely what Luther opposed, regarding it as a distortion of original Christianity. Reaching back over the centuries and past the Catholic era, Luther derived from Augustine his concept of the believer whose conscience stands in a direct relationship with God.

Although the *Confessions* have no psychological intent, Augustine is nonetheless the founding father of the modern psychological and auto-biographical novel. In Germany, this development took a detour by way of pietism. With increasing secularization, religious self-reflection before God lost its meaning. There was no longer an authority to confess to, and religious self-reflection therefore became simply reflection on one's own life, devoid of the religious element. The first novel in Germany to exemplify this clearly is Karl Philip Moritz's *Anton Reiser*. Although Moritz's own roots were pietistic, it was his work that marked the final turning away from "edifying" life stories in the pietistic mode. The concept of grace gave way entirely to one of autonomous self-development, and we find the culmination of this change in Goethe, who conceived of personal history as "an image cast in constant, living change."

Philosophy and Sociology

T HE THOUGHTS DEVELOPED in this essay are based on Karl Mannheim's *Ideology and Utopia*.[1] What I am attempting here is an analysis of the theoretical basis presented in that book and of the claims made for sociology that derive from that theoretical basis. My arguments will not directly address Mannheim's analyses of individual historical cases, analyses at which he is far more competent than this reviewer. Instead, I will confine myself exclusively to the book's basic philosophical intent. This article assumes that the reader is familiar with Mannheim's book, the importance of which lies in pointing up, from a historical perspective, the questionable nature of all modern thought (*Geistigkeit*).[2] What are the implications for philosophy of this perceived questionable nature? What is the nature of the problems it raises that they can so disturb philosophy?

The reason why the book is disturbing to philosophy is that Mannheim—while demonstrating that all thought is "situation-bound," that is, tied to a specific social situation and even to a specific political

Published in German as "Philosophie und Soziologie: Anlässlich Karl Mannheim, *Ideologie und Utopie*," *Die Gesellschaft*, VII/2, Berlin, 1930. English translation by Robert and Rita Kimber. The numbered notes are at the end of the essay.

position—takes no position himself, unless we regard as a kind of position-taking his inquiry into the social situation in which "non-situation-boundness" is even possible. Only in this context does sociology bear on philosophical issues and have something to say to philosophy. Only in this context is sociology with all its analytical destructuring[3] of reality still in search of "reality"[4]—reality itself, not some socio-economic interest that can be seen as underlying individual theories, reality as "something that helps us orient ourselves in the world."[5] But the will to orient ourselves in the world implies recognition of the intellectual realm as significant; refusal to commit oneself to any one position implies awareness of the potential fruitfulness of neutrality. It is here that the basic difference between Mannheim's position and that of Georg Lukács lies. Lukács, like Mannheim, challenges the intellectual sphere's claim to absolute validity,[6] but he does so from a specific position, namely, that of the proletariat, and thereby imperceptibly and without any qualms adopts its altogether justified concept of interest (which turns out to be very fruitful for concrete interpretation).

The detachment from any historical position, together with the awareness that even this refusal to take a position is historically conditioned, bears on philosophy in two ways. First of all, Mannheim inquires into the nature of reality, that is, into what the true origin of thought might be; second, by taking into account *all* positions and radically relativizing them he comes to see that all "interpretations of existence"[7] ultimately serve as means of orientation in a specific, historically given world and thus place the significance of the world in the realm of human communal life.

Put in philosophical terms, the underlying problem in Mannheim's sociology is the uncertain nature of the relationship between the ontic and the ontological.[8] Whereas philosophy inquires into the "Being of the What Is" (Heidegger's *Sein des Seienden*) or into "existence" (*Existenz* in Jaspers) dissociated from everyday life, sociology does just the opposite, inquiring into the "What Is" that underlies our "interpretations of existence"; that is, sociology focuses on the very thing that philosophy deems irrelevant.

According to Mannheim, all human thought is "existentially bound" and can be properly understood only by taking into account the particular situation from which it arises. This applies even to philosophical thought, which claims to be unaffected by particular points of view and to embody truth as such, thus assuming *absolute* validity for itself. But this claim to absolute validity cannot be refuted simply by pointing out that all thinking is situation-bound. It can be seriously undermined only by tracing specific philosophies back to their origins in particular situations. Situation-boundness is not just the *conditio sine qua non* but the *conditio per quam*. If situation-boundness were just the *conditio sine qua non* of all thought, it would have nothing to say about the objective content of thought seen apart from its genesis. Genesis in the real world cannot simply be turned into genesis of meaning. Only if existential-boundness is accepted not just abstractly but concretely as the driving force behind thought, that is, if thought is defined as nothing more than a special type of transformation which is itself existentially bound (as in the assertion that philosophy is possible only in the context of a certain social position), only then can the absolute separation of ontology and the ontic be overcome and an ontic posited that in its historical transmutations creates and destroys various ontologies. The demonstration of the inevitable connectedness of the two spheres—that of Being and that of the What Is, to use Heidegger's terms—takes the most radical form where consciousness of the absolute can be traced back to its ontic determinants and thus refuted. We see, then, that sociological destructuring not only *relativizes*, which would be fairly harmless, but also is capable of *refuting*. Refutation takes the form of unmasking consciousness of the absolute as *ideology* (in the sense of "total ideology,"[9]) that is, as a consciousness that is unaware of being bound to the ontic precisely because of ontic conditions and thus lays claim to absoluteness. The decisive point here, then, is not just that ontology is bound to the ontic but that unmasking ontology as ideology means that ontology as such can arise only because of limits to perception *imposed by the What Is itself*.

Thus, the nature of philosophy proves to be not transcendent and above everyday reality; rather, the vital motivation for philosophy originates in that very reality. Reality is the *conditio per quam*. From a sociological point of view philosophy can no longer yield any answers about the "Being of the What Is," but is now revealed as one What Is among others, bound to and entangled in the world of What Is and its motivations. The absolute reality of philosophy is called into question here by tracing philosophy back to a "more original" reality, a reality it has forgotten. Indeed, philosophy's transcendence is interpreted as a mere case of forgetfulness, its claim to absolute answers as the result of having forgotten its historical roots. This not only negates the claim of philosophy as such to absolute validity but even challenges it in its specific manifestations. Sociology thus raises the philosophical question of what the point of philosophy is.

Before we go into Mannheim's answer to this question, it will be helpful to consider briefly two modern philosophical approaches against which Mannheim's book seems to be directed. I will deliberately limit myself to only those aspects that are pertinent to this discussion.

Karl Jaspers has made human existence the primary subject of philosophy. By "existence" he means not ordinary everyday life in its continuity but those few moments during which alone we experience our authentic selves and recognize the uncertainty of the human situation as such. These are "border situations,"[10] in comparison to which all of everyday life is merely a "falling away." We are authentically ourselves only when, detached and freed from the daily here and now where we have always to prove ourselves to others, we experience the absolute solitude of the "border situations." The fact that Jaspers regards everyday life and "falling away" into it as a necessary part of human life is immaterial in this context. The term "falling away" implies a negative assessment of everydayness, and the negative quality is further brought out by the comparison to non-everyday experience. Sociology attempts just the opposite: It tries to comprehend the non-everyday as a mode inherent in everyday life. We will examine later to what extent this attempt is successful. What matters here is that sociology assigns the status of concrete reality to the here and now and brings even "peak moments" down to the level of this reality, making them subject to its historical continuity and its laws. In this view solitude can be understood, if at all, only as a negative mode of human existence (fear of and escape from the world or, as Mannheim puts it, a consciousness "that is not congruous with the world around it"[11]).

In this basic assessment of everyday life, sociology seems to approach Heidegger's view in *Being and Time*. Heidegger takes as his starting point the everydayness of human existence—Mannheim's everydayness of human communal life or what Heidegger terms the "they" (*das Man*)—in which "existence (*Dasein*) most immediately and most commonly manifests itself."[12] Communal human life, that is, the historical world, is so much a condition of being oneself that "*authentic Being-one's-Self* does not rest upon an exceptional condition of the subject, a condition that has been detached from the 'they'; *it is, rather, an existentiell modification of the 'they'—of the 'they' as an essential existentiale.*"[13] Being human necessarily means "Being-in-the-world."[14] In this basic philosophical premise, *Dasein* is thus understood as existence in a particular world. What links Heidegger to Jaspers is that he calls the "basic form of Being in everydayness" a "falling away from *Dasein*." Authenticity, "*Dasein's* potential for being itself," becomes possible only if the self extricates itself from its inevitable state of "being lost in the publicness of the 'they.' "[15] From these considerations, Mannheim develops a double polemic. On the one hand, he doubts—as he did above in connection with Jaspers—the possibility of being free from the 'they' and, by extension, of attaining the authentic existence that Heidegger circumscribes with his phrase "Being-towards-death"[16] and Jaspers, with his "border situations." Mannheim thereby implicitly questions the admissibility of the categories authenticity and non-authenticity altogether and favors instead a concept of existence that lies beyond the alternatives of authentic and non-authentic, genuine and non-genuine. All these categories appear to Mannheim to be totally arbitrary. He sees no reason why being oneself should have priority over being "they." The indeterminacy in which all categories of this kind are left follows from a radical relativizing and historicizing. It is not just the phenomenon of the "they" that interests the sociologist, but "how this 'they' came to exist. . . . Where the philosopher's questions end, the sociological problem begins."[17] This suggests at the same time that there may not always have been and may not always be something like the "they." Not only can "the extent to which its dominion becomes compelling and explicit . . . change in the course of history"[18] but there can be a human existence in which the "they"—that is, an interpretation of existence that is in this sense public—has not just not been *discovered* but in fact does not *exist*. The sociologist does not inquire into "being in the world" as a formal structure of existence as such but into the specific historically determined world in which any given human being lives. This delimiting of sociology appears harmless, as if all it did was define the discipline's field of competence. It becomes a threat to philosophy only at the point when it claims the world can be investigated only in its particulars, not as a formal structure of human existence. This calls into question the possibility of an *ontological* understanding of being. The ontological structures of human existence in the world, to the extent that they remain unquestionably constant—examples are hunger and sexuality—are the very things that are unimportant, that do not concern us. In any attempt we make to understand our own existence, we are thrown back upon the ever changing ontic realm, which represents *real* reality as opposed to the "theories" of the philosophers. Thus, although Mannheim never explicitly says so, he denies reality to thought as a matter of principle.[19]

Everything in the mental or intellectual realm is regarded as ideology or utopia. Both ideology and utopia are "transcendent to being."[20] They rise from a consciousness "that is not congruous with the world around it."[21] This *mistrust* of the mind evident in sociology and its destructuring mode arises from the homelessness to which the mind in our society is condemned.[22] This homelessness and apparent rootlessness ("socially unattached intelligentsia"[23]) renders everything intellectual suspicious from the outset. Sociology is in search of a reality that is more original than the mind itself, and all intellectual products are to be interpreted or destructured in its light. Destructuring does not mean destruction, but, rather, a tracing back of any claim to validity to the specific situation from which it rises.

Mannheim's attempt at destructuring differs from that of psycho-analysis—which also claims to penetrate to a more original reality—in two respects (quite apart from the fact that psychoanalysis can be only a "partial" and never a "total ideology."[24] First, in sociology the situation-bound validity of the mental world is to a certain extent pre-served. In psychoanalysis, however—which regards everything in the mental or intellectual realm as nothing but "repression" or "sublima-tion"—that realm no longer has any validity at all, and would never even appear in an uninhibited, that is, a properly functioning consciousness. Second—and this is the key point—the reality for the sake of which psychoanalysis does its destructuring is totally alien to meaning and thought. In its working back toward the unconscious, psychoanalysis penetrates to that very realm over which human beings do not have, and never have had, control, i.e., to the realm of the ahistorical. By contrast, sociology does its destructuring precisely in terms of the historical, in terms of what still is or once was within the realm of human freedom. But both sociology and psychoanalysis promote a mode of *understanding* fundamentally different from that of the humanities: not a *direct* under-standing that takes what it understands at face value, not a direct con-frontation, but a detour by way of a reality that they consider *more original*. Both disciplines share a conception of thought as secondary and alien to reality. But the "reality" of psychoanalysis is far more alien to thought than is that of sociology, which requires that the detour of understanding be by way of the "collective subject" and therefore requires understanding based on a historical and social context.[25] In conceiving of its central task as destructuring in terms of the historical, sociology becomes a historical discipline.

This raises two questions: first, the philosophical question of the reality from which all thought derives and in what way thought is transcendent in relation to reality; and, second, the question of competence in historical research.

The reality of primary importance to thought, the vital ground from which thought itself springs, is the "concretely operative order of life"; and this in turn can "best be understood and characterized by means of the particular economic and political structure on which it is based."[26] At first glance it would appear that the economic and political structure from which we can distill the particular operative order of life, that is, the reality of concern to us, is no more than a heuristic principle. Of crucial importance here is the fact that the economic and political structure *is* the heuristic principle, that we distill from it, that it is a more reliable indicator of reality than any intellectual position. A tracing back to the existential-boundness of any philosophical insight would not only say nothing against philosophy but might say something for it, even if this tracing back relativizes and destructures philosophy's claim to absolute validity—a claim that philosophy can relinquish without giving up its meaning. Mannheim himself says that it is precisely existential-boundness that offers a "chance for knowledge,"[27] that only knowledge of that kind escapes the vacuity and vagueness of supposedly universal insights.[28] By tracing its roots back to its existential-boundness, to its *specific* boundness, this knowledge can substantiate its originality. In the confrontation of knowledge with its specific situation, the question of meaning can and will emerge. The genesis of truth in itself says nothing about its originality and "genuineness." (Thus *Ideology and Utopia*, 149: ". . . it is easily possible that there are truths or correct intuitions which are accessible only to a certain personal disposition or to a definite orientation of interests of a certain group.") That can be denied only by those who equate "origins" known to us historically, e.g., the origins of occidental history, with origins per se. A simple example shows how impossible that is: We know that it was often more natural for the early Greeks to express themselves in verse rather than in prose, but for us today to regard this as the "more original" practice and to prefer verse to prose would be extremely mannered and just the opposite of original. This example illustrates that origin and originality are two different things. Every age has its own originality. Relativizing in the context of existential-boundness is the same thing as *relativism* only—and Mannheim stresses this[29]—to the extent that historical understanding is consistent with a concept of truth that is itself traditionally bound and goes back to an era in which "existentially bound thinking" had not yet been discovered. Mannheim's term *"relationism"* provides, by contrast, a new epistemological concept discovered by means of historical understanding, a concept that envisions truth emerging only in existential-boundness. But the existence to which every intellectual position is bound is defined as the social existence of the human community that is in turn inferred from the "economic power structure." It is therefore taken for granted that the existence to which thought is bound, the reality to which it is traced back, is "public existence." The basis for this assertion is that only this existence is capable of undergoing historical change, in contrast to "such natural limitations as birth and death."[30] The individual's own being is determined by its confrontation with this public existence, which is seen as *the* world. Only through this confrontation does the individual human existence become a *historical* one.[31] However, that the historical world manifests itself most clearly in the economic sphere indicates that it is most unequivocally itself where it is at the farthest remove from meaning and thought. Thought therefore necessarily "transcends reality" and is itself not, or is at least only secondarily, reality. It can partake of reality only if it is able somehow to recognize the existing economic and social reality, even if only by deriving from it the impulses for a revolution. Sociology's mission of destructuring takes for granted that thought is homeless, that is, lives in a world inherently alien to it.[32] Thought transcends this alien world and if, in spite of its transcendent nature, it is applied to this world, it becomes *ideology* or *utopia*.

Pursuing this line of thought further would lead to this conclusion: The perception of all thought as either ideological or utopian is based on the conviction that "thought" can exist only where consciousness is incongruent with the social situation in which it is placed and of which it attempts to make sense. Consciousness and thought are "true" if they "contain neither more nor less than the reality in whose medium [they] operate."[33] In this sphere of congruence, however, the possibility of thought as transcendent has not yet been discovered. Thought in this sense arises only when reality has become questionable for the specific consciousness confronting it and when the question of what reality is becomes an inquiry into the nature of genuine reality. Such a consciousness is then a "false consciousness" "if in a given practical situation it uses concepts and categories which, if taken seriously, would prevent man from adjusting himself at that historical stage."[34] Every ideology arises from a "false consciousness," usually one that thinks in "outmoded categories."[35] In other words, ideology lends an absolute authority to a past social situation to which the individual in question is still bound and which he uses to combat a new world situation he finds himself at odds with. Destructuring can therefore be applied only against outmoded ideas "with which we no longer identify."[36] By contrast, a utopian consciousness is one that tends to "shatter, either partially or wholly, the order of things prevailing at the time"[37] for the sake of a coming order it advocates. We distinguish utopia from ideology by applying the criterion of "relevance to reality."[38] As utopia, thought's transcendence of reality tries to translate itself into reality and therefore has a certain power over it, even though thought will always range beyond any specific reality. For ideology, on the other hand, a past world is transcendent because ideology, by its very nature, does not attempt to translate itself into reality (e.g., the Romantic idealizing of the Middle Ages), or it postulates from the outset a categorically transcendent, otherworldly world (e.g., the Christian religion) and therefore renounces any interest in the world as it is. It is utopia's will to affect reality that distinguishes it from ideology. Utopia creates a new reality and therefore becomes a source of power. Only as utopia can thought confront the reality to which it is bound with a different reality that it has itself created. Sociology is thus not concerned with reality as such but with *reality that exerts power over thought*. Reality exerts power over thought because thought is at its origins alien to reality, as is shown by the example of ideology, which *forgets* the actual world that determines it. Thought thus forgets that which made it thought in the first place and to which it remains implicitly bound. Sociology uncovers the determinants of thought, in which thought itself takes no interest, and suggests at the same time that thought's passion for the absolute is simply an unacknowledged forgetting of the conditional. (Both ideology and utopia are characterized by a passion for the absolute, for utopia too believes in the absoluteness of the world it evokes. Both forms of thought can therefore be destructured.) Sociology claims to be the "key science"[39] because it alone is capable of revealing the determinants of thought.

But now this attempt at radical determination encounters "spheres of irresolvability."[40] What remains as a residue of the freedom of thought are "metaphysical, ontological value judgments," which no ideological destructuring can truly dispel and which no analysis of the current state of the economic system can really replace. "Increased knowledge" can only postpone the forming of such judgments.[41] What also remains is that "ecstatic dimension" beyond history that "somehow exists as a constant stimulus, as it were, to the creation of meaning in history and social experience." Mannheim admits that "history constantly lapses from this dimension, too." Both the "postponed metaphysical value judgment" and the ecstatic dimension, which Mannheim finally comes to recognize, exist at the outer limits of what we can know through sociology. This marginal status gives them their peculiar character. Because sociology claims to be the key science, these barely perceptible borderline factors acquire a special status. Sociology claims to encounter them only after destructuring all the interpretations of reality available to us through history. Because sociology assumes that thought (ideology and utopia) is by nature not at home in the world, thought, which is generated by freedom, can exist only *outside historical communal life*. This leads us to an odd conclusion that is, however, paradoxical only on its surface: Thought exists authentically in its ahistorical context ("ecstatic dimension") totally divorced from concrete reality. It is only the impact of thought that belongs to history and is accessible to research. In its essential unrelatedness, thought can be characterized only in negative and deliberately vague terms ("somehow," "so to speak," "human existence is more than").[42]

In its unknowable authorship, thought can be defined only in terms of negatives, and it therefore stands in the same relationship to the concretely experienced and investigable human community as the God of negative theology stands to the concrete world he has created and from which his existence can be inferred only by means of negative statements that define him as one who is *not* thus and so. Indeed, this parallel to negative theology can be pursued even further if we also consider that on the evidence of the real world negative theology was able to infer only the *existence* of God, an existence that by its very nature lies at the outer limits of what human beings can experience. In similar fashion, human freedom, and with it the freedom of thought as such, becomes for sociology a mythical borderline phenomenon in the realm of human understanding. Human thought thus transcends the human world itself and transcends it to an even greater extent than sociology had originally assumed. For if at the beginnings of sociological research (as Mannheim practices it), thought *saw itself* as transcending reality, the sociologist saw it as rooted in and arising from a constantly shifting reality. Thus, the very transcendence that thought appropriated to itself with its claim to absoluteness sociology attempted to destructure by interpreting this transcendence as conditioned by the What Is. Sociology argued here that human existence transcended reality by thought only when it could no longer endure reality and could no longer orient itself in it (thought as escape from a reality that consciousness no longer finds acceptable: false consciousness). Because sociology, by interpreting the transcendence of thought as *escape*, fails to do justice to certain possibilities of human existence and only appears to be able to unmask them, destructuring leaves residues that sociology had not anticipated and to which it therefore attributed a much more radical transcendence than thought would have claimed on its own. From this failure to anticipate the possible primacy of thought, i.e., from the destructuring itself, which does not from the outset define the limits of its competence (which it could not meaningfully do, for only in the process of destructuring could it encounter that which could not be destructured), comes the strange result that thought remains as the final residue after all but becomes transcendent and ahistorical because the reality of history is understood in such a way that there is no place in it for thought.

Sociology thus declares inexplicable and inaccessible to illumination a phenomenon that for philosophy is in no way condemned to remain in this state of indeterminacy and negativity. The "ecstatic dimension" is ultimately identical with human existence, about which philosophy has a great deal to say; it is identical with "existence" in the sense that Kierkegaard used that term. The courage and virtue initially required to deny transcendence and attempt a universal destructuring ultimately forces sociology to admit that a non-destructurable residue remains, to equate the non-destructurable with transcendence, and to assign to the sphere of irreducibility phenomena that philosophy with good reason does not regard as transcendent at all.

Sociology's inherent *mistrust* of thought, however, eliminates thought in another way. Just as this mistrust forces thought into absolute transcendence on the one hand, so on the other it reduces it to the level of a "collective subject" that is regarded as the true vehicle of history. In my view this "collective subject" is at a relatively *greater remove from history* than is thought. The individual not only exists to the extent that he is subsumed under the collective subject and helps constitute it, but also exists—and this is perhaps particularly true of individuals whose lives have an impact on history—at *a remove from the collective subject* that becomes apparent when he finds himself not in congruence with the social world to which he belongs. At this remove, the historical world into which he is born appears to him not as immutable but, from this detached perspective, as changing and changeable. Mannheim calls this freedom from public existence—a freedom that sees the world as alterable—"utopian consciousness." In his analysis of this consciousness he is guided by the following implicit premise: Only because a particular public existence is such that consciousness is incongruous with it does the will to change it arise and, with that will, a relative freedom from the world. Even detachment itself is understood as derived from the given world. Thus, the experience that underlies *freedom from* arises from *boundness to*. *Solitude* is never regarded as a positive and genuine possibility of human life. Correct as it is to stress, in opposition to philosophy, that absolute detachment from communal life is not a prerequisite of genuineness, it is nevertheless questionable to say—though Mannheim does not state this explicitly; he only implies it—that genuineness in life arises only from rootedness in communal life and that solitude is only escape from reality (ideology) or escape into the future (utopia) and in either case is deemed negative.

Then too, Mannheim's criterion of "relevance to reality" for the modes of transcendence, namely, ideology and utopia, is not always adequate. Transcendence can be a *positive* way of saying no to the world without being utopian. Christian brotherly love is an example. Mannheim would interpret it as ideology if *homo religiosus* thinks he can realize it only in absolute transcendence, or as utopia if *homo religiosus* wants to realize the kingdom of God on earth. But there is a third possibility that is not an arbitrary special case but one absolutely crucial to the concept of brotherly love in early Christianity. This is the possibility of living in the world but being guided by a transcendence that does not conceive of itself as realizable on earth (eschatological consciousness). This remove from the world does not give rise to any will to change the world, but at the same time it does not represent an escape from the world, i.e., a world historically structured in a particular way and one whose historicity is seen as absolute. Saint Francis of Assisi, for example, lived in the world *as if it did not exist* and *realized* this "as-if-it-did-not-exist" in his concrete life.

Sociology can always object here that to interpret something as "ideology" indicates precisely that thought is unaware of the ideological nature of its existence. Its own self-conception is therefore nothing but *material* for sociological interpretation and has nothing it can directly offer to the interpreter. But it is surely open to question whether the *self-conception* of thought can be ignored in this way. It is possible that self-interpretation itself, in its intellectual content, is part of that process by which understanding ourselves creates something new, making us into that which we understand ourselves to be. The transcendence inherent in all thinking is inconceivable without detachment and distance. The detachment that is a *fact* underlying every mental act can, however, be interpreted in various ways. This interpretation is not—at least not always—something simply added to the fact (an ideological superstructure, as critiques of ideology would have it). It is what makes the fact understandable and consequently enables it to have an impact in the historical world. In short, only specific "ideologies" enter into "history."

Max Weber has demonstrated in his essay "The Protestant Ethic and the Spirit of Capitalism"[43] how a specific public order (capitalism) arose from a specific type of solitude and its self-understanding (Protestantism). An originally religious boundness for which the world is not home has created a world of everyday life in which there is in fact no longer any place for the individual in his uniqueness. Unlike the chiliastic movement,[44] this religious-boundness does not do this out of a utopian consciousness but does it merely as the *expression* of a basic not-being-in-the-world yet having-to-come-to-terms-with-it. The world is understood here as an essentially negative one in which one's only role is to do one's duty, and the world has to be this way in reality as well because it would otherwise reassert its claims on man. Only after the religious bond is lost does the public order become so all-powerful that solitude is possible only in the form of flight from the world. This process requires in turn a primary definition of this self-created world as economy and society, a world that did not exist in this form during its creation. We are perhaps so much at the mercy of this public order today that even our possibilities of detachment can be defined only as freedom from it. That does not mean, however, that the public order must always have primacy. Only if the "economic power structure" has become so overwhelming that the mind that created it has no longer any home at all in it[45] is it possible to understand thought as ideology or utopia.

Sociology itself, then, is bound to a historical moment without which it could not have arisen in the first place, the moment when a justified mistrust of the mind was awakened through its homelessness. As a historical discipline it can operate only within the given limits of its historical competence. The interpretation of mental life purely in terms of reducing it to ideology or utopia is justified only when the economic component has gained such predominance in life that thought in fact can and must become "ideological superstructure." The primacy of the "economic power structure" in reality has its own history and is part of the history of modern thought. "Groups of pre-capitalistic origin, in which the communal element prevails, may be held together by traditions or by common sentiments alone," according to Mannheim. "In such a group, theoretical reflection is of entirely secondary importance. On the other hand, in groups which are not welded together primarily by such organic bonds of community life, but which merely occupy similar positions in the social-economic system, rigorous theorizing is a prerequisite of cohesion."[46] Only when people no longer see their existence in community as given, only when, as by means of economic advancement, the individual suddenly finds himself belonging to a completely different community does something like ideology arise as a justification of one's own position against the position of others. Only at this point does the question of *meaning* arise, a question born of the questionableness of one's own situation. Only when the individual's place in the world is determined by economic status and not by tradition does he become homeless. And only in this homelessness can the question of the rightfulness and meaning of his position emerge. This question of meaning is, however, older than capitalism because it goes back to an earlier experience of human insecurity in the world, that is, to Christianity. The concept of ideology, indeed the fact of ideological thinking, points to a positive factor, to the question of meaning. Reduction of this question to the "more original" reality of economic life becomes possible only when the world and life of human beings are indeed primarily determined by economic factors and when the reality to which mental life is bound has become fundamentally alien to thought and meaning. Originally this was not the case in sociology, as it was from the start in the psychoanalytic conception of reality. Before we can pose Mannheim's question concerning the social and historical locus of sociological inquiry, we need to inquire first into the existential situation in which sociological analyses are historically legitimate.

NOTES

1. Karl Mannheim, *Ideologie und Utopie*, Bonn: Verlag Fr. Cohen, 1929, cited hereafter as *Ideologie*.

2. *Geist, Geistigkeit*, and *das Geistige* are key terms in this essay. They suggest "spirit" or "spirituality," not in any religious or supernatural sense but only in the sense of "the sum total of human mental life," and have been translated here as "mind," "intellect," "intellectual activity," or "thought," whichever was most appropriate in context. —Trans.

3. Mannheim's term *Destruktion* (here "destructuring") does not mean "destruction," but the dismantling of ideological or utopian propositions to reveal their origins in specific sociological situations. —Trans.

4. Mannheim, *op. cit.*, 54.

5. *Verhandlungen des 6. Deutschen Soziologentages in Zurich, 1928*, Tubingen: Mohr, 1929, 80; cited hereafter as *Verhandlungen*.

6. Georg Lukács, *Geschichte und Klassenbewusstsein*, Berlin: Malik, 1923.

7. *Verhandlungen*, 45.

8. Martin Heidegger, *Sein und Zeit*, Halle: Niemeyer, 1927, 6ff; cited hereafter as *Sein und Zeit*.

9. *Ideologie*, 8.

10. Karl Jaspers, *Psychologie der Weltanschauungen*, Berlin: Springer, 1925, 229ff.

11. *Ideologie*, 169. Cf., too, 52.

12. *Sein und Zeit*, 117.

13. *Ibid.*, 130. Cf., too, 43, 175.

14. *Ibid.*, 52ff.

15. *Ibid.*, 175.

16. *Ibid.*, 260ff.

17. *Verhandlungen*, 46.

18. *Sein und Zeit*, 129.

19. Cf. Max Scheler's expression "the powerlessness of thought" in "Probleme einer Soziologie des Wissens" in *Die Wissensformen und die Gesellschaft*, Leipzig: Der neue Geist Verlag, 1926.

20. *Ideologie*, 169.

21. *Ibid.*

22. *Ibid.*, 128.

23. *Ibid.*, 123.

24. *Ibid.*, 9ff.

25. *Ibid.*, 8.

26. *Ibid.*, 171.

27. *Ibid.*, 35.

28. *Ibid.*, 41.

29. *Ibid.*, 33.

30. *Ibid.*, 167.

31. *Ibid.*, 141.

32. *Ibid.*, 128. Mannheim speaks explicitly only about the homelessness of thought in the present-day world.

33. *Ibid.*, 54.

34. *Ibid.*, 51.

35. *Ibid.*, 53.

36. *Ibid.*, 43, fn. 1.

37. *Ibid.*, 169.

38. *Ibid.*, 29.

39. *Ibid.*, 233.

40. *Ibid.*, 163.

41. *Ibid.*, 165, 43.

42. *Ibid.*, 47.

43. Max Weber, *Religionssoziologie*, vol. I, Tübingen: Mohr, 1921.

44. *Ideologie*, 191. In Mannheim's view, the first example of thought consciously aligning itself with certain social classes occurs in the chiliastic movement. Only from this moment on can there be such a thing as utopia in Mannheim's sense.

45. On the homelessness of present-day thought, which seems least bound to social class, see *Ideologie*, 123ff.

46. *Ibid.*, 93–94.

Søren Kierkegaard

S EVENTY-FIVE YEARS ago, Kierkegaard died alone in a hospital in Copenhagen at the age of forty-three. During his lifetime he enjoyed not so much fame as notoriety. Peculiarities of his person and his way of life became, in the public eye, occasions for scandal, and only long after his death did his influence begin to make itself felt. If we were to write a history of his fame with Germany as our focus, only the last fifteen years would concern us, but in those years his fame has spread with amazing rapidity. This fame rests on more than the discovery and belated appreciation of a great man who was wrongly neglected in his own time. We are not just making amends for not having done him justice earlier. Kierkegaard speaks with a contemporary voice; he speaks for an entire generation that is not reading him out of historical interest but for intensely personal reasons: *mea res agitur*.

Even as short a time as twenty-five years ago—fifty years after his death—Kierkegaard was hardly known in Germany. One reason is that not all of his work had been translated into German, even though Chris-

Published in German in *Frankfurter Zeitung*, No. 75–76, 29 January 1932. English translation by Robert and Rita Kimber.

toph Schrempf had called attention to Kierkegaard's importance as early as the late 1880s. The far more important reason is that the intellectual and cultural climate in Germany was simply not hospitable to him. In the unbroken façade of self-assurance that each of the humanistic disciplines presented to the world, there was not the slightest breach through which Kierkegaard's unsettling message could have slipped and begun to undermine that complacency. It was not until the post-war years, which brought a willingness to tear down outmoded intellectual structures, that Germany would offer a soil in which Kierkegaardian thought could take root. Nietzsche and the so-called life philosophy (*Lebensphilosophie*), Bergson, Dilthey, and Simmel had prepared the way for Kierkegaard in Germany. In Nietzsche, systematic philosophy saw its fundamental tenets threatened for the first time, for Nietzsche's destruction of old psychological assumptions revealed the extra-philosophical, psychic, and vital energies that actually motivated philosophers to philosophize. This revolt of a philosopher against philosophy clarified the situation of philosophizing itself and insisted that philosophizing *was* philosophy. This meant the salvation of the individual's subjectivity. In a parallel development, experience philosophy (*Erlebnisphilosophie*) was attempting to comprehend concrete objects not from a generalized perspective but on the basis of "experience." This called for a personal apprehension of the object itself rather than the placing of it in a general category. The crucial point here is not the methodological innovation but the opening up of dimensions of the world and of human life that had previously remained invisible to philosophy or that had had only a derivative shadow existence for it.

So Germany appeared to be prepared—but for a Kierkegaard, a man whose existence was shaped by Christianity? What did the revolt in philosophy have to do with Christianity? The late eruption of his fame is more surprising the more we contemplate his resolutely Christian position and attempt to understand him from that perspective. This fragile link between philosophy and Christianity takes on substance from Kierkegaard's polemic against Hegel, which is not so much a critique of one specific philosopher as it is a rejection of philosophy as such. In Kierkegaard's view, philosophy is so caught up in its own systematics that it forgets and loses sight of the actual self of the philosophizing subject: it never touches the "individual" in his concrete "existence." Hegel indeed trivializes this very individual and his life, which are for

Kierkegaard the central concern. This trivialization occurs because Hegel's dialectic and synthesis do not address the individual in his specific existence but, rather, treat individuality and specificity as abstractions. Against the Hegelian doctrine of thesis, antithesis, and synthesis Kierkegaard sets the fundamental paradoxicality of Christian existence: to be an individual—insofar as one stands alone before God (or death)—and yet no longer to have a self—insofar as this self as an individual is nothing before God if its existence is denied. For Kierkegaard, this paradox is the fundamental structure of human existence. In Hegel, the paradox of thesis and antithetis is "reconciled" at the higher level of synthesis. As such it is not the unresolvable paradox inherent in being, which Kierkegaard calls "existence," the paradox in which human life, in Kierkegaard's view, is rooted. Kierkegaard always speaks only of himself. Hegel speaks only as the exponent of his system. Kierkegaard can, in a certain sense, speak in general, too, but his general statements are not generalizations. He speaks, rather, "in generalities that apply to all by virtue of the fact that they apply to the single human being," for everyone is an individual. In Kierkegaard's view, Hegel negates concrete reality, contingency, and therefore the individual when he interprets history as a logically comprehensible sequence of events and a process that follows an inevitable course. This polemic against Hegel is a polemic against any and every philosophical system.

The situation today is this: The most varied and heterogeneous schools of thought look to Kierkegaard as a prime authority; they all meet on the ambiguous ground of radical skepticism, if, indeed, one can still use that pallid, now almost meaningless term to describe an attitude of despair toward one's own existence and the basic principles of one's own scientific or scholarly field.

The most resolute adherents of the most diversified camps nonetheless share Kierkegaard's basic concept of "choice," which has in the meantime also taken on a somewhat abstract quality. There is, however, still another reason why the Protestant and Catholic camps both call on the authority of Kierkegaard. This reason does not lie in Kierkegaard's specific, subjective character, but, rather, in the milieu in which he as a religious being lived and had to live. Kierkegaard was the first thinker to live in a world constituted much like our own, that is, in a wholly secularized world stemming from the Enlightenment. In its polemic, an unconditionally religious life—the very kind of life that Schleier-macher,* for example, did not lead—had to deal with just about the same world in which we are living today. If the Christian from Paul to Luther defended himself against worldliness and the secularization of existence, that "evil" world was a world fundamentally different from the one we actually inhabit. To the extent that such a thing as a religious existence is possible at all in the modern world, it has to turn to Kier-kegaard as its forebear. The differences between Protestantism and Ca-tholicism pale in comparison with the gigantic abyss that has opened up between a self-contained atheistic world and a religious existence in that same world. To be radically religious in such a world means to be alone not only in the sense that one stands alone before God but also in the sense that no one else stands before God.

The existence that concerns Kierkegaard is his own life and it is in this his life that the Christian parodox has to be realized. The "indi-vidual" renounces his self, his individuality, his worldly possibilities, over against which—and from without, as it were—stands the inexorable reality of God. From its very beginnings, his life is not determined by his own desires, his own possibilities; it is only a consequence, a con-sequence of being-determined-by-God. But this being-determined-by-God remains curiously suspended between being close to and being far from God. In his diaries, Kierkegaard says that the determining factor in his life was a sin committed by his father. Kierkegaard's father had, when still a child, once cursed God. This curse was decisive for the life of the son; he inherited, as it were, that curse. The only task of concern to him as a writer was to comprehend this ambiguous condition of being-determined-by-God. This vulnerability, of which one can never say whether it is a curse or a blessing, accounts for Kierkegaard's breaking off his engagement with Regine Olsen and thus forgoing the possibility of a "normal" life, the possibility of not being an "exception."

What determined his life, then, was not what was inherent in it, not the law immanent in his individual life alone and in no other, but what was totally external to it, what it would experience only later, namely, the curse of his father. And from his perspective this curse was

*Friedrich D. E. Schleiermacher (1768–1834), Protestant theologian and philoso-pher of religion. —Ed.

carried over to him in the fact that he could not know if he himself had not fathered a child. This possibility, which, as Theodor Häcker* said of it, "we would have to call almost abstract," was a "thorn in his side." In his vulnerability, this abstract possibility became the most burdensome of realities. Chance is what is outside the self, which draws into itself through this outsideness the entire obligation of the transcendent, of that which is willed by God alone. In being taken with absolute seriousness, a seriousness that is identical with ultimate logic, the contingent becomes the last locus in which God himself speaks, however distant he may be.

To the degree that this vulnerable life can be maintained only by the most ferocious of commitments to logic, so to that same degree Kierkegaard's concrete self succumbs to a cruel psychological addiction to reflection. Taking one's own possibilities seriously is what gives rise to this compulsive reflection; hence, the essential task is to eradicate those possibilities and to be nothing more than an anonymous incarnation of logic. But writing is always the product of a specific person, of someone with a name, and if a writer is to achieve this desired anonymity publicly and, so to speak, as witness to his own namelessness, then his name has to hide behind a pseudonym. But every pseudonym threatens to take the place of the author's real name and so to take possession of the author. And so it is that one pseudonym follows on the heels of another and that hardly any two of Kierkegaard's works appeared under the same name. This changing of pseudonyms reveals, of course, an aesthetic playing with possibility, that seductive possibility that Kierkegaard himself, under the name "Victor Eremita," presented in *Either/Or*.

Both Kierkegaard and Nietzsche mark the end of Romanticism, each of course in a very different way, but despite those differences there is a common element in their advance beyond it. The richness of life and the world that the Romantics regarded in terms of aesthetic opportunity and possibility is, in Kierkegaard and Nietzsche, wrenched out of the aesthetic context. In Kierkegaard, what the Romantics saw as aesthetic possibility becomes the essential existential problem. For the realm of the inner life and the inescapable obligations it imposes, possibility be-

---

*Th. Häcker's *Sören Kierkegaard und die Philosophie der Innerlichkeit* was published in 1913 and his *Sören Kierkegaard, Kritik der Gegenwart* (2nd edition) in 1922. —Ed.

comes reality, namely, the reality of sin. In Nietzsche, art becomes the most essential moral and morally symptomatic fact. Kierkegaard represents, in a sense, an atonement for, and the vengeance of, Romanticism. In him, the aesthetic possibility Romanticism employed ironically as a pretext to excuse itself in the eyes of the world takes its vengeance and becomes inescapable inner reality, indeed, becomes reality per se. Kierkegaard paid back with his life the debts that Romanticism piled up with noncommittal abandon.

Friedrich von Gentz

ON THE 100TH ANNIVERSARY OF
HIS DEATH, JUNE 9, 1932

"He seized upon untruth with a passion for truth." — Rahel Varnhagen

RARELY HAS A great writer been more thoroughly forgotten. When, in the mid-1830s, Varnhagen von Ense erected a monument to Gentz in a portrait summarizing his life and work, and when a little later Gustav Schlesier published a first selection of his writings and letters, the *Hallish Annual* opined even then that nothing Gentz had produced could rescue him from the neglect he so richly deserved. It was not worthwhile to argue against him, the periodical claimed; he was passé and forgotten. And even Rudolf Haym's much more objective and fair-minded assessment found that Gentz's "combining of literary and political talents"—a combination rarely seen in Germany—was the only thing about him of significance to posterity.

This neglect is all the more remarkable when we consider that Gentz was the only member of his generation and, more important, of his circle to play an active role in European politics. He was born in Breslau in 1764, studied with Kant in the 1780s, then went to Berlin to begin a career in the Prussian civil service. In Berlin, he first befriended Wil-

Published in German in *Kölnische Zeitung*, No. 308, June 8, 1932. English translation by Robert and Rita Kimber.

helm von Humboldt, then joined the circle that gathered around Henriette Herz and later around Rahel Varnhagen. He belonged to the generation that consciously experienced the French Revolution as the triumph of philosophy over history. More rapidly than the others of his circle, Gentz shifted his initial enthusiasm for the Revolution into a more enduring admiration for the stature and historical durability of the English constitution. He was the first to translate Burke and by doing so created the first foundations for the conservative position in Germany. An open letter he wrote in 1797 to Friedrich Wilhelm III, on the occasion of Friedrich's assumption of the throne, calling for freedom of the press and the citizen's right to exercise any trade he chose, made him so unpopular in Prussia that further promotion was closed to him.

Because he was not willing to spend the rest of his life in the rank of military councillor, he went to Vienna in 1802, at first as a "freelance" writer—as a "volunteer," as he later described himself—in the service of the Austrian government. Before that he traveled to England and reinforced the ties that already bound him to English politicians. He received money from the English government for his work as a writer, and from this time on he was never able to rid himself of the reproach that he could be bought.

On his return to Austria, his major goal was to unite the European cabinets against Napoleon. All his writings from this period—especially the famous *Fragments from the Recent History of the European Balance of Power*—are only nominally addressed to the nations of Europe, but the audience he was really addressing was the cabinets to which he did not yet have any access. From 1812 on he was a loyal and devoted follower of Metternich and adherent of Austrian restoration policy. He wrote justifications for government policies; he wrote the minutes of the Congress of Vienna; he was an untiring mediator there and Metternich's secret adviser. This role he continued to play at the Carlsbad Congress and the later congresses at Troppau and Laibach. He became the conservative spokesman for the status quo, the most bitter opponent of freedom of the press, the most intelligent advocate of those who wanted to see the contribution of the people to the wars of liberation forgotten in favor of cabinet politics. Metternich's policy, the policy of calm at any price, celebrated only brief triumphs. The rebellions in Spain, Italy, and Greece, and the July Revolution in France, appeared to render Gentz's life's work illusory.

When Gentz died in 1832, he knew that he had fought for a lost cause, that "the spirit of the times would prove stronger" than he and those in whose service he had placed himself, that "art is no more able than political power . . . to slow the turning of the world's wheel." The spirit of the times, which Gentz so passionately hated, was stronger than the art of the diplomat and the power of the statesman. In his defense of cabinet government, Gentz had fought against two enemies, neither of which actually emerged victorious in his lifetime, but both of which unofficially shaped the life of the times. These two were *liberalism* and *conservatism*.

Liberalism and its "insidious claim that everyone may regard his own reason as a source of law" meant anarchy to him, the end of a moral and political world order. He played against this liberalism a "feudalism, even though of a mediocre order" suggested to him in the Romantic formulation of his friend Adam Müller. But conservatism cannot claim him as its own either, for he used it only as a foil against anything that smacked of reform. He did not advocate it for its own sake, but used it only as a means of maintaining a "balance." He tried to perpetuate the status quo, to suspend the course of history in order to create a "stable system" in which tradition and reason would exist in equilibrium. When he gave up his life as a free-lance writer to achieve specific goals in the service of a specific state, he threw in his lot with reality—and consequently against the Enlightenment and the possible "triumph of philosophy over history." But he turned just as decisively against Romanticism, whose world seemed illusionistic to him. As a corrective to the arrogance of reason, he held up "human frailty," and as a corrective to conservatism, to the principle of legitimacy, he maintained that this principle was not "absolute" but had been "born in time," was "caught up in time," and had to be "modified by time." He promoted neither one principle nor the other, but devoted his efforts entirely to the "magnificent old world" whose decline he was witnessing. This "magnificent old world" was Europe. He remained untouched by patriotism, the new national feeling, that momentarily allied dying feudalism with the emerging liberal Prussian patriots.

It was no coincidence that the liberal Varnhagen was the first to argue with Gentz. Gentz's mode of argumentation was drawn from the Enlightenment; his mode of life was early Romantic. Both these factors place him in the generation he seemed to be turning away from when he opted for reality, the generation of Wilhelm von Humboldt and Friedrich Schlegel. And indeed he never fully turned away from his old friends—not from Humboldt any more than from Rahel Varnhagen or Pauline Wiesel. Despite his friendship with Adam Müller, he did not convert to Catholicism, nor did he experience any inner change equivalent to such a step. He may have lived in the world of Viennese diplomacy, but to the extent he wanted to be understood, he had to turn to a liberal intellectual world whose political incarnation he was fighting against. As Rudolf Haym wrote, "He continued living like Mirabeau, but he began thinking like Burke." His virtuosity consisted in his ability to be a different person than the cause he was advocating demanded he be. He did not understand that the life of the Enlightenment man, which he was, required an Enlightenment politics (at that time, liberal politics) as well. For him, politics was merely the art of guiding states and ruling populations, an art the liberals dabbled in as dilettants; the Romantics, as victims of their own illusions.

All the criticisms of Gentz take as their basic assumption that politics is a matter of character, of principle. That is precisely what politics for Gentz was not. Heinrich von Stein called him a man with a "rotten heart and a dried-up brain," objecting, in other words, to the very principles of his politics. His friend Adam Müller, on the other hand, who was in total agreement with the principles of Austria's politics, always appealed nonetheless to "something better in him." His principles, Müller thought, could not be reconciled with his life. Gentz was regarded as the greatest egoist, as "the living principle of hedonism" (*Hallisch Annual*), and his work as available to any who would pay his price. In more objective portraits he appears sometimes as the cavalier of the eighteenth century, sometimes as "the spirit of *Lucinde* incarnate."* All these criticisms are directed at the ambiguity of Gentz's character, but they miss the mark because they fail to understand the reason for that ambiguity, because they do not understand that he is not a "hypocrite." Rahel Varnhagen, who stood by him despite all the personal disappointments she experienced at his hands, recognized this when she spoke repeatedly of his incredible "naïveté."

Toward the end of his life, Gentz wrote a genuine apologia for his political activities. To the challenge of Amalie Imhof, a woman with

---

Lucinde, a novel of free love by Friedrich Schlegel. —Ed.

whom he had been very much in love in his youth, he responded with his "political confession."

"World history," he wrote, "is a constant transition from the old to the new. In this never-ending cycle of things, everything destroys itself, and the fruit that has ripened falls from the plant that produced it. But if this cycle is not to lead to the rapid demise of everything that exists and of everything just and good as well, then there must be, along with the large and ultimately always greater number of those who work to bring in the new, a smaller number of those who try to maintain the old and to contain the freshets of the times, neither being able nor wanting to hold them back altogether, within fixed banks. In eras of great civil convulsions, such as our own, the contest between these two parties assumes a passionate, excessive, an often wild and destructive character. The principle, however, remains the same, and the better forces on both sides know how to guard against the follies and errors of their allies. In my twenty-fifth year, I made my choice. Earlier, influenced by recent German philosophy and also no doubt by some presumably new discoveries in the field of political science, which was however still very alien to me at the time, I had recognized with utter clarity from the outbreak of the French Revolution what my role would be. I had felt initially, then later had understood and known, that I, by virtue of the inclinations and abilities with which nature had equipped me, was called to be a defender of the old and an opponent of innovation."

Gentz justifies himself here by means of an appeal to the role that fell to him in reality, but at the same time, in this self-justification, he distances himself from the world in which he played a definite part. As a pure observer of the world, he assigns himself a place in it. He does not seek to render an account for any cause but only for himself or, rather, for the role he played.

Whether one can ever succeed in finding a place in the world, in reality, is one of the basic questions raised by early Romanticism, which was a formative influence for Gentz's generation.

The remove of fantasy from reality, the imagination's dalliance among infinite possibilities, accounts for the wreckage of Friedrich Schlegel's life. By contrast, a genuine engagement with the world, even if only in the form of experimentation, provided Humboldt with a chance at success; for in experimenting with himself and the world Humboldt broke free from himself and his purely imaginative impulses. He gave the world the opportunity to take him by surprise. Gentz gave himself to the world immediately and directly, and it consumed him. His hedonism was only the most radical way open to him to let the world consume him; indeed, his relationship to himself was one of "enjoying his own self." Even his own ego was a reality he did not control but to which he could submit. His "greatest virtuosity" was that of "enjoying his own self." This total passivity is why he could be called "the spirit of *Lucinde* incarnate."

Gentz himself called this being-consumed-by-the-world his "unbounded receptivity." He wrote to Rahel Varnhagen: "Do you know, dear, why we developed such a grand and complete relationship? You are an infinitely productive being; and I am an infinitely receptive one. You are a great man; I am the most womanly of all women who have ever lived. I know that if I had been a woman physically, I would have had the world at my feet. . . . Consider this remarkable fact: From my own being I cannot strike even the most pathetic spark. . . . My receptivity is completely without limits. Your constantly active, constantly fruitful spirit (I don't mean your mind alone but your soul, everything) encountered this unbounded receptivity, and so we gave birth to ideas and emotions and loves and languages all never heard of before. No mortal has any inkling of what we two know." The idea that the androgynous human being is the perfect human being, an idea familiar to us from *Lucinde*, appears here in real and concrete form. If this "affair" had ever been consummated, Gentz might have found in it the possibility of holding a second self-contained world up against the real world and so have created for himself a way to isolate himself from reality.

When Friedrich Schlegel found access to a larger world by way of Catholicism, he called his relationship to the political events of his time one of "engaged participatory thinking." In a similar vein, Gentz stressed his *participatory knowledge* as his highest achievement. "I know *everything*. No one on earth knows what *I* know of contemporary history." This remark and others like it recur over and over again in Gentz. But he was, as he himself said, "delighted by nothing, instead very cold, blasé, scornful of the foolishness of just about everyone else and of my own, not wisdom, but perspicacity, my insight, my keen and profound understanding, and, in myself, almost fiendishly pleased that the so-called great historical events ultimately came to such a ridiculous conclusion." This blasé attitude did not leave him as long as he remained completely involved in politics. (It disappeared only in the final years of his life when he was completely possessed by his passion for the dancer Fanny Elssler.) But what still kept drawing him back to the "affairs of the world" was the possibility of knowing what was going on. To take part in the world, though only in the form of knowledge, to be a witness to it, appears to be the greatest opportunity available to the Romantics. Gentz sacrificed to it his philosophical outlook, his status, and his fame as a writer. His success at knowing all there really was to know left him ultimately indifferent toward the destruction of everything he had sought to achieve in his political life. From his distancing himself from every-thing specific—and not from any fixed conviction or determinate point of view—comes the sentence with which he closed his apologia to Amalie Imhof: "*Victrix causa deis placuit, sed victa Catoni*" (The victorious cause pleased the gods, but the defeated one pleases Cato).

Berlin Salon

*"Je serai cet après-diné entre six et sept heures chez vous, chère et aimable Ma-
demoiselle Lévi, pour raisonner et déraisonner avec vous pendant deux heures.*
— I said to Gentz that you are a moral midwife who provided one with so
gentle and painless a confinement that a tender emotion remained from
even the most tormenting ideas. — Until then, be well.   Louis"

MADEMOISELLE LÉVI IS Rahel Lewin, known in her
time as "Little Lévi," later as Rahel Varnhagen or simply
Rahel. And Louis is Prussian Prince Louis Ferdinand. The
social circle that made this intimate note and many letters possible is
known by the name "Berlin Salon."

This Berlin social life had a brief genesis and a short duration. It
arose from the "scholarly Berlin" of the Enlightenment, which accounts
for its social neutrality. In its effective and representative form, it lasted
only from the French Revolution until the outbreak of the unfortunate
war of 1806. The fact that this society, which was more a product of
the Frederickian Enlightenment, was somewhat behind the times accounts for its peculiar isolation and, consequently, its private nature. It

Published in German as "Berliner Salon" in *Deutscher Almanach für das Jahr 1932*,
Leipzig. English translation by Robert and Rita Kimber.

encompasses the two classes that have a certain public aspect in daily life: actors and the nobility. Those are the two extremes between which the bourgeoisie stands and from which it is in a certain sense excluded. But now an ever more powerful bourgeoisie would begin appropriating those classes to itself. That is evident in the portrayal of Wilhelm Meister, who owes his education and orientation in the world to those very two groups; and it is evident, too, in the nobility's practice of entrusting the education of their children to bourgeois tutors. It is no coincidence that the first Berlin social circle that was headed by a woman (Henriette Herz), and could therefore rightly be termed a salon, included both Humboldts, who had been educated by the Berlin Enlightenment educator Joachim Heinrich Campe, and the Counts Dohna, in whose home Friedrich Schleiermacher had been a tutor.

Because the salon was socially neutral ground, it was accessible to Berlin's Jews, whose social status was indeterminate but who were adapting to the current social situation with amazing rapidity. The Jews did not now have to free themselves from all manner of social ties: they stood outside society to begin with. And though Jewish men were to some degree limited by their professions, Jewish women—once they were emancipated—were free from all convention to an extent difficult to imagine today. These Jewish houses became the meeting places of the intellectual world, and their owners did not have to feel themselves either compromised or honored by the fact.

The Tugendbund (League of Virtue), founded by Henriette Herz in the 1780s, was still completely a product of the Enlightenment. It included both Humboldts, Alexander von Dohna, Karl de Laroche, Brendel Veit, and Friedrich Schlegel's wife-to-be, Dorothea Mendelssohn Veit. Except for Brendel Veit, who was a friend of Henriette Herz's youth, they were all students of Marcus Herz and came regularly to his house for lectures. The two women played the role of older confidantes. The League was based on the pursuit of virtue and on the premise of the equality of all "good" human beings. It is important to note that this idea of the equal rights of all good human beings first gave rise to the kind of indiscretion we have come to regard as typically Romantic. All the members of the League were obliged, for example, to show each other important letters, even ones from individuals not known to the rest of the group. The reason for this rule was, as we know from Caroline von Dacheröden, "that those people who entrust a secret to us would just as readily entrust it to the rest of the group if they knew them as well as they know us." Wilhelm von Humboldt's fiancée, Caroline, voiced strong objections to this reduction of the individual generated by a superficial understanding of Lessing, and she would soon convince Wilhelm to leave this circle of virtue worshipers. The circle fell apart rapidly. Dorothea went to Jena with Friedrich Schlegel; Wilhelm von Humboldt's engagement took him away from it; Dohna remained as a personal friend of Henriette Herz. Through him she became acquainted with Schleiermacher. What the tone of the League must have been, however, we can gather from a remark Friedrich Schlegel made years later to Caroline Schlegel. "Schleiermacher's association with Henriette Herz is ruining him in himself and for me and for our friendship. . . . They puff up each other's vanity. There is no real pride there but only a silly intoxication, as if from some barbaric punch. They preen themselves for every little exercise of virtue, no matter how paltry. Schleiermacher's mind is shriveling up. He is losing his sense for what is truly great. In short, this damned wallowing in petty emotion is driving me wild!"

About four or five years after the founding of the League of Virtue, Rahel Lewin's reputation began to grow. Her circle was the first to separate itself from the Enlightenment and to reveal the emerging consciousness of a new generation that was finding its own mode of expression in its reverence for Goethe. Rahel established the Goethe cult in Berlin, which was fundamentally different from that of the Romantics. If it was characteristic for Jena society, at the center of which were the two Schlegel brothers and Caroline Schlegel, that every member of it considered himself and everyone else in it a genius and that Goethe was the prototype and standard of the genius, Goethe's role in the Berlin circle was only that he expressed what everyone else felt: He was their spokesman. Infused with Goethe's spirit, people of the most varied classes and personalities gathered at Rahel's. They formed a circle "for admission to which royal princes, foreign ambassadors, artists, scholars, and businessmen of every rank, countesses, and actresses all vied with the same zeal; and in which each of them acquired neither more nor less value than he himself was able to establish by virtue of his cultivated personality"—thus wrote Brinckmann, the Swedish ambassador in Berlin, to Varnhagen[1] after Rahel's death. The condition for acceptance,

---

[1] The notes are at the end of the essay.

then, was "a cultivated personality." That excludes from the outset the idea that accomplishment or social position could qualify one for membership in the salon. If we let pass in review before us those who frequented Rahel's "attic" in the 1790s, we will see how wide the range of possibilities was and to what extent they were often all held together only by Rahel's *goût* itself. Along with the Jewish doctor David Veit there was von Burgsdorf, the Brandenburg nobleman, who passed his time with that refined dilettantism that from time immemorial had been regarded as the privilege of the aristocracy but now, as self-improvement, acquired new value. Peter von Gualtieri, who belonged to the court circle, had never written anything, and offered nothing but his personal fascination—a welcome social talent. Rahel numbered him among the "four vain ones." How did he find his way to her? "He was capable of experiencing a higher level of suffering than anyone I have ever known before, for he simply could not bear it." This one mark of excellence was enough. Then there was Hans Genelli, a young architect with a mixture of shyness, irony, and impeccable cleanliness that is hard to describe, withal a charm that could make the most serious things appear light and delicate. And the famous actress Unzelmann, who was loved by all; and Henriette Mendelssohn, of whom Schlegel said, her "beautiful soul would surely be more beautiful if it were not so exaggeratedly and exclusively beautiful"; the Bohemian Countess Josephine Pachta, who left her husband and lived with a commoner for eighteen years; Countess Karaline Schlabrendorf, who sometimes wore men's clothes and traveled to Paris with Rahel because she was expecting an illegitimate child. Then Friedrich Gentz; Pauline Wiesel, the lover of Prince Louis Ferdinand; Christel Eigensatz, the actress and lover of Gentz. Friedrich Schlegel, Schleiermacher, Humboldt, Jean Paul, and other major figures sometimes appeared, too, but they were not representative of the tone and nature of this circle.

Self-education was essential for those whose social traditions had been shaken. Caught up in this process of detachment were not only the young nobility who had been enlightened by bourgeois tutors and alienated from the ideals of their own class, yet at the same time could not identify with middle-class ones, but also the recently emancipated Jews who had still not had time enough to form a new tradition. Both were consequently thrown back on their own lives. The veneration and esteem of women that is documented in this salon is the result of taking private life seriously, a realm that appears more congenial to woman by nature than to man—and that was revealed to the public in almost shameless fashion in Schlegel's *Lucinde*.

Initially, this indiscretion was guided in Henriette Herz's Tugend-bund by an apparent ideal, namely, virtue—though in Wilhelm von Humboldt this ideal pales completely beside the interest in the "interesting human being." Now, in the 1790s, this interest became general. Everything intimate thus acquired a public character; everything public, an intimate one. (Even today, speaking in a mode at once both public and private, we refer to the women who became famous at that time by their first names: Rahel, Bettina, Caroline.) One could be indiscreet because private life lacked the element of intimacy, because private life itself had acquired a public, objective quality. But what is thus forcibly removed from the sphere of intimacy is not so much the individual person and his individuality, but his life. "But to me life itself was the assignment," Rahel wrote, much like Wilhelm von Humboldt, who said of himself in his autobiography that his "true sphere is life itself." From this attitude arises that personal historicity that makes one's own life, the data of which can be recorded, into a sequence of objective events, whatever those events may be. If we call this objectification of the personal with Rahel "destiny," we can see how relatively modern this category is that we take for granted today. Destiny is where one's own life is historicized or, as Rahel says, "when one knows what kind of destiny one has." The noblest example of such a historicized life was that of Goethe, whose works are "fragments of a great confession." "Goethe and life are always one for me; I am working my way into both."

In this concern for personal life, the bearer of that life is forgotten; hence the fact of a lack of discrimination. We consequently have, for example, an extensive correspondence containing innumerable intimate details that Rahel conducted with a certain Rebekka Friedländer,[2] whom Rahel herself described as "pretentious and of an unnatural poverty of spirit."[3] But this person of poor spirit was unhappy, and her unhappiness, her pain, was as it were more real than she herself. The only "consolation" is that what has happened is preserved in the communication of it. "Consolation is dreadful!" Rahel wrote to Friedländer, "but it is your task to convey your pain to the most sympathetic heart." In this way one can acquire a witness for oneself, a witness who can attest to one's reality when all public esteem has disappeared. "Let *this* be your consolation for the horror you have experienced: that there is a living creature who is a loving witness to your existence. . . ." Bearing witness takes the form of true sympathy with the life of the other. To be a witness to many lives and many events is the only justification for, and the true origin of, this indiscretion and thus for the salon society as such.

The catastrophe of 1806 was a catastrophe for this society as well.[4] The public events, the dimensions of the general misfortune, could no longer be absorbed into the private realm. The intimate was once again separated from the public, and what of the intimate remained "known" became gossip. The possibility of living without social status as an "imaginary romantic person, one to whom true *goût* could be given!"[5] was lost. Rahel never again succeeded in being the focal point of a representative circle without representing something other than herself. As early as 1808 Humboldt wrote from Berlin to his wife that Rahel was completely isolated. "What has become of our time," Rahel wrote to Pauline Wiesel in 1818, "when we were all together. It went under in 1806, went under like a ship, carrying life's loveliest treasures, life's greatest joys."

The salons did not simply cease to exist; they just formed around different people, people of status and name. The best known of these salons are those of Privy Councillor Stägemann, Countess Voss, and Prince Radziwill. They were frequented by Adam Müller,[6] Heinrich von Kleist, Wilhelm von Humboldt, Achim von Arnim, Ferdinand von Schill. The meetings had the character of secret patriotic leagues and were therefore very exclusive. It was typical of them that together with the landed aristocracy, the higher levels of the civil service and the older generation came to the fore again. Until that time, the civil servants had not been able to compete socially with the Jewish salons of Berlin. Adam Müller set the intellectual tone for this older generation and its conservatism. Arnim, Müller, Clemens Brentano—the younger generation of the Romantics, born around 1780 and ten to fifteen years younger than Rahel's circle—defined the physiognomy of Berlin society after 1809. In keeping with the pronounced political nature of the new salons, they were not content to be simply salons. They sought instead a form that could bring the members of the circle closer together. A first attempt in this direction was Zelter's Singing Circle, "in which men from all classes of respectable Berlin society came together to cultivate the art of song and further the national idea."[7] This was the origin of that odd mixture—found only in Germany—of patriotism and men's glee clubs. Originally, however, this link was only a disguise to let what was really a political club evade the censors. Wilhelm von Humboldt wrote in 1810: "I was at Zelter's Singing Circle today, but things are too serious there to permit of any singing."

The Christian-German Table Society was the direct descendant of the Singing Circle and counted some of the same figures among its members. Arnim founded it. Brentano, Kleist, and Adam Müller belonged to it, along with members of the aristocracy and the upper ranks of the military and the bureaucracy. This produced a strange transitional organization in which Romantic and Prussian elements came together in a brief marriage. The Table Society had established laws and was almost like a club. The Romantic element was represented here by means of an unusual institution: It was a rule that at each meeting a serious story would be read that "recounted a relatively unknown incident demonstrating patriotic loyalty and courage."[8] Immediately on the heels of this story came a comic one that retold the same story but gave it an ironic or grotesque twist. This Romantic impulse to treat serious attitudes ironically was still tolerated by the group. The main requirements for admission were that the candidate not be "a Jew, a Frenchman, or a philistine." The tossing together of Jews, Frenchmen, and philistines seems odd at first glance. But what it indicates—apart from the predictable anti-Semitism of the aristocracy and the predictable hostility toward the French of the patriots—is that the three groups are representatives of the Enlightenment. Karl August von Hardenberg, because of his reform initiatives, was the prototype of the philistine; Goethe, the prototype of the non-philistine. Everything we know about the antiphilistine ideology of this society can be found in Brentano's essay "The Philistine Before, In, and After History." There we learn that philistines "scorn old folk festivals and legends and everything that, somehow preserved from the impudence of modern ways, has grown gray with age," "that they constantly busy themselves with destroying everything that gives their fatherland a distinctive, individual character." "They call Nature anything that falls within the sphere of their vision, or, rather, the square of their vision, because they can comprehend only four-sided things. . . . A beautiful landscape, they say, nothing but thoroughfares! They prefer Voltaire to Shakespeare, Wieland to Goethe, Ramler to Klopstock; Voss is their favorite of all time." France was seen as the classic country of the Enlightenment, and the Jews owed entirely to the Enlightenment and its belief in equal rights for all men the arguments for social emancipation and the demand for the equality of Jews as citizens. Then, too, women were excluded from the Table Society, which can be read as a direct protest against the earlier salons. Altogether characteristic of the style of the meetings is that they were held at the noon meal, in contrast to the salons that came together at tea time or in the evening. It is a crucial difference whether one drinks beer or tea. For the Prussian aristocracy, this strange union of Romanticism and Prussian patriotism would find its natural end in the wars of liberation, and for the Romantics in the Romantic conversions to Catholicism.

The Varnhagen salon of the 1820s is no longer representative of the intelligentsia. Rahel Lewin, as Frau Varnhagen von Ense, became a member of society, and her social contacts were therefore essentially determined for her. She was acutely aware of that. She still maintained some important friendships—Heinrich Heine was one of them—and some major figures of the time still found her fascinating. But her essentially conventional invitations no longer carried any special significance. When Rahel died, her first salon had been scattered for twenty-five years. Some of its members had sunk into anonymity; some had gone over to the Table Society; some had been converted; the best of them, like Prince Louis and Alexander von der Marwitz, had died in the wars. The only person who remained to her from earlier times was the one who from the very beginning had stood outside any given intellectual, political, or social order: Pauline Wiesel. The only thing remaining to Rahel from the old salon was what had always existed outside society.

NOTES

1. Karl August Varnhagen, born 1758, was a liberal diplomat in post-Napoleonic Prussia. He is known for editing his wife Rahel's letters and diaries. —Ed.

2. In Varnhagen's edition of her letters, *Rahel, ein Buch des Andenkens*, the letters to Rebekka Friedländer are identified as letters to "Frau v. F." It was Varnhagen's usual practice in his coded edition of the correspondence to equip Jewesses as quickly as possible with a "von." Henriette Herz, for example, appears as "Frau von Bl." An even more common practice is to take excerpts from letters without indicating when or to whom the letters were written. This causes statements made with reference to specific situations to appear to be "general thoughts." This obviously distorts their original intent and makes interpretation more difficult.

3. From an unpublished letter to Pauline Wiesel. The correspondence with Pauline Wiesel, Rahel's only real friend, is stored unpublished in the Berlin State Library, and Varnhagen did not prepare it for publication. One reason for this is that in the 1830s he felt that Rahel's friendship with this irresistible "apparition from the world of the Greek gods" who, despite the innumerable scandals surrounding her, remained loved by all, seemed embarrassing to the memory of Rahel, whom he was intent on putting on a pedestal. He could of course have coded her name, too, and in fact did so in a few of the published letters, as Frau v. V. A more telling reason for his suppression of these letters was that a very different Rahel appears in them, particularly in those from the 1820s, than the one he liked to present to the world. These letters also reveal that the Varnhagens' marriage did not in reality coincide with the picture of it projected in the published passages from the letters. Varnhagen proceeded here, though less rigorously, as he did with Clemens Brentano's letters, from which he cut everything and anything that might have reflected unfavorably on himself.

4. This was the year Napoleon entered Berlin; it marked the end of the Holy Roman Empire. —Ed.

5. From an unpublished letter to Pauline Wiesel.

6. Adam Müller, 1779–1829, belonged to the Arnim and Brentano generation of the Romantics. Influential political conservative, and his writings were "revived" by early Nazi apologists. —Ed.

7. Reinhold Steig, *Kleists Berliner Kämpfe*, 14.

8. Cf. Reinhold Steig, 21ff.

On the Emancipation of Women

T HE EMANCIPATION OF women has to a certain extent
become a fact: almost all professions stand open to today's
woman, who, socially and politically, enjoys the same rights as
man, including the right to vote and the right to run for office. In contrast
to these tremendous steps forward, the restrictions imposed on women
—especially in marriage, where their right to earn a living and acquire
property still depends on their husband's consent—appear to be the
"inconsequential" remains of a previous era, no matter how important
they may be in individual cases. Looked at closely, however, women's
emancipation, guaranteed in principle, has something formal about it.
For, although today's women have the same rights legally as men, they
are not valued equally by society. Economically, their inequality is reflected in the fact that in many cases they work for a considerably lower
wage than men. If they were to work on the same pay scale, they
would—in keeping with their social value—simply lose their positions
of employment. This would definitely be a reactionary development, since

A review of *Das Frauenproblem der Gegenwart: Eine Psychologische Bilanz* (Contemporary Women's Issues: A Psychological Balance Sheet), by Dr. Alice Rühle-Gerstel,
in *Die Gesellschaft*, 2, 1933. English translation by Elisabeth Young-Bruehl.

at least for the time being the independence of women is economic independence from men. Only the so-called higher professions, such as medicine and law, are exempt from this paradoxical situation of having partially to renounce equality for the sake of equality. These professions are numerically unimportant, however, even if strictly speaking they are the ones that owe their privileges to the women's movement. The working woman is an economic fact, beside which the ideology of the women's movement marches along.

The average situation of the professional woman is much more complicated. Not only must she accept, despite her legal equality, less remuneration for her work, but also she must continue to do socially and biologically grounded tasks that are incompatible with her new position. In addition to her profession, she must take care of her household and raise her children. Thus a woman's freedom to make her own living seems to imply either a kind of enslavement in her own home or the dissolution of her family.

These "contemporary women's issues" constitute the starting point of A. Rühle-Gerstel's book. She describes the many ways by which women characteristically try to deal with their situations. Proceeding from the correct insight that the biological factor of motherhood is not simply a *factum brutum* but can also be modified by social changes, she follows a method that is based on an individual psychology and its global claim that all human achievements, positive and negative, are the result of an original overcompensation. This theory, applied not just to the life history of a given individual, but to an entire class, makes it possible to recognize typical overcompensations and even to discern their models. The description of these models—the housewife, the princess, the demoness; the compassionate, the childish, the capable, the shrewd, the overstressed—is the strongest and most original contribution of this book.

The author sees the position of women in contemporary society as doubly complicated. First, apart from her own social class, as a housewife she is the propertyless employee of a male employer, especially when she lives in a bourgeois or petty bourgeois environment. She is not even a proletarian, not even an independent salaried worker. Second, as a working woman she is almost always a salaried employee. The ambivalence of these conditions becomes especially clear when considered from a political point of view. Women in this situation have not gone forward on political fronts, which are still masculine fronts. And, furthermore, whenever the women's movement crosses a political front it does so only as a unified, undifferentiated whole, which never succeeds in articulating concrete goals (other than humanitarian ones). The vain attempt to found a women's political party reveals the problem of the movement very sharply. The problem is like that of the youth movement, which is a movement only for the sake of youth. A women's movement only for the sake of women is equally abstract.

If women saw their situation clearly, they would, according to Rühle-Gerstel, associate themselves with the mass of the working classes, despite their constant struggle for equality in that realm. This way their political coordination would rest upon the social situation sketched above. But both this political recommendation and the analysis of the social situation are problematic. The typical housewife becomes a propertyless employee only when her marriage breaks up. At that point, for the first time, she can enter the proletarian situation (the author means to say: for the first time, her proletarian situation becomes clear to her). But this analysis does not take into account the reality that, even in the case of divorce, the woman is in most cases still caught up in the social unit to which she belongs. Identifying woman's dependence on a man with that of the employee on the employer proceeds from a definition of the proletarian much too oriented on the individual. The individual should not be the unit of analysis, but, rather, the family, which is either proletarian or bourgeois, regardless of whether in one case a proletarian woman may be treated like a princess and in another case a bourgeois housewife like a slave.

Despite its verbosity, this book is instructive and stimulating. Its conclusion, "The Balance Sheet of Femininity," is presented with a slightly tasteless pathos. Further, the main basis for her study, a research sample which included only 155 subjects, was not large enough to support the sweeping conclusions the author draws. The statistics frequently lack the kind of sociological and geographical spread that would legitimate her generalizations.

Franz Kafka: A Revaluation

ON THE OCCASION OF THE

TWENTIETH ANNIVERSARY OF HIS DEATH

TWENTY YEARS AGO, in the summer of 1924, Franz Kafka died at the age of forty. His reputation grew steadily in Austria and Germany during the twenties and in France, England, and America during the thirties. His admirers in these countries, though strongly disagreeing about the inherent meaning of his work, agree, oddly enough, on one essential point: All of them are struck by something new in his art of storytelling, a quality of modernity which appears nowhere else with the same intensity and unequivocalness. This is surprising, because Kafka—in striking contrast with other favorite authors of the intelligentsia—engaged in no technical experiments whatsoever; without in any way changing the German language, he stripped it of its involved constructions until it became clear and simple, like everyday speech purified of slang and negligence. The simplicity, the easy naturalness of his language may indicate that Kafka's modernity and the difficulty of his work have very little to do with that modern complication of the

Originally published in *Partisan Review*, XI/4, 1944. Two somewhat different German versions of this essay were published, the first in *Die Wandlung*, I/12, 1945–46, and the second in Arendt's *Sechs Essays*, 1948 (which was reprinted in her *Die verborgene Tradition: Acht Essays*, 1976).

inner life which is always looking out for new and unique techniques to express new and unique feelings. The common experience of Kafka's readers is one of general and vague fascination, even in stories they fail to understand, a precise recollection of strange and seemingly absurd images and descriptions—until one day the hidden meaning reveals itself to them with the sudden evidence of a truth simple and incontestable.

Let us begin with the novel *The Trial*, about which a small library of interpretations has been published. It is the story of a man who is tried according to laws which he cannot discover and finally is executed without having been able to find out what it is all about.

In his search for the real reasons for his ordeal, he learns that behind it "a great organization is at work which . . . not only employs corrupt wardens, stupid inspectors, and examining magistrates . . . but also has at its disposal a judicial hierarchy of high, indeed of the highest, rank, with an indispensable and numerous retinue of servants, clerks, police and other assistants, perhaps even hangmen." He hires an advocate, who tells him at once that the only sensible thing to do is to adapt oneself to existing conditions and not to criticize them. He turns to the prison chaplain for advice, and the chaplain preaches the hidden greatness of the system and orders him not to ask for the truth, "for it is not necessary to accept everything as true, one must accept it as necessary." "A melancholy conclusion," said K.; "it turns lying into a universal principle."

The force of the machinery in which the K. of *The Trial* is caught lies precisely in this appearance of necessity, on the one hand, and in the admiration of the people for necessity, on the other. Lying for the sake of necessity appears as something sublime; and a man who does not submit to the machinery, though submission may mean his death, is regarded as a sinner against some kind of divine order. In the case of K., submission is obtained not by force, but simply through increase in the feeling of guilt of which the unbased accusation was the origin in the accused man. This feeling, of course, is based in the last instance on the fact that no man is free from guilt. And since K., a busy bank employee, has never had time to ponder such generalities, he is induced to explore certain unfamiliar regions of his ego. This in turn leads him into confusion, into mistaking the organized and wicked evil of the world surrounding him for some necessary expression of that general guiltiness which is harmless and almost innocent if compared with the ill will that turns "lying into a universal principle" and uses and abuses even man's justified humbleness.

The feeling of guilt, therefore, which gets hold of K. and starts an interior development of its own, changes and models its victim until he is fit to stand trial. It is this feeling which makes him capable of entering the world of necessity and injustice and lying, of playing a role according to the rules, of adapting himself to existing conditions. This interior development of the hero—his *education sentimentale*—constitutes a second level of the story which accompanies the functioning of the bureaucratic machine. The events of the exterior world and the interior development coincide finally in the last scene, the execution, an execution to which, although it is without reason, K. submits without struggle.

It has been characteristic of our history-conscious century that its worst crimes have been committed in the name of some kind of necessity or in the name—and this amounts to the same thing—of the "wave of the future." For people who submit to this, who renounce their freedom and their right of action, even though they may pay the price of death for their delusion, anything more charitable can hardly be said than the words with which Kafka concludes *The Trial*: "It was as if he meant the shame of it to outlive him."

That *The Trial* implies a critique of the pre-war Austro-Hungarian bureaucratic regime, whose numerous and conflicting nationalities were dominated by a homogeneous hierarchy of officials, has been understood from the first appearance of the novel. Kafka, an employee of a workmen's insurance company and a loyal friend of many eastern European Jews for whom he had had to obtain permits to stay in the country, had a very intimate knowledge of the political conditions of his country. He knew that a man caught in the bureaucratic machinery is already condemned; and that no man can expect justice from judicial procedures where interpretation of the law is coupled with the administering of lawlessness, and where the chronic inaction of the interpreters is compensated by a bureaucratic machine whose senseless automatism has the privilege of ultimate decision. But to the public of the twenties, bureaucracy did not seem an evil great enough to explain the horror and terror expressed in the novel. People were more frightened by the tale than by the real thing. They looked therefore for other, seemingly deeper, interpretations, and they found them, following the fashion of the day, in a mysterious depiction of religious reality, the expression of a terrible theology.

The reason for this misinterpretation, which in my opinion is as fundamental, though not as crude, a misunderstanding as the psychoanalytical variety, is of course to be found in Kafka's work itself. It is true, Kafka depicted a society which had established itself as a substitute for God, and he described men who looked upon the laws of society as though they were divine laws—unchangeable through the will of men. In other words, what is wrong with the world in which Kafka's heroes are caught is precisely its deification, its pretense of representing a divine necessity. Kafka wants to destroy this world by exposing its hideous and hidden structure, by contrasting reality and pretense. But the modern reader, or at least the reader of the twenties, fascinated by paradoxes as such, and attracted by mere contrasts, was no longer willing to listen to reason. His understanding of Kafka reveals more about himself than about Kafka—reveals his fitness for this society, even if it be the fitness of an "élite"; and he is quite serious when it comes to Kafka's sarcasm about the lying necessity and the necessary lying as divine law.

Kafka's next great novel, *The Castle*, brings us back to the same world, which this time is seen not through the eyes of somebody who finally submits to necessity and who learns of its government only because he has been accused by it, but through the eyes of quite another K. This K. comes to it out of his own free will, as a stranger, and wants to realize in it a very definite purpose—to establish himself, to become a fellow-citizen, build up a life and marry, find work, and be a useful member of society.

The outstanding characteristic of K. in *The Castle* is that he is interested only in universals, in those things to which all men have a natural right. But while he demands no more than this, it is quite obvious that he will be satisfied with nothing less. He is easily enough persuaded to change his profession, but an occupation, "regular work," he demands as his right. The troubles of K. start because only the Castle can fulfill his demands; and the Castle will do this either as an "act of favor" or if he consents to become its secret employee—"an ostensible village worker whose real occupation is determined through Barnabas," the court messenger.

Since his demands are nothing more than the inalienable rights of man, he cannot accept them as an "act of favor from the Castle." At this point the villagers step in; they try to persuade K. that he lacks experience and does not know that the whole of life is constituted and dominated by favor and disfavor, by grace and disgrace, both as inexplicable, as hazardous as good and bad luck. To be in the right or in the wrong, they try to explain to him, is part of "fate," which no one can alter, which one can only fulfill.

K.'s strangeness therefore receives an additional meaning: He is strange not only because he does not "belong to the village, and does not belong to the Castle," but because he is the only normal and healthy human being in a world where everything human and normal, love and work and fellowship, has been wrested out of men's hands to become a gift endowed from without—or, as Kafka puts it, from above. Whether as fate, as blessing or as curse, it is something mysterious, something which man may receive or be denied, but never can create. Accordingly, K.'s aspiration, far from being commonplace and obvious is, in fact, exceptional and scandalous. He puts up a fight for the minimum as if it were something which embraced the sum total of all possible demands. For the villagers, K.'s strangeness consists not in his being deprived of the essentials of life but in his asking for them.

K.'s stubborn singleness of purpose, however, opens the eyes of some of the villagers; his behavior teaches them that human rights may be worth fighting for, that the rule of the Castle is not divine law and, consequently, can be attacked. He makes them see, as they put it, that "men who suffered our kind of experiences, who are beset by our kind of fear . . . who tremble at every knock at the door, cannot see things straight." And they add: "How lucky are we that you came to us!" The fight of the stranger, however, had no other result than his being an example. His struggle ends with a death of exhaustion—a perfectly natural death. But since he, unlike the K. of *The Trial*, did not submit to what appeared as necessity, there is no shame to outlive him.

The reader of Kafka's stories is very likely to pass through a stage during which he will be inclined to think of Kafka's nightmare world as a trivial though, perhaps, psychologically interesting forecast of a world to come. But this world actually has come to pass. The generation of the forties and especially those who have the doubtful advantage of having lived under the most terrible regime history has so far produced know that the terror of Kafka adequately represents the true nature of the thing called bureaucracy—the replacing of government by administration and of laws by arbitrary decrees. We know that Kafka's construction was not a mere nightmare.

If Kafka's description of this machinery really were prophecy, it would be as vulgar a prediction as all the other countless predictions that have plagued us since the beginning of our century. It was Charles Péguy, himself frequently mistaken for a prophet, who once remarked: "Determinism as far as it can be conceived . . . is perhaps nothing else but the law of residues." This sentence alludes to a profound truth. In so far as life is decline which ultimately leads to death, it can be foretold. In a dissolving society which blindly follows the natural course of ruin, catastrophe can be foreseen. Only salvation, not ruin, comes unexpectedly, for salvation and not ruin depends upon the liberty and the will of men. Kafka's so-called prophecies were but a sober analysis of underlying structures which today have come into the open. These ruinous structures were supported, and the process of ruin itself accelerated, by the belief, almost universal in his time, in a necessary and automatic process to which man must submit. The words of the prison-chaplain in *The Trial* reveal the faith of bureaucrats as a faith in necessity, of which they themselves are shown to be the functionaries. But as a functionary of necessity, man becomes an agent of the natural law of ruin, thereby degrading himself into the natural tool of destruction, which may be accelerated through the perverted use of human capacities. Just as a house which has been abandoned by men to its natural fate will slowly follow the course of ruin which somehow is inherent in all human work, so surely the world, fabricated by men and constituted according to human and not natural laws, will become again part of nature and will follow the law of ruin when man decides to become himself part of nature, a blind though accurate tool of natural laws, renouncing his supreme faculty of creating laws himself and even prescribing them to nature.

If progress is supposed to be an inevitable superhuman law which embraces all periods of history alike, in whose meshes humanity inescapably got caught, then progress indeed is best imagined and most exactly described in the following lines quoted from the last work of Walter Benjamin:

The angel of history . . . turns his face to the past. Where we see a chain of events, he sees a single catastrophe which unremittingly piles ruins on ruins and hurls them at his feet. He wishes he could stay— to awaken the dead and to join together the fragments. But a wind blows from Paradise, gets caught in his wings and is so strong that the angel cannot close them. This wind drives him irresistibly into the future to which he turns his back, while the pile of ruins before him towers to the skies. What we call progress is this wind.*

In spite of the confirmation of more recent times that Kafka's nightmare of a world was a real possibility whose actuality surpassed even the atrocities he describes, we still experience in reading his novels and stories a very definite feeling of unreality. First, there are his heroes who do not even have a name but are frequently introduced simply by initials; they certainly are not persons whom we could meet in a real world, for they lack all the many superfluous detailed characteristics which together make up a real individual. They move in a society where everybody is assigned a role and everybody has a job, and with whom they are contrasted only by the very fact that their role is indefinite, lacking as they do a defined place in the world of jobholders. And all of this society, whether small fellows like the common people in *The Castle*, who are afraid of losing their jobs, or big fellows like the officials in *The Castle* and *The Trial*, strive at some kind of superhuman perfection and live in complete identification with their jobs. They have no psychological qualities because they are nothing other than jobholders. When, for instance, in the novel *Amerika*, the head porter of a hotel mistakes somebody's identity, he says: "How could I go on being the head porter here if I mistook a person for another. . . . In all my thirty years of service I've never mistaken anyone yet." To err is to lose one's job; therefore, he cannot even admit the possibility of an error. Jobholders whom society forces to deny the human possibility of erring cannot remain human, but must act as though they were supermen. All of Kafka's employees, officials, and functionaries are very far from being

---

Theses on the Philosophy of History, IX. A close friend of Arendt, Benjamin took his own life on the French-Spanish border while fleeing the Nazis in 1940. See Arendt's "Walter Benjamin 1892–1940" in *Men in Dark Times,* Harcourt, Brace & Company, New York, 1968. —Ed.

perfect, but they act on an identical assumption of omnicompetence.

An ordinary novelist might describe a conflict between someone's function and his private life; he might show how the function has eaten up the private life of the person, or how his private life—the possession of a family, for example—has forced him into abandoning all human traits and into fulfilling his function as though he were inhuman. Kafka confronts us at once with the result of such a process, because the result is all that counts. Omnicompetence is the motor of the machinery in which Kafka's heroes get caught, which is senseless in itself and destructive, but which functions without friction.

One of the main topics of Kafka's stories is the construction of this machinery, the description of its functioning and of the attempts of his heroes to destroy it for the sake of simple human virtues. These nameless heroes are not common men whom one could find and meet in the street, but the model of the "common man" as an ideal of humanity; thus they are intended to prescribe a norm to society. Like the "forgotten man" of Chaplin's films, Kafka's "common man" has been forgotten by a society which consists of small and big fellows. For the motor of his activities is good will, in contrast to the motor of the society with which he is at odds, which is functionality. This good will, of which the hero is only a model, has a function too; it unmasks almost innocently the hidden structures of society which obviously frustrate the most common needs and destroy the best intentions of man. It exposes the misconstruction of a world where the man of good will who does not want to make a career is simply lost.

The impression of unreality and modernity with which Kafka's stories strike us is mainly due to this supreme concern of his with functioning, combined with his utter neglect of appearances and his lack of interest in the description of the world as phenomenon. Therefore, it is a misunderstanding to class him with the surrealists. While the surrealist tries to give as many and contradictory aspects of reality as possible, Kafka invents freely only in relation to function. While the surrealist's favorite method is always photomontage, Kafka's technique could best be described as the construction of models. If a man wants to build a house or if he wants to know a house well enough to be able to foretell its stability, he will get a blueprint of the building or draw one up himself. Kafka's stories are such blueprints; they are the product of thinking rather than of mere sense experience. Compared with a real house, of course, a blueprint is a very unreal affair; but without it the house could not have come into being, nor could one recognize the foundations and structures that make it a real house. The same imagination—namely, that imagination which in the words of Kant creates "another nature out of the material that actual nature gives it"—is to be used for the building of houses as for the understanding of them. Blueprints cannot be understood except by those who are willing and able to realize by their own imagination the intentions of architects and the future appearances of buildings.

This effort of imagination is demanded from the readers of Kafka's stories. Therefore, the mere receptive reader of novels, whose only activity is identification with one of the characters, is at a complete loss when reading Kafka. The curious reader who out of a certain frustration in life looks for the ersatz in the romantic world of novels, where things happen which do not happen in his life, will feel even more deceived and frustrated by Kafka than by his own life. For in Kafka's books there is no element of daydreaming or wishful thinking. Only the reader for whom life and the world and man are so complicated, of such terrible interest, that he wants to find out some truth about them and who therefore turns to story-tellers for insight into experiences common to us all may turn to Kafka and his blueprints, which sometimes in a page, or even in a single phrase, expose the naked structure of events.

In the light of these reflections we may consider one of the most simple of Kafka's stories, a very characteristic one which he entitled:

A COMMON CONFUSION

A common experience resulting in a common confusion. A. has to transact important business with B. in H. He goes to H. for a preliminary interview, accomplishes the journey there in ten minutes, and the journey back in the same time, and in returning boasts to his family of his expedition. The next day he goes again to H., this time to settle his business finally. As that is expected to require several hours, A. leaves very early in the morning. But although all the accessory circumstances, at least in A.'s estimation, are exactly the same as the day before, it takes him ten hours this time to reach H. When he arrives there quite exhausted in the evening he is informed that B., annoyed at his absence, had left an hour before to go to A.'s village, and they must have passed each other on the road. A. is advised to wait. But in his anxiety about his business he sets off at once and hurries home.

This time he achieves the journey, without paying any particular attention to the fact, exactly in a second. At home he learns that B. had arrived quite early, immediately after A.'s departure, indeed that he had met A. on the threshold and reminded him of his business; but A. had replied that he had no time to spare, he must go at once.

In spite of this incomprehensible behavior of A., however, B. had stayed on to wait for A.'s return. It is true, he had asked several times whether A. was not back yet, but he was still sitting up in A.'s room. Overjoyed at the opportunity of seeing B. at once and explaining everything to him, A. rushes upstairs. He is almost at the door, when he stumbles, twists a sinew, and almost fainting with the pain, incapable even of uttering a cry, only able to moan faintly in the darkness, he hears B.—impossible to tell whether at a great distance or quite near him—stamping down the stairs in a violent rage and vanishing for good.

The technique here seems very clear. All essential factors involved in this common experience of failure to carry out an appointment—such as overzealousness (which makes A. leave too early and overlook B. on the doorstep), misconcentration on details (A. thinks of the journey instead of his essential purpose in meeting B., which makes the way far longer than it was when measured without paying attention), and finally the typical mischievous tricks by which objects and circumstances conspire to make such failures final—are found in the story. These are the author's raw material. Because his stories are built up out of factors contributing to typical human failure, and not out of a real event, they seem at first like a wild and humorous exaggeration of actual happenings or like some inescapable logic gone wild. This impression of exaggeration, however, disappears entirely, if we consider the story as what it actually is: not the report of a confusing event, but the model of confusion itself. What remains is cognition of confusion presented in such a way that it will stimulate laughter, a humorous excitement that permits man to prove his essential freedom through a kind of serene superiority to his own failures.

From what has been said so far it may become clear that the novel-writer Franz Kafka was no novelist in the classical, the nineteenth-century, sense of the word. The basis for the classical novel was an acceptance

of society as such, a submission to life as it happens, a conviction that
greatness of destiny is beyond human virtues and human vice. It presupposed the decline of the citizen, who, during the days of the French
Revolution, had attempted to govern the world with human laws. It
pictured the growth of the bourgeois individual for whom life and the
world had become a place of events and who desired more events and
more happenings than the usually narrow and secure framework of his
own life could offer him. Today these novels which were always in
competition (even if imitating reality) with reality itself have been supplanted by the documentary novel. In our world real events, real destinies, have long surpassed the wildest imagination of novelists.

The pendant to the quiet and security of the bourgeois world in
which the individual expected from life his fair share of events and
excitements, and never quite got enough of them, was that of great men,
the geniuses and exceptions who in the eyes of that same world represented the wonderful and mysterious incarnation of something superhuman, which could be called destiny (as in the case of Napoleon), or
history (as in the case of Hegel), or God's will (as in the case of Kierkegaard, who believed God had chosen him to serve as an example), or
necessity (as in the case of Nietzsche, who declared himself to be "a
necessity"). The highest idea of man was the man with a mission, a call,
which he had to fulfill. The greater the mission, the greater the man.
All that man, seen as this incarnation of something superhuman, could
achieve was *amor fati* (Nietzsche), love of destiny, conscious identification
with what happened to him. Greatness was no longer sought in the work
done but in the person himself; genius was no longer thought of as a
gift bestowed by the gods upon men who themselves remained essentially
the same. The whole person had become the incarnation of genius and
as such was no longer regarded as a simple mortal. Kant, who was
essentially the philosopher of the French Revolution, still defined genius
as "the innate mental disposition through which Nature gives the rule
to Art." I do not agree with this definition; I think that genius is, rather,
the disposition through which Mankind gives the rule to Art. But this
is beside the point. For what strikes us in Kant's definition as well as
in his fuller explanation is the utter absence of that empty greatness
which during the entire nineteenth century had made of genius the
forerunner of the superman, a kind of monster.

What makes Kafka appear so modern and at the same time so strange among his contemporaries in the pre-war world is precisely that he refused to submit to any happenings (for instance, he did not want marriage to "happen" to him as it merely happens to most); he was not fond of the world as it was given to him, not even fond of nature (whose stability exists only so long as we "leave it at peace"). He wanted to build up a world in accordance with human needs and human dignities, a world where man's actions are determined by himself and which is ruled by his laws and not by mysterious forces emanating from above or from below. Moreover, his most poignant wish was to be part of such a world—he did not care to be a genius or the incarnation of any kind of greatness.

This of course does not mean, as it is sometimes asserted, that Kafka was modest. It is he who once, in genuine astonishment, noted in his diaries, "Every sentence I write down is already perfect"—which is a simple statement of truth, but was certainly not made by a modest man. He was not modest, but humble.

In order to become part of such a world, a world freed from all bloody apparitions and murderous magic (as he tentatively attempted to describe it at the end, the happy end, of his third novel, *Amerika*), he first had to anticipate the destruction of a misconstructed world. Through this anticipated destruction he carried the image, the supreme figure, of man as a model of good will, of man the *fabricator mundi*, the world-builder who can get rid of misconstructions and reconstruct his world. And since these heroes are only models of good will and left in the anonymity, the abstractness of the general, shown only in the very function good will may have in this world of ours, his novels seem to have a singular appeal, as though he wanted to say: This man of good will may be anybody and everybody, perhaps even you and me.

Foreign Affairs in the Foreign-Language Press

WITH THE APPROACH of the presidential elections, American public opinion discovers once more one of the most puzzling and important political factors of the country: the existence of the foreign-language groups in general and the role of voters who are influenced by foreign issues in particular. Although it would be rather hazardous to guess the weight of this electorate in exact numbers and though the claims of the different groups in this respect certainly are exaggerated, the fact remains that "nearly half of the white inhabitants are descended from post-colonial foreign stock,"* that most of these are the sons of recent immigrants, and that therefore a very considerable part of the "descendants" keep and cherish the memory of their origin.

No American statesman can afford to overlook the fact that the population of his country has come from the four corners of the world. These people may one day form a kind of international relationship between this country and the rest of the world. For the time being, however, they do not make life any easier for the government; on the

Part of this essay was published as "Our Foreign-Language Groups" in *The Chicago Jewish Forum*, III/1, Fall 1944.

*Marcus Lee Hansen, *The Immigrant in American History*, Preface.

contrary, reaching political decisions is much more complicated and carrying out commitments much more difficult here than is the case for any government with a wholly homogeneous population. The main trouble is that necessarily and without the ill will of anybody each decision of foreign policy is apt to become a domestic issue of immediate importance.

In terms of her population alone, isolationism would be an absurdity for America. Slogans such as "America First" have been preached throughout the country by German and Italian newspapers because they wanted America to stay out of the war for the benefit of their respective homelands. If some descendant-groups went isolationist without sincerely putting America first, others became interventionist without any connotation of international broad-mindedness or general liberal or even anti-fascist conviction, which this attitude usually indicated on the American scene. As a matter of fact, all these labels become almost devoid of sense when we come to foreign-language groups. The American Polish press is only one case in point. In this case, loyalty to the old country together with adherence to a decidedly semi-fascist government demanded interventionism, and, sure enough, intervention at any price was the battle cry of the most reactionary parts of the Polish press when Germany occupied the homeland. When in the summer of 1941 two Congressmen of Polish extraction—out of nine—voted against the government bill extending military service, a storm went through the Polish papers which nobody could accuse of being "liberal." The Congressmen were denounced as having voted against the interests of American Poles, who would "henceforth have no desire to vote for these Polish candidates." Characteristically enough, nobody thought of accusing them of having placed America first—but of having succumbed to German and Irish influences in Congress.

As it sometimes happens in very troublesome aspects of public life, the important role of the foreign-language vote is all too often either ignored or wildly exaggerated. Thus we are told that there are five million Polish votes which can be successfully used to force an open declaration of the government on behalf of Poland's pre-war frontiers, or—to take an entirely different instance—that the recent dismissal of the Yugoslav Ambassador to Washington, Constantin Fotitch, was principally due to his disagreements with the Yugoslav Committee in the United States headed by Louis Adamic. In both instances, the influence of the descendant-groups is certainly exaggerated. But it would be almost as bad judgment to deny this influence altogether.

For the interest of American citizens of non-American descent in the welfare of the lands of their origin is a matter of record. In the last analysis, it may be found that this sentiment formed the realistic basis for the humanitarian tradition of American foreign policy, of the numerous interventions of the government on behalf of freedom and against oppression in other countries. For a long time the foreign-language groups acted as safeguards of a liberal and humanitarian foreign policy, together with their fellow-citizens who, however, were rather more interested in the domestic field. They had been driven to the coast of the New World by a spirit of rebellion against the governments of their home-countries or by a thirst for opportunity and adventure—in any event, by some love for freedom and by some hate of oppression. If they did not speak the same language as their fellow-citizens or if they had a different past and different habits, they shared with them the same political ideas and ideals. They did more than any official policy to win for America the wide popular confidence and good will she is enjoying today among all European nations. Their interest in the affairs of the Old Country was not "un-American" if we understand by the much abused slogan "true Americanism" the political doctrines of the Founding Fathers. On the contrary, they wanted for their former countries no more and no less than the same benefits of freedom and opportunity they themselves enjoyed in the New World.

Through her foreign-language groups, the share of America in the history of European freedom has been considerable indeed. For during the whole nineteenth century, most of the national liberation movements were financed by descendants of immigrants. An outstanding example is the Irish struggle for independence which was well-nigh operated from an American base. The same holds true, though in a somewhat lesser degree, of the Hungarian, Polish, and Italian patriotic movements, which were furthered by financial support and political pressure from the respective groups in the United States. Prior to 1914, many German immigrants here were proud that they or their fathers had left the political regime of the Hohenzollern. Organized as Social Democrats, they enjoyed the reputation of being the most advanced and the most radical sons of the fatherland. During the First World War, Czechs and Slovaks joined hands in America and helped to bring the Czechoslovak Republic into being because they both felt themselves members of oppressed peoples and wanted liberation from the Hapsburg yoke. The last instance of such a liberation movement which hardly would have been possible without active help from citizens of this country is the upbuilding of the Jewish National Home in Palestine.

This long and honorable history of immigrant groups in the United States makes it all the more surprising that during the past few decades a substantial section of those groups has supported and sometimes initiated an utterly reactionary political policy in their former homelands. Many different factors have contributed to bringing about this most unfortunate change. Among them must be counted the radical change in general outlook which, after the turn of the century, distinguished the immigrant from his forefathers. This new immigrant, whose influence was to be felt only about twenty years after his arrival, came for economic reasons only, was not politically minded, and had little knowledge of the traditional meaning of America for European political thought as the land of freedom and self-government. He looked forward to a kind of promised land of money-making and material well-being rather than to new political forms. His relationship to the Old Country was no longer characterized by criticism of her government, but by homesickness in the first generation and a curious mixture of sentimentality and pride in the second.

The consequences of this change in the character of the descendant-groups have been considerable. Recent immigrants, sadly lacking the political education of their predecessors, no longer were able to make a distinction between the Old Country and the government it happened to have. For many Italians, Mussolini simply became synonymous with Italy, as for many Germans Hitler became identical with Germany; for Lithuanians, Smetona with Lithuania; for Poles, Pilsudski with Poland; for Spaniards, Franco with Spain, and so on. A sentimental longing for national pride has supplanted former political criticism, and the empty boasting of the fascist and semi-fascist dictators swelled the hearts of descendants abroad. This trend was equally discernible in those groups that belonged to the defeated in the First World War as in those that met with discrimination in America and had some reasons not to feel accepted as full-fledged Americans. The hollow words with which dictators of the post-war period labelled their respective people as superior, glorious, and unique above all others, made a deep impression on national groups, in which they soothed the wounds of hurt self-respect, and were even more effective here than in the home countries, where people soon had ample opportunity to experience the ugly terror and the utter contempt hiding behind the smokescreen of propaganda speeches. This means that the descendant-groups in spite of their violent interest in the future of their former countries have but little in common with the actual present state of mind of their former fellow-citizens.

II

Since the times of Homer, great tales have followed in the footsteps of great wars, and great storytellers have crept from the ruins of destroyed cities and devastated landscapes. Newspapers today employ storytellers, calling them reporters or correspondents, and storytelling itself has become organized by modern techniques. Word by word, tales are brought home by telephone or wireless, and sometimes, buried in an abundance of reading material, they emerge as sparkling as precious diamonds from a heap of worthless stones.

When the invasion ship on which Ernie Pyle served as storyteller came within shooting distance of Sicily, five bright, terrifying bands of searchlight, one after the other, closed down on the little ship, exposing a helpless target to the coastal batteries. For some frightful moments sailors and soldiers waited for what must have seemed, according to the rules of military practice, like the end. But then, the first searchlight slowly slid away, followed in close succession by the next three. Only the last one remained for an extra minute, as though reluctant to part from what it had found. The men almost believed in a miracle, but searchlights are handled by men, and so are coastal batteries. Italian soldiers, as well as they could, had given their first greetings to those whom they, by their own free will, no longer considered their enemies. The searchlights had turned out to be signals of welcome, an enormous, grotesque, and powerful twinkling of the eyes. Through the night of war, the light of a secret understanding had flashed a message of unexpected friendship and alliance awaiting the invaders on these foreign shores. If white flags mean surrender, this maneuver of searchlights meant invitation. Yet it was an admonition, too, which, translated into words, would have said: "See what we could do to you if we wanted. Don't forget that we did not want to."

The essence of this story has been reinforced time and again during the whole Sicilian campaign. The surrender of the Badoglio government was the official legitimation of numerous acts of solidarity with the Allied cause shown by the Italian people upon the invasion of their land. But if we were deprived of our storytellers, and if we tried to guess what is going on in Italy by reading the Italian press in this country, we never would have been able to foretell this course of events. Of the four leading Italian dailies, it was only the newly converted *Progresso Italo-Americano* of Generoso Pope—up to Pearl Harbor an ardent fascist—which supported Eisenhower's appeal to the Italian people to surrender to the Allied armies. Others scorned "these 'prominent' Italian-Americans" who dared to approve such "useless invitations" (*La Notizia*), even wanted Italy to continue her fight "as befits an honorable nation" which "cannot, must not surrender" (*La Gazetta Italiana*), boasted of Italian pilots who, "contemptuous of danger, leaped upon the invaders," or warned openly against surrender by publishing the Axis version of the armistice conditions (*La Gazetta del Massachusetts*).

While the fall of Mussolini brought Italy into an ecstasy of joy and hope, the opinion of the six million American Italians was, to say the least, divided, with the majority hiding their distress under a vigorous defense of the monarchy and a minority stubbornly harping on the old string that Mussolini had acted as bulwark against communism in Italy. There is, of course, a small section within the Italian community that is, and always was, anti-fascist. The members of the Mazzini Society, the readers of Count Sforza's *Nazione Unita* or Don Luigi Sturzo's *La Voce Del Popolo* welcomed the Sicilian invasion as unequivocally as the majority of Sicilians, and have hailed the downfall of Mussolini as enthusiastically as the citizens of Rome. But these groups are small and powerless, led by anti-fascist refugees without strong roots within the community of those who are American citizens and who rather feel that they have "enough leadership in this country to guide the Italian groups without having to call upon discarded elements from Italy," as one of their papers put it about a year ago.

Recent events in Italy itself have proved these "discarded elements" to be much closer to the feelings of the Italian masses than anybody would have dared to expect. But this does not suffice to change the situation right here, and since American foreign policy is necessarily influenced by the attitude of "descendants," it must be expected that the six million American citizens of Italian descent will have more say and carry more weight than the small anti-fascist groups. This is recognized by leaders of the latter, who desperately try to make contact with and win influence among the Italian community in this country. In this respect it is rather significant that an anti-fascist labor leader of long standing like Luigi Antonini, vice-president of the International Ladies' Garment Workers' Union and chairman of the Italian American Labor Council, saw fit to join hands with Generoso Pope, in the recently founded American Committee for Italian Democracy, as soon as the question of direct influence on Italian affairs assumed pressing importance. Mr. Antonini must have been aware that this new association would earn him considerable trouble with his former friends. Yet apparently he realized that his only chance lay in joining the outfit of the formerly pro-fascist leaders of Italian-Americans. And after a few weeks of violent attacks against this new body, even Count Sforza came out with a statement that for him it would be sufficient to bridge the abyss between them if Pope were to acknowledge his past mistakes.

There have been numerous complaints in the anti-fascist Italian press about the apparent reluctance of the United States government to deal with the truly anti-fascist elements in this country and about its eagerness to win the support of those whose attitude even during the war was not dictated by unequivocal loyalty. There had been repeated attempts in the past to move the most powerful Italian organization, the Order of the Independent Sons of Italy, to issue a statement calling upon the the people of Italy to surrender unconditionally. These attempts have been frustrated, and various resolutions respectively shelved. With the downfall of Mussolini, however, the picture seemed to change. The Pennsylvania Lodge of the Sons of Italy, under the leadership of Judge Alessandroni, has offered to sponsor a special broadcast to Italy, which would be operated jointly with the OWI [Office of War Information]. And if one is to trust the information in Drew Pearson's column, "Washington Spotlight," "Government officials were delighted . . . they considered this one of the most patriotic moves made by any Italian group to date." These are perhaps indications that the American government in its handling of Italian affairs may be more inclined to rely on the recently and very superficially converted Italian-Americans of long-standing prominence in the Italian community in this country than on those who have a reputation as old fighters against fascism but are newcomers on the American scene.

This probable course of events is certainly deplorable, especially since these Italian-Americans (who in contrast to their former compatriots have not yet overcome the disease of fascism) will not be true spokesmen for the Italian people, but on the contrary might artificially strengthen those very elements in Italy that have been closely tied to the fascist party-and-government machinery. Possessing both Italian origin and American citizenship, they will command considerable respect and influence on the hopes and political decisions of a defeated people. These men, the Fortes, the Alessandronis, the Popes, and, worse still, the Gorrasis, the anti-Semite Scala, *et al.*, have successfully discarded all those who, having left Italy more recently, could have told the Italian community in America something about the true feelings of the Italian people. The argument that "LaGuardia [?], Sforza, Salemini, Borgese, Ascoli and company . . . should have stayed in Italy . . . and kept the light of liberty shining"—as the influential New York financier Luigi Criscuolo once put it (in *La Gazetta del Massachusetts*)—though showing a surprising ignorance of modern police methods, has proved very effective. There is no use hiding the fact that this whole state of affairs is not due only to the fascist leanings of a few influential individuals or to the ambitions of isolated "leaders." When Generoso Pope, after America's entry into the war, changed the editorial policy of his *Progresso Italo-Americano*, the circulation was said to have dropped considerably, and his example was not followed by the other Italian dailies. More conclusive still appears the result of his widely publicized contest "Why should Italy join the United Nations?" which took place just some six months ago: not a single Italian-American, or even Italian alien, was among the prize winners. Certainly an anti-fascist would not compete in the contest of a man with Mr. Pope's past. But the large mass of readers of the largest Italian daily in this country apparently did not approve wholeheartedly of the new pro-democratic policy of its editor.

III

During the last twenty-five years, the foreign-language press in the United States has considerably decreased in circulation. But the proportion of natives to foreign-born in each of the foreign-language groups has increased in a far larger ratio. This signifies that these groups are today largely made up of American citizens who have more actual power and more semi-official relations with the government and the political bodies than they had a couple of decades ago. The Italian press writes for and speaks in the name of six million American Italians of whom only about 1.5 million are foreign-born. The Polish foreign-born population numbers only about one million, but the Polish press, with a combined circulation of about 800,000 copies, is apparently read by a population of about five and a half million Americans of Polish descent. It would be rather ridiculous to assume that 52,000 foreign-born Croats could subscribe to about 25,000 copies of the Croat daily or that 35,000 foreign-born Ukrainians could afford two dailies with a combined circulation of 27,000 copies—in addition, by the way, to four weeklies with a combined circulation of about 15,000. It has already been pointed out that "in general the attitude of the third-generation Americans toward the language or languages of their grandparents is more sympathetic than that of the preceding generations."* And the circulation figures of the foreign-language press are eloquent proof of the truth of this remark.

What adds to the importance and influence of this press is the fact that a majority of papers are organs of clubs, societies, benefit and fraternal organizations, insurance companies, churches, and parishes. They can reckon with the support and speak in the name of organized members upon whose agreement, on the other side, they are largely dependent. They can be said to be as expressive of the opinions of their readers as the few English-language newspapers with a definite "party-line" or political "angle." The editors, in contrast to their English-speaking colleagues, are frequently the political leaders of their respective communities, the presidents of the insurance companies, secretaries of the Workers' Benefit Leagues, or outstanding members of the newly founded national councils which among such groups as Czechoslovaks, Poles, and Yugoslavs have the function of backing homeland governments

---

*Hannibald Gerald Duncan, *Immigration and Assimilation*, Boston, 1933.

(as is the case of the Slovak League and the Hungarian Association Abroad) or governments-in-exile. Most of these societies have local branches throughout the country. The newspaper that goes to every member is one of the most important links between the national groups dispersed all across the continent. The Rumanian tri-weekly *Amerika*, for instance, is published in Cleveland; but as the "official organ of the Union and League of Rumanian Societies of America," an insurance company which comprises fifteen units, it goes to the Rumanian-speaking groups in Detroit and Youngstown, as well as in Chicago and New York. Through this insurance company, to belong to which is a vital interest of every Rumanian, the Rumanian Orthodox Church was able to exercise considerable influence—influence which prior to Pearl Harbor manifested itself in full support of the Rumanian fascists—the Iron Guard—and violent attacks against Jews.

Without these insurance companies and clubs of long standing, recent outright political foundations would have been without the necessary bases. The Hungarian World Association, founded in 1938 under the presidency of Horthy, the head of the Hungarian government, did not need to base itself on individual membership. It simply used the Hungarian insurance associations and the newspapers closely associated with them, such as the 47,000 members of Verhovay and the New York daily *Amerikai Magyar Nepszava*, or the 14,000 members of Bridgeporter and the Cleveland daily *Szabadsag*. The president of the Verhovay Fraternal Insurance Association, Joseph Darego, is at the same time editor of the weekly organ of that organization—*Verhovayak Lapja*—and an honorary president of the Hungarian World Association.

The same holds true for other groups. The chief bodies of the very controversial Polish politics in America, the "Polish American Council" (which supports the Polish government-in-exile), as well as the National Committee of Americans of Polish Descent (which is violently opposed to it), are composed of fraternal or other non-political societies such as the Polish Roman Catholic Union or the Polish National Alliance. The Czech government-in-exile is supported by the Czechoslovak National Council, which is made up of organizations to which Americans of Czech origin of the third and fourth generation still adhere. And so is the Slovak League, its most uncompromising foe.

On the other hand, what has been said about the lack of influence of the Italian anti-fascist refugees is not an isolated instance. Reactionary or semi-fascist politicians have usually found access and a field for their activities if only they once had an official standing with their governments. The case of Tibor von Eckhardt among the Hungarians is the best known. Another such case is that of Mr. Matuszewski—erstwhile Minister of Finance of the Pilsudski regime, later director of the Municipal Credit Society in Warsaw—who is now permitted to play a leading part in the right-wing opposition against the Polish government-in-exile and has been cordially invited to be an illustrious guest writer by the important New York daily *Nowy Swiat* and the Detroit daily *Dziennik Polski*. Conversely, it has been the fate of the outright anti-fascists to remain isolated with their recently founded, small, and uninfluential publications. How difficult conditions are for these refugees, who for obvious reasons cannot boast of having secured official positions in the semi-fascist pre-war regimes of their homelands, can be seen in the sad fact that they sometimes have not even been able to win the confidence of the more democratic organizations of their national groups. Thus, when the Hungarian democrats of the Vambery group—who publish the excellent New York weekly *Harc*, which has a ridiculously low circulation—recently tried to win the support of the rather democratic insurance company Rakoczi, they met with little success. Even if a certain amount of political agreement can be achieved, newcomers from Europe, if they are not more or less officially delegated by the governments of the old countries, are looked down upon as nuisances. As far as public opinion is concerned, this general distrust of newcomers and refugees has had some serious consequences for the governments-in-exile. Since the war brought about the divorce of governments from their peoples, it has been only natural for all the refugee governments to attempt to win over not only American public opinion in general but primarily to gain the support of their own descendant-groups—groups which were so well organized and whose old loyalties were so deeply aroused through the catastrophes that had ruined their homelands.

In this, however, they have not been very successful. Whenever one of their representatives in America, being in the disagreeable position of representing a government without a people, has tried to enlist their united support, he was almost invariably advised by important sections that it was rather doubtful whether he had a right to speak to and for anybody at all, and that he was abusing the rules of diplomatic privilege. Very few papers, on the other side, share the healthy view (once expressed by the Polish weekly *Trybuna*) that "the safeguarding of Polish interests has to be left to the government-in-exile." Most of them would agree (with *Nowiny Polskie*, a Polish daily) that under present circumstances only the American Polish press can openly approve or criticize the political actions of the refugee governments, with quite a few claiming "equal rights in affairs concerning the Polish nation" (as *Nowy Swiat* put it a few years ago).

The fact that immigrant groups are passionately interested in the future of their homelands but feel themselves under no obligation whatsoever as regards the exiled governments, makes things somewhat difficult for the various ambassadors in Washington. American Slovenians, because of their American citizenship, can write to Churchill, asking his support for a united Slovenia after the war, without paying the slightest attention to the Yugoslav government; and American Slovaks can ask the authorities of this country to look to them for their information instead of to the Czech government. It is rather hard to ascertain whether or not the New York Slovak bi-weekly *Slovak V Amerike* was right when it indicated that the alleged indifference with which Beneš was met in the State Department (according to reports in *Time*) was due to the successfully disseminated "information" of Slovak-Americans.

It is certainly no accident that governments without large and well-organized groups of descendants, such as the Dutch or the Belgians, enjoy a better reputation and awake more confidence in their claims to be representative of their countries than the Czecho-Slovaks, the Yugoslavs, or the Poles. Opposition of dissenting bodies against the activities of the Czechoslovak and Polish National Councils has been extremely violent and was supported by organizations firmly rooted within their communities. Under these conditions, official representatives or resolutions of exiled governments are often not taken seriously by neutral or even benevolent observers. When for instance, more than a year ago, the Yugoslav government resolved not to divide Yugoslavia, the Serb National Defense Council passed a resolution demanding a partition of the homeland and the establishment of Greater Serbia. This statement caused Wm. Philip Simms (in his column in the *New York World Telegram*) to wonder whether the Yugoslav government really did represent the Yugoslav nation. In other words, the Serb National Defense Council, and similarly the Croatian and Slovenian organizations, though composed mainly of American citizens, were held more representative of the people of Yugoslavia than the official decision of a recognized government. The case of the Czechoslovaks is not less complicated. Since American Czechs and Slovaks had been of greater help to Masaryk during and after the First World War, it is all the more disturbing that now, when it comes to restore what once had been won with their support, the very same organizations refuse to help and even attack and denounce.

In each of the respective groups there exist one or several papers on whose unswerving support the exiled governments can rely. But these papers are rarely those with the highest circulation figures. They frequently lack popular support in the form of fraternal or other societies and they have therefore sometimes been suspected of receiving substantial subsidies from the embassies. It is questionable whether other methods of achieving unity are more fortunate. Consider this instance: Among the American Slovak press the New York daily *New Yorski Dennik* is outstanding in its wholehearted support of Beneš; its owner is Mr. Richard Vogel—who also owns the Czech New York daily *New Yorske Listy*, which is the mouthpiece of the Czechoslovak government. The arguments employed against exiled governments show a striking resemblance to the usual accusations made against refugees. By losing their countries, they have lost that official standing which commanded authority. The descendants simply won't recognize any "refugee" and even prefer puppet governments—but acting governments nevertheless—as happened in the case of the Slovaks.

IV

With America at war, these conditions would be more discomforting and would give rise to more serious concern as regards the future of a more democratic Europe were it not for the fact that the sometimes peculiar behavior of certain parts of immigrant groups is less dictated by ideological conviction than by a deformed and ill-comprehended sense of loyalty to the Old Country. This sentiment usually is well understood and even strengthened by public opinion in this country, which again has made things very difficult for refugees who oppose the government of their Old Country and who are mainly particularly loyal to their new country's government. At least one may doubt the wisdom of the judge who, a year ago, refused American citizenship to a Finn because he had solicited names for a petition to the United States government to declare war on Finland. Said his Honor: "You will never be granted American citizenship. One who hates the country of his birth is unfit to be a citizen of any country." (The Astoria Finnish semi-weekly *Lannen Suometar*, still unequivocally supporting the Finnish government, of course rejoiced over this when reporting the case to its readers.)

The fact is, however, that the frequent pro-fascist leanings of foreign-language papers are not too deeply rooted. That might again be seen from the Italian example. It is perhaps not a very pleasant discovery in itself that many Italian newspapers that for two decades had praised Mussolini and had been hardly disturbed at all by America's entry into the war changed their attitudes within a few days after Mussolini's dismissal and came out with wholehearted support for Badoglio. But it does indicate the probability of overnight changes, which, after a careful reading of these papers, one would not have thought likely.

There are more indications of inconsistency in what might appear as the political convictions of certain foreign-language groups. There are the odd but by no means isolated cases of newspapers giving all-out support to fascist governments in the Old Country, and then, in the domestic field of the new land—where they actually live, work, and occasionally cast a vote—they support the New Deal, President Roosevelt and sometimes even his Administration, and his Social Security program. After all, the bulk of the foreign-language population is made up of workers who, with the exception of the German-Americans and the Scandinavians, are democratic voters by tradition. It is true that the Poles, the overwhelming majority of whom once worked in America's heavy industry, have in recent years developed a growing middle class. This may or may not have strengthened the reactionary elements in that group, although that fact in itself can hardly suffice to explain the extreme violence of their nationalistic argumentation. At any rate, even those papers that, in the field of homeland politics, enjoy the collaboration of such outstanding Polish reactionaries as Mr. Matuszewski, in the American domestic field back all those measures that are usually considered liberal—such as the order freezing prices, wages, and salaries, and the Social Security program. The Hungarian workers in Detroit and elsewhere are patrons of the Hungarian Himler-chain papers. That these papers vaguely favor a Hapsburg restoration and approve of Tibor von Eckhard apparently does not bother them much; but they have to be given precisely the opposite political line when it comes to domestic politics: support of Roosevelt's social reforms, coupled with violent attacks on "millionaires" and big business.

Such inconsistencies are by far more typical of the foreign-language press in general than of papers that consciously follow the fascist or communist party-line. The latter convey the impression of publishing elaborate translations, in a variety of languages, of identical texts. Fascist papers, regardless of their language, invariably attack Great Britain and promulgate a negotiated peace. Communist papers monotonously urge the opening of a second front and register every shift and trend of Soviet foreign policy. Both have, moreover, a consistent political line in the domestic field, the former spreading confusion by calling all social measures "Nazism," and the latter by unequivocally supporting the war effort with special emphasis on help for Russia.

The inconsistency of most of the foreign-language press, however, is honest and candid. Only recently has the innocence of the sharp line drawn between measures approved in the Old Country and the politics supported in the new been slightly blurred. The American press has repeatedly stressed that the innumerable European boundary conflicts will probably play a role in the coming elections. These fears have been caused by threats of certain Polish papers, after the Polish-Russian break, that they would no longer support the Democratic ticket "should the Democratic members of the Administration accept the imperialistic claims of Russia" (the New Jersey weekly *Glos Narodu*). Although the Polish community in general continued to support Mr. Kelly in the municipal election in Chicago, the fact that he was elected with a comparatively small majority has aroused comment linking his loss of votes to the problem of Poland's post-war boundaries.

However insignificant these signs may be in themselves, they may indicate, if connected with other symptoms of revitalized interest in the destinies of the Old Countries, a growing impact of homeland politics on the general political outlook of national splinter groups. The terrible catastrophe that has befallen the European nations has strengthened the feeling that it is a matter of simple decency not to forget the worries and the misery of the Old Country. As a Lithuanian paper once put it: "It is the duty of countrymen in the United States who enjoy the privilege of free people to speak [for their enslaved brethren]." Those who were driven by economic emergency to the shores of this country—which for a long time they considered a kind of "promised land"—feel today like outposts saved for a time of national emergency. For they consider themselves the "only true interpreters and proxies in a position freely to declare [their] natural, historical and human rights," as expressed in a recent letter from the Ukrainian Catholic Brotherhood of Alberta, Canada, addressed to the Governor-General of Canada, demanding him to support a "free Ukraine." These sentiments, frequently nourished by an exalted belief in the freedom America offers to each of her citizens, are too strong to be weighed down by so reasonable a desire, allegedly uttered by the government, that citizens of foreign descent in this time of war be only "very slightly active" on behalf of the interests of their former countries (as reported by the Cleveland Polish daily *Wiadomosci Codzienne*).

So let us not forget that among other motives it is also decency that leads occasionally to such absurd attitudes that, after reading certain newspapers, one might think Americans of Slovenian descent fight this war for Trieste and Fiume, Americans of Serb origin for "Greater Serbia," and those of Hungarian extraction for the revision of the Trianon Treaty. Not all go as far as the representatives of the Slovak League, who allegedly dream of attending the coming peace conference as Slovak delegates (reported by the Slovak daily *New Yorski Dennik*); maybe they want to submit their request for Madagascar (sic!) which another Slovak paper, *Katolicki Sokol*, has already claimed as a colony for independent Slovakia. But American Lithuanians are asked, by the Chicago Lithuanian daily *Draugas*, to buy more war bonds "for Lithuanian independence"; and at a meeting that took place in Waterbury, Connecticut, on June 27th, it was resolved to support only such a peace as "will safeguard the territorial integrity and freedom of Lithuania." American Serbs maintain that they "are ready to defend with equal reverent love both our Americanism and our Serbianism" (the Pittsburgh daily *Amerikanski Srbobran*). A few Polish papers have even advocated a plan of re-emigration to Poland of American Poles in connection with the tasks of post-war reconstruction. This topic originally emerged in the columns of the Milwaukee daily *Kurier Polski* in 1941, and was taken up again in June of this year in the New York daily *Nowy Swiat* by P. P. Yolles, who insisted that Polish-American organizations should take the matter into their hands, so that re-emigration, which he apparently expects to be spontaneous, may become an organized exodus.

This last example shows the great gift of imagination which characterizes many politicians and journalists of our foreign-language groups. This talent was not impaired, apparently, by the utter failure of the campaign for volunteer enlistment of Americans of Polish descent in the Polish Legion before America's entry into the war. And then, there is something in this mad utopian dream which is almost certain to strike popular feeling, and this is the old glorious picture of the homecoming rich uncle from America who has not forgotten his poor family and now returns with the legendary gifts of the New World—riches and liberty.

V

When one first enters the strange land of the foreign-language press, desperately trying to determine the true aims to which its varying and bewildering ways might lead, one can hardly escape the impression that the plan of the Polish extremists for re-emigration may not be such a stupid idea after all. Consider the fact that so many of the "descendants" not only sympathize with and worry about the unspeakable misery of the Old Countries, but are actually worrying their heads off over the pettiest boundary disputes in a Europe thousands and thousands of miles away—such as whether Teschen belongs to Poland or Czechoslovakia, or Vilna to Lithuania instead of to Poland!

And then, after a certain time, the novice will detect that he was all wrong, and the better acquainted he is with homegrown European politics, the quicker he will realize his mistake. He might have been led astray by those overoptimistic advocates of the melting pot who insist that the foreign-language press is as "American" as any English-language paper in the country and that, indeed, its papers are only translated American papers. Or he may have been too much impressed by the peculiarly aggressive and sometimes vicious style in which feuds between the groups are fought out. In both cases, he will soon correct his judgment.

There are two basic facts about the foreign-language groups' quarrels that are easily overlooked, both of which tend rather to make these conflicts part of the American political scene, even though their contents are wholly European. First, there is the fact that every dispute is argued in terms of American foreign policy or in terms of slogans that dominate the whole life of the nation. Second, there is the fundamental change all European national conflicts must undergo when they are fought out by people who, for the first time, live in such close proximity to one another as, since the turn of the century, they do in all our large towns and cities. It is not only New York that has to be considered as one of the largest points of concentration of all existing European nationalities, but Detroit, Chicago, Cleveland, and all the densely populated places in Pennsylvania, Illinois, Ohio, and Michigan. This new problem of living together within the framework of a growing nation in which all of them are to become integral parts accounts, on the one hand, for the peculiar violence of nationalistic arguments, and, on the other, creates unexpected alliances, awakening the consciousness of common interests. This would hardly have been possible on the old continent and, sometime in the future, may play an important if not decisive role in shaping the political sentiments of the European peoples.

Both these trends, in the last analysis, mean assimilation, and if this assimilation works much slower than the prophets of the melting pot have expected, it will prove much less superficial than those who were satisfied with mere adjustment to the "American way of life" have made us fear. People get adjusted to the use of icebox and automobile in less than two years; it is only normal that it take several generations to instill in them the political traditions of the American Republic.

VI

The political ideas that in recent times have been even more decisive for the foreign-language press than for the usual papers are: Isolationism prior to the war, Atlantic Charter during the war, and, in the last months, Federation. Not one of these slogans has escaped considerable distortions of its genuine meaning. Isolationism was preached throughout the country by German newspapers and frequently by German agents. Nearly the whole of the German-American press was openly isolationist and openly pro-fascist before America's entry into the war, and there still are papers, like the *Chicagoer Abendpost*, the *Milwauker Deutsche Zeitung*, the semi-weekly *Staatsanzeiger* in Bismarck, North Dakota, and, among others, the National Weeklies chain, which more or less cautiously follow the old line. The same could be said of the Italian-language press and, as a rule, of all groups whose homelands during the present war have either preserved their neutrality or, in the initial stages of the conflict, profiteered from Hitler's conquests. Ironically enough, for the groups that used isolationism only as a means of protecting what they believed to be national interests of European countries, the America First Committee gave the best possible excuse. Foreign influences, especially from immigrant groups, were certainly stronger in these circles than they were among those who a few years ago still were called "warmongers." Under the smokescreen of discussing plans of former members of the America First Committee, such as the plan published by Col. Robert R. McCormick suggesting the inclusion of the British Commonwealth in United States territories, the *Chicagoer Abendpost* still feels safe enough to wage an anti-British propaganda campaign. For the German-Americans, "America First" meant protection of German interests and they became America Firsters because they thought first of Germany. The case of the Scandinavian press, which sympathized with isolationism out of a firm tradition of neutrality in their former homelands, is different; their attitude has almost disappeared since the occupation of Norway.

While the slogan "America First" even in its deforming interpretation by the foreign-language press still kept its aspect of being a controversial issue, and its content of unequivocal opposition to war, the next watchword that penetrated every group suffered a different fate. There is hardly a single nationality or a single political faction or paper from the extreme right to the extreme left wing which has not adopted the Atlantic Charter as the new "Bill of Rights," according to which exactly everything can be claimed and exactly every political line can be justified. In the name of the Atlantic Charter, the Czechs want the restoration of Czechoslavakia, the Slovaks the independence of Slovakia, the Hungarians the revision of the Trianon frontiers, the Ukranians an independent Western Ukraine with the inclusion of parts of Russia, and the Carpatho-Russians want reunion with Russia. The Atlantic Charter is upheld by all leftist papers because it grants self-determination; and it has, at the same time, been the very nucleus of anti-Russian campaigns for the Finns and the Lithuanians, the Latvians and the Poles. In the midst of this bewildering situation in which at first glance nobody can possibly decide who is who, it has been gratifying that at least one paper has been candid enough to confess the veritable clue to the puzzle. The Hungarian daily *Amerikai Magyar Nepszava*, when supporting General Giraud against De Gaulle, admitted: "We who in the Hungarian question have set our hopes on the Atlantic Charter, that is the principle of non-intervention, would like to say that in the case of the French intervention is not only justified but necessary."

The existence of descendant-groups as clearly separated bodies within the general life of the nation has been noted as far back as the thirties of the last century, when efforts were made to secure the German or the Irish vote locally. For over a century, however, these groups have existed fairly unrelated one to another, and though all of them simultaneously followed a rather progressive line until the close of the last war and though most of them turned violently pro-fascist during the last two decades, these coincidences happened rather by the accident of a similar European background than through concerted action of any kind.

This state of things seems, however, about to change. There are certain indications in the foreign-language press of the last two years that cross-relations are existent and that even the formation of blocs is not out of the picture. It all dates back to the day when Russia made it known to the world that she regarded the Baltic States, parts of Poland, and Bessarabia as prospective republics of the Soviet Union. Since then it has dawned upon most of the smaller nations that sovereignty and independence alone will give neither national security nor economic prosperity. The growing use of the new fashionable word "federation" has made this fact perfectly clear. Groups which, like the Polish and Lithuanians, only a few years ago would notice each other only in order to prolong age-old feuds in the most abusive language are trying hard to come to terms. The same is true for Poles and Ukrainians and even for Hungarians and Slovaks. Everybody began to plan for "regional federations."

The talk about regional federations was in full swing when the Soviet Union for the second time gave out a clear statement about her future foreign policy. She declared herself simply opposed to all types of federations in Europe, but most of all to the so-called Eastern Federation, which she considered a "cordon sanitaire" against her. It is an open question whether the "federations" will leave the scene of political argument as quickly as did the Atlantic Charter more than a year ago. But it is true that most of the federation talk had been made with an eye to the "common enemy," who more often than not was Russia for the

Eastern nations and the Czechs for the Central European nations—
with sometimes the rather perfunctory addition of Germany.

The authentic political problem of the reorganization of Europe after
this war is hidden, rather than indicated, by the use of the word federation in the descendant-groups. The post-war plans offered by the
various newspapers have already exhausted each and every imaginable
combination of states and nationalities. When it comes to planning, the
Czechs readily forget that the Slovaks broke away from them and hold
that Czechoslovakia should be the "cornerstone" of Central Europe. The
Hungarians and the Slovaks forget their bitter quarrels and think of
combining against the Czechs. The Serbs in certain instances seemed
to know only one enemy, the Croats, and prepare for close alliance with
Greece and eventually Bulgaria. Poles, Lithuanians, and Ukrainians
preach unity against the "Bolshevik aggressor." The Slovaks discover
that they "always had more friendly relations with the Poles than with
the Czechs" (in *Slovenska Obrana*) and Poles are reported (by the Hungarian weekly *Harc*) to have cultivated this new friendship so far as to
propose inclusion of Slovakia in a new Greater Poland. It is obvious that
this combination game might or might not point to possible future alliances. With federations it has nothing in common but an ill-chosen
name. History, to be sure, has still left a few new possibilities to cut
the European pudding, but as far as these propositions go, there is no
sign that those who have to share it will be more satisfied with their
new slices than they had been with the old ones.

If the different proposals of "federations" were nothing but post-war
planning, it would hardly be worthwhile to discuss them. What constitutes their importance for the American scene is that they represent an
attempt to create working alliances between different descendant-groups
in this country rather than a serious effort to reorganize Europe. In
contrast to the once so popular Atlantic Charter, which actually aimed
at definite goals on the European scene—though in the interpretation
of the foreign-language press mostly the restoration of semi-fascist
regimes—the "federations" are to be realized right here. A "political
bloc" formed by "the American descendants of the small nations abroad"
and "acting in unison" (as the Lithuanian weekly *Lietuviu Zinios* put it)
is in the making. If such a bloc should succeed, the descendant-groups
would be able to combine and to act as pressure groups at the conclusion

of peace treaties. Advocates of the "formation of a federation of states from the Baltic to the Adriatic"* might not have a very clear vision of the future European political structure they propose; they can, nevertheless, hope to mobilize under the cover of a regional federation in Europe, the American descendants of Lithuanians, Poles, Slovaks, Hungarians, Croats, and Slovenes for organized influence and concerted action in America.

The "federations" have the great advantage that they are nowhere easier to realize than right here, where Ukrainians and Slovaks, Croats and Poles, Lithuanians and Hungarians live on the same spot. The time is gone when Czechoslovak quarrels were fought between Czechs and Slovaks alone and when attacks on Beneš were led by Slovaks with the possible assistance of only some Hungarian newspapers. Now the Ukrainians discover their "kinship" with the Slovaks, having known a similar fate: what the Slovaks suffered at the hands of the Czechs, the Ukrainians suffered from either the Poles or the Russians. Gone, too, are the times when the struggles which tore Yugoslavia apart concerned Croats, Slovenes, and Serbs alone. Now the Croats and the Slovak press exchange news and propaganda items and the Serbs complain that there is more to this than appears on the surface.

The alarming thing about these cross-relations which still are in the first stages of development is that there exists no definite unifying program of any kind, though certain similar traits can be discerned. It is certainly characteristic that the descendants of none of the greater nations, whether they be our enemies, like the Germans, or our friends, like the French, or neutrals such as the Spaniards, can be found among these working alliances. To be sure, there is some discussion in the foreign-language press about federalizing Europe; but these discussions are merely theoretical, really concerned with Europe, and their proponents have so far made no tangible attempts to start the federation of Europe through a federation of descendants in this country. What is in the making seems to be a bloc of the descendants of the smaller nations as such, no matter whether their former countries are at war or at peace with the United States.

The second characteristic trait which they have in common is the

---

*In this form proposed by the Slovak writer Peter Privadok in *A Good Word to Slovaks*, Pamphlet No. 2, published by the Slovak Catholic Union of Pennsylvania.

fact that the descendants of these small nations are predominantly Catholic. The Scandinavian nations are conspicuously absent and without connections with Eastern and Central European descendant groups. This factor is far from negligible. Catholic unions, parishes, associations, and orders (the latter especially in the Polish press) play a big role as publishers of the foreign-language press. These societies again are connected with large Catholic American bodies, such as the Catholic National Welfare Conference. The articles released by the press-bureau of the CNWC are reprinted by Catholic papers in different languages throughout the country and have certainly an important unifying influence on the political views of certain issues that would otherwise be rather controversial.

This influence is due to increase in almost the same proportion as the appeal of the Atlantic Charter has decreased. In this respect it appears rather significant that Bishop Bohachewsky, who has some influence on *Ameryka*, the official organ of the Providence Association of the Ukrainian Catholics in America, has recommended closer cooperation with American Catholic organizations and has ceased collaboration with other Ukrainian nationalist groups. This situation means that a heavy burden of responsibility is laid on the shoulders of American Catholicism. Deeply rooted in the political life of the nation, it represents an important link between foreign-language groups and America. For a long while, Catholic organizations have helped immigrants and members of underprivileged groups to adjust themselves to American traditions. This mostly has been done by priests who were of the same origin as their flock, and who were careful and probably wise in conserving certain heritages from the Old Country. This task had been assigned to them almost automatically for immigrants from countries in which the Church is still held in great authority by the masses of the people. And emigration to America in many cases has not weakened but, rather, strengthened this authority, precisely because the immigrants in a new and confusing environment came to regard Catholic institutions as representative of and sometimes identical with their various national traditions. The new tendency toward collaboration among these groups might bring about additional weight to this authority, although up to now nobody can possibly foretell in which direction this weight and this influence will make itself felt.

VII

It is obvious from the preceding remarks that the case of the Jewish descendants and their press is somehow different from all others. No real homeland of their own was there to stimulate a special interest in foreign policies. More than that, Jews came to this country because of persecutions suffered at the hands of European peoples and, consequently, felt some natural distrust of their descendants and a much greater readiness to cut loose from the Old Country, and to think only in terms of America, than any other immigrant group. And it is a matter of course—and, incidentally, luck—that American Jewry escaped the influences of fascist and chauvinistic trends which played so great a part in the more recent history of other descendant-groups.

This does not mean, as some superficial observers are inclined to think, that Jews are about to give up their identity more readily than other immigrant groups from Europe. But it does mean that the changes which American Jewry has undergone since the end of the last war are much less abrupt, that old idealistic traditions are much better kept. To be sure, here, too, the changes are considerable. The old European influences on the Jewish masses, especially from Poland, have declined in strength. The Bundist kind of socialism and anti-Zionism is about to disappear, and newspapers with formerly strong anti-Zionist traditions have turned recently rather pro-Zionist, while the formerly pro-Zionist press has left behind the old sentimental attitudes, together with the old quarrels among the various Zionist factions, in order to turn outright political with the accent strongly on foreign policies.

Within the political structure of American Jewry, Palestine takes more and more the place which other descendant-groups reserve to their respective homelands. But here, too, the Jewish attitude shows more resemblance to the attitude of descendant-groups prior to the First World War than with those of their contemporaries, who are divided between shameless expansion at the cost of other small nations and regional federations. The fact that the slogan of "federation" is conspicuously absent from Jewish newspapers is due not only to the geographical position of Palestine, where, seemingly, only a federation with the Arabs would be possible, but also to those peculiar circumstances which made the Jews almost the only small European people to whom the Versailles Treaty failed to give either a state of their own or a co-responsibility in one of the multi-national states. Logically enough, they claim today, with the slogan of a Jewish Commonwealth, which according to Weizmann means "a state of their own," a degree of independence and sovereignty whose impracticability and dangers other small nations have already had the opportunity to experience.

The Jewish people of America even more than other descendant-groups feel themselves today as outposts saved for the cause of supreme national emergency. This has fastened their links with Palestine as it has fastened the links of all descendant-groups with their homelands, and it has added a strong feeling of responsibility for the future of the people as a whole. The old sentiment of living in the "promised land" which once was so predominant among American Jews has given way to a more sober feeling of the indivisibility of the Jewish destiny all over the globe. Paradoxical as it may sound, these new tendencies tend to liquidate the old exceptional position of American Jewry as the only immigrant group without a homeland and may lead them into a process of true Americanization. The ultimate success, however, of such a development will depend much less on the Jews than on the attitudes of other descendant-groups.

There is reason to hope that these groups, with the liquidation of fascism in their homelands, will give up the strange and dangerous trends which have marked their public utterances during a certain period. With peace and freedom in Europe, they may recover their own peace of mind. With the liquidation of anti-Semitism which is already notably in decline on the European scene, they may learn to look upon the Jews not only as their fellow-citizens but also as fellows in a very similar destiny. To be sure, none of these groups will as rapidly and as easily disappear or lose its interest in homeland politics as the advocates of the melting pot have believed. They will continue for a while to constitute for the policy-makers of this country both the most dangerous source of trouble and the most hopeful asset of ultimate success. For in terms of foreign politics, their presence means the possibility of a natural relationship with almost all nations of the world, and therefore a chance for world policy without imperialistic connotations such as no other nation with a homogeneous population ever could enjoy.

Approaches to the
"German Problem"

T HE "GERMAN PROBLEM" as we hear about it today has
been resurrected from the past, and if it is now presented simply
as the problem of Germanic aggression it is because of the tender
hopes for restoration of the status quo in Europe. To achieve this in the
face of the civil war sweeping the continent it appeared necessary, first,
to "restore" the meaning of the war to its nineteenth-century sense of
a purely national conflict, in which countries rather than movements,
peoples rather than governments, suffer defeats and win victories.

Thus the literature on the "German problem" reads for the most part
like a revised edition of the propaganda of the last war, which merely
embellished the official viewpoint with the appropriate historical learning, and was actually neither better nor worse than its German counterpart. After the armistice, the papers of the erudite gentlemen on both
sides were allowed to pass into charitable oblivion. The only interesting
aspect of this literature was the eagerness with which scholars and
writers of international renown offered their services—not to save their
countries at the risk of their lives but to serve their governments with
a complete disregard for truth. The one difference between the propa-

Partisan Review, XII/1, Winter 1945.

gandists of the two world wars is that this time quite a few of the former dispensers of German chauvinism have made themselves available to the Allied powers as "experts" on Germany and have lost through this switch not a bit of their zeal or subservience.

These experts on the "German problem," however, are the only remnants of the last war. But while their adaptability, their willingness to serve, their fear of intellectual and moral responsibility remain constant, their political role has changed. During the First World War, a war not ideological in character, the strategies of political warfare had not yet been discovered, its propagandists were little more than morale-builders, arousing or expressing the national sense of the people. Perhaps they failed even in this task, if we are to judge by the fairly general contempt in which they were held by the fighting forces; but beyond it, they were surely quite unimportant. They had no voice in politics and they did not voice the policy of their respective governments.

Today, however, propaganda as such is no longer effective, especially if it is couched in nationalist and military, rather than ideological or political, terms. Hatred, for example, is conspicuously absent. The only propaganda result of the revival of the "German problem" is therefore negative: Many who have learned to discount the atrocity stories of the last war simply refuse to believe what this time is a gruesome reality because it is presented in the old form of national propaganda. The talk of the "eternal Germany" and its eternal crimes serves only to cover Nazi Germany and its present crimes with a veil of skepticism. When in 1939—to take one instance—the French government took out of storage the slogans of the First World War and spread the bogey of Germany's "national character," the only visible effect was an incredulity about the terror of the Nazis. So it was all over Europe.

But if propaganda has lost much of its inspirational power, it has acquired a new political function. It has become a form of political warfare and is used to prepare public opinion for certain political steps. Thus the posing of the "German problem" by spreading the notion that the source of international conflict lies in the iniquities of Germany (or Japan) has the effect of masking the actual political issues. By identifying fascism with Germany's national character and history people are deluded into believing that the crushing of Germany is synonymous with the eradication of fascism. In this way it becomes possible to close one's eyes to the European crisis which has by no means been overcome and which made possible the German conquest of the continent (with the aid of quislings and fifth columnists). Thus all attempts to identify Hitler with German history can only lead to the gratuitous bestowal upon Hitlerism of national respectability and the sanction of a national tradition.

Whether you compare Hitler with Napoleon, as English propaganda did at times, or with Bismarck, in either case you exonerate Hitler and make free with the historical reputations of Napoleon or Bismarck. Napoleon, when all is said, still lives in the memory of Europe as the leader of armies moved by the image, however distorted, of the French Revolution; Bismarck was neither better nor worse than most of Europe's national statesmen who played the game of power politics for the sake of the nation but whose aims were clearly defined and clearly limited. Though he tried to expand some of Germany's frontiers, Bismarck did not dream of annihilating any of the rival nations. He agreed reluctantly to the incorporation of Lorraine into the Reich because of Moltke's "strategical reasons," but he did not want foreign splinters within the German frontiers and had not the slightest ambition to rule foreign peoples as subject races.

What is true of German political history is even more true of the spiritual roots attributed to Nazism. Nazism owes nothing to any part of the Western tradition, be it German or not, Catholic or Protestant, Christian, Greek, or Roman. Whether we like Thomas Aquinas or Machiavelli or Luther or Kant or Hegel or Nietzsche—the list may be prolonged indefinitely as even a cursory glance at the literature of the "German problem" will reveal—they have not the least responsibility for what is happening in the extermination camps. Ideologically speaking, Nazism begins with no traditional basis at all, and it would be better to realize the danger of this radical negation of any tradition, which was the main feature of Nazism from the beginning (though not of fascism in its first Italian stages). It was, after all, the Nazis themselves who were the first to surround their utter emptiness with the smoke-screen of learned interpretations. Most of the philosophers at present slandered by the over-zealous experts of the "German problem" have long been claimed by the Nazis as their own—not because the Nazis cared about responsibility but simply because they realized that there is no better hiding-place than the great playground of history and no better bodyguard than the children of that playground, the easily employed and easily deluded "experts."

The very monstrosities of the Nazi regime should have warned us that we are dealing here with something inexplicable even by reference to the worst periods of history. For never, neither in ancient nor medieval nor modern history, did destruction become a well-formulated program or its execution a highly organized, bureaucratized, and systematized process. It is true that militarism has a relation to the efficiency of the Nazi war machine and that imperialism has much to do with its ideology. But to approach Nazism you have to empty militarism of all its inherited warrior's virtues and imperialism of all its inherent dreams of empire-building, such as the "white man's burden." In other words, one may easily find certain trends in modern political life which in themselves point toward fascism and certain classes which are more easily won and more easily deceived than others—but all must change their basic functions in society before Nazism can actually make use of them. Before the war is over the German military caste, certainly one of the most disgusting institutions, ridden by stupid arrogance and an upstart tradition, will be destroyed by the Nazis together with all other German traditions and time-honored institutions. German militarism as represented in the German army scarcely had more ambition than the old French army of the Third Republic: the German officers wanted to be a State within a State, and they foolishly assumed that the Nazis would serve them better than the Weimar Republic. They were already in a state of dissolution when they discovered their mistake—one part was liquidated and the other adjusted itself to the Nazi regime.

It is true that the Nazis have occasionally spoken the language of militarism, as they have spoken the language of nationalism; but they have spoken the language of every existing ism—socialism and communism not excluded. This has not prevented them from liquidating socialists and communists and nationalists and militarists, all of them dangerous bedfellows for the Nazis. Only the experts, with their fondness for the spoken or written word and incomprehension of political realities, have taken these utterances of the Nazis at face value and interpreted them as the consequence of certain German or European traditions. On the contrary, Nazism is actually the breakdown of all German and European traditions, the good as well as the bad.

2

Many premonitory signs announced the catastrophe which has threat-ened European culture for more than a century and which was divined though not correctly described in Marx's well-known words regarding the alternative between socialism and barbarism. During the last war this catastrophe became visible in the form of the most violent destruc-tiveness ever experienced by the European nations. From then on ni-hilism changed its meaning. It was no longer a more or less harmless ideology, one of the many competing ideologies of the nineteenth century; it no longer remained in the quiet realm of mere negation or mere skepticism or mere foreboding despair. Instead it began basing itself on the intoxication of destruction as an actual experience, dreaming the stupid dream of producing the void. The devastating experience was enormously strengthened during the aftermath of the war, when through inflation and unemployment the same generation was thrown into the opposite situation of utter helplessness and passivity within the frame-work of a seemingly normal society. When the Nazis appealed to the famous *Fronterlebnis* (battlefront experience), they not only aroused mem-ories of the *Volksgemeinschaft* (people's community) of the trenches, but even more the sweet recollections of a time of extraordinary activity and power of destruction enjoyed by the individual.

It is true that the situation in Germany lent itself more readily than anywhere else to the breaking of all traditions. This is connected with the late development of the Germans as a nation, their unfortunate political history and lack of any kind of democratic experience. It is more closely connected with the fact that the post-war situation of inflation and unemployment—without which the destructive power of the *Fron-terlebnis* might have remained a temporary phenomenon—took hold of more people in Germany and affected them more profoundly than elsewhere.

But though it may have been easier to break European traditions and standards in Germany, it is still true that these had to be broken, so that it was not any German tradition as such but the violation of all traditions which brought about Nazism. How strongly Nazism appealed to the veterans of the last war in all countries is shown by the almost universal influence it wielded in all veteran organizations of Europe. The veterans were the first sympathizers, and the first steps the Nazis took in the field of foreign relations were frequently calculated to arouse those "comrades-in-arms" beyond the frontiers who were sure to understand their language and to be moved by like emotions and a like desire for destruction.

This is the only tangible psychological meaning of the "German problem." The real trouble lies not in the German national character but, rather, in the disintegration of this character, or at least in the fact that it no longer plays any role in German politics. It is as much a thing of the past as German militarism or nationalism. It will not be possible to revive it by copying out mottoes from old books or even by adopting extreme political measures. But a greater trouble still is this, that the man who has replaced *the German*—namely, the type who in sensing the danger of utter destruction decides to turn himself into a destroying force—is not confined to Germany alone. The Nothing from which Nazism sprang could be defined in less mystical terms as the vacuum resulting from an almost simultaneous breakdown of Europe's social and political structures. Restoration is so violently opposed by the European resistance movements precisely because they know that the very same vacuum would thus be produced, a vacuum of which they live in mortal fear even though by now they have learned that it is the "lesser evil" to fascism. The tremendous psychological appeal exercised by Nazism was due not so much to its false promises as to its frank recognition of this vacuum. Its immense lies fitted the vacuum; these lies were psychologically efficient because they corresponded to certain fundamental experiences and even more to certain fundamental cravings. One can say that to some extent fascism has added a new variation to the old art of lying—the most devilish variation—that of *lying* the truth.

The truth was that the class structure of European society could no longer function; it simply could no longer work either in its feudal form in the East or in its bourgeois form in the West. Not only did its intrinsic lack of justice become more obvious daily, but it was constantly depriving millions and millions of individuals of any class status whatever (through unemployment and other causes). The truth was that the national State, once the very symbol of the sovereignty of the people, no longer represented the people, becoming incapable of safeguarding either its external or internal security. Whether Europe had become too small for this form of organization or whether the European peoples had outgrown the organization of their national states, the truth was that they no longer behaved like nations and could no longer be aroused by national feelings. Most of them were unwilling to wage a national war—not even for the sake for their independence.

This social truth of the breakdown of European class-society was answered by the Nazis with the lie of the *Volksgemeinschaft*, based on complicity in crime and ruled by a bureaucracy of gangsters. The declassed could sympathize with this answer. And the truth of the decline of the national State was answered by the famous lie of the New Order in Europe, which debased peoples into races and prepared them for extermination. The gullibility of the European peoples—who in so many cases let the Nazis into their countries because the Nazi lies alluded to certain fundamental truths—has cost them an enormous price. But they have learned at least one great lesson: that none of the old forces which produced the maelstrom of the vacuum is so terrible as the new force which springs from this maelstrom and whose aim is to organize people according to the law of the maelstrom—which is destruction itself.

3

The European resistance movements arose among the same peoples who in 1938 had hailed the Munich agreements and in whom the outbreak of the war aroused only dismay. These movements came into being only when the nationalists of all shades and the preachers of hate had had their opportunity to turn collaborationist, so that the almost inevitable inclination of nationalists toward fascism and of chauvinists toward subservience to the foreign invader had been proven to entire populations. (The few exceptions were such old-fashioned nationalists as De Gaulle and the journalist Henri de Kérillis; but they only proved the rule.) The underground movements, in other words, were the immediate product of the collapse, first, of the national State, which was replaced by a quisling government, and second, of nationalism itself as the driving force of nations. Those who emerged to wage war fought against fascism and nothing else. And this is not surprising; what is surprising precisely because of its strict, almost logical, consequence is, rather, that all of these movements at once found a positive political slogan which plainly indicated the non-national though very popular character of the new struggle. That slogan was simply EUROPE.

Hence it is natural that the "German problem," as presented by the experts, should have awakened very little interest in the European Resistance. It was recognized at once that the old insistence on the "German problem" would only becloud the issues of the "ideological war" and that the outlawing of Germany would prevent a solution of the European question. Members of the underground were therefore concerned with the "German problem" only to the extent that it is part and parcel of the European problem. Many a well-meaning correspondent, who has learned his lesson from the experts on Germany, was shocked by the absence of personal hatred against Germans and by the presence, in the liberated countries, of political hatred for fascists, collaborationists, and their like, of no matter what nationality.

The words which Georges Bidault, former chief of the French Resistance and now foreign minister, spoke to the wounded German soldiers immediately after the liberation of Paris, sound like a simple and splendid expression of the sentiments of those who fought against Nazi Germany not with their pens but with their lives. He said: "German soldiers, I am the chief of the Resistance. I have come to wish you good health. May you soon find yourselves in a free Germany and a free Europe."

The insistence on Europe even at such a moment is characteristic. Any other words would not have corresponded to the conviction that the European crisis is first of all a crisis of the national State. In the words of the Dutch underground: "We are experiencing at present . . . a crisis of state sovereignty. One of the central problems of the coming peace will be: how can we, while preserving cultural autonomy, achieve the formation of larger units in the political and economic field? . . . A good peace is now inconceivable unless the States surrender parts of their economic and political sovereignty to a higher European authority: we leave open the question whether a European Council, or Federation, a United States of Europe or whatever type of unit will be formed."

It is obvious that for these men, the true *homines novi** of Europe, the "German problem" is not, as it is for De Gaulle, the "center of the universe," not even the center of Europe. Their main enemy is fascism, not Germany; their main problem is the crisis of all State organizations

---

*New men: In ancient Rome the term designated a family or clan that had never before attained curule office. Cicero, *De Officiis* I, xxxix, 138. Cicero himself was a "new man." —Ed.

of the Continent, not merely the German or Prussian State; their center of gravity is France, the country which has truly been, culturally as well as politically, the heart of Europe for centuries and whose more recent contributions to political thought have again put her at the spiritual head of Europe. In this connection it was more than significant that the liberation of Paris was celebrated in Rome with more enthusiasm than even its own liberation; and that the message of the Dutch Resistance to the French Forces of the Interior after the liberation of Paris concluded with the words "So long as France lives, Europe will not die."

For those who have known Europe intimately during the period between the two wars it must have come almost as a shock to see how quickly the same peoples that only a few years ago were not at all concerned with questions of political structure have now discovered the primary conditions for the future existence of the European continent. Under Nazi oppression they have not only relearned the meaning of freedom but also won back their self-respect as well as a new appetite for responsibility. This is clearly enough manifested in all the former monarchies where—to the surprise and dismay of some observers—the people want most of all a republican regime. In France, a country of mature republican traditions, the repudiation of old centralized forms of government, which left very little responsibility to the individual citizen, is gaining ground; the search for some new form, giving the citizen more of the duties as well as the rights and honors of public life, is characteristic of all factions.

The cardinal principle of French resistance was *liberer et federer*; and by federation was meant a federated structure of the Fourth Republic (in opposition to the "centralist State which is bound to become totalitarian") integrated in a European Federation. It is in almost identical terms that the French, Czech, Italian, Norwegian, and Dutch underground papers insist on this as the primary condition of a lasting peace—although, so far as I know, only the French underground has gone so far as to state that a federative structure of Europe must be based on similarly federated structures in the constituent states.

Equally universal, though not equally new, are the demands of a social and economic nature. All want a change in the economic system, control of wealth, nationalization, and public ownership of basic resources and major industries. Here again, the French have some ideas of their own. As Louis Saillant put it, they do not want "a rehash of some socialist or other kind of program," for they are mainly concerned with "the defense of that human dignity for which the men of the Resistance fought and sacrificed." The danger of an *étatisme envahissant* they hope to avert by giving the workers and the technical personnel of each factory a stake in the results of production and the consumers a decisive voice in the management.

It was necessary to sketch at least this general programmatic framework because only in its terms does the answer to the "German problem" make sense. Conspicuous by its absence is Vansittartism of any kind. A French officer, one of those who with the help of the German underground escape daily from the Nazi prisoner-camps, draws a distinction in this respect between prisoners and the people at home, who hate the Germans more than they do. "Our hatred, the violent hatred of the prisoners, is aimed at the collaborationists, the profiteers and their like, at all who have helped the enemy—and there are three millions of us. . . ."

The Polish socialist paper *Freedom* has warned against the yearning for revenge because this "can easily change into the desire to dominate other nations, and thus, after the defeat of Nazism, its very methods and ideas would again triumph." Very similar statements have been made by the movements of all other countries. This fear of falling into some kind of racism after the defeat of its German variety motivates the general renunciation of the idea of dismembering Germany. In this as in many other questions the disagreement between the underground movements and the governments-in-exile is nearly complete. Thus De Gaulle claimed the annexation of the Rhineland while still in exile, only to reverse his position a few weeks later when, upon entering Paris after its liberation, he stated that all that France wanted was an active share in the occupation of the Rhineland.

However, the Dutch, the Poles, the Norwegians, and the French stand as one behind the program of nationalizing German heavy industry, liquidating the Junkers and industrialists as social classes, complete disarmament, and control of industrial output. Some look forward to the establishment of a German federal administration. The French Socialist Party has declared that this program "must be put into effect with the closest fraternal collaboration of German democrats"; and all programs conclude with the admonition that to deliver "seventy million people in the heart of Europe to economic misery" (the Norwegians) is to vitiate the ultimate aim of "receiving Germany into the community of European nations and a planned European economy" (the Dutch).

To think in terms of the European underground is to realize that the much debated alternatives of a soft or hard peace for Germany have little bearing on the problem of her future sovereignty. Thus the Dutch contend that "the problem of equality of rights should not be a matter of restoring sovereign rights to the defeated state but of granting it a limited influence within the European Council or Federation." The French, planning for a period when the non-European armies of occupation will have left the continent and when they would again be faced by issues of strictly European reference, have warned that "essential restrictions on German sovereignty can be envisaged without difficulty only if all the states likewise accept significant limitations on their own sovereignty."

Long before the Morgenthau plan became known, the underground movements rejected any such idea of destroying German industry. The rejection is so general that it becomes superfluous to quote special sources. The reasons are obvious: There is an overwhelming and altogether justified fear that half of Europe would starve if German industry ceased to function.

Instead of destroying this industry, what is proposed is control of it, not so much by any particular country or people as by a European advisory council which together with German representatives would assume the responsibility of its management for the purpose of stimulating production and directing distribution. Most remarkable among the economic plans for the European use of German industry is the French program which was tentatively discussed before the liberation. This program calls for the combining in one single economic system, without changing national borderlines, the industrial regions of western Germany, the Ruhr, the Saar, the Rhineland, and Westphalia, with the industrial regions of eastern France and Belgium.

But this willingness to come to terms with a future Germany is not to be explained merely by calculations of economic welfare or even by the natural feeling that no matter what the Allied governments may decide the Germans will stay in Europe for good. It is also necessary to take into account the fact that the European Resistance had in many instances fought side by side with German anti-fascists and deserters from the Reichswehr. The Resistance knows of the existence of a German underground, for the millions of foreign workers and prisoners of war in the Reich have had ample opportunities to avail themselves of its services. A French officer, describing how French prisoners in Germany made contact with French forced labor and with the underground in France proper, speaks of the German underground in matter-of-fact terms, emphasizing that such contact would have been impossible "without the active help of German soldiers and workers." He speaks, too, of having left "many good friends among the Germans before we cut through the barbed wire." Even more striking is his disclosure that the German underground counts on the help of Frenchmen in Germany "at the moment of the final coup" and that organized cooperation between the two groups had led to the divulgence to the French of the location of the arms stored by the German underground.

These details are cited in order to make clear the actual experiences underlying the programs of the Resistance with respect to Germany. This experience has in turn made more cogent the attitude that has for some years now been characteristic of European anti-fascists and which has recently been defined by Georges Bernanos as "l'espoir en des hommes dispersés à travers l'Europe, séparés par les frontières et par la langue, et qui n'ont guère de commun entre eux que l'expérience du risque et l'habitude de ne pas céder à la menace."

4

The return of the governments-in-exile may quickly put a stop to this new feeling of European solidarity, for the very existence of these governments depends on the restoration of the status quo. Hence their inveterate tendency is to weaken and disperse the resistance movements with the aim of destroying the political renaissance of the European peoples.

Restoration in Europe appears today in the form of three fundamental concepts. First there arose the concept of collective security, which is in reality not a new concept but one taken over from the happy times of the Holy Alliance; it was revived after the last war in the hope that it would serve as a check on nationalistic aspirations and aggression. If this system went to pieces, however, it was not because of such aggression but because of the intervention of ideological factors. Thus Poland, for instance, though threatened by Germany, refused the help of the Red Army in spite of the fact that in her case collective security could hardly go into effect without such help. The strategical security of frontiers was sacrificed because the main aggressor—Germany—stood as the embodiment of the struggle against Bolshevism. It is plain that the system of collective security can be restored only on the presupposition that the obstructive ideological factors no longer exist. Such presuppositions are illusory, however.

In order to avert clashes between the ideological forces which are to be found in all nations, the second policy was introduced—that of clearly demarcated spheres of interest. This is a policy that derives from colonial imperialist methods, methods that now recoil upon Europe. It is not likely, however, that anyone will succeed in treating Europeans like colonials at a time when even the colonial countries are manifestly on their way to independence. Still more unrealistic is the hope that on so small and so thickly populated a territory as Europe it will prove possible to erect walls that shut off nation from nation and prevent the interaction of ideological forces.

At this moment we are witnessing the resurrection of the good old bilateral alliance, which seems to have become the favored political instrument of the Kremlin. This last piece borrowed from the vast arsenal of power-politics has only one meaning, and that is the re-employment of nineteenth-century political instruments whose ineffectiveness was discovered and denounced after the last war. Actually, what such bilateral agreements come to in the end is that the stronger partner of any so-called alliance dominates the weaker, politically and ideologically.

The governments-in-exile, being interested only in restoration as such, waver pitifully between these alternatives and are ready to accept almost anything offered by one of the Big Three—collective security, sphere of interest, or alliance. Among their leaders, De Gaulle must be conceded a special position. Unlike the others, he represents not the forces of yesterday but is, rather, a solitary reminder of the forces of the day before yesterday—a time which, whatever its faults, was considerably more propitious to human purposes than the recent past. In other words, he alone truly represents patriotism and nationalism in the old sense. When his former comrades in the French Army and the Action Française turned traitors, and pacifism seized France like a fever and the ruling classes rushed to collaborate, he did not even understand what was happening. In a sense, he had the good fortune to be unable to believe his eyes—to believe, that is, that Frenchmen did not want a national war against Germany. All that he has done since, he has done for the sake of the nation, and his patriotism is so deeply rooted in the popular will that the Resistance, i.e., the people, was able to support and influence his policies. De Gaulle, who is the only national statesman left in Europe, is the only one who is sincere when he says that the "German problem is the center of the universe." For him the war is really a national and not an ideological conflict. What he wants for France is as large a share as possible in the defeat of Germany. His appetite for annexation has been checked by the Resistance; the new proposal, allegedly accepted by Stalin, which looks towards the creation of a separate German state in the Rhineland under Allied or French control, suggests a compromise between his previous plans for annexations and the hopes of the Resistance for a federated Germany and a European-controlled German economy.

Restoration has started very logically with restoring the endless borderline disputes in which only a few old-time nationalists are vitally interested. Despite the strong protests of the underground movements of their respective countries, all governments-in-exile have put forth territorial demands. These demands, backed and possibly inspired by London, can be fulfilled only at the expense of the defeated, and if there is not much joy at the prospect of acquiring new territories it is because no one seems to know how to solve the inherent population problems. The minority treaties which were expected to work miracles after the last war are utterly disregarded today, though no one has any confidence in the only alternative, which is assimilation. This time one hopes to solve the problem by means of population-transfers; the Czechs were the first to announce their determination to liquidate the minority treaties and to deport two million Germans to the Reich. The other governments-in-exile have followed suit and pronounced similar plans for the Germans found on the ceded territories—many millions of them.

But if such population-transfers actually take place they will be followed not only by an indefinite prolongation of chaos but perhaps by something even more sinister. The ceded territories will prove to be underpopulated and the neighbors of Germany will find themselves unable to populate them properly and to profit from the available resources. This would in turn lead either to re-immigration of German manpower, thus reproducing the old dangers, or to a situation where an over-crowded country with highly skilled labor-power and a highly developed technique is forced into developing ingenious industrial methods to keep going. The result of such "punishment" would prove to be exactly the same as that of the Versailles Treaty, also thought of as a reliable instrument for crushing Germany's economic power but which turned out to be the very cause of the over-rationalization and amazing growth of Germany's industrial capacity. Since in our time manpower is far more important than territories, and technical skill combined with a high level of scientific research more promising than raw materials, we may very well be on the way to creating in the midst of Europe a gigantic powder-keg whose explosive capacity will surprise tomorrow's statesmen as much as the rise of defeated Germany surprised the statesmen of yesterday.

The Morgenthau plan, finally, seems to offer a definitive solution. But this plan can hardly be relied on to convert Germany into a nation of small farmers—because no power would undertake to exterminate the thirty or so million Germans too many. Any serious attempt to do so would in all probability bring about that "revolutionary situation" which those who want restoration fear more than anything else.

Restoration thus promises nothing. If it succeeded, the process of the past thirty years might commence again, this time at a greatly accelerated tempo. For restoration must begin precisely with the restoration of the "German problem"! The vicious circle in which all discussions of the "German problem" move shows clearly the utopian character of "realism" and power-politics in their application to the real issues of our time. The only alternative to these antiquated methods, which could not even preserve peace, let alone guarantee freedom, is the course taken by the European Resistance.

Organized Guilt
and Universal Responsibility

T HE GREATER THE military defeats of the Wehrmacht in
the field, the greater becomes that victory of Nazi political
warfare which is so often incorrectly described as mere propaganda. It is the central thesis of this Nazi political strategy that there
is no difference between Nazis and Germans, that the people stand united
behind the government, that all Allied hopes of finding part of the people
uninfected ideologically and all appeals to a democratic Germany of the
future are pure illusion. The implication of this thesis is, of course, that
there is no distinction as to responsibility, that German anti-Fascists
will suffer from defeat equally with German Fascists, and that the Allies
had made such distinctions at the beginning of the war only for propaganda purposes. A further implication is that Allied provisions for punishment of war criminals will turn out to be empty threats because they
will find no one to whom the title of war criminal could not be applied.

That such claims are not mere propaganda but are supported by very
real and fearful facts, we have all learned in the past seven years. The
terror organizations which were at first strictly separated from the mass

Published in *Jewish Frontier*, No. 12, 1945, as "German Guilt."

of the people, admitting only persons who could show a criminal past or prove their preparedness to become criminals, have since been continually expanded. The ban on party membership for members of the army has been dissolved by the general order which subordinates all soldiers to the party. Whereas those crimes which have always been a part of the daily routine of concentration camps since the beginning of the Nazi regime were at first a jealously guarded monopoly of the SS and Gestapo, today members of the Wehrmacht are assigned at will to duties of mass murder. These crimes were at first kept secret by every possible means and any publication of such reports was made punishable as atrocity propaganda. Later, however, such reports were spread by Nazi-organized whispering campaigns and today these crimes are openly proclaimed under the title of "measures of liquidation" in order to force "Volksgenossen"—whom difficulties of organization made it impossible to induct into the "Volksgemeinschaft" of crime—at least to bear the onus of complicity and awareness of what was going on. These tactics, as the Allies abandoned the distinction between Germans and Nazis, resulted in a victory for the Nazis. In order to appreciate the decisive change of political conditions in Germany since the lost battle of Britain, one must note that until the war, even until the first military defeats, only relatively small groups of active Nazis, among whom not even the Nazi sympathizers were included, and equally small numbers of active anti-Fascists really knew what was going on. All others, whether German or non-German, had the natural inclination to believe the statements of an official, universally recognized government rather than the charges of refugees, which, coming from Jews or Socialists, were suspect in any case. Even of those refugees, only a relatively small proportion knew the full truth and even a smaller fraction was prepared to bear the odium of unpopularity involved in telling the truth.

As long as the Nazis expected victory, their terror organizations were strictly isolated from the people and, in time of war, from the army. The army was not used to commit atrocities and SS troops were increasingly recruited from "qualified" circles of whatever nationality. If the planned New Order of Europe had succeeded, we would have been witnesses of an inter-European organization of terror under German leadership. The terror would have been exercised by members of all European nationalities, with the exception of Jews, in an organization graded according to the racial classification of the various countries. The German people, of course, would not have been spared by it. Himmler was always of the opinion that authority in Europe should be in the hands of a racial élite, organized in SS troops without national ties.

It was only their defeats which forced the Nazis to abandon this concept and pretend to return to old nationalist slogans. The active identification of the whole German people with the Nazis was part of this turning. National Socialism's chances of organizing an underground movement in the future depend on no one's being able to know any longer who is a Nazi and who is not, on there being no visible signs of distinction any longer, and above all on the victorious powers' being convinced that there really are no differences between Germans. To bring this about, an intensified terror in Germany, which proposed to leave no person alive whose past or reputation proclaimed him an anti-Fascist, was necessary. In the first years of the war the regime was remarkably "magnanimous" to its opponents, provided they remained peaceful. Of late, however, countless persons have been executed even though, for the reason that for years there has been no freedom of movement, they could not constitute any immediate danger to the regime. On the other hand, prudently foreseeing that in spite of all precautionary measures the Allies might still find a few hundred persons in each city with an irreproachable anti-Fascist record—testified to by former war prisoners or foreign laborers, and supported by records of imprisonment or concentration-camp internment—the Nazis have already provided their own trusted cohorts with similar documentation and testimony, making these criteria worthless. Thus in the case of inmates of concentration camps (whose number nobody knows precisely, but which is estimated at several million), the Nazis can safely either liquidate them or let them escape: in the improbable event of their survival (a massacre of the type which occurred in Buchenwald is not even punishable under the war-crimes provisions), it will not be possible to identify them unmistakably.

Whether any person in Germany is a Nazi or an anti-Nazi can be determined only by the One who knows the secrets of the human heart, which no human eye can penetrate. At any rate, those who actively organize an anti-Nazi underground movement in Germany today would meet a speedy death if they failed to act and talk precisely like Nazis. In a country where a person attracts immediate attention by failing either to murder upon command or to be a ready accomplice of murderers, this is no light task. The most extreme slogan which this war has evoked among the Allies, that the only "good German" is a "dead German," has this much basis in fact: the only way in which we can identify an anti-Nazi is when the Nazis have hanged him. There is no other reliable token.

II

These are the real political conditions which underlie the charge of the collective guilt of the German people. They are the consequences of a policy which, in the deepest sense, is a- and anti-national; which is utterly determined that there shall be a German people only if it is in the power of its present rulers; and which will rejoice as at its greatest victory if the defeat of the Nazis involves with it the physical destruction of the German people. The totalitarian policy, which has completely destroyed the neutral zone in which the daily life of human beings is ordinarily lived, has achieved the result of making the existence of each individual in Germany depend either upon committing crimes or on complicity in crimes. The success of Nazi propaganda in Allied countries, as expressed in the attitude commonly called Vansittartism, is a secondary matter in comparison. It is a product of general war propaganda, and something quite apart from the specific modern political phenomenon described above. All the documents and pseudo-historical demonstrations of this tendency sound like relatively innocent plagiarism of the French literature of the last war—and it makes no essential difference that a few of those writers who twenty-five years ago kept the presses rolling with their attacks on "perfidious Albion" have now placed their experience at the Allies' disposal.

Yet even the best-intended discussions between the defenders of the "good" Germans and the accusers of the "bad" not only miss the essence of the question, but also plainly fail to apprehend the magnitude of the catastrophe. Either they are betrayed into trivial general comments on good and bad people, and into a fantastic over-estimation of the power of education, or they simply adopt an inverted version of Nazi racial theory. There is a certain danger in all this only because, since Churchill's famous declaration,* the Allies have refrained from fighting an ideological war and have thus unconsciously given an advantage to the Nazis (who, without regard to Churchill, are organizing their defeat ideologically) and a chance of survival to all racial theories.

The true problem however is not to prove what is self-evident, namely, that Germans have not been potential Nazis ever since Tacitus' times, nor what is impossible, that all Germans harbor Nazi views. It is, rather, to consider how to conduct ourselves and how to bear the trial of confronting a people among whom the boundaries dividing criminals from normal persons, the guilty from the innocent, have been so completely effaced that nobody will be able to tell in Germany whether in any case he is dealing with a secret hero or with a former mass murderer. In this situation we will not be aided either by a definition of those responsible, or by the punishment of "war criminals." Such definitions by their very nature can apply only to those who not only took responsibility upon themselves, but also produced this whole inferno—and yet strangely enough are still not to be found on the lists of war criminals. The number of those who are responsible *and* guilty will be relatively small. There are many who share responsibility without any visible proof of guilt. There are many more who have become guilty without being in the least responsible. Among the responsible in a broader sense must be included all those who continued to be sympathetic to Hitler as long as it was possible, who aided his rise to power, and who applauded him in Germany and in other European countries. Who would dare to brand all these ladies and gentlemen of high society as war criminals? And as a matter of fact they really do not deserve such a title. Unquestionably they have proved their inability to judge modern political organizations, some of them because they regarded all principles in politics as moralistic nonsense, others because they were affected by a

---

*Speaking to the House of Commons on May 24, 1944, Churchill said: "As this war has progressed, it has become less ideological in its character in my opinion." On August 2 of that year he noted the "confusion" this statement had caused, and went on to defend it. He was becoming increasingly convinced not only that the defeat of Germany must be total and her surrender "unconditional," but also that after the war the German state should be restructured in such a way as to prevent its re-emergence as a continental power for at least fifty years. *The War Speeches of Winston S. Churchill,* compiled by Charles Eade, vol. III, Boston: Houghton Mifflin, 1953, 149–50, 196. —Ed.

romantic predilection for gangsters whom they confused with "pirates" of an older time. Yet these people, who were co-responsible for Hitler's crimes in a broader sense, did not incur any guilt in a stricter sense. They, who were the Nazis' first accomplices and their best aides, truly did not know what they were doing nor with whom they were dealing.

The extreme horror with which persons of good will react whenever the case of Germany is discussed is not evoked by those irresponsible co-responsibles, nor even by the particular crimes of the Nazis themselves. It is, rather, the product of that vast machine of administrative mass murder, in whose service not only thousands of persons, not even scores of thousands of selected murderers, but a whole people could be and was employed: In that organization which Himmler has prepared against the defeat, everyone is either an executioner, a victim, or an automaton, marching onward over the corpses of his comrades—chosen at first out of the various Storm Troop formations and later from any army unit or other mass organization. That everyone, whether or not he is directly active in a murder camp, is forced to take part in one way or another in the workings of this machine of mass murder—that is the horrible thing. For systematic mass murder—the true consequence of all race theories and other modern ideologies which preach that might is right—strains not only the imagination of human beings, but also the framework and categories of our political thought and action. Whatever the future of Germany, it will not be determined by anything more than the inevitable consequences of a lost war—consequences which in the nature of the case are temporary. There is no political method for dealing with German mass crimes, and the destruction of seventy or eighty million Germans, or even their gradual death through starvation (of which, of course, nobody except a few psychotic fanatics dream), would simply mean that the ideology of the Nazis had won, even if power and the rights of might had fallen to other peoples.

Just as there is no political solution within human capacity for the crime of administrative mass murder, so the human need for justice can find no satisfactory reply to the total mobilization of a people for that purpose. Where all are guilty, nobody in the last analysis can be judged.*

---

*That German refugees, who had the good fortune either to be Jews or to have been persecuted by the Gestapo early enough, have been saved from this guilt is of course not their merit. Because they know this and because their horror at what might

For that guilt is not accompanied by even the mere appearance, the mere pretense of responsibility. So long as punishment is the right of the criminal—and this paradigm has for more than two thousand years been the basis of the sense of justice and right of Occidental man—guilt implies the consciousness of guilt, and punishment evidence that the criminal is a responsible person. How it is in this matter has been well described by an American correspondent,* in a story whose dialogue is worthy of the imagination and creative power of a great poet.

Q. Did you kill people in the camp? A. Yes.

Q. Did you poison them with gas? A. Yes.

Q. Did you bury them alive? A. It sometimes happened.

Q. Were the victims picked from all over Europe? A. I suppose so.

Q. Did you personally help kill people? A. Absolutely not. I was only paymaster in the camp.

Q. What did you think of what was going on? A. It was bad at first but we got used to it.

Q. Do you know the Russians will hang you? A. (Bursting into tears) Why should they? *What have I done?* [Italics mine. PM, Sunday, Nov. 12, 1944.]

Really he had done nothing. He had only carried out orders and since when has it been a crime to carry out orders? Since when has it been a virtue to rebel? Since when could one only be decent by welcoming death? What then had he done?

In his play *The Last Days of Mankind*, about the last war, Karl Kraus rang down the curtain after Wilhelm II had cried, "I did not want this." And the horribly comic part of it was that this was the fact. When the curtain falls this time, we will have to listen to a whole chorus calling out, "We did not do this." And even though we shall no longer be able to appreciate the comic element, the horrible part of it will still be that this is the fact.

have been still haunts them, they often introduce into discussions of this kind that insufferable tone of self-righteousness which frequently, and particularly among Jews, can turn into the vulgar obverse of Nazi doctrines—and in fact already has.

*Raymond A. Davies, a correspondent for the Jewish Telegraph Agency and broadcaster for the Canadian Broadcasting Corporation, gave the first eyewitness account of the death camp at Maidanek. —Ed.

III

In trying to understand what were the real motives which caused people to act as cogs in the mass-murder machine, we shall not be aided by speculations about German history and the so-called German national character, of whose potentialities those who knew Germany most intimately had not the slightest idea fifteen years ago. There is more to be learned from the characteristic personality of the man who can boast that he was the organizing spirit of the murder. Heinrich Himmler is not one of those intellectuals stemming from the dim No Man's Land between the Bohemian and the Pimp, whose significance in the composition of the Nazi élite has been repeatedly stressed of late. He is neither a Bohemian like Goebbels, nor a sex criminal like Streicher, nor a perverted fanatic like Hitler, nor an adventurer like Goering. He is a "bourgeois" with all the outer aspect of respectability, all the habits of a good *paterfamilias* who does not betray his wife and anxiously seeks to secure a decent future for his children; and he has consciously built up his newest terror organization, covering the whole country, on the assumption that most people are not Bohemians nor fanatics, nor adventurers, nor sex maniacs, nor sadists, but first and foremost jobholders, and good family men.

It was Péguy, I believe, who called the family man the "grand aventurier du 20e siècle." He died too soon to learn that he was also the great criminal of the century. We had been so accustomed to admire or gently ridicule the family man's kind concern and earnest concentration on the welfare of his family, his solemn determination to make life easy for his wife and children, that we hardly noticed how the devoted *paterfamilias*, worried about nothing so much as his security, was transformed under the pressure of the chaotic economic conditions of our time into an involuntary adventurer, who for all his industry and care could never be certain what the next day would bring. The docility of this type was already manifest in the very early period of Nazi "Gleichschaltung." It became clear that for the sake of his pension, his life insurance, the security of his wife and children, such a man was ready to sacrifice his beliefs, his honor, and his human dignity. It needed only the Satanic genius of Himmler to discover that after such degradation he was entirely prepared to do literally anything when the ante was raised and the bare existence of his family was threatened. The only condition he put was that he should be fully exempted from responsibility for his acts. Thus that very person, the average German, whom the Nazis notwithstanding years of the most furious propaganda could not induce to kill a Jew on his own account (not even when they made it quite clear that such a murder would go unpunished) now serves the machine of destruction without opposition. In contrast to the earlier units of the SS men and Gestapo, Himmler's over-all organization relies not on fanatics, nor on congenital murderers, nor on sadists; it relies entirely upon the normality of jobholders and family men.

We need not specially mention the sorry reports about Latvians, Lithuanians, or even Jews who have participated in Himmler's murder organization in order to show that it requires no particular national character in order to supply this new type of functionary. They are not even all natural murderers or traitors out of perversity. It is not even certain that they would do the work if it were only their own lives and future that were at stake. They felt (after they no longer needed to fear God, their conscience cleared through the bureaucratic organization of their acts) only the responsibility toward their own families. The transformation of the family man from a responsible member of society, interested in all public affairs, to a "bourgeois" concerned only with his private existence and knowing no civic virtue, is an international modern phenomenon. The exigencies of our time—"Bedenkt den Hunger und die grosse Kälte in diesem Tale, das von Jammer schallt" (Brecht)*— can at any moment transform him into the mob man and make him the instrument of whatsoever madness and horror. Each time society, through unemployment, frustrates the small man in his normal functioning and normal self-respect, it trains him for that last stage in which he will willingly undertake any function, even that of hangman. A Jew released from Buchenwald once discovered among the SS men who gave him the certificates of release a former schoolmate, whom he did not address but yet stared at. Spontaneously the man stared at remarked: You must understand, I have five years of unemployment behind me. They can do anything they want with me.

---

*"Think of the hunger and the great cold in this valley that rings with lamentations." Arendt apparently quoted from memory the final verses of the *Dreigroschenoper*, substituting "hunger" for "darkness": *"Bedenkt das Dunkel und die grosse Kälte / In diesem Tale, das von Jammer schallt."* —Ed.

It is true that the development of this modern type of man, who is the exact opposite of the "citoyen" and whom for lack of a better name we have called the "bourgeois," enjoyed particularly favorable conditions in Germany. Hardly another country of Occidental culture was so little imbued with the classic virtues of civic behavior. In no other country did private life and private calculations play so great a role. This is a fact which the Germans in time of national emergency disguised with great success, but never altered. Behind the façade of proclaimed and propagandized national virtues, such as "love of the Fatherland," "German courage," "German loyalty," etc., there lurked corresponding real national vices. There is hardly another country where on the average there is so little patriotism as Germany; and behind the chauvinistic claims of loyalty and courage, a fatal tendency to disloyalty and betrayal for opportunistic reasons is hidden.

The mob man, however, the end-result of the "bourgeois," is an international phenomenon; and we would do well not to submit him to too many temptations in the blind faith that only the German mob man is capable of such frightful deeds. What we have called the "bourgeois" is the modern man of the masses, not in his exalted moments of collective excitement, but in the security (today one should say the insecurity) of his own private domain. He has driven the dichotomy of private and public functions, of family and occupation, so far that he can no longer find in his own person any connection between the two. When his occupation forces him to murder people he does not regard himself as a murderer because he has not done it out of inclination but in his professional capacity. Out of sheer passion he would never do harm to a fly.

If we tell a member of this new occupational class which our time has produced that he is being held to account for what he did, he will feel nothing except that he has been betrayed. But if in the shock of the catastrophe he really becomes conscious that in fact he was not only a functionary but also a murderer, then his way out will not be that of rebellion, but suicide—just as so many have already chosen the way of suicide in Germany, where it is plain that there has been one wave of self-destruction after another. And that too would be of little use to us.

IV

For many years now we have met Germans who declare that they are ashamed of being Germans. I have often felt tempted to answer that I am ashamed of being human. This elemental shame, which many people of the most various nationalities share with one another today, is what finally is left of our sense of international solidarity; and it has not yet found an adequate political expression. Our fathers' enchantment with humanity was of a sort which not only light-mindedly ignored the national question; what is far worse, it did not even conceive of the terror of the idea of humanity and of the Judeo-Christian faith in the unitary origin of the human race. It was not very pleasant even when we had to bury our false illusions about "the noble savage," having discovered that men were capable of being cannibals. Since then peoples have learned to know one another better and learned more and more about the evil potentialities in men. The result has been that they have recoiled more and more from the idea of humanity and become more susceptible to the doctrine of race, which denies the very possibility of a common humanity. They instinctively felt that the idea of humanity, whether it appears in a religious or humanistic form, implies the obligation of a general responsibility which they do not wish to assume. For the idea of humanity, when purged of all sentimentality, has the very serious consequence that in one form or another men must assume responsibility for all crimes committed by men and that all nations share the onus of evil committed by all others. Shame at being a human being is the purely individual and still non-political expression of this insight.

In political terms, the idea of humanity, excluding no people and assigning a monopoly of guilt to no one, is the only guarantee that one "superior race" after another may not feel obligated to follow the "natural law" of the right of the powerful, and exterminate "inferior races unworthy of survival"; so that at the end of an "imperialistic age" we should find ourselves in a stage which would make the Nazis look like crude precursors of future political methods. To follow a non-imperialistic policy and maintain a non-racist faith becomes daily more difficult because it becomes daily clearer how great a burden mankind is for man.

Perhaps those Jews, to whose forefathers we owe the first conception of the idea of humanity, knew something about that burden when each year they used to say "Our Father and King, we have sinned before you," taking not only the sins of their own community but all human offenses upon themselves. Those who today are ready to follow this road in a modern version do not content themselves with the hypocritical confession "God be thanked, I am not like that," in horror at the undreamed-of potentialities of the German national character. Rather, in fear and trembling, have they finally realized of what man is capable—and this is indeed the precondition of any modern political thinking. Such persons will not serve very well as functionaries of vengeance. This, however, is certain: Upon them and only upon them, who are filled with a genuine fear of the inescapable guilt of the human race, can there be any reliance when it comes to fighting fearlessly, uncompromisingly, everywhere against the incalculable evil that men are capable of bringing about.

Nightmare and Flight

AMONG RECENT PUBLICATIONS, I know of very few that come so close to the experiences of modern man. Whoever wants to catch a glimpse of the postwar, post-Fascism state of mind of Europe's intellectuals should not miss reading *The Devil's Share*— carefully, patiently and (meaning no offense) with charity. The shortcomings of author and book are obvious, glaring to an irritating degree. They confuse the reader as they have confused the author. But the point is that this confusion is the direct result of experiences to which the author bears witness and from which he does not try to escape. Such experience as well as confusion will be common to all who survive and refuse to return to the deceptive security of those "keys to history" that pretended to explain everything, all trends and tendencies, and that actually could not reveal any single real event. Rougemont is speaking of the "nightmare of reality" before which our intellectual weapons have failed so miserably; and if he is confused, it is because in a desperate attempt not to be confronted with this nightmare in spiritual nakedness, he picks up from the great and beautiful arsenal of time-honored figures

A review of *The Devil's Share*, by Denis de Rougemont, translated from the French by Haakon Chevalier, *Partisan Review*, XII/2, 1945.

and images anything that seems to correspond to or to interpret the new shocks that rock the old foundations.

The reality is that "the Nazis are men like ourselves"; the nightmare is that they have shown, have proven beyond doubt what man is capable of. In other words, the problem of evil will be the fundamental question of postwar intellectual life in Europe—as death became the fundamental problem after the last war. Rougemont knows that ascribing all evils and evil as such to any social order or to society as such is "a flight from reality." But instead of facing the music of man's genuine capacity for evil and analyzing the nature of man, he in turn ventures into a flight from reality and writes on the nature of the Devil, thereby, despite all dialectics, evading the responsibility of man for his deeds.

The flight from reality, incidentally, is not a flight to theology, as the title and repeated quotations from the Bible suggest. It is a flight into literature, and occasionally very bad literature. There are not only little parables in which the author imitates Nietzsche at his worst—like "Woman beats man"—or essays on modern human behavior which imitate Chesterton on a much less brilliant level. There are such phrases as "I like to write only dangerous books," which in their puerile vanity make it hard for the reader to take the whole thing seriously.

More serious than immaturity (Rougemont belongs to the generation which, raised between two wars, never had sufficient opportunity to mature and has something of a birthright to immaturity) is the basic confusion of the whole approach. This consists of identifying man's capacity for evil and the problem of evil as such with the "evils of our time" loosely and generally speaking. This leads to the introduction of the Devil in person, who serves simply as common denominator. Although his existence is proved with a nice trick of Chestertonian logic ("Those who stick to old wives' tales—'I can't believe in a gent with red horns and a long tail'—are those who refuse to believe in the Devil because of the image they form of him which is drawn from old wives' tales"), he is nothing but a personification of Heidegger's Nothingness that already through its "begetting nothingness" was something of an acting subject. (The Devil is the "messenger of Nothingness," "serves Nothing," is "the agent of Nothingness," "tends to Nothingness," etc.)

This, of course, would be simply an attempt to explain the new experiences with the categories of the nineteen-twenties. But Rougemont does not stop there: his "flight from reality" is more complicated and more interesting to watch. Much against his will and though fearing and predicting "modern gnosticism," he falls into the worst pitfalls of gnostic speculation. His ultimate consolation is his confidence that in an eternal fight between God and the Devil, the good and the evil forces, victory is already won "from the point of view of eternity," that "our misdeeds and those of the Devil change nothing in the Order of this world" and that, consequently, "what concerns us in this century is to make ourselves immediate participants in this victory." This can but lead to the conclusion that all we have to do is "sanctify ourselves" for the purpose of joining the right, the eternally winning side. It is precisely this metaphysical opportunism, this escape from reality into a cosmic fight in which man has only to join the forces of light to be saved from the forces of darkness, this confidence that the order of the world cannot be changed no matter what man does, which makes gnosticism so attractive to modern speculation and may promote it to the place of the most dangerous and widespread "heresy" of tomorrow.

When all this has been said, one has the duty of recommending the book anew. Whether one likes it or not, it is a true *document humain*. Whether one agrees with Denis de Rougemont or not, he belongs to those who, in his own words, "are all in the sinking ship, and at the same time . . . are all in the ship that has launched the torpedo." Those who know this, who do not want to get away from this not very comfortable position, are not numerous, and they are the only ones who matter.

Dilthey as Philosopher
and Historian

D ILTHEY'S LIFE STRETCHED through the entire nineteenth century. When he was born in 1833, the German eighteenth century had just come to an end with the death of Hegel
and Goethe; when he died in 1911, the European nineteenth century
had three more years to live. These biographical data remain essential
for the evaluation of the man and his work. For although Dilthey in
many respects represented the best aspects of the "spirit of his age," he
never went beyond it and he never left the narrow framework of academic
life. He had nothing to do with the great rebels of and against the
nineteenth century, and his antipathy to Nietzsche was anything but a
matter of "temperament" (Hodges). The great hatred of men like Kierkegaard, Marx, Nietzsche for mere contemplation as the supreme content of intellectual life must have shocked and horrified Dilthey, whose
ruling passion was very much like the passion of the famous collectors
of the nineteenth century, although he did not collect objects. His collection was a more precious and more refined one: it was a collection of
inner experiences (*Erlebnisse*) whose main concern was to present a
complete exhibition of "life itself."

A review of *Wilhelm Dilthey: An Introduction*, by H. A. Hodges, *Partisan Review*,
XII/3, 1945.

Dilthey has been best known for his attempt to lay the foundations of the human studies (*Geisteswissenschaft*) as different and even opposed to the methods of natural science. History in which all other branches of the humanities are comprehended presupposes a secure method of "hermeneutics," the establishment of a science and art of interpretation. At the core of historical science as of history itself lies for him the problem of understanding. He had planned (and never achieved) a Critique of Historical Reason; the main function of this reason was man's capacity to understand. The objects of the understanding reason are the expression of *Erlebnisse* ("lived experience" in Hodges' translation), as they are presented in history and culture, because Life expresses and "objectifies" itself. History becomes for Dilthey a series of objectified experiences which we can understand insofar as we can "re-live" (*nacherleben*, Hodges' translation) them. Understanding, interpretation, hermeneutics are the art of deciphering signs of expression.

The main point about this art of reproduction is that it enables one to share in experiences that are ordinarily beyond the bounds of an individual life and a specific historical time. "Dilthey instances the effect of his own study of Luther and the Reformation in enabling him at least to understand a religious experience of a depth and intensity such as in his own person he was not capable of sharing" (Hodges). It is this somehow parasitical attitude to life which makes Dilthey's general reflections on history so highly characteristic of the spirit of the nineteenth century, and it is quite in accordance with this spirit that Dilthey found the highest type of man in the artist. For the general genius-worship of his time was actually based on the conviction that only the artist who possesses the capacity of expressing his "lived experiences" is truly "alive," a conviction which Dilthey shared and from which he concluded that if the Gods have refused a man the necessary talents his second-best chance to become "alive" is to decipher "expressions," thus partaking in the experiences of others. In Dilthey's concept, the historian becomes a kind of artist who has missed his calling.

The artist as the prototype of man is an old topic of philosophy. The difference, however, between the older concepts and the nineteenth-century genius-worship that started with German romanticism is marked. For the former the artist was the supreme guarantee of man's creative capacities, whereas romanticism already saw in art only the expression of experiences and in the artist only a human being with more and more interesting experiences. In Germany, Schleiermacher was the first to detect in the "lived experiences" the central interest of man and he transformed, accordingly, religion into religiosity, faith into religious sentiments, and the "reality of God" into the feeling of dependence. It is by no means accidental that Dilthey's greatest admiration went to Schleiermacher and that one of his most elaborate and best-known works was devoted to his biography.

It is a matter of course that insofar as this hunger for life and lived experiences of the nineteenth century was genuine, the passion for understanding, for "re-living" has produced some great achievements. These, however, do not belong to the realm of philosophy, and the most serious shortcoming of Hodges' introduction to the work of Dilthey (the first book in English to deal with his work) is that he places the main accent on Dilthey the philosopher and leaves Dilthey the historian, who was a far more important man, almost entirely out of his picture. For Dilthey's *Interpretation and Analysis of Man in the Fifteenth and Sixteenth Century* and his *Experience and Poetry* (*Erlebnis und Dichtung*) are indeed standard works of the history of ideas—both of which are omitted from the introductory text as well as from the Selected Passages, which, on the other hand, contain a badly organized choice of fragmentary general ideas and reflections which appear today rather antiquated.

A similar error in judgment seems to be that Hodges highly overrates Dilthey's influence on modern existential philosophers. He calls Karl Jaspers a disciple of Dilthey and quotes in support of this thesis the *Psychologie der Weltanschauungen*. As far as I can find out, Jaspers quotes Dilthey but once among many other authors as one of his historical sources. It may have been easier to prove an influence on Heidegger (whom Hodges does not name), for Heidegger expressly states (in *Sein und Zeit*) that his treatment of the problem of history has grown out of an interpretation of Dilthey's work, although even in this case a closer examination shows that it was York von Wartenburg's letters to Dilthey, rather than Dilthey himself, which influenced Heidegger's analysis.

The literature on Dilthey in Germany is tremendous and Hodges' bibliography is a service to all students. From this literature, the few pages which Hofmannsthal wrote on the occasion of Dilthey's death convey best, in their carefully balanced briefness, the greatness of comprehension that was the hallmark of Dilthey's contemplation. Dilthey's tremendous erudition was something more than extensive knowledge, and Hofmannsthal honors him rightly when he evokes the lines of Goethe's *Lynkeus-lied*:

> *Er schaut in die Ferne,*
> *er sieht in die Näh',*
> *den Mond und die Sterne,*
> *den Wald und das Reh.*

> [He beholds what is far,
> He observes what is near,
> The moon and the stars,
> The wood and the deer.*]

---

*Cf. *Faust*, II, v, 11292–295. —Ed.

The Seeds of a
Fascist International

O N   A L L   S I D E S we hear fascism lightly disposed of with the remark that nothing will remain of it but anti-Semitism. And as for anti-Semitism, the whole world, including the Jews, has of course long since learned to put up with it, so that today anyone who concerns himself with it seriously seems slightly ridiculous. Yet, anti-Semitism was indubitably the feature which gave the fascist movement its international appeal, equipping fellow-travelers in every country and class. As a global conspiracy, fascism was essentially based on anti-Semitism. If one says, therefore, that anti-Semitism will be the only relic of fascism, it amounts to no more and no less than saying that the major reliance of fascist propaganda and one of the most important principles of fascist political organization will survive.

It is a highly dubious achievement of Jewish counter-propaganda to have exposed anti-Semites as mere crackpots, and to have reduced anti-Semitism to the banal level of a prejudice not worth discussing. This had the consequence that Jews never became aware—not even when they had already been fatally injured—that they were being drawn into the very storm center of the political perils of our time. Non-Jews too

Jewish Frontier, June 1945.

still imagine, as a result, that they can deal with anti-Semitism by a few words of sympathy. Both stubbornly confuse the modern version of anti-Semitism with mere discrimination against minorities, not even being sobered by the reflection that it burst forth most frightfully in a country where there was relatively little discrimination against Jews, while in other countries, with much more active social discrimination (as for example the United States), it has failed to develop into a significant political movement.

Actually, anti-Semitism is one of the most important political movements of our time, the fight against it is one of the most vital duties of the democracies, and its survival is one of the most significant indications of future perils. In order to judge it correctly, one should remember that the first anti-Semitic parties on the continent in the 1880s had already (in contrast to the practice of all other rightist parties) combined on an international scale. In other words, modern anti-Semitism was never a mere matter of extremist nationalism: from the very beginning it functioned as an International. The textbook of this International, after the last war, was the *Protocols of the Elders of Zion*, which was distributed and read in all countries, whether there were many Jews there, or few Jews, or none at all. Thus, to cite a little noted example, Franco had the *Protocols* translated during the Spanish Civil War, even though Spain for lack of Jews could claim no Jewish problem.

Repeated demonstrations of the falsity of the *Protocols* and the tireless exposés of its true origin are of little significance. It is of much greater utility and importance to explain not what is obvious but what is mysterious about the *Protocols*: namely, why, despite the obvious fact that it is a forgery, it continues to be believed. Here and here alone lies the key to the question which no one apparently asks any longer, why the Jews were the spark which enabled Nazism to flare up, and why anti-Semitism was the nucleus around which the fascist movement crystallized all over the world. The importance of the *Protocols*, even in countries without any real Jewish problem, is strong proof of the correctness of a thesis put forward by Alexander Stein (*Adolf Hitler: Schüler der Weisen von Zion*) without making the slightest impression, in the thirties: that the organization of the suppositious Elders of Zion was a model followed by the fascist organization, and that the *Protocols* contain the principles which fascism adopted in order to seize power. Thus, the secret of the success of this forgery was not primarily Jew-hatred, but, rather, boundless admiration for the cunning of an allegedly Jewish technique of global world organization.

Disregarding the cheap Machiavellianism of the *Protocols*, their essential characteristic, politically, is that they are, in principle, antinational; that they show how the nation and the national state can be subverted; that they are not satisfied with the conquest of a particular country, but aim at the conquest and rule of the whole world; and, finally, that the international global conspiracy which they describe has an ethnic and racist foundation, enabling a people without a state or a territory to rule the whole world by means of a secret society.

In order to believe that Jews actually used such an ingenious device (there are many people who still believe in the essential truth of the *Protocols*, even though they concede they are forgeries), one need (or should) know no more about the Jews than that, dispersed everywhere, they have managed to persist for two thousand years, without state or territory, as an ethnic entity; and that for all that time they have played a far from insignificant role in the government of national states by way of private influence; and that they are connected internationally by business, family, and philanthropic ties. It is difficult for peoples who are accustomed to politics to understand that so great an opportunity for political power should actually never have been exploited, or used only to the smallest extent for purposes of defense (how hard it must be to understand this may be realized by any Jew who will read attentively Benjamin Disraeli, one of the first of cultivated Europeans to believe in a sort of Jewish secret society engaged in world politics—and even to be proud of it). This small quantity of facts which everybody knows, including those who have never actually seen a Jew, is enough to give the picture of the *Protocols* considerable plausibility; enough, moreover, to provoke imitation of the pattern, in an imaginary competition for world rule with—of all peoples—the Jews.

An even more important element in the *Protocols* than the plausibility of their picture of the Jews is the extraordinary fact that, in their own crackpot manner, they touch on every essential political problem of our time. Their generally anti-national tenor and semi-anarchist antagonism to the state corresponds most significantly to major modern developments. In showing how the national state may be undermined, the *Protocols* plainly indicate that they regard it as a colossus with feet of clay, an outmoded form of political power concentration. In this they express, in their own vulgar fashion, what imperialist statesmen and parties since the end of the past century have thought sedulously to hide under their nationalistic phraseology: that national sovereignty is no longer a working concept of politics, for there is no longer a political organization which can represent or defend a sovereign people, within national boundaries. Thus the "national state," having lost its very foundations, leads the life of a walking corpse, whose spurious existence is artificially prolonged by repeated injections of imperialistic expansion.

The chronic crisis of the national state became acute immediately after the end of the First World War. The unmistakable failure of the attempt to reorganize Eastern and Southeastern Europe, with their mixed populations, according to the model of the Western national states was a significant contributory factor. The lower the prestige of the national state fell, the higher rose the popular interest in the *Protocols*. During those years of the twenties, the masses began to feel themselves peculiarly attracted by all the anti-national movements. The fact that in the thirties both fascist and communist movements were denounced in all countries except Germany, the Soviet Union, and Italy as fifth columnists, as the *avant-garde* of the external policy of foreign powers, did not harm their cause, but perhaps even aided it. The masses knew very well what was the nature and purpose of these movements; but in any case, nobody believed in national sovereignty any longer, and one was inclined to prefer the frankly anti-national propaganda of the new Internationals to an outmoded nationalism, which was felt to be at once hypocritical and weak.

The motif of global conspiracy in the *Protocols* also corresponded, and still corresponds, to the altered power situation in which, for past decades, politics have been conducted. There are no longer any powers but world powers, and no power politics but global politics. These have been the conditions of modern political life for the past century—conditions, however, to which Western civilization has so far found no adequate response. At a time when full political information, necessarily worldwide in scope, is available only to the professional, and when statesmen have found no other clue to world politics than the blind alley of imperialism, it is almost a matter of course for the others, who vaguely sense our worldwide interdependence but are unable to penetrate into the actual working of this universal relationship, to turn to the dramatically simple hypothesis of a global conspiracy and a secret worldwide organization. If, therefore, they are called upon to align themselves also with another, supposedly secret, and in fact semi-conspiratorial, world organization, they are far from being repelled by the idea—or even from seeing anything out of the ordinary in it. They are manifestly of the opinion that this is the only way in which one can become politically active.

Finally, the conception of a worldwide organization whose members constitute an ethnic entity dispersed all over the globe is suited not to the Jewish situation alone. As long as the Jewish destiny was a unique curiosity, anti-Semitism relied upon the familiar nineteenth-century arguments against the intruder and was limited to the dread of the universal stranger. At the same time, no other people was much interested in speculating on just how the Jews had managed to survive without state or territory. However, since the last war, with its aftermath of minority questions and statelessness, the Jewish demonstration that nationality, the bond to a people without benefit of political organization, can be maintained without a state or a territory has been repeated by almost all European peoples. Therefore they are even more inclined than before to accept those methods which purportedly preserved the Jewish people for two thousand years. It is no accident that the Nazis had so strong a following among Germans abroad, that, indeed, the most characteristic phases of the ideology of National Socialism as an International Movement derive from *Auslands-Deutschen*.

II

Only when fascism is understood as an anti-national international movement does it become intelligible why the Nazis, with unparalleled coolness, not distracted by national sentimentality or humane scruples as to the welfare of their people, allowed their land to be transformed into a shambles. The German nation has gone down in ruins together with its terrorist regime of twelve years' duration, whose policing apparatus functioned unfailingly until the last minute. The line of demarcation which, for the next decades, and perhaps still longer, will divide Europe more sharply than all the national boundaries of the past goes straight through the middle of Germany.

The public opinion of the world cannot comprehend this self-staged ruin. It can be only partially explained by the long-pilloried nihilistic tendencies of Nazism, by their *Götterdämmerungs* ideology whose innumerable variations forecast cataclysmic disaster in the event of defeat. What remains unexplained is that the Nazis have apparently left none of the occupied countries so ravaged as Germany itself. It seems as if they maintained their terrorist machine, and through it their (from a military standpoint) completely useless resistance, solely in order to avail themselves of every opportunity to provoke complete destruction. However correct it may be to regard the purely destructive tendency of fascism as one of the most active forces of the movement, it would be dangerously misleading to interpret these destructive impulses as culminating in a theatrical, suicidal urge directed against the movement as such. The Nazis may have planned to destroy Germany completely, they may have calculated on impoverishing the whole European continent by ruining German industry, they may hope to leave the Allies the burden and responsibility of governing ungovernable chaos, but certainly they have never wished to liquidate the fascist movement.*

It is obvious that, in the opinion of the Nazis, a mere *defeat* of Germany would mean the ruin of the fascist movement; but on the other hand, the thorough *destruction* of Germany offers fascism an opportunity to turn the outcome of this war into a merely temporary defeat of the movement. That is, the Nazis have offered up Germany as a sacrifice to the future of fascism—though the question remains, of course, whether this sacrifice will "pay" in the long run. All the discussions and conflicts between the Party and High Command, between the Gestapo and the Wehrmacht, between representatives of the so-called ruling classes and the real rulers of the party bureaucracy involved nothing

---

*Shortly before the German defeat, reports were published that new and unknown persons had been selected for the organization and leadership of an underground fascist movement. It seems probable that Himmler and some of his closest co-workers had hoped they would be able to go underground, to retain the illegal leadership, and to proclaim Hitler a martyr. At any rate, the rapid succession in which prominent leaders of the party and police machine have been captured by the Allies indicates that something went wrong with their plan. The events of the last weeks have not yet been cleared up and perhaps never will be. The most plausible explanation, however, can be found in the report of the last meeting Hitler held immediately before his death, during which he allegedly asserted that the SS troops could no longer be trusted.

other than this sacrifice—which was as self-evident a necessity to the Nazi political strategists as it was unimaginable to the military and industrialist fellow-travelers.

However one may assess the chances of this policy for the survival of the fascist International, it became clear immediately after the announcement of Hitler's death that the ruin of Germany, that is the destruction of the strongest power center of the fascist movement, was by no means identical with the disappearance of fascism from international politics. Undeterred by the present power situation, the Irish government expressed its sympathy to the (no longer existing) German government, while Portugal even proclaimed two days of mourning, which would have been a very unusual step even under ordinary circumstances. The striking feature of the attitude of these "neutrals" is that, at a time when nothing seems to be as highly regarded as brute power and sheer success, they have dared to act so cavalierly towards the great, victorious powers. De Valera and Salazar are no quixotic fools. They simply evaluate the situation somewhat differently and do not believe that power is identical with military force and industrial capacity. They speculate on Nazism and all its affiliated ideological elements' having lost only a battle, not the war. And since they know from experience that they have to do with an international movement, they do not take the destruction of Germany as a decisive blow.

III

It was always a too little noted hallmark of fascist propaganda that it was not satisfied with lying but deliberately proposed to transform its lies into reality. Thus, *Das Schwarze Korps** conceded several years before the outbreak of the war that people abroad did not completely believe the Nazi contention that all Jews are homeless beggars who can only subsist as parasites in the economic organism of other nations; but foreign public opinion, they prophesied, would in a few years be given the opportunity to convince itself of this fact when the German Jews would be driven out across the borders like a pack of beggars. For such a fabrication of a lying reality no one was prepared. The essential char-

*A Nazi publication. —Ed.

acteristic of fascist propaganda was never its lies, for this is something more or less common to propaganda everywhere and of every time. The essential thing was that they exploited the age-old Occidental prejudice which confuses reality with truth, and made that "true" which until then could only be stated as a lie. It is for this reason that any argumentation with fascists—the so-called counter-propaganda—is so extremely senseless: it is as though one were to debate with a potential murderer as to whether his future victim were dead or alive, completely forgetting that man can kill and that the murderer, by killing the person in question, could promptly provide proof of the correctness of this statement.

This was the spirit in which the Nazis destroyed Germany—in order to be proved in the right: an asset which may be of the greatest value for their future activity. They destroyed Germany to show that they were right when they said the German people were fighting for its very existence; which was, at the outset, a pure lie. They instituted chaos in order to show that they were right when they said that Europe had only the alternative between Nazi rule and chaos. They dragged out the war until the Russians actually stood at the Elbe and the Adriatic so as to give their lies about the danger of Bolshevism a *post facto* basis in reality. They hope of course, that in a short time, when the peoples of the world really comprehend the magnitude of the European catastrophe, their politics will be proved completely justified.

If National Socialism were really in essence a German national movement—like, for instance, Italian fascism in its first decade—it would gain little by such proofs and arguments. In that case success alone would be decisive, and their failure as a national movement has been overwhelming. The Nazis themselves know this very well, and therefore several months ago they retired from the governmental apparatus, separated the party from the state once again, thereby relieving themselves of all those nationalistic chauvinist elements who joined them partly for opportunistic reasons, partly out of a misunderstanding. The Nazis also know, however, that even if the Allies should be so foolish as to implicate themselves with new Darlans, the influence of these groups would remain unavailing simply because the German nation itself no longer existed.

Actually, the National Socialist Party, since the end of the 1920s, was no longer a purely German party, but an international organization with its headquarters in Germany. Through the outcome of the war it has lost its strategic base and the operational facilities of a particular state machinery. This loss of a national center is not exclusively disadvantageous for the continuation of the fascist International. Freed of every national tie and the inevitable extraneous concerns connected therewith, the Nazis can try once more in the postwar era to organize as that true and undiluted secret society dispersed all over the world which has always been the pattern of organization towards which they have striven.

The factual existence of a Communist International, growing in power, will be of great assistance to them. They have been arguing for a long time (for months past their propaganda has been based exclusively upon this) that this is nothing other than the Jewish global conspiracy of the Elders of Zion. There will be many whom they can convince that this global menace can be met only by organizing in the same manner. The danger of such a development will become greater to the extent that the democracies continue to operate with purely national conceptions, renouncing any ideological strategy of war and peace and thereby giving rise to the impression that, in contrast to the ideological Internationals, they stand only for the immediate interests of particular peoples.

In this enterprise, far more dangerous than a mere underground movement of purely German character, fascism will find highly useful the racist ideology which in the past was developed only by National Socialism. It is already becoming obvious that colonial problems will remain unsolved, and that, as a result, the conflicts between white and colored peoples, i.e., the so-called racial conflicts, will become even more acute. Furthermore, competition between the imperialistic nations will remain a feature of the international scene. In this context the fascists, who even in their German version never identified the master race with any nationality but spoke of "Aryans" generally, could easily make themselves the protagonists of a unified White Supremacy strategy capable of out-bidding any group not unconditionally advocating equal rights for all peoples.

Anti-Jewish propaganda will surely remain one of the most important points of attraction for fascism. The terrible losses of the Jews in Europe have made us lose sight of another aspect of the situation: though numerically weakened, the Jewish people will emerge from the war far more widely dispersed geographically than before. In contrast to the pre-

1933 era, there is hardly a spot on earth any longer where Jews do not live, in larger or smaller number, but always watched more or less distrustfully by the non-Jewish environment.

As the counterpart of an Aryan fascist International, the Jews, conceived as the ethnic representative of the Communist International, are today perhaps even more useful than before. This is particularly true for South America whose strong fascist movements are sufficiently well known.

The opportunities in Europe itself for a fascist International organization not bound by problems of state and territory are even greater. The so-called refugee population, product of the revolutions and wars of the last two decades, is growing daily in number. Driven from territories to which they are unwilling or unable to return, these victims of our time have already established themselves as national splinter groups in all European countries. Restoration of the European national system means for them a rightlessness compared to which the proletarians of the nineteenth century had a privileged status. They might have become the true vanguard of a European movement—and many of them, indeed, were prominent in the Resistance; but they can easily fall prey, also, to other ideologies if appealed to in international terms. The 250,000 Polish soldiers, who are offered no other solution than the precarious status of mercenaries under British command for the occupation of Germany, are clearly a case in point.

Even without these relatively new problems, "restoration" would be extremely dangerous. Yet in all areas not under immediate Russian influence, the forces of yesterday have placed themselves in the saddle, more or less undisturbed. This restoration, proceeding with the aid of intensified nationalist chauvinist propaganda, particularly in France, is in sharp opposition to the tendencies and aspirations begotten by the resistance movements, which were genuinely European movements. These aspirations are not forgotten, even though for a time they have been forced into the background by the release of liberation and the misery of day-to-day living. At the beginning of the war it was obvious to any student of European conditions, including the numerous American correspondents, that no people in Europe was any longer prepared to go to war over national conflicts. The resurrection of territorial disputes may vouchsafe the victorious governments brief triumphs of prestige and give the impression that the European nationalism of old, which alone could offer a secure foundation for a restoration, has come back to life. It will soon become apparent, however, that all this is merely a short-lived bluff from which the nations will turn with fanaticism redoubled by their embitterment to those ideologies which can propose purportedly international solutions, that is to fascism and to communism.

Under these conditions it may prove an advantage to the Nazis to be able to operate all over Europe at once, without having to be bound to a particular country and rely upon a particular government. No longer concerned with the weal or woe of one nation, they might all the more quickly assume the appearance of a genuine European movement. There is the danger that Nazism might pose successfully as the heir of the European resistance movement, taking over from them the slogan of a European federation and exploiting it for its own purposes. One should not forget that even when it was unmistakably clear that it would mean merely a Europe ruled by Germans, the slogan of a United Europe proved to be the Nazis' most successful propaganda weapon. It will hardly lose its power in an impoverished post-war Europe, rent by nationalistic governments.

These are, in general, the perils of tomorrow. Unquestionably, fascism has been once defeated, but we are far from having completely eradicated this arch-evil of our time. For its roots are strong and they are called—Anti-Semitism, Racism, Imperialism.

Christianity and Revolution

W HILE IT IS already obvious that the Christian churches in Europe have survived fascism, war, and occupation in their religious as well as their organizational aspects, it is still a question whether we shall see a general Christian and especially Catholic revival in French and intellectual life. There is no doubt about the part played by various Catholic movements and individuals in the Resistance or about the impeccable attitude of the greater part of the lower clergy. This does not mean, however, that these Catholics have a political position of their own. At the moment it looks rather as if the old anti-clerical passions are no longer alive in France—in contrast to Spain and probably Italy—and as if one of the most important issues in French domestic politics since the days of the Revolution is about to depart quietly from the political scene.

We have witnessed one wave of neo-Catholic revival after another since the period of *fin de siècle* decadence by which they were partly engendered. It started at the time of the Dreyfus Affair with the famous "Catholics without faith," who later developed into the Action Française, were condemned by the Pope in 1926, and ended by bowing before their

The Nation, 161/12, September 22, 1945.

real master, Mr. Hitler. With their boundless admiration of organization for organization's sake, they were the degenerated disciples of de Maistre, that great champion of reaction and greater master of French prose. And one must admit that they brought into the dead boredom of reactionary theories the violence of polemic and some passion of argument.

The "Catholics without faith" loved the church—which is still the greatest example of authoritarian organization and as such has withstood two thousand years of history; they had an open contempt for the content of Christian faith precisely because of its inherent democratic elements. They were Catholics because they hated democracy; they were as much attracted by de Maistre's hangman as the most reliable pillar of society, and by the possibility of domination through a hierarchy, as they were disgusted by the teachings of charity and the equality of man.

But side by side with these dilettantes of fascism there sprang up a very different Catholic revival movement, whose greatest representatives were Péguy and Bernanos in France and Chesterton in England. These too sought escape from the modern world and, therefore, sometimes stumbled into unhappy alliances with the "Catholics without faith," alliances in which they naturally were destined to play the role of suckers. Witness Jacques Maritain's relations with the Action Française, or the strange friendship between G. K. Chesterton and Hilaire Belloc. For what these men hated in the modern world was not democracy but the lack of it. They saw through the appearances of democracies which might be more accurately described as plutocracies and through the trimmings of a republic which was much more a political machine. What they sought was freedom for the people and reason for the mind. What they started from was a deep hatred of bourgeois society, which they knew was essentially anti-democratic and fundamentally perverted. What they fought against always was the insidious invasion of bourgeois morals and standards into all walks of life and all classes of the people. They were indeed struggling against something very ominous, which scarcely a socialist—whose political party, according to Péguy, "is completely composed of bourgeois intellectuals"—clearly realized, namely, the all-pervading influence of bourgeois mentality in the modern world.

It is a remarkable phenomenon, and something to start our progressives thinking, that as far as polemics go these Catholic converts or neo-Catholics have come out as victors. There are no more devastating,

amusing, or better-written polemics against the host of modern superstitions, from Christian Science to gymnastics as a means of salvation,
to teetotalism, and Krishnamurti, than Chesterton's essays. It was Péguy
who discovered and defined the essential difference between poverty—
which was always a virtue, for Roman republicans as well as for medieval
Christians—and destitution, which is the modern plague reserved for
those who refuse the pursuit of money and the humiliations of success.
And it was, finally, Bernanos who wrote the most passionate denunciation of fascism—*Les grandes Cimetières sous la lune*—a knight without
fear or reproach, unhampered by any admiration for "historical greatness" and untouched by any secret desire for the necessity of evil.

On the other hand, it must be admitted that none of these individuals
was a great philosopher and that this movement did not produce a single
great artist. Although both Chesterton and Péguy wrote good poetry,
neither will be remembered primarily for his poems. With the exception
of *The Man Who Was Thursday*, Chesterton's novels are only another
form of the essay, and Bernanos's novels are of little interest. Nor was
there among them a great theologian. The only neo-Catholic of importance who ventured into this field was Léon Bloy—with rather crude
and absurd results, which, theologically speaking, were always on the
borderline of heresy and sometimes approached the borderline of bohemian *Kitsch*: he maintained, for instance, that women should be either
saints or whores, for while saints may be forced by circumstances to
descend to the level of the whore, and whores may always become saints,
the honest woman of bourgeois society is lost beyond salvation.

Since the turn of the century these converts, it would seem, have
felt that their proper field was politics and their task to become true
revolutionaries, that is, more radical than the radicals. And in a sense
they were right, right at least as long as they remained in the negative
and took the offensive. It certainly was more radical to repeat that "it
is easier for a camel to go through the eye of a needle than for a rich
man to enter into the kingdom of God" than to quote economic laws.
When Chesterton describes the rich man who for the pretended sake of
humanity has adopted some fancy new vegetarian rule as the man who
does not go "without gardens and gorgeous rooms which poor men can't
enjoy" but has "abolished meat because poor men like meat," or when
he denounces the "modern philanthropist" who does not give up "petrol
or . . . servants" but rather "some simple universal things" like "beef

or sleep, because these pleasures remind him that he is only a man"—
then Chesterton has better described the fundamental ambitions of the
ruling classes than have all the academic discussions of the functions of
capitalists. And in Péguy's endless repetition, "All evil comes from the
bourgeoisie," is more elementary hatred than in the collected speeches
of Jaurès.

With the whole of Western culture at stake once bourgeois rule had
entered the path of imperialism, it is not surprising that the oldest
weapons, the fundamental convictions of Western mankind, sufficed to
show at least the extent of the evil. The great advantage of these neo-
Catholic writers was that when they went back to Christianity they
broke with the standards of their surroundings more radically than any
other sect or party. It was their instinct as publicists which pushed them
into the church. They were looking for arms, and were ready to take
them wherever they found them; and they found better ones in the oldest
arsenal than in the half-baked half-truths of modernity. Publicists and
journalists are always in a hurry—that is their occupational disease.
Here were arms that one could take up in a hurry; had not two thousand
years proved their utility? The best among the converts knew from bitter
experience how much better it was, how much freer one could remain,
and how much more reasonable, if one accepted the single great assumption which Christian faith exacts than if one remained in the
turmoil of modernism, which enforces every other day, with a maximum
of fanaticism, another absurd doctrine.

There was something more in Christianity than its highly useful
denunciation of the rich man as a wicked man. The insistence of the
Christian doctrine on man's limited condition was somehow enough of
a philosophy to allow its adherents a very deep insight into the essential
inhumanity of all those modern attempts—psychological, technical,
biological—to change man into the monster of a superman. They realized
that a pursuit of happiness which actually means to wipe away all tears
will pretty quickly end by wiping out all laughter. It was again Christianity which taught them that nothing human can exist beyond tears
and laughter, except the silence of despair. This is the reason why
Chesterton, having once and for all accepted the tears, could put real
laughter into his most violent attacks.

If this is the case of the publicists and journalists among the neo-
Catholics, the case of the philosophers is slightly different and slightly

embarrassing. The point is that philosophers by definition are supposed not to be in a hurry. If one is to judge by the book recently published by Raïssa Maritain,* it was not hatred of bourgeois society which brought the Maritains into the church—although M. Maritain was a socialist in his youth; it was, as Mme Maritain insists time and again, the need for "spiritual guidance." At the time of their conversion it is probable that both of them, and not only Mme Maritain, "had by instinct an insuperable apprehension toward anything concerning political activity, in which I saw—and still do—the domain of what St. Paul calls the evil of time." What separated them from Péguy—a former friendship broke up, strangely enough, because of their conversion—was precisely that they wanted first of all to save their souls, a preoccupation which played no great role in either Péguy's or Chesterton's Catholicism.

The Maritains became converts after having been exposed to the anti-intellectualism of Bergson. It is all to Jacques Maritain's credit that Bergson's attack on reason frightened him so much; the question is only whether a philosopher is allowed to seek shelter so quickly and so desperately. It is true that the teachings of the church still represent a stronghold of human reason, and it is quite understandable that in the day-by-day fight publicists like Péguy and Chesterton took cover as quickly as possible. They were no philosophers, and all they needed was a fighting faith. What Maritain wanted was one certainty which would lead him out of the complexities and confusions of a world that does not even know what a man is talking about if he takes the word truth into his mouth.

But the truth is a rather difficult deity to worship because the only thing she does not allow her worshipers is certainty. Philosophy concerned with truth ever was and probably always will be a kind of *docta ignorantia*—highly learned and therefore highly ignorant. The certainties of Thomas Aquinas afford excellent spiritual guidance and are still much superior to almost anything in the way of certainties which has been invented in more recent times. But certainty is not truth, and a system of certainties is the end of philosophy. This is the reason why one may be allowed to doubt very strongly that Thomism will ever be able to bring about a revival of philosophy.

Adventures in Grace, New York, 1945.

Power Politics Triumphs

W HEN THIS BOOK was published, some six months ago, its basic thesis—for all its logic and sanity—was a dead issue. Mr. Gross conclusively proves that federation for Eastern Europe is an economic necessity; and he insists on the political desirability of a federated Europe because a "world-wide organization," without which "there can be no lasting peace," can be achieved only through "regional organizations." Confident of the "natural trend of history toward world economy" and well acquainted with the desperate situation of the "pulverized states inhabited by Poles, Czechoslovaks, Rumanians, Serbs, Croats . . . and others," he surveys the history of the idea of federation, gives very valuable material on economic conditions in Eastern Europe and adds a much needed selection from contemporary accounts to show that all the peoples who joined the Resistance did not do so just to fight the German invader but had gotten it into their heads that they were fighting *for* something. What they were fighting for was a federated Europe.

But then came Soviet Russia and declared that any federation not

A review of *Crossroads of Two Continents: A Democratic Federation of East-Central Europe,* by Feliks Gross, *Commentary,* No. 1, 1945–46.

dominated by herself was a hostile *cordon sanitaire*. And then came the rest of the Big Three and found out that in spite of all their internal differences there was one point upon which all three agreed, and this was that no new political structure was to be allowed in Europe. And then came the governments back from their exile and told their peoples that what they had fought against was the Germans and what they had fought for was the status quo. And that was that.

The obsoleteness of this book is, however, not merely a result of the changed situation. It is also a consequence of the author's pathetic faith in the validity of economic arguments. It is true, and almost self-evident, that the whole Continent is likely to collapse because of the principle of national sovereignty, and it is beyond doubt that great sections of Eastern Europe will be ruined by a state of affairs which nobody has quite the courage to call peace. The transfers of population make no economic sense whatsoever and can result only in the depopulation and devastation of vast agricultural regions, which may weaken Europe permanently. The point the author overlooks, and which is all-important for modern politics, is that nobody cares. Everything is decided from the point of view of politics. In the present instance the restoration of national states with homogeneous ethnic populations is the chief issue. President Beneš and his abruptly changed approach to all these questions is a perfect case in point, precisely because Beneš is not a fool and knows the key importance of economics to the European situation as well as Mr. Gross does.

Even more damaging to Mr. Gross's argument is another oversight. To this new neglect of economic factors on the part of those who make politics must be added the new over-emphasis on power. Mr. Gross takes Russia's arguments against a possibly non-democratic federation at their face value and solemnly reassures her of the longing of the peoples concerned for truly democratic and peaceful institutions. He completely overlooks what, after all, is obvious, namely, that Russia being a big Power wants nothing so much as to become an even bigger Power. Therefore, she feels—rightly—that no matter how peaceful and democratic and friendly an Eastern European or a general European federation would be, it still would almost automatically check—not Russia's present power, but her plans—judging by the facts of every postwar Soviet move—for an ever increasing accumulation of power.

No Longer and Not Yet

HUME ONCE REMARKED that the whole of human civilization depends upon the fact that "one generation does not go off the stage at once and another succeed, as is the case with silkworms and butterflies." At some turning-points of history, however, at some heights of crisis, a fate similar to that of silkworms and butterflies may befall a generation of men. For the decline of the old, and the birth of the new, is not necessarily an affair of continuity; between the generations, between those who for some reason or other still belong to the old and those who either feel the catastrophe in their very bones or have already grown up with it, the chain is broken and an "empty space," a kind of historical no man's land, comes to the surface which can be described only in terms of "no longer and not yet." In Europe such an absolute interruption of continuity occurred during and after the First World War. All the loose talk of intellectuals about the necessary decline of Western civilization or the famous lost generation, as it is usually uttered by "reactionaries," has its basis of truth in this break, and consequently has proved much more attractive than the corresponding

A review of *The Death of Virgil*, by Hermann Broch, translated by Jean Starr Untermeyer, *The Nation*, September 14, 1946.

triviality of the "liberal" mind that puts before us the alternative of going ahead or going backward, an alternative which appears so devoid of sense precisely because it still presupposes an unbroken chain of continuity.

Speaking merely in terms of European literature, this gap, this opening of an abyss of empty space and empty time, is most clearly visible in the disparity between the two greatest literary masters of our time, Marcel Proust and Franz Kafka. Proust is the last and the most beautiful farewell to the world of the nineteenth century, and we return to his work, written in the key of the "no longer," again and again when the mood of farewell and of sorrow overwhelms us. Kafka, on the other hand, is our contemporary only to a limited extent. It is as though he wrote from the vantage point of a distant future, as though he were or could have been at home only in a world which is "not yet." This puts us at a certain distance whenever we are to read and discuss his work, a distance which will not grow smaller, even though we may know that his art is the expression of some future world which is our future, too—if we are to have any future at all.

All other great European novelists and poets find their place and their standard of measurement somewhere in between these dead masters. But Hermann Broch's book falls in a different category from the rest. That he has in common with Proust the form of the inner monologue and with Kafka the utter and radical renunciation of entertainment, as well as a preoccupation with metaphysics, that he shares with Proust a deep fondness for the world as it is given to us, and that he shares with Kafka the belief that the "hero" of the novel is no longer a character with certain well-defined qualities but, rather, man as such (for the real life of the man and poet Virgil is no more than an occasion for Broch's philosophical speculations)—all this is true, and the histories of literature may say it later.

What is more important, at least at this moment, is that Broch's work—through its subject matter and through its entirely original and magnificent poetic diction—has become something like the missing link between Proust and Kafka, between a past which we have irretrievably lost and a future which is not yet at hand. In other words, this book is by itself the kind of bridge with which Virgil tries to span the abyss of empty space between the no longer and the not yet. And since this abyss is very real; since it has become deeper and more frightful every single year from the fateful year of 1914 onward, until the death factories erected in the heart of Europe definitely cut the already outworn thread with which we still might have been tied to a historical entity of more than two thousand years; since we are already living in the "empty space," confronted with a reality which no preconceived traditional idea of the world and man can possibly illuminate—dear as this tradition may have remained to our hearts—we must be profoundly grateful for the great work of poetry which clings so desperately to this one subject.

Curiously enough, very little in Broch's earlier work indicates the future author of *The Death of Virgil*. *The Sleepwalkers*, apart from its qualities as a novel, shows only that its author is fed up with story-telling, thoroughly impatient with his own work: he tells his readers that they had better find for themselves the end of the story, and neglects character and plot in order to squeeze into his book long speculations about the nature of history. Up to a certain date Broch was a good, playful, amusing story-teller, not a great poet.

The event which made of Broch a poet seems to have coincided with the last stage of darkening in Europe. When the night arrived, Broch woke up. He awoke to a reality which so overwhelmed him that he translated it immediately into a dream, as is fitting for a man roused in the night. This dream is *The Death of Virgil*.

Critics have said that the book is written in lyrical prose, but this is not quite correct. The style, unique in its concentrated tension, bears more of a resemblance to those invocations of the Homeric hymns in which the God is summoned over and over again, each time with another residence, another mythological setting, another place of worship—as though the worshiper had to make sure, absolutely sure, that he could not miss the God. In the same way Broch invokes Life, or Death, or Love, or Time, or Space, as if he wanted to make sure, absolutely sure, that he would not miss the mark. This gives the monologue its passionate urgency, and brings out the tense, concentrated action of all true speculation.

In the "O"s of the invocations are imbedded the exciting descriptions, the extensive landscape painting in which the work is so very rich. These read like a long and tender song of farewell to all Western painters, and they transcend through their form of invocation these described objects, as though they embraced all that is beautiful or all that is ugly, all that is green or all earthly dustiness, all nobility or all vulgarity.

The subject of Broch's book, as the title indicates, is the last twenty-four hours of Virgil's life. But death is treated not merely as an event but as the ultimate achievement of man—whether in the sense that moments of dying are one's last and only chance for knowing what life was all about or in the sense that it is then one passes judgment upon one's own life. This judgment is not self-accusation, for it is too late for that, nor self-justification, for it is, in a way, too early for that; it is the ultimate effort to find the truth, the last definitive word for the whole story. This makes of the last judgment a human affair, to be settled by man himself, though at the limits of his forces and possibilities—as if he wanted to spare God this whole trouble. The "no longer and not yet" on this level means the no longer alive and the not yet dead; and the task is the conscious achievement of judgment and truth.

This grandiose concept of death as an ultimate task instead of as an ultimate calamity prevents Broch's speculations from falling into the trap of modern death-philosophy, for which life has in itself the germ of death and for which, consequently, the moment of death appears as the "goal of life." If death is the last task of the living man, then life has been given, not as a death-infected gift, but, rather, under certain conditions—that we forever "stand on the bridge that is spanned between invisibility and invisibility and nevertheless . . . are caught in the stream."

The actual subject matter of the book is the position of the artist in the world and in history: of the man who does not "do" like a human being; but "creates" like God—though in appearance only. The artist is forever excluded from reality, and banished into the "empty province of beauty." His playing at eternity—and this bewitching game that we call beauty—turns into the "laughter that destroys reality," the laughter that springs from the terrible intuition that the Creation itself, and not merely man's playing at creating, can be destroyed. With this laughter the poet "descends to the mob-patterns," to the cynical, debased vulgarity over which he had been carried on his litter through the slums of Brundisium. Mob and artist alike are greedy with self-idolatry, caring only for themselves, and excluded from all true community, which is based on helpfulness. "Intoxicated with loneliness," from which spring in equal part "the intoxication of blood, the intoxication of death, and . . . the intoxication of beauty," they are both equally treacherous, equally unconcerned with truth, therefore entirely unreliable and in need of forgetting reality, by means of beauty or circus games; both are intoxicated with "empty forms and empty words."

Because the "no longer and not yet" cannot be bridged with the rainbow of beauty, the poet is bound to fall "into vulgarity . . . where vulgarity is at its worst, into literarity." From this insight rises the decision which becomes the central plot of the story, the decision to burn the *Aeneid*, to have the work "consumed by the fire of reality." This deed, this sacrifice, suddenly appears as the only escape left from the "empty province of beauty," the only door through which, even when dying and in the very last moment, the poet may still perceive the promised land of reality and human fellowship.

It is at this moment that the friends enter the scene, trying to prevent what clearly are mere fever delusions of the dying man. There follows the long dialogue between Virgil and Octavian—one of the most truthful and impressive pieces of writing in all historical fiction—which ends with the abandonment of this sacrifice. The sacrifice, after all, would have been made only for the salvation of the soul, out of anxiety about the self, for the sake of the symbol—while the abandonment of the plan and the gift of the manuscript win from the face of the imperial friend a last happy smile.

Then comes death, the boat ride down to the depths of the elements when gently, one after another, the friends disappear, and man returns in peace from the long voyage of freedom into the quiet waiting of an inarticulate universe. His death seemed to him a happy death: for he had found the bridge with which to span the abyss that yawns between the "no longer and not yet" of history, between the "no longer" of the old laws and the "not yet" of the new saving word, between life and death: "Not quite here but yet at hand; that is how it has sounded and how it would sound."

The book is written in a very beautiful and extremely complicated German; the achievement of the translator is beyond praise.

What Is Existential Philosophy?

T HE HISTORY OF existential philosophy goes back at least a hundred years. It began with Schelling's late work and with Kierkegaard. From Nietzsche, it took innumerable new directions, many of which still remain unexplored today. It was a major element in Bergson's thought and in so-called life philosophy, and in post-war Germany it has reached, in the work of Scheler, Heidegger, and Jaspers, a previously unattained clarity in articulating the central concerns of modern philosophy.

The term "existence" denotes simply the Being (*Sein*) of man, independent of all the qualities and capabilities that any individual may possess and that are accessible to psychological investigation. What Heidegger once correctly remarked of "life philosophy" also applies, then, to existential philosophy. The name is as redundant and therefore as meaningless as "botany" is for the study of plants. It is, however, no coincidence that the word "existence" has taken the place of the word

Published in German as "Was ist Existenz-Philosophie?" in Arendt's *Sechs Essays*, Heidelberg, 1948. A version in English, "What Is Existenz Philosophy?," appeared in *Partisan Review*, XVIII/1, 1946. The version given here was translated by Robert and Rita Kimber.

"Being," and in this terminological change one of the fundamental problems of modern philosophy is contained.

With a comprehensiveness never achieved before him, Hegel provided a philosophical explanation for all the phenomena of nature and history and brought them together in a strangely unified whole. His philosophy, of which no one could ever be quite sure whether it provided a residence or a prison for reality, was truly the "owl of Minerva that takes flight only at dusk." For immediately after Hegel's death it became apparent that his system represented the last word of all western philosophy, at least to the extent that, since Parmenides, it had not—for all its diverse turns and apparent internal contradictions—ever dared call into question the unity of thought and Being: *to gar auto esti noein te kai einai*. Those who came after Hegel either followed in his footsteps or rebelled against him, and what they were rebelling against, and despairing of, was philosophy itself, the postulated identity of thought and Being.

This epigonal character is common to all the so-called schools of modern philosophy. They all attempt to re-establish the unity of thought and Being, whether they achieve that harmony by proclaiming the primacy of matter (materialism) or of mind (idealism) or whether they play with various perspectives to create a whole that bears the stamp of Spinoza.

The Phenomenological Attempt at Reconstruction

Pragmatism and phenomenology are the most recent and interesting of the epigonal philosophical schools of the last hundred years. Phenomenology has been particularly influential in contemporary philosophy, a fact due neither to coincidence nor solely to this school's methodology. Husserl's attempt to re-establish the ancient tie between Being and thought that had always guaranteed man his home in the world made use of a detour that postulates the intentional structure of consciousness. Because every act of consciousness has by nature an object, I can be sure of at least one thing, namely, that I "have" the objects of my consciousness. The question of Being, not to mention the question of reality, can thus be "bracketed." As a conscious being I can conceive of all beings, and as consciousness I am, in my human mode, the Being of the world. (The seen tree, the tree as object of my consciousness, does not have to be the "real" tree; it is in any case the real object of my consciousness.)

The modern sense of the world's discomfiting nature has always originated in the perception that individual things have been torn out of their functional context. Modern literature and much of modern painting offers incontrovertible evidence of this. However one chooses to interpret this sense of unease sociologically or psychologically, its philosophical basis is this: The functional context of the world in which I too am included can always explain and justify why, for example, there are tables or chairs at all. But it will never be able to make me understand why *this* table *is*. And it is the existence of *this* table, quite apart from tables in general, that evokes the philosophical shock.

Phenomenology seemed to solve this problem, which is much more than a purely theoretical one. In its phenomenological description of consciousness, it defined these isolated things that had been torn out of their functional context as the objects on which arbitrary acts of consciousness seized; and by virtue of the "stream of consciousness," it seemed to reintegrate them into human life. Indeed, Husserl even claimed that by means of this detour via consciousness and of a comprehensive gathering together of all the factual material of consciousness (a *mathesis universalis*) he would be capable of reconstituting this world now shattered into pieces. Such a reconstituting of the world by consciousness would amount to a second creation in the sense that through this reconstitution the world would lose its contingent character, which is to say its character of reality, and it would no longer appear to man as a world given, but as one created by him.

This basic tenet of phenomenology comprises the most original and most modern attempt to provide a new intellectual foundation for humanism. Most intimately bound up with the sense of life that gave rise to phenomenology is Hofmannsthal's famous letter of farewell to Stefan George, in which he takes sides with the "little things" and against big words because it is in those little things that the mystery of reality lies hidden. Husserl and Hofmannsthal are both classicists if classicism is the attempt—by means of an utterly rigorous imitation of the classic vision, which is to say, of man's sense of being at home in the world— to conjure up a new home from a world perceived as alien. Husserl's phrase "to the things themselves" is no less a magic formula than Hofmannsthal's "little things." If we still could achieve anything by magic—in an age whose only good is that all magic fails in it—we would indeed have to begin with the smallest and seemingly most modest of things, with unpretentious "little things," with unpretentious words.

It was of course this apparent unpretentiousness that made Husserl's analyses of consciousness (analyses that Jaspers always considered irrelevant for philosophy because he had no use for either magic or classicism) so influential for both Heidegger and Scheler in their youth, even though Husserl would contribute little of its concrete content to existential philosophy. The widely accepted belief that Husserl's influence was only of methodological importance is correct in the sense that he liberated modern philosophy, to which he did not really belong, from the bonds of historicism. In the wake of Hegel and under the influence of an extremely intense interest in history, philosophy threatened to degenerate into speculation on the possibility that some kind of inherent law was manifested in history. It is irrelevant here whether this speculation was optimistic or pessimistic in tone, whether it tried to see progress as inevitable or decline as predestined. The key point in either case was simply, as Herder put it, that man was like an "ant" that "only crawls on the wheel of destiny." Because Husserl's focus on "the things themselves" cut off this kind of idle speculation and insisted on separating the phenomenally verifiable content of an event from its genesis, it had a liberating influence in the sense that man himself, not the historical or natural or biological or psychological flow in which he was caught up, once again became the main concern of philosophy.

This liberation of philosophy had great repercussions, but Husserl himself, who was totally devoid of any sense of history, never really grasped the implications of this his negative accomplishment. This accomplishment has become much more important than Husserl's positive philosophy, in which he tries to comfort us about the very point in which all of modern philosophy can take no comfort whatsoever, namely, that man is forced to affirm a Being that he did not create and that is alien to his very nature. By transforming this alien Being into consciousness, he tries to give the world a human face again, just as Hofmannsthal, with the magic of little things, tries to reawaken in us the old tenderness toward the world. But what dooms this modern humanism, this expression of good will toward modesty, is the equally modern hubris that underlies it and that hopes—either secretly, as in Hofmannsthal, or openly and naively, as in Husserl—to become after all and in this quite inconspicuous way what man cannot be: the creator of the world and of himself.

In contrast to Husserl's arrogant modesty, non-derivative modern philosophy attempts in a number of different ways to reconcile itself to the fact that man is not the creator of the world. On the other hand, and always where it is best, it tries to place man where Schelling, in a typical misunderstanding of his own thinking, placed God: in the role of the "lord of Being."

Kant's Destruction of the Old World and Schelling's Call for a New One

To my knowledge, the word "existence" used in the modern sense appears for the first time in Schelling's late work. Schelling knew precisely what he was rebelling against when he proposed his "positive philosophy" as a counterforce to "negative philosophy," to the philosophy of pure thought. His positive philosophy took as its point of departure "existence . . . [which] initially it possesses only in the form of the pure That." He knew that with this step philosophy had taken its final leave of the "contemplative life." He knew that it was "the I that had given the signal for this change of direction" because the philosophy of pure thought, in its failure "to explain the arbitrariness of events and the reality of things," had brought "the I to the point of utter despair." This despair underlies all modern irrationalism, all modern hostility to mind and reason.

Modern philosophy begins with the realization that the What will never be able to explain the That; it begins with the overpowering and shocking perception of an inherently empty reality. The more empty of all qualities reality appears, the more immediately and nakedly appears the only thing about it that remains of interest: *that* it is. That is why from its very outset this philosophy has celebrated chance as the form in which reality directly accosts man as uncertain, incomprehensible, and unpredictable. And that is why Jaspers identifies death, guilt, fate, and chance as the philosophical "border situations" that drive us to philosophize, because in all these experiences we find we cannot escape reality or solve its mysteries by thought. In these situations man realizes that he is dependent not on anything specific or even on his own general limitations but simply on the fact that he *is*.

Because *essentia* therefore appears to have nothing more to do with *existentia*, modern philosophy turns away from the sciences, which investigate the What of things. From Kierkegaard's perspective, the objective truth of science is irrelevant because it does not bear on the question of existence. And subjective truth, the truth of "that which exists," is a paradox because it can never be objective, never universally valid. If Being and thinking are no longer the same, if thinking no longer enables me to penetrate the true reality of things because the nature of things has nothing to do with their reality, then science can be whatever it likes; it no longer yields up any truth to man, no truth of any interest to man. This turning away from science has often been misunderstood, primarily because of Kierkegaard's example, as an attitude deriving from Christianity. But for this philosophy, intent on reality as it is, the point is not that, in view of a truer and better world, preoccupation with the things of this world (as *curiositas* or *dispersio*) detract from the salvation of the soul. What this philosophy wants is clearly this world, whose only great failing, however, is that it has lost its reality.

The unity of thought and Being presupposed the pre-established coincidence of *essentia* and *existentia*; that is, everything thinkable also existed, and everything extant, because it was knowable, also had to be rational. Kant, who is the real, though secret, as it were, founder of modern philosophy and who has also remained its secret king until this very day, shattered that unity. Kant robbed man of the ancient security in Being by revealing the antinomy inherent in the structure of reason; and by his analysis of synthetic propositions, he proved that in any proposition that makes a statement about reality, we reach beyond the concept (the *essentia*) of any given thing. Even Christianity had not impinged on this security, but only reinterpreted it into a "divine plan for salvation." But now one could not be certain of the meaning, or the Being, of the earthly Christian world, nor could one be certain of the eternally present Being of the ancient cosmos, and even the traditional definition of truth as *aequatio intellectus et rei* no longer held.

Well before Kant's revolutionizing of the western concept of Being, Descartes posed the question of reality in a very modern way, only to answer it in a thoroughly traditional way. The question of whether Being as such *is*, is every bit as modern as the answer of *cogito ergo sum* is pointless, for as Nietzsche noted, this answer in no way proves the existence of the *ego cogitans* but, at best, only the existence of *cogitare*.

In other words, no truly living I can ever emerge from "I think," but only an I that is a creation of thought. This is the crucial thing we have known since Kant.

More derives from Kant's destruction of the ancient unity of thought and Being than we generally realize in the history of secularization. Kant's refutation of the ontological proof of God's existence destroyed any rational belief in God based on the proposition that anything accessible to reason had to exist, a belief that is not only older than Christianity but also probably much more firmly rooted in the European mind since the Renaissance. This so-called disappearance of God from the world, the knowledge that we cannot rationally prove the existence of God, had as serious implications for the concepts of ancient philosophy as it did for the Christian religion. In a godless world, man in his "abandonment" or in his "individual autonomy" is accessible to interpretation. For every modern philosopher—and not just for Nietzsche—this interpretation becomes the touchstone of his philosophy.

Hegel can be regarded as the last of the old philosophers because he was the last to evade this question successfully. Schelling marks the beginning of modern philosophy because he explicitly states that he is concerned with the individual who "wants a providential God" . . . who "is the lord of Being," and by "individual" here Schelling means "the individual freed of the universal," that is, the real human being, for "it is not the universal in man that desires happiness but the individual." This astonishingly forthright articulation of the individual's claim on happiness (after Kant's contempt for the old desire for happiness made it by no means a simple matter to declare one's allegiance to it again) contains more than a desperate wish to return to the security of Providence. What Kant had not understood when he destroyed the classical concept of Being was that he called into question the reality not only of the individual but also of everything. Indeed, he implied what Schelling now stated explicitly: "Nothing universal exists at all, only the individual, and the *universal being* (*Wesen*) exists only if it is the *absolute individual* (*Einzelwesen*)."

With this position, which followed directly from Kant, man was cut off from the absolute, rationally accessible realm of ideas and universal values and left in the midst of a world where he had nothing left to hold onto—not his reason, which was obviously inadequate for an understanding of Being, nor the ideals of his reason, whose existence could not be proved, nor the universal, which in turn existed only in the form of himself.

From this time on the word "existing" has been used as the opposite of what is only thought, only contemplated; used as the concrete as opposed to the merely abstract, as the individual as opposed to the merely universal. The consequence of this was that philosophy, which had been thinking exclusively in concepts ever since Plato, had now lost its faith in concepts; and, ever since, philosophers have never quite been able to shake, as it were, the guilty conscience they feel for indulging in philosophy at all.

The purpose of Kant's destruction of the ancient concept of Being was to establish the autonomy of man, what he himself called the dignity of man. He is the first philosopher to attempt to understand man entirely within the context of laws inherent in man and to separate him out from the universal context of Being in which he is only one thing among others (even though he is a *res cogitans* as opposed to a *res extensa*). This represents the philosophical articulation of what Lessing regarded as man's intellectual coming-of-age, and it is no coincidence that this philosophical declaration coincides with the French Revolution. Kant is truly *the* philosopher of the French Revolution. Just as it was decisive for the historical development of the nineteenth century that nothing disappeared as quickly as did the new revolutionary concept of the *citoyen*, so it was decisive for the development of post-Kantian philosophy that nothing disappeared as quickly as did this new concept of man that had just barely begun to emerge.

Kant's destruction of the ancient concept of Being went only halfway. Kant destroyed the old identity of Being and thought and, along with it, the idea of a pre-established harmony between man and the world. What he did not destroy, but, instead, implicitly retained, was another concept equally old and intimately linked to the idea of harmony. This was the concept of Being as a given, to whose laws man was always subject. Man could bear to live with this idea only if he had a sense of security in Being and of belonging to the world and felt certain that he could at least comprehend Being and the world's course. On this feeling rested the ancient world's and indeed the whole western world's concept of fate up to the nineteenth century (i.e., until the emergence of the novel). Without this pride of man's, neither tragedy nor western philosophy would have been possible. Nor did Christianity deny that man had insight into God's plan of salvation; and whether man owed this insight to his own godlike capacity for reason or to God's revelation was of no great importance. In either case, man remained privy to the secrets of the cosmos and of the course of the world.

What is true of Kant's destruction of the classic concept of Being holds even more for his new concept of the freedom of man, a concept in which the modernistic view of man's lack of freedom is anticipated. For Kant, man has the possibility, based in the freedom of his good will, to determine his own actions; the actions themselves, however, are subject to nature's law of causality, a sphere essentially alien to man. Once a human act leaves the subjective sphere, which is man's sphere of freedom, it enters the objective sphere, which is the sphere of causality, and loses its element of freedom. Man, who is free in himself, is nonetheless hopelessly at the mercy of the workings of a natural world alien to him, of a fate opposing him and destroying his freedom. This unfree freedom represents once again the antinomical structure of human being as it is situated in the world. At the same time that Kant made man the master and the measure of man, he also made him the slave of Being. Every modern philosopher since Schelling has protested against this degradation, and modern philosophy has remained preoccupied up to the present day with this paradoxical legacy of Kant's: just as man comes of age and is declared autonomous, he is also utterly debased. Man never seemed to have risen so high and at the same time to have fallen so low.

Since Kant, every philosophy has contained, on the one hand, an element of defiance and, on the other, either an open or hidden concept of fate. When Marx declared he no longer wanted to interpret the world but to change it, he stood, so to speak, on the threshold of a new concept of Being and world, by which Being and world were no longer givens but possible products of man. But even he, when he declared that freedom was achieved through insight into necessity, beat a quick retreat into the old safety and thus gave back to man, who in losing his hold on the world had also lost his pride, a measure of dignity that was now of little use to him. Nietzsche's *amor fati*, Heidegger's resoluteness, Camus's defiant attempt to take life on its own terms despite the absurdity of a human condition rooted in man's rootlessness in the world are all attempts at self-rescue by means of a retreat into the old safety. It is no coincidence that since Nietzsche the heroic gesture has become the characteristic pose of philosophy, for it does indeed require no little heroism to live in the world Kant left us. Modern philosophers with their modernistic heroic pose show only too clearly that they have been able to carry Kant's thinking through to its logical conclusions but have not been able to go one step beyond him. Indeed, in their logical consistency and their despair, they have mostly fallen a few steps behind him, for they have all, with the one great exception of Jaspers, at some point given up Kant's basic concept of human freedom and dignity.

When Schelling voiced his demand for a "real lord of Being," he wanted once again to have an active role in determining the course the world took, a role from which free man had been excluded since Kant. Schelling took refuge again in a philosophical god, because he accepted with Kant "the fact of man's fall (*Abfall*)" but did not share the extraordinary equanimity that allowed Kant to make his peace with that fact. For Kant's equanimity, which we find so imposing, derives ultimately from his firm rootedness in a tradition that regards philosophy as essentially identical with contemplation, a tradition that Kant himself, half unknowingly, helped to destroy. Schelling's "positive philosophy" took refuge in God so that God could "counteract the fact of the fall," that is, so that he could help man recover the reality he had lost at the very moment that he found his freedom.

The reason Schelling is usually neglected in discussions of existential philosophy is that no philosopher has adopted Schelling's resolution of the Kantian aporias posed by subjective freedom and objective nonfreedom. Instead of resorting to a "positive philosophy," later philosophers (with the exception of Nietzsche) have tried to reinterpret the human situation in order to somehow fit man back again into this world that has robbed him of his dignity. His ruin was not determined solely by fate but was part and parcel of his own Being. His downfall was not the fault of a hostile natural world completely ruled by the law of causality but was already anticipated in his own nature. That is why these philosophers relinquished Kant's concepts of the freedom and dignity of man as well as his ideas of humanity as the regulating principle in all political activity, and this in turn gave rise to that distinctive melancholy that has characterized all but the most superficial philosophy since Kierkegaard. It seemed still more acceptable to be subject to the "fall" as an inherent law in human existence than to fall at the hands of an alien world ruled by causality.

The Birth of the Self: Kierkegaard

Modern existential philosophy begins with Kierkegaard. There is not a single existential philosopher who does not show evidence of his influence. As we know, Kierkegaard's point of departure was a critique of Hegel (and, we might add, a conscious neglect of Schelling, with whose late philosophy Kierkegaard was familiar from lectures). Against Hegel's system, which presumed to comprehend and explain the "whole," Kierkegaard set the "individual," the single human being, for whom there is neither place nor meaning in a totality controlled by the world spirit. In other words, Kierkegaard's point of departure is the individual's sense of being lost in a world otherwise totally explained. The individual stands in constant contradiction to this explained world because his "existence," that is, the very fact of his altogether arbitrary existing (that I am *I* and no one else and that I *am* rather than not am) can neither be foreseen by reason nor resolved by it into something purely thinkable.

But this existence that I am living at this moment and that I cannot rationally comprehend is the only thing of which I can be really certain in the sense that I have incontrovertible evidence for it. It is therefore man's task "to become subjective," a consciously existing being constantly aware of the paradoxical implications of his life in the world. All essential questions of philosophy—such as those concerning the immortality of the soul, the freedom of man, the unity of the world—which is to say, all the questions whose antinomical structure Kant demonstrated in the antinomies of pure reason, can be comprehended only as "subjective truths," not known as objective ones. Socrates exemplifies the "existing" philosopher with his *"If* there is an immortality." "Was he therefore a doubter?" Kierkegaard continues in one of the greatest interpretations of a work rich in great interpretations. "By no means. On this 'if' he risks his entire life, he has the courage to meet death. . . . The Socratic ignorance . . . was thus an expression for the principle that the eternal truth is related to an existing individual, and that this truth must therefore be a paradox for him as long as he exists."[1]

The universal, with which philosophy had so long been preoccupied in its mode of pure cognition, was thus to be brought into a real

[1]The notes are at the end of the essay.

relationship to man. That relationship has to be a paradoxical one to the extent that man always remains an individual. The individual may well be able, by way of paradox, to comprehend the universal, make it the content of his existence, and so lead that paradoxical life that Kierkegaard reports himself as leading. If the universal is to become real at all and thus meaningful for man, man has to try to realize in his paradoxical life the contradiction that "the universal takes the form of the individual." Kierkegaard later interprets such a life with reference to the category of the "exception," the exception from the general, average, everyday life; an exception, furthermore, which man chooses to accept for himself only because God has called him to it to make him an example of what the paradox of human life in the world really means. In the exception, man as individual realizes the universal structures of existence per se. It is characteristic for all existential philosophy that it understands by "existential" essentially what Kierkegaard illustrated in the category of the exception. The key point of existential conduct is the constant realization (in contrast to mere contemplation) of the most universal elements of life.

The passion to become subjective is set in motion for Kierkegaard with the realized fear of death. Death is the event in which I am definitely alone, an individual cut off from everyday life. Thinking about death becomes an "act" because in it man makes himself subjective and separates himself from the world and everyday life with other men. Psychologically, the assumption underlying this inner technique of reflection is simply the idea that once I no longer exist my interest in what is must also come to an end. It is altogether characteristic of modern philosophy that so many thinkers have accepted this assumption innocently, as it were, and without closer inspection. On this premise rests not only the modern preoccupation with the inner life but also the fanatical determination, which also begins with Kierkegaard, to take the moment seriously, for it is the moment alone that guarantees existence, that is reality.

This new serious engagement with life that uses death as a point of departure does not, however, necessarily imply an affirmation of life or of human existence as such. In fact, only Nietzsche and, in his footsteps, Jaspers have explicitly made such an affirmation the basis of their philosophical thought, and this is why their philosophical deliberations have found a positive path into philosophy. Kierkegaard and Heidegger after him have always interpreted death as the incontrovertible "objection" to man's Being, as the proof of man's "nothingness." And in this Heidegger's analysis of death and of the characteristics of human life linked to it may well exceed Kierkegaard's in its force and precision.

It is clear that the inner activity characteristic of Kierkegaard, his "becoming subjective," leads directly out of philosophy. It has to do with philosophy only in the sense that philosophical reasons have to be found for the philosopher's rebellion against philosophy. Marx presents a similar case but at the opposite extreme, as it were. Philosophically, he likewise declared that man could change the world and should therefore stop interpreting it. They both wanted to move directly to action, and it did not occur to either of them to find a new basis for philosophy once they had begun to doubt the prerogative of contemplation and to despair of the possibility of purely contemplative cognition. The result was that Kierkegaard turned to psychology in the description of internal activity; Marx, to political science in the description of external activity, with the difference, however, that Marx did in fact return to and accept again the security of Hegelian philosophy, which he changed less by "turning it on its head" than he assumed he had. For philosophy, the replacement of Hegel's principle of spirit by Marx's principle of matter was not as significant as the restoration of the unity of man and world in a doctrinaire and purely hypothetical way, hence, one that would never prove convincing to modern man.

Kierkegaard became much more important than Marx for the later development of philosophy because he clung to his despair of philosophy. From him above all philosophy adopted its new concrete contents. The most important of these are as follows: *Death* as the guarantor of the *principium individuationis* because death, even though it is the most universal of all universals, nonetheless inevitably strikes me alone; *Chance* as the guarantor of a reality that is given and that, precisely because of its incalculability and the impossibility of reducing it to thought, overwhelms me; *Guilt* as the category of all human activity, which is doomed to failure not because of the world but by its own nature, in that I always take on responsibilities whose implications I cannot foresee, and in that, by the decisions I make, I am always obliged to neglect something else. Guilt thus becomes the mode by which I become real, by which I entangle myself in reality.

In Jaspers's *Psychologie der Weltanschauungen*, these new contents of philosophy appear for the first time in the utmost clarity. There, Jaspers calls them "border situations," in which the antinomical nature of man's being places him and which provide him with his real motive to pursue philosophy. Even in his early work, Jaspers tries to found an entirely new kind of philosophy on the basis of these situations, and he adds to those contents taken over from Kierkegaard another that he sometimes calls struggle and sometimes love but that in any case later becomes for him in his theory of "communication" the new form of philosophical discourse. Unlike Jaspers, Heidegger attempts to use these new elements to revive systematic philosophy in the most traditional sense.

The Self as Being and Nothingness: Heidegger

Heidegger's attempt to re-establish an ontology, against and in spite of Kant, led to far-reaching changes in traditional philosophical terminology. For this reason, Heidegger always appears to be, at first glance, far more revolutionary than Jaspers, and this terminological façade has interfered a great deal with the correct assessment of his philosophy. He has said explicitly that he wants to re-establish an ontology, and all he can mean by that is that he intends to reverse the destruction of the classical concept of Being initiated by Kant. There is no reason not to take this intention seriously, even if one should arrive at the conclusion that ontology in the traditional sense cannot be re-established on the basis of the new contents derived from the rebellion against philosophy.[2]

Heidegger has never really established his ontology, because the second volume of Being and Time (Sein und Zeit) has never appeared. To the question of the meaning of Being he has provided the provisional and inherently unintelligible answer that temporality is the meaning of Being. This implies—and his analysis of Dasein (i.e., the being of man) as conditioned by death spells out—that the meaning of Being is nothingness. Heidegger's attempt to provide a new foundation for metaphysics has not ended, then, with the promised second volume in which he intended to use an analysis of man's being to elucidate the meaning of Being as such. It has ended instead with a thin brochure titled What Is Metaphysics? (Was ist Metaphysik?), in which Heidegger shows with reasonable consistency and despite all his obvious verbal tricks and sophistries that Being in a Heideggerian sense is Nothing.

The fascination that the idea of nothingness has held for modern philosophy does not necessarily suggest a nihilistic bias in that philosophy. If we consider the problem of nothingness in our context of a philosophy in revolt against philosophy as pure contemplation and if we see it as an attempt to make us the "master of Being" and thus enable us to pose the philosophical questions that will enable us to progress immediately to action, then the idea that Being is really nothingness is of inestimable value. Proceeding from this idea, man can imagine that he stands in the same relationship to Being as the Creator stood before creating the world, which, as we know, was created *ex nihilo*. Then too, designating Being as nothingness brings with it the attempt to put behind us the definition of Being as what is given and to regard human actions not just as god-like but as divine. This is the reason—though it is not one Heidegger admits to—why in his philosophy nothingness suddenly becomes active and begins to "nihilate" (*nichten*). Nothing tries, as it were, to destroy the givenness of Being and "nihilatingly" (*nichtend*) to usurp Being's place. If Being, which I have not created, is the business of a being that I am not and do not know, then nothingness is perhaps the truly free domain of man. Since I cannot be a world-creating being it could perhaps be my role to be a world-destroying being. (Camus and Sartre are openly and clearly exploring these possibilities today.) This is, in any case, the philosophical basis of modern nihilism, with its origins reaching back into the old ontology; in it, the arrogant attempt to fit new questions and elements into the old ontological framework has come home to roost.

But regardless of how Heidegger's experiment has turned out, its great accomplishment was to pick up again the questions Kant had broached and that no one after him had developed further. In the ruins of the pre-established harmony of Being and thought, of *essentia* and *existentia*, of existents and the What of existents that can be comprehended by reason, Heidegger claims to have found a being in whom essence and existence are identical, and that being is man. His essence is his existence. "The substance of man is not spirit . . . but existence." Man has no substance; he consists in the fact *that* he is. We cannot inquire into the What of man the way we can into the What of a thing. We can only inquire into the Who of man.

Man as the identity of existence and essence seemed to provide a new key to the question of Being in general. To understand how seductive this idea was, we need only recall that for traditional metaphysics God was the being in whom essence and existence were one, in whom thinking and action were identical, and who therefore was declared the other-worldly fundament of all this-worldly Being. This was in fact an attempt to make man the "master of Being." Heidegger calls this the "ontically ontological pre-eminent rank of *Dasein*," a formulation that should not prevent us from understanding that it puts man in the exact same place that God had occupied in traditional ontology.

Heidegger calls the being of man *Dasein*. This lets him avoid using the term "man" and is by no means an example of arbitrary terminology. Its purpose is to resolve man into several modes of being that are phe-nomenologically demonstrable. That dispenses with all those human characteristics that Kant provisionally defined as freedom, human dig-nity, and reason, that arise from human spontaneity, and that therefore are not phenomenologically demonstrable because as spontaneous char-acteristics they are more than mere functions of being and because in them man reaches beyond himself. Behind Heidegger's ontological ap-proach lies a functionalism not unlike Hobbes's realism. If man consists in the fact that he is, he is no more than his modes of Being or functions in the world (or in society, Hobbes would say). Heidegger's functionalism and Hobbes's realism both end up proposing a model of the human being that says man would function even better in a preordained world because he would then be "freed" of all spontaneity. This realistic functionalism that sees man only as a conglomerate of modes of being is essentially arbitrary because no idea of man guides the selection of the modes of being. The "Self" takes the place of man in that the main characteristic of *Dasein* (the being of man) is that "in its Being it is concerned with itself." This self-reflective quality of *Dasein* can be comprehended "ex-istentially," and that is all that remains of man's power and freedom.

For Heidegger, this comprehension of one's own existence constitutes the philosophical act itself: "Philosophical inquiry itself has to be under-stood existentially as a possibility of being for every existing *Dasein*." Philosophy is the outstanding existential mode of *Dasein*. Ultimately, this is only a reformulation of the Aristotelian *bios theoretikos*, of the contemplative life as the highest possibility man can attain. This is all the more serious a matter because Heidegger's philosophy makes man a kind of *summum ens*, a "master of Being," to the extent that existence and essence are identical in him. Once man was discovered to be the being he had for so long considered God to be, it then turned out that such a being is also, in fact, powerless and that there is consequently no "master of Being." All that remains are anarchistic modes of being.

The nature of *Dasein* is not that it simply *is* but, rather, that in its being its primary concern is its being itself. This basic element is called "care," which underlies all the daily care-taking in the world. Care-taking has a genuinely self-reflective character. It only appears to be directed at whatever it happens to be occupied with at the moment. It actually does everything in the mode of the for-the-sake-of (*Um-willen*).

The Being for which *Dasein* cares is "existence," which is constantly threatened by death and is ultimately condemned to destruction. *Dasein* is in a constant relationship with this threatened existence. Only from the perspective of existence can all modes of behavior be understood and a unified analysis of man's being be derived. The structures of man's existence, that is, the structures of his That, Heidegger calls "existentials" and their structural interrelatedness he calls "existentiality." Heidegger calls "existentiell" the individual possibility of comprehending these existentials and thus existing in an explicit sense. In this concept of "existentiell" the question never laid to rest since Schelling and Kierkegaard, namely, how the universal can *be*, reappears again, together with the answer Kierkegaard had already given.

Apart from Nietzsche, who at least made an honest effort to make man a genuine "master of Being," Heidegger's is the first absolutely and uncompromisingly this-worldly philosophy. The crucial element of man's being is its being-in-the-world, and what is at stake for his being-in-the-world is quite simply survival in the world. That is the very thing that is denied man, and consequently the basic mode of being-in-the-world is alienation, which is felt both as homelessness and anxiety. In anxiety, which is fundamental fear of death, is reflected the not-being-at-home in the world. Being-in (*In-Sein*) enters into the existentiell mode of not-being-at-home. This is alienation.

Dasein could be truly itself only if it could pull back from its being-in-the-world into itself, but that is what its nature can never permit it to do, and that is why, by its very nature, it is always a falling away from itself. "*Dasein* is always at a remove from itself as genuine being-able-to-be-Self; it has fallen into the 'world.' " Only at death, which will take him out of the world, does man have the certainty of being himself. This Self is the Who of *Dasein*. ("With the term 'Self' we answer the question of the Who of *Dasein*.")

By bringing *Dasein* back to the Self without any detour by way of man, the question of the meaning of Being has fundamentally been given up and replaced with the question more fundamental to this philosophy, that is, the question of the meaning of the Self. But this question seems truly unanswerable, because a Self, taken in its absolute isolation, is meaningless; and if it is not isolated but is involved in the everyday life of the They, it is no longer Self. This ideal of the Self follows as a consequence of Heidegger's making of man what God was in earlier ontology. A being of this highest order is conceivable only as single and unique and knowing no equals. What Heidegger consequently designates as the "fall" includes all those modes of human existence in which man is not God but lives together with his own kind in the world.

Heidegger himself has refuted this passionate desire, bred of hubris, to become a Self, for never before has a philosophy shown as clearly as his that this goal is presumably the one thing that man can never achieve.

In the framework of Heidegger's philosophy man comes to his "fall" as follows: As being-in-the-world, man has not made himself but is "thrown" (*geworfen*) into this his being. He attempts to escape this thrown-into-ness (*Geworfenheit*) by means of a "projection" (*Entwurf*) in anticipation of death as his utmost possibility. But "in the structure of thrown-into-ness as well as in the structure of the projection lies essentially a nothingness": Man has not manipulated himself into being, and he does not ordinarily manipulate himself out of it again. (Suicide has no place in Heidegger's thought. But when Camus claims, "Il n'y a qu'un problème philosophique vraiment sérieux: c'est le suicide," he draws the logical conclusion from this position, but it is contrary to Heidegger's view, which does not leave man even the freedom to commit suicide.) In other words, the character of man's being is determined essentially by what man is *not*, his nothingness. The only thing that the Self can do to become a Self is "resolutely" to take this fact of its being upon itself, whereby, in its existence, it "is the negative ground of its nothingness."

In his "resolve" to become what man, because of his "nothingness," cannot become, namely, a Self, man realizes that "*Dasein as such* is guilty." Man's being is such that in constantly falling into the world it at the same time constantly hears the "call of conscience from the ground of its being." To live existentially therefore means: "Willing-to-have-conscience commits itself to this being-guilty." In this resolve, the Self constitutes itself.

The essential character of the Self is its absolute Self-ness, its radical separation from all its fellows. Heidegger introduced the anticipation of death as an existential in order to define this essential character, for it is in death that man realizes the absolute *principium individuationis*. Death alone removes him from connection with those who are his fellows and who as "They" constantly prevent his being-a-Self. Though death may be the end of *Dasein*, it is at the same time the guarantor that all that matters ultimately is myself. In experiencing death as nothingness as such, I have the opportunity to devote myself exclusively to being-a-Self and, in the mode of axiomatic guilt, to free myself once and for all from the world that entangles me.

What emerges from this absolute isolation is a concept of the Self as the total opposite of man. If since Kant the essence of man consisted in every single human being representing all of humanity and if since the French Revolution and the declaration of the rights of man it became integral to the concept of man that all of humanity could be debased or exalted in every individual, then the concept of Self is a concept of man that leaves the individual existing independent of humanity and representative of no one but himself—of nothing but his own nothingness. If Kant's categorical imperative insisted that every human act had to bear responsibility for all of humanity, then the experience of guilty nothingness insists on precisely the opposite: the destruction in every individual of the presence of all humanity. The Self in the form of conscience has taken the place of humanity, and being-a-Self has taken the place of being human.

Later, and after the fact, as it were, Heidegger has drawn on mythologizing and muddled concepts like "folk" and "earth" in an effort to supply his isolated Selves with a shared, common ground to stand on. But it is obvious that concepts of that kind can only lead us out of philosophy and into some kind of nature-oriented superstition. If it does not belong to the concept of man that he inhabits the earth together with others of his kind, then all that remains for him is a mechanical reconciliation by which the atomized Selves are provided with a common ground that is essentially alien to their nature. All that can result from that is the organization of these Selves intent only on themselves into an Over-self in order somehow to effect a transition from resolutely accepted guilt to action.

Characteristics of Human Existence: Jaspers

Historically speaking, it would have been more appropriate to begin this discussion of contemporary existential philosophy with Jaspers. His *Psychologie der Weltanschauungen*, the first edition of which appeared in 1919, is without doubt the first book of the new "school." But other good reasons spoke against starting with Jaspers, a purely external one being that Jaspers's major *Philosophy* (in three volumes) appeared some five years after *Sein und Zeit*. More important, however, is the fact that Jaspers's philosophy is still evolving and remains much more modern, whereby "modern" means simply that it continues to provide direct impulses for contemporary philosophical thought. Such impulses can be found in Heidegger too, of course, but it is inherent in their nature that they lead only to polemic or to radicalizations of Heidegger's position, such as we are witnessing in current French philosophy. In other words, Heidegger has either contributed his last word to contemporary philosophy, or he will have to break with his own philosophy. By contrast, the continuity of Jaspers's thought remains unbroken; he is an active participant in modern philosophy, and he will continue to contribute to its development and speak with a decisive voice in it.

In his *Psychologie der Weltanschauungen*, Jaspers breaks with traditional philosophy. In that work, he portrays and relativizes all philosophical systems as mythologizing structures to which man flees seeking protection from the real questions of his existence. Jaspers sees *Weltanschauungen* that claim to have grasped the meaning of life and systems that present themselves as "coherent theories of the Whole" as mere hollow "shells" that interfere with the experiencing of "border situations" and confer a false peace of mind that is inherently unphilosophical. Using the border situations as his point of departure, he attempts to develop a new type of philosophizing based on Kierkegaard and Nietzsche. The primary mission of this philosophizing is not to instruct; it consists of a "perpetual agitation, a perpetual *appeal* [italics mine] to the life force in oneself and in others." This is Jaspers's way of participating in that revolt against philosophy with which modern philosophy began. He attempts to transform philosophy into philosophizing and to find ways by which philosophical "results" can be communicated in such a way that they lose their character as results.

Communicability itself therefore becomes one of the central issues of this philosophy. In Jaspers's view, communication is the pre-eminent form of philosophical participation, which is at the same time communal philosophizing whose purpose is not to produce results but to "illuminate existence." The similarity of this method to Socrates's maieutic method is obvious, except that what Socrates would have called maieutic method, Jaspers calls appeal. This shift in emphasis is deliberate. Jaspers does indeed make use of the Socratic method, but in such a way that he removes from it its pedagogical character. In Jaspers, as in Socrates, there is no "philosopher" who has, since Aristotle, been thought to lead an existence distinct from that of other men. Jaspers does not retain even the Socratic priority of the questioner, for in communication the philosopher moves, as a matter of principle, among his equals, to whom he can appeal and who can in turn appeal to him. This consequently removes philosophy from the realm of scientific and scholarly disciplines with their specialized fields, and the philosopher consequently gives up special prerogatives of any and every kind.

To the extent that Jaspers communicates results, he expresses them in the form of a "playful metaphysics," presenting certain thought processes in a way that is always experimental and never rigidly fixed, having at the same time the character of suggestions that induce others to join with him in thought, to philosophize with him.

For Jaspers, existence is not a form of Being but a form of human freedom, the form in which "man as potential spontaneity rejects the conception of himself as mere result." Existence is not man's being as such and as a given; rather, "man is, in *Dasein*, possible existence." The word "existence" here means that man achieves reality only to the extent that he acts out of his own freedom rooted in spontaneity and "connects through communication with the freedom of others."

This gives new meaning to the inquiry into the That of reality, which cannot be resolved into thought without losing its character as reality. The That of given Being—whether as the reality of the world or as the unpredictability of our fellow human beings or as the fact that I have not created myself—becomes the backdrop from which human freedom declares itself distinct, becomes, as it were, the stuff from which it takes fire. That I cannot resolve reality into thought becomes the triumph of my potential freedom. Expressed paradoxically: Only because I have not made myself am I free. If I had made myself, I would have been able to foresee myself and therefore would have become unfree. Seen in this light, the question of the meaning of Being can be left in an abeyance that permits the following answer to it: "Being is so constituted that *Dasein* is possible."

We become aware of Being by proceeding in thought from the "imagined world of the merely thinkable" to the border of reality, which as a pure object of thought or pure possibility can no longer be grasped. This thinking our way to the borders of the thinkable Jaspers calls transcending, and his "playful metaphysics" is an orderly, sequential naming of such self-transcending movements of thought. Crucial to these movements is that man, as "master of his thoughts," is more than any of these movements of thought. Philosophizing itself consequently does not become the highest "existential" mode of man's being, but, rather, a preparation for encountering the reality of both myself and the world. "By passing beyond all knowledge of the world that would fit Being into fixed categories, philosophizing enters a state of suspension in which it appeals to my freedom and, in invoking transcendence, creates an arena of unlimited action." This "action" that arises from the "border situations" comes into the world through communication with others who as my fellows and through an appeal to the powers of reason common to us all guarantee us something universal. Through action, philosophizing creates the freedom of man in the world and thus becomes "the seed, however small, of a world's creation."

For Jaspers, thinking has the function of leading man to certain experiences in which thinking itself (but by no means thinking man) fails. In the failure of thought (but not of man) man—who as a real and free being is more than thought—experiences what Jaspers calls the "cipher of transcendence." That transcendence is experienced as a cipher only in failure is itself a sign of an existence that "realizes not only that it has not created its own *Dasein* and that as *Dasein* it is powerless to prevent its own certain destruction but also that even as freedom it does not owe its existence to itself alone."

Failure in Jaspers should not be confused with what Heidegger called falling or falling-into and what Jaspers himself calls "falling away (*Abgleiten*)." What Jaspers means is a fall away from real human being, a fall that he has often described, explaining it psychologically but not designating it (as Heidegger does) as a structurally inevitable phenomenon. For Jaspers, any ontology that claims it can say what Being really is is a falling away into an absolutizing of individual categories of being. The existential significance of such a falling away would be that it robs man of his freedom, which can only be maintained if man does not know what Being really is.

To put this in formal terms: Being is transcendence, and as such it is a "reality that cannot be transformed into potentiality," a reality I cannot imagine as not being—which I can imagine about individual beings. Not until my thinking comes up short against the That of reality do I experience the "weight of reality." The failure of thought is consequently the condition that makes existence possible, free existence that is constantly trying to transcend this merely given world—the condition that makes it possible for existence, encountering the "weight of reality," to find its way into reality and to belong to it in the only way in which human beings can belong to it, namely, by choosing it.

In failing, man learns that he can neither know nor create Being and therefore is not God. This experience makes him aware of the limitations of his existence, the extent of which he attempts to define by philosophizing. In his failure to transcend all limits he experiences the reality given him as the cipher of a Being that he himself is not.

It is the task of philosophy to free man "from the illusory world of what is only thinkable" and to let him "find his way home to reality." Philosophic thought can never get around the fact that reality cannot be resolved into what can be thought; indeed, the very purpose of philosophic thought is to "heighten . . . the intellectually irresolvable." This is all the more urgent in that the "reality of the thinker precedes his thinking" and his real freedom alone determines what he will and will not think.

The real essence of Jaspers's philosophy cannot be captured in a report like this one, because it is primarily found in the paths and movements his philosophizing itself takes. By way of these paths Jaspers has dealt with all the basic questions of contemporary philosophy without, however, answering or settling even a single one of them. He has, as it were, mapped the paths on which modern philosophizing has to travel if it does not want to end up in the blind alleys of a positivistic or a nihilistic fanaticism.

Of these paths, the most important would appear to be the following. Being as such is not knowable; it can be experienced only as something "all encompassing." This makes superfluous the ancient ontological search which, so to speak, kept a lookout in beings hoping to find Being, as if Being were a magical, omnipresent substance that makes present everything that is and that is manifest linguistically in the little word "is." Once the concrete world was freed from this specter of Being and from the illusion that we are capable of knowing that specter, philosophy was likewise freed from the necessity of having to explain everything monistically on the basis of one principle, that is, of this one omnipresent substance. Instead, we can accept the "fragmentation of Being" (in which context Being no longer means the Being of the ontologies), and we can accommodate the modern sense of alienation in the world and the modern desire to create, in a world that is no longer a home to us, a human world that could become our home. It is almost as if with the concept of Being as the "All-Encompassing," there were sketched in rough outline an island on which man, no longer threatened by the dark, inexplicable aura that in traditional philosophy clung to all beings like an extra quality, finally can have free rein.

The dimensions of this island of human freedom are marked by the border situations in which man experiences the limitations that directly determine the conditions of his freedom and provide the basis for his actions. Working from those dimensions he can "illuminate" his existence and define what he can and cannot do. And thus he can pass from mere "being-a-result" to "existence," which for Jaspers is only another term for being human in a determinate sense.

Existence itself is, by its very nature, never isolated. It exists only in communication and in awareness of others' existence. Our fellow-men are not (as in Heidegger) an element of existence that is structurally necessary but at the same time an impediment to the Being of Self. Just the contrary: Existence can develop only in the shared life of human beings inhabiting a given world common to them all. In the concept of communication lies a concept of humanity new in its approach though not yet fully developed that postulates communication as the premise for the existence of man. Within "all-encompassing" Being in any case, human beings live and act with each other; and in doing so, they neither pursue the phantom of Self nor live in the arrogant illusion that they constitute Being itself.

The movement of transcendence in thought, a movement basic to man's nature, and the failure of thought inherent in that movement bring us at least to a recognition that man as "master of his thoughts" is not only more than what he thinks—and this alone would probably provide basis enough for a new definition of human dignity—but is also constitutionally a being that is more than a Self and wills more than himself. With this understanding, existential philosophy has emerged from its period of preoccupation with Self-ness.

NOTES

1. Translation adapted from *Concluding Unscientific Postscript*, Princeton, NJ, 1941. —Ed.

2. Another question and one certainly worthy of discussion is whether Heidegger's philosophy has not been taken unduly seriously simply because it concerns itself with very serious matters. In his political behavior, in any case, Heidegger has provided us with more than ample warning that we should take him seriously. [As is well known, he entered the Nazi Party in a very sensational way in 1933—an act which made him stand out pretty much by himself among colleagues of the same calibre. Further, in his capacity as rector of Freiburg University, he forbade Husserl, his teacher and friend, whose lecture chair he had inherited, to enter the faculty, because Husserl was a Jew. Finally, it has been rumored that he has placed himself at the disposal of the French occupational authorities for the re-education of the German people.]

In view of the truly comic aspect of this development and in view of the no less genuinely abysmal state of political thought in German universities, one is tempted simply to dismiss the whole business. What speaks against such a dismissal is, among other things, that this entire mode of behavior has such exact parallels in German Romanticism that one can hardly believe them to result from the sheer coincidence of a purely personal failure of character. Heidegger is really (let us hope) the last Romantic—an immensely talented Friedrich Schlegel or Adam Müller, as it were, whose complete lack of responsibility is attributable to a spiritual playfulness that stems in part from delusions of genius and in part from despair.

[The bracketed passage is added from the English-language version of this essay published in 1946. It was apparently deleted from the original—but subsequently published—German version. See letters 40 and 42 (June 9 and July 9, 1946) in *Hannah Arendt–Karl Jaspers Correspondence 1926–1969*, edited by Lotte Kohler and Hans Saner, New York, 1992. —Ed.]

French Existentialism

A LECTURE ON philosophy provokes a riot, with hundreds crowd-
ing in and thousands turned away. Books on philosophical problems preaching no cheap creed and offering no panacea but, on
the contrary, so difficult as to require actual thinking sell like detective
stories. Plays in which the action is a matter of words, not of plot, and
which offer a dialogue of reflections and ideas run for months and are
attended by enthusiastic crowds. Analyses of the situation of man in the
world, of the fundaments of human relationship, of Being and the Void
not only give rise to a new literary movement but also figure as possible
guides for a fresh political orientation. Philosophers become newspa-
permen, playwrights, novelists. They are not members of university
faculties but "bohemians" who stay at hotels and live in the café—leading
a public life to the point of renouncing privacy. And not even success,
or so it seems, can turn them into respectable bores.

This is what is happening, from all reports, in Paris. If the Resistance
has not achieved the European revolution, it seems to have brought about,
at least in France, a genuine rebellion of the intellectuals, whose docility
in relation to modern society was one of the saddest aspects of the sad

The Nation, 162, February 23, 1946.

spectacle of Europe between wars. And the French people, for the time being, appear to consider the arguments of their philosophers more important than the talk and the quarrels of their politicians. This may reflect, of course, a desire to escape from political action into some theory which merely talks about action, that is, into activism; but it may also signify that in the face of the spiritual bankruptcy of the left and the sterility of the old revolutionary élite—which have led to the desperate efforts at restoration of all political parties—more people than we might imagine have a feeling that the responsibility for political action is too heavy to assume until new foundations, ethical as well as political, are laid down, and that the old tradition of philosophy which is deeply imbedded even in the least philosophical individual is actually an impediment to new political thought.

The name of the new movement is "Existentialism," and its chief exponents are Jean-Paul Sartre and Albert Camus, but the term Existentialism has given rise to so many misunderstandings that Camus has already publicly stated why he is "not an Existentialist." The term comes from the modern German philosophy which had a revival immediately after the First World War and has strongly influenced French thought for more than a decade; but it would be irrelevant to trace and define the sources of Existentialism in national terms for the simple reason that both the German and the French manifestations came out of an identical period and a more or less identical cultural heritage.

The French Existentialists, though they differ widely among themselves, are united on two main lines of rebellion: first, the rigorous repudiation of what they call *l'esprit de sérieux*; and, second, the angry refusal to accept the world as it is as the natural, predestined milieu of man.

L'esprit de sérieux, which is the original sin according to the new philosophy, may be equated with respectability. The "serious" man is one who thinks of himself *as* president of his business, *as* a member of the Legion of Honor, *as* a member of the faculty, but also *as* father, *as* husband, or as any other half-natural, half-social function. For by so doing he agrees to the identification of himself with an arbitrary function which society has bestowed. *L'esprit de sérieux* is the very negation of freedom, because it leads man to agree to and accept the necessary deformation which every human being must undergo when he is fitted into society. Since everyone knows well enough in his own heart that he is not identical with his function, *l'esprit de sérieux* indicates also bad faith in the sense of pretending. Kafka has already shown, in *Amerika*, how ridiculous and dangerous is the hollow dignity which grows out of identifying oneself with one's function. In that book the most dignified person in the hotel, upon whose word the hero's job and daily bread depend, rules out the possibility that he can make an error by invoking the argument of the "serious" man: "How could I go on being the head porter if I mistook one person for another?"

This matter of *l'esprit de sérieux* was first touched upon in Sartre's novel *La Nausée*, in a delightful description of a gallery of portraits of the town's respectable citizens, *les salauds*. It then became the central topic of Camus's novel *L'Etranger*. The hero of the book, the stranger, is an average man who simply refuses to submit to the serious-mindedness of society, who refuses to live as any of his allotted functions. He does not behave as a son at his mother's funeral—he does not weep; he does not behave as a husband—he declines to take marriage seriously even at the moment of his engagement. Because he does not pretend, he is a stranger whom no one understands, and he pays with his life for his affront to society. Since he refuses to play the game, he is isolated from his fellow-men to the point of incomprehensibility and isolated from himself to the point of becoming inarticulate. Only in a last scene, immediately before his death, does the hero arrive at some kind of explanation which conveys the impression that for him life itself was such a mystery and in its terrible way so beautiful that he did not see any necessity for "improving" upon it with the trimmings of good behavior and hollow pretensions.

Sartre's brilliant play *Huis Clos* belongs to the same category. The play opens in hell, appropriately furnished in the style of the Second Empire. The three persons gathered in the room—"L'enfer c'est les autres"—set the diabolical torture in motion by trying to pretend. Since, however, their lives are closed and since "you are your life and nothing else," pretense no longer works, and we see what would go on behind closed doors if people actually were stripped of the sheltering cover of functions derived from society.

Both Sartre's play and Camus's novel deny the possibility of a genuine fellowship between men, of any relationship which would be direct, innocent, free of pretense. Love in Sartre's philosophy is the will to be loved, the need for a supreme confirmation of one's own existence. For

Camus love is a somewhat awkward and hopeless attempt to break through the isolation of the individual.

The way out of pretense and serious-mindedness is to play at being what one really is. Again Kafka indicated in the last chapter of *Amerika* a new possibility of authentic life. The great "Nature Theater" where everyone is welcome and where everybody's unhappiness is resolved is not by accident a theater. Here everybody is invited to choose his role, to play at what he is or would like to be. The chosen role is the solution of the conflict between mere functioning and mere being, as well as between mere ambition and mere reality.

The new "ideal" becomes, in this context, the actor whose very profession is pretending, who constantly changes his role, and thus can never take any of his roles seriously. By playing at what one is, one guards one's freedom as a human being from the pretenses of one's functions; moreover, only by playing at what he really is, is man able to affirm that he is never identical with himself as a thing is identical with itself. An inkpot is always an inkpot. Man is his life and his actions, which are never finished until the very moment of his death. He *is* his existence.

The second common element of French Existentialism, the insistence upon the basic homelessness of man in the world, is the topic of Camus's *Le Mythe de Sisyphe: Essai sur l'Absurde*, and of Sartre's *La Nausée*. For Camus man is essentially the stranger because the world in general and man as man are not fitted for each other; that they are together in existence makes the human condition an absurdity. Man is the only "thing" in the world which obviously does not belong in it, for only man does not exist simply as a man among men in the way animals exist among animals and trees among trees—all of which necessarily exist, so to speak, in the plural. Man is basically alone with his "revolt" and his "clairvoyance," that is, with his reasoning, which makes him ridiculous because the gift of reason was bestowed upon him in a world "where everything is given and nothing ever explained."

Sartre's notion of the absurdity, the contingency, of existence is best represented in the chapter of *La Nausée* which appears in the current issue of the *Partisan Review* under the title "The Root of the Chestnut Tree." Whatever exists, so far as we can see, has not the slightest reason for its existence. It is simply *de trop*, superfluous. The fact that I can't even imagine a world in which, instead of many too many things, there would be nothing only shows the hopelessness and senselessness of man's being eternally entangled in existence.

Here Sartre and Camus part company, if we may judge from the few works of theirs which have reached this country. The absurdity of existence and the repudiation of *l'esprit de sérieux* are only points of departure for each. Camus seems to have gone on to a philosophy of absurdity, whereas Sartre seems to be working toward some new positive philosophy and even a new humanism.

Camus has probably protested against being called an Existentialist because for him the absurdity does not lie in man as such or in the world as such but only in their being thrown together. Since man's life, being laid in the world, is absurd, it must be lived as absurdity—lived, that is, in a kind of proud defiance which insists on reason despite the experience of reason's failure to explain anything; insists on despair since man's pride will not allow him the hope of discovering a sense he cannot figure out by means of reason; insists, finally, that reason and human dignity, in spite of their senselessness, remain the supreme values. The absurd life then consists in constantly rebelling against all its conditions and in constantly refusing consolations. "This revolt is the price of life. Spread over the whole of an existence, it restores its grandeur." All that remains, all that one can say yes to, is chance itself, the *hazard roi* which has apparently played at putting man and world together. " 'I judge that everything is well,' said Oedipus; and this word is sacred. It resounds in the ferocious universe which is the limit of man. . . . It makes of destiny an affair of men which should be settled among men." This is precisely the point where Camus, without giving much explanation, leaves behind all modernistic attitudes and comes to insights which are genuinely modern, the insight, for instance, that the moment may have arrived "when creation is no longer taken tragically; it is only taken seriously."

For Sartre, absurdity is of the essence of things as well as of man. Anything that exists is absurd simply because it exists. The salient difference between the things of the world and the human being is that things are unequivocally identical with themselves, whereas man— because he sees and knows that he sees, believes and knows that he believes—bears within his consciousness a negation which makes it impossible for him ever to become one with himself. In this single respect—in respect of his consciousness, which has the germ of negation in it—man is a creator. For this is of man's own making and not merely given, as the world and his existence are given. If man becomes aware of his own consciousness and its tremendous creative possibilities, and renounces the longing to be identical with himself as a thing is, he realizes that he depends upon nothing and nobody outside himself and that he can be free, the master of his own destiny. This seems to be the essential meaning of Sartre's play *Les Mouches* (*The Flies*), in which Orestes, by taking upon himself the responsibility for the necessary killing of which the town is afraid, liberates the town and takes the Flies—the Erinyes of bad conscience and of the dark fear of revenge—with him. He himself is immune because he does not feel guilty and regrets nothing.

It would be a cheap error to mistake this new trend in philosophy and literature for just another fashion of the day because its exponents refuse the respectability of institutions and do not even pretend to that seriousness which regards every achievement as a step in a career. Nor should we be put off by the loud journalistic success with which their work has been accompanied. This success, equivocal as it may be in itself, is nevertheless due to the quality of the work. It is also due to a definite modernity of attitude which does not try to hide the depth of the break in Western tradition. Camus especially has the courage not even to look for connections, for predecessors and the like. The good thing about Sartre and Camus is that they apparently suffer no longer from nostalgia for the good old days, even though they may know that in an abstract sense those days were actually better than ours. They do not believe in the magic of the old, and they are honest in that they make no compromises whatever.

Yet if the revolutionary élan of these writers is not broken by success, if, symbolically speaking, they stick to their hotel rooms and their cafés, the time may come when it will be necessary to point out "seriously" those aspects of their philosophy which indicate that they are still dangerously involved in old concepts. The nihilistic elements, which are obvious in spite of all protests to the contrary, are not the consequences of new insights but of some very old ideas.

The Ivory Tower
of Common Sense

T HIS BOOK IS a collection of thirty-two essays, most of them gathered from Dewey's writings during the past ten years. The exceptions are the introductory chapter, written especially for this volume, and one essay which dates back to the end of the last century. The selection is excellent and offers a consistent picture of Dewey's philosophy.

What makes it so difficult to review this philosophy is that it is equally hard to agree or to disagree with it. How could one possibly agree with a philosophy, priding itself on its closeness to reality and experience, which is actually so lost in abstract argument that, following it, and its evaluation of past and present history, one feels oneself happily inside a paradise which rapidly turns out to be a fool's paradise? Dewey earnestly holds that the source of all the social and political evils of our time is laissez-faire (supposed to have caused the outstripping of social knowledge by scientific knowledge); but a glance at today's or yesterday's newspaper invariably teaches us that hell can be properly established only through the very opposite of laissez-faire, through scientific planning. (This, of course, does not say anything against science as such.) Even

A review of *Problems of Men*, by John Dewey, *The Nation*, 163, October 19, 1946.

more out of tune with reality are Dewey's complacent judgments on those evil times of the past in which men were still slaves and serfs; only a great scholar living in the ivory tower of common sense could be so completely unaware of the fact that certain categories of men today are far worse off than any slave or serf ever was. Nor do we need to evoke the extremities of the death factories. Concentration camps have outlived the downfall of the Nazi regime and are accepted as a matter of course; their inmates belong to a new class of human beings who have lost even the elementary human usefulness for society as a whole of which slaves and serfs were never deprived.

But hard as it is to agree with Dewey, it seems even harder to disagree with him, for such disagreement is to disagree with common sense personified. And who would dare or like to do that? Dewey's arguments, taken in themselves, without any reflection upon reality and experience, and without any remembrance of the commonplace philosophical questions as they appear and have appeared throughout all time (in proverbs, in prophecy, in tragedy, in art, up to the highest philosophical speculations)—those arguments are always sound and obvious, as though one simply could not think otherwise. This fantastic disparity between the argumentation itself, which in an abstract sense is always right, and the basis of experience, which in its historical actuality is always wrong, may be understood in the light of Dewey's central concept, which is not a concept of Man but a concept of Science. Dewey's main effort aims at applying to the social sciences the scientific concepts of truth as a working hypothesis. This is supposed to put the social sciences on a sound epistemological basis from which they and we will progress until the supposed gap between natural and social science is closed.

The intention of this approach is certainly humanistic in essence; it tries sincerely to humanize science, to make scientific results usable for the human community. The trouble is only that, at the same time, science, and not man, takes the lead in the argument, with the result that man is degraded into a puppet which through education—through "formation of attitudes," through "techniques for dealing with human nature"—has to be fitted into a scientifically controlled world. As though it was not man who invented science but some superhuman ghost who prepared this world of ours and only, through some incomprehensible obliviousness, forgot to change man into a scientific animal; as though man's problem were to conform and to adjust himself to some abstract niceties. As though science could ever be more than man; and, conse-quently, as though such a gap between scientific and social knowledge could ever be more than wishful thinking.

Superstition lies at the basis of all radical optimism and all radical pessimism, whose basic concepts of progress and decline resemble each other like hostile brothers. Both are truths in Dewey's sense, for both are working hypotheses in the historical sciences. Both stem from old and time-honored myths without which they cannot be understood or properly appreciated. The myth of progress presupposes that the begin-ning of mankind was hell and that we move forward to some kind of paradise; the myth of decline presupposes that the beginning was paradise and that from then on, possibly with the help of the original sin, we come closer and closer to hell. There is no doubt that great historians have used the progress myth while others, no less great, have used the other. But if we are serious about truth in history, we had better leave the delightful playground of mythology.

Apart from these considerations, which are concerned only with Dewey as a philosopher and not with Dewey as a great scholar, this book becomes excellent as soon as it deals with analyses of the scientific mind and the functioning of scientific experience. Here Dewey is extremely modern, in the best sense of the word, especially when he tries to "discover in terms of an experienced state of affairs the connection that exists between physical subject-matter and the common-sense objects of everyday experience," and when he shows that "modern experience is expansive since it is marked off by its constant concern for potentialities of experience as yet unrealized." In other words, what Dewey can and does give is a kind of logic for the scientific mind. That this is an important subject for science and scientists is beyond doubt. That it is the only concern of philosophy, or even one of its chief concerns, is a highly controversial question.

The Image of Hell

AS THE FORMAL accusers of the German people before the bar of the civilized world, it may be properly demanded of the Jews that they prepare . . . a bill of indictment. It is easily done. . . . The blood of Hitler's victims cries from the ground. The purpose of our bill is to make the cry articulate."

But if the authors of *The Black Book* thought the story of the last decade an easy one to tell, they are sadly mistaken. The awkwardness of their book, for all its good intentions, is sufficient proof of that. It is not, however, simply a matter of technical skill. True, the material could have been better organized, the style less journalistic, and the sources selected more scientifically. But such and other improvements would have made even more obvious the discrepancy between the facts themselves and any possible use of them for political purposes. *The Black Book* fails because its authors, submerged in a chaos of details, were

A review of *The Black Book: The Nazi Crime Against the Jewish People*, compiled and edited by the World Jewish Congress, the Jewish Anti-Fascist Committee, the Vaad Leumi, and the American Committee of Jewish Writers, Artists and Scientists, New York, 1946, and *Hitler's Professors*, by Max Weinreich, New York, 1946, *Commentary*, II/3, 1946.

unable to understand or make clear the nature of the facts confronting them.

The facts are: that six million Jews, six million human beings, were helplessly, and in most cases unsuspectingly, dragged to their deaths. The method employed was that of accumulated terror. First came calculated neglect, deprivation, and shame, when the weak in body died together with those strong and defiant enough to take their own lives. Second came outright starvation, combined with forced labor, when people died by the thousands but at different intervals of time, according to their stamina. Last came the death factories—and they all died together, the young and the old, the weak and the strong, the sick and the healthy; not as people, not as men and women, children and adults, boys and girls, not as good and bad, beautiful and ugly—but brought down to the lowest common denominator of organic life itself, plunged into the darkest and deepest abyss of primal equality, like cattle, like matter, like things that had neither body nor soul, nor even a physiognomy upon which death could stamp its seal.

It is in this monstrous equality without fraternity or humanity—an equality in which cats and dogs could have shared—that we see, as though mirrored, the image of hell.

Beyond the capacities of human comprehension is the deformed wickedness of those who established such equality. But equally deformed and beyond the reach of human justice is the innocence of those who died in this equality. The gas chamber was more than anybody could have possibly deserved, and in the face of it the worst criminal was as innocent as the new-born babe. Nor is the monstrousness of this innocence made any easier to bear by such adages as "better to suffer ill than do ill." What mattered was not so much that those whom an accident of birth condemned to death obeyed and functioned to the last moment as frictionlessly as those whom an accident of birth condemned to life (this is so well known, there is no use hiding it). Even beyond that was the fact that innocence and guilt were no longer products of human behavior; that no possible human crime could have fitted this punishment, no conceivable sin, this hell in which saint and sinner were equally degraded to the status of possible corpses. Once inside the death factories, everything became an accident completely beyond control of those who did the suffering and those who inflicted it. And in more than one case, those who inflicted the suffering one day became the sufferers the next.

Human history has known no story more difficult to tell. The monstrous equality in innocence that is its inevitable *leitmotif* destroys the very basis on which history is produced—which is, namely, our capacity to comprehend an event no matter how distant we are from it.

The spell is broken only when we come to the story of Jewish resistance and the Battle of the Warsaw Ghetto. *The Black Book*, however, deals with these events even more inadequately than with the others, devoting a mere nine poorly written pages to the Ghetto battle—and without even mentioning Shlomo Mendelsohn's masterful analysis of the event that appeared in the *Menorah Journal* of spring, 1944. No conceivable chronicle of any kind could succeed in turning six million dead people into a political argument. The attempt of the Nazis to fabricate a wickedness beyond vice did nothing more than establish an innocence beyond virtue. Such innocence and such wickedness have no bearing on that reality where politics exists.

Yet Nazi policy, realized best in the phony world of propaganda, was well served by the fabrication. Had the Nazis been content merely to draw up a bill of indictment against the Jews and propagandize the notion that there are subhuman and superhuman peoples, they would hardly have succeeded in convincing common sense that the Jews were subhuman. Lying was not enough. In order to be believed, the Nazis had to fabricate reality itself and make Jews *look* subhuman. So that even today, when faced by the atrocity films, common sense will say: "But don't they look like criminals?" Or, if incapable of grasping an innocence beyond virtue and vice, people will say: "What terrible things these Jews must have done to have the Germans do this to them!"

In drawing up a bill of indictment on the part of the absolutely innocent Jewish people against the absolutely guilty German people, the authors of *The Black Book* overlook the fact that they lack the power to make the whole German nation *look* as guilty as the Nazis made Jews *look*—and God forbid that anyone should ever again have such power! For to establish and maintain such distinctions would mean installing hell permanently on earth. Without such power, without the means of fabricating a false reality according to a lying ideology, propaganda and publicity of the style embodied in this book can only succeed in making a true story sound unconvincing. And the account grows all the more unconvincing as the events themselves become more atrocious. Told as propaganda, the whole story not only fails to become a political argument—it does not even sound true.

Politically speaking, the death factories did constitute a "crime against humanity" committed on the bodies of the Jewish people; and had the Nazis not been crushed, the death factories would have swallowed up the bodies of quite a number of other peoples (as a matter of fact, Gypsies were exterminated along with Jews for more or less the same ideological reasons). The Jewish people is indeed entitled to draw up this bill of indictment against the Germans, but provided it does not forget that in this case it speaks for all the peoples of the earth. It is as necessary to punish the guilty as it is to remember that there is no punishment that could fit their crimes. For Goering the death penalty is almost a joke, and he, like all his fellow-defendants at Nuremberg, knows that we can do no more than make him die but a little earlier than he would have done anyhow.

From innocence beyond virtue and guilt beyond vice, from a hell where all Jews were of necessity angelic and all Germans of necessity diabolical, we must return to the reality of politics. The real story of the Nazi-constructed hell is desperately needed for the future. Not only because these facts have changed and poisoned the very air we breathe, not only because they now inhabit our dreams at night and permeate our thoughts during the day—but also because they have become the basic experience and the basic misery of our times. Only from this foundation, on which a new knowledge of man will rest, can our new insights, our new memories, our new deeds, take their point of departure. Those who one day may feel strong enough to tell the whole story will have to realize, however, that the story *in itself* can yield nothing but sorrow and despair—least of all, arguments for any specific political purpose.

Only a common subject matter justifies reviewing Max Weinreich's book together with *The Black Book*. His book possesses all the qualities the other so glaringly lacks, and, in its implications and honest presentation of the facts, constitutes the best guide to the nature of Nazi terror that I have read so far.

Soberly written from an expert knowledge of the organizational set-up of the Nazi machine, its larger part deals with the steps by which the Nazis carried out their "scientifically" planned program. Many documents that the Yiddish Scientific Institute ingeniously acquired for its archives are reproduced and, in addition, correctly evaluated. However, the list of the German scholars who collaborated with Hitler is not complete: many more names, especially from the humanities, could have been added. But even in this case, the book provides a good trunk to which supplements and additions can be grafted. The same holds true for the short bibliographies in the index. In his— understandable—excitement about many hitherto unknown documents marked "top secret" and many newly discovered sources. Dr. Weinreich has failed to pay enough attention to more easily accessible books and sources.

This happens to be more than a technical question. Dr. Weinreich's main thesis is that "German scholarship provided the ideas and techniques which led to and justified unparalleled slaughter." This is a highly controversial statement. It is true that some outstanding scholars went out of their way and did more to aid the Nazis than the majority of German professors, who fell into line simply for the sake of their jobs. And quite a few of those outstanding scholars did their utmost to supply the Nazis with ideas and techniques: prominent among them were the jurist Carl Schmitt, the theologian Gerhard Kittel, the sociologist Hans Freyer, the historian Walter Frank (former director of the Reich Institute for Research into the Jewish Question, in Munich), and the existentialist philosopher Martin Heidegger. These names are lost, however, amid the mass of material Dr. Weinreich's book provides on lesser-known scholars and scholars of bad reputation. Moreover, only a careful and complete bibliography of all these scholars' pre-Hitler publications would have shown their real standing in the world of scholarship. (Conspicuous by their absence are Walter Frank's books on the Stoecker movement and on the Third Republic, both of which already showed a strong anti-Semitic bias before Hitler.)

It is also true, and Dr. Weinreich is right to insist thereon, that Hitler showed one of his crucial insights into the nature of modern propaganda when he asked for "scientific" arguments and refused to use the standard crackpot ones of traditional anti-Semitic propaganda. The reason for this surprising inclination of his for "scientificality" is simple and can be explained by the same example Hitler himself uses in *Mein*

Kampf: He begins by stating that the advertiser of a new brand of soap would be doing a bad job if he admitted that there were other good soaps on the market. It is obvious, as every businessman knows, that the usual claim, "My soap is better than any other soap in the world," can be greatly improved by adding a little threat like: "If you don't use my soap you'll get pimples instead of a husband." And what you do, as long as you can't deprive all the girls who don't use your soap of husbands, is back up your claim "scientifically." But once you succeed in acquiring the power and put all girls with the wrong kind of soap beyond the reach of boys or, even better, monopolize soap-fabrication, "science" is no longer necessary.

So while it is perfectly true that quite a few respectable German professors volunteered their services to the Nazis, it is equally true—which was rather a shock to these gentlemen themselves—that the Nazis did not use their "ideas." The Nazis had their own ideas—what they needed were techniques and technicians with no ideas at all or educated from the beginning in only Nazi ideas. The scholars first put to one side by the Nazis as of relatively little use to them were old-fashioned nationalists like Heidegger, whose enthusiasm for the Third Reich was matched only by his glaring ignorance of what he was talking about. After Heidegger had made Nazism respectable among the élite at the universities, Alfred Bäumler, well known as a charlatan in pre-Hitler times, stepped into his place and received all the honors. The last to fall into disgrace with the Nazis were people like Walter Frank who had been anti-Semites even before Hitler rose to power but nevertheless managed to cling to some remnants of scholarship. In the early forties Frank had to surrender his position to the notorious Alfred Rosenberg, whose *Myth of the Twentieth Century* had revealed no inclinations whatsoever toward "scholarship" on its author's part. The point here is that the Nazis most likely mistrusted Frank precisely because he was *not* a charlatan.

The only science the Nazis appear to have actually trusted to some extent was racial "science," which, as we know, has never yet gone beyond the stage of somewhat crude superstition. But even racial "scientists" had a rather hard time of it under the Nazis, being asked at first to prove the inferiority of all Semites, chiefly the Jews; then the high standing of all Semites, chiefly the Arabs (for the Jews as a "*Mischrasse*" did not belong to the Semites)—and then, finally, even having to abandon their pet notion of "Aryan" superiority for the sake of Japanese susceptibilities. More interesting, however, than all these "results of research" that changed according to political necessity was the unchanging docility of the "scholars" concerned. And to finish the picture, there is the fantastic ease with which the victorious Allies were able to persuade top German scientists, who had held the key to important military inventions and worked with more or less devotion for the German war effort, to transfer the scene of their activities to the enemy's country.

Dr. Weinreich's book pays too great a compliment to these professors by taking them too seriously. Their shame is pettier than that and they were hardly ever guilty of having "ideas." That not one of the first-rate German scholars ever attained to a position of influence is a fact, but this fact does not mean that they did not try to. And even so, the majority of them were soon taken aback more or less by the outspoken vulgarity of the representatives of the Nazi regime—not, however, by their crimes. If anybody wants a real glance at the physiognomy of the average German professor under Hitler he should read the candid confession of Gerhard Ritter, professor of history at Freiburg, in the April, 1946, *Review of Politics*. This anti-Nazi professor kept his real opinions so secret and had so little knowledge of what was going on that he could feel that "the machinery of the Hitler Reich . . . did not function well." And he was so involved in the "deeper life of the intellect," so busy preventing "the inevitable damage from becoming too great," and so convinced of his chances to "publish . . . independent views on historico-political questions"—although "there were certain impassable limits to [his] freedom as teacher"—that the Gestapo, to his own great surprise, decided to use him for propaganda abroad. . . .

One of the most horrible aspects of contemporary terror is that, no matter what its motives or ultimate aims, it invariably appears in the clothes of an inevitable logical conclusion made on the basis of some ideology or theory. To a far lesser degree this phenomenon was already to be seen in connection with the liquidation of the anti-Stalinists in Russia—which Stalin himself predicted and justified in 1930. He argued at that time that, since parties are nothing but the expression of class interests, factions inside the Communist party could not possibly be anything else than the expression of the interests of "dying classes" in the Soviet Union or of the bourgeoisie abroad. The obvious conclusion was that one had to deal with these factions as one would with a hostile class or with traitors. The trouble is, of course, that nobody except Stalin knows what the "true interests of the proletariat" are. Yet there is available an infallible doctrine on the course of history and the origin of human opinions that makes it possible for anyone not feeble-minded to obtain this knowledge—so why not Stalin? Besides, he holds the power. The expression "dying classes" makes the argument even more convincing because it is attuned to historical progress—in accordance with whose laws man does only what would happen anyhow. The point at issue is not whether this is still true Marxism—or true Leninism either—but the fact that terror should appear as a logical, matter-of-course conclusion from a pseudo-scientific hypothesis.

This "scientificality" is indeed the common feature of all the totalitarian regimes of our time. But it means nothing more than that purely man-made power—mainly destructive—is dressed in the clothes of some superior, superhuman sanction from which it derives its absolute, not-to-be-questioned force. The Nazi brand of this kind of power is more thorough and more horrible than the Marxist or pseudo-Marxist, because it assigns to nature the role Marxism assigns to history. While the basis and source of history is still man, the basis and source of nature seems to be nothing at all or consists only in nature's own laws and functioning. The Nazi interpretation of these laws culminated in the tautology that the weak have an inclination to die and the strong an inclination to live. By killing the weak, we merely obey the orders of nature, which "sides with the strong, the good, and the victorious." And Himmler would add: "You may call this cruel, but nature is cruel." By killing the weak and the helpless, one proves by implication that one belongs to the strong. A rather important by-product of this kind of reasoning is that it takes victory and defeat out of the hands of man and makes any opposition to the verdicts of reality hopeless by definition, since one no longer fights against man but against History or Nature—and thus to the reality of power itself is added a superstitious belief in the eternity of that power.

It was a general atmosphere of "scientificality" of this sort, coupled with efficient modern technique, that the Nazis needed for their death factories—but not science itself. Charlatans who sincerely believed the will of nature to be the will of God and felt themselves allied with superhuman and irresistible forces served Nazi purposes best—not real scholars, no matter how little courage real scholars may have shown and how great the attraction they may have felt towards Hitler.

But neither science nor even "scientificality," neither scholars nor charlatans, supplied the ideas and techniques that operated the death factories. The ideas came from politicians who took power-politics seriously, and the techniques came from modern mob-men who were not afraid of consistency.

The Nation

N OTHING IN THE historical sciences is more obscure than
its terminology. The arbitrariness with which the same groups
are alternatively called peoples or races or nations, the loose
talk which uses terms such as nationalism, patriotism and imperialism
as equivalents, the many parallels which are used to explain away everything that may be new under the sun—the best as well as the worst—
all these very well-known features of current historiography tend to
produce easy and readable books, which leave the reader's peace of mind
quite undisturbed. Those few students, on the other side, who have left
the field of surface descriptions behind them, who are no longer interested in any particular aspect nor in any particular new discovery because
they know that the whole is at stake, are forced into the adventure of
structural analyses and can hardly be expected to come forward with perfect books. There is no doubt that Delos's study belongs to this latter category where it is outstanding through the rich and deep thoughtfulness of
its content; and it certainly shares all the shortcomings of those authors
who do not pass their lives in the inner security of the ivory tower of sci-

A review of *La Nation*, by J.-T. Delos, 2 vols., Montreal, 1944, *The Review of Politics*, VIII/1, January 1946.

ence and therefore somehow find neither the time nor the patience to organize their material and to explain their thought in a systematic order. Superficially and conventionally speaking, Delos's book suffers from too long quotations, from repetitions and omissions, from too many cross-references. This, however, is not said for the sake of criticism; it is meant only as a side remark for the highly desirable case of an English translation.

The fundamental political reality of our time is determined by two facts: on the one hand, it is based upon "nations" and, on the other, it is permanently disturbed and thoroughly menaced by "nationalism." The leading questions of Delos's study, therefore, which in its broadest aspect is concerned with the phenomenon of civilization, is to find a political principle which would prevent nations from developing nationalism and would thereby lay the fundamentals of an international community, capable of presenting and protecting the civilization of the modern world.

Civilization is called that part of the world which as the product of human work and human thought—the "human artifice"—is ruled through institutions and organization. One of the main phenomena of the modern world is that civilization has renounced its old claim to universality and presents itself in the form of a particular, a national civilization. Another aspect of modern civilization is its reconstitution of the state (after the period of feudalism), reconstitution, however, which does not solve the fundamental problem of the state: the origin and the legality of its power. A third aspect is the new phenomenon of masses, with which each civilization has to be concerned since it consists primarily in social organization.

The present analysis of the nation starts with the discussion of the question: "Nations or races?" and comes to the conclusion that the student of the social sciences (who knows families and nations, ethnic and religious groups) has still to run across any human society which is based on the "facial or cephalic index." The right observation that almost all modern brands of nationalism are racist to some degree has tempted the author into an overlong presentation of all current scientific and genetic arguments which, unfortunately, are taken at their face-value. (Darré,* for instance, is quoted *in extenso*.) This strange seriousness—

---

*Walter Darré, author of *The Peasantry as the Life Source of the Nordic Race*, was German Minister for Food and Agriculture, 1933–42, and also chief of the SS Central Office for Race and Resettlement. —Ed.

as far as I can see the only important mistake in emphasis—is based upon Delos's conviction that imperialism is a somehow logical development of nationalism, which in the opinion of this reviewer is only partially true. For if Delos is right in his statement that "races are classifications based on physical and biological standards which artificially unite men without taking into account their social links, or the communities to which they belong," he is wrong in assuming that this is a kind of scientific mistake. It is, rather, the ultimate, political aim of the racial pseudo-sciences to prepare the destruction of societies and communities whose atomization is one of the prerequisites of imperialistic domination.

What now follows is a highly welcome clarification of some of the basic notions of historical writing. A people becomes a nation when "it takes conscience of itself according to its history"; as such it is attached to the soil which is the product of past labor and where history has left its traces. It represents the "milieu" into which man is born, a closed society to which one belongs by right of birth. The state on the other hand is an open society, ruling over a territory where its power protects and makes the law. As a legal institution, the state knows only citizens no matter of what nationality; its legal order is open to all who happen to live on its territory. As a power institution, the state may claim more territory and become aggressive—an attitude which is quite alien to the national body which, on the contrary, has put an end to migrations. The old dream of the innate pacifism of the nations whose very liberation would guarantee an era of peace and welfare was not all humbug.

Nationalism signifies essentially the conquest of the state through the nation. This is the sense of the national state. The result of the nineteenth-century identification of nation and state is twofold: while the state as a legal institution has declared that it must protect the rights of men, its identification with the nation implied the identification of the citizen as national and thereby resulted in the confusion of the rights of men with the rights of nationals or with national rights. Furthermore, insofar as the state is an "enterprise of power," aggressive and inclining to expansion, the nation through its identification with the state acquires all these qualities and claims expansion now as a national right, as a necessity for the sake of the nation. "The fact that modern nationalism has frequently and almost automatically led to imperialism or to conquest, is due to the identification of state and nation."

The conquest of the state through the nation started with the dec-

laration of the sovereignty of the nation. This was the first step transforming the state into an instrument of the nation, which finally has
ended in those totalitarian forms of nationalism in which all laws and
the legal institutions of the state as such are interpreted as a means for
the welfare of the nation. It is therefore quite erroneous to see the evil
of our times in a deification of the state. It is the nation which has
usurped the traditional place of God and religion.

This conquest of the state was made possible through the liberal
individualism of the nineteenth century. The state was supposed to rule
over mere individuals, over an atomized society whose very atomization
it was called upon to protect. The modern state was on the other hand
a "strong state" which through its growing tendency towards centralization monopolized the whole of political life. This discrepancy between
a centralized state and an atomized (individualized, liberal) society was
to be bridged through the solid cement of national sentiment, which
proved to be the only working living connection between the individuals
of the national state. As the sovereignty of the nation was shaped after
the model of the sovereignty of the individual, so the sovereignty of the
state as national state was the representative and (in its totalitarian forms)
the monopolizer of both. The state conquered by the nation became the
supreme individual before which all other individuals had to bow.

It is this personification of the state, achieved through its conquest
by the nation and shaped after the model of the autonomous individual,
which first brought into existence that "individualization of the moral
universal within a collective," that concretization of the Idea which was
first conceived in Hegel's theory of state and history. After the specific
Hegelian idealism disappeared, "the idea of the nation, the spirit of the
people, the soul of the race, or other equivalents took the place of Hegel's
Spirit; but the conception as a whole remained."

The main aspect of this conception is that the Idea, no longer recognized as an independent entity, finds its realization in the movement
of history as such. Since then, all modern political theories which lead
to totalitarianism present an immersion of an absolute principle into
reality in the form of a historical movement; and it is this absoluteness,
which they pretend to embody, which gives them their "right" of priority
over the individual conscience.

It is only logical that the rise and the functioning of all one-party
systems follow the basic pattern of "movements." These movements are

"charged with philosophy" which is realized in the movement itself, whereas the old parties, though they frequently were inspired by some political theory, thought of their objectives as some ends outside themselves. The identification of means and ends—so characteristic for modern "movements"—lies in the structure of an assumed eternal dynamism. "The characteristic of totalitarianism is not only to absorb man within the group, but also to surrender him to becoming." Against this seeming reality of the general and universal, the particular reality of the individual person appears, indeed, as a *quantité négligeable*, submerged in the stream of public life which, since it is organized as a movement, is the universal itself.

This is the way in which nationalism becomes fascism: the "Nation-State" transforms or, rather, personifies itself into the totalitarian State. There is little doubt that civilization will be lost if after destroying the first forms of totalitarianism we do not succeed in solving the basic problems of our political structures. "The relations between Nation and State—or in more general and exact terms, between the political order and that of nationality—raise one of the essential problems which our civilization has to solve." The state, far from being identical with the nation, is the supreme protector of a law which guarantees man his rights as man, his rights as citizen and his rights as a national. "The real function of the state is the establishment of a legal order which protects all rights," and this function is not at all affected through the number of nationalities which are protected within the framework of its legal institutions. Of these rights, only the rights of man and citizen are primary rights, whereas the rights of nationals are derived and implied in them. For "the nation presents man in his dependence upon time, history and the universal becoming," his rights are "affected by relativity in their very source," because after all "being French, Spanish or English is not a means of becoming a man, it is a manner of being a man."

While these distinctions between the citizen and the national, between the political order and the national one, would take the wind out of the sails of nationalism by putting man as a national in his right place in public life, the larger political needs of our civilization, with its "growing unity" on one side, and its growing national consciousness of peoples, on the other, would be met with the idea of federation. Within federated structures, nationality would become a personal status rather than a territorial one. The state, on the other side, "without losing its legal personality would appear more and more as an organ charged with competencies to be exerted on a limited territory."

This is certainly not the place to go into a discussion of Delos's work, which is much too important to be criticized within the limits of a review. We may, however, be allowed to add one remark. Delos's brilliant analyses of the development of nationalism into totalitarianism overlook its equally intimate connection with imperialism—which is mentioned only in a footnote. And neither the racism of modern nationalism nor the power-craziness of the modern state can be explained without a proper understanding of the structure of imperialism.

Dedication to Karl Jaspers

L IEBER VEREHRTESTER, *

    Thank you for permitting me to dedicate this little book to you, and thank you, too, for the opportunity to say to you what I have to say on its publication in Germany.

For it is not an easy thing for a Jew to publish in Germany today, even if he is a German-speaking Jew. In the face of what has happened, the appealing opportunity to write in one's own language again counts for very little, although this is the only return home from exile that one can never entirely ban from one's dreams. But we Jews are not or are not any longer exiles and hardly have a right to such dreams. Quite apart from how our expulsion appears and is understood in the context of German or European history, the fact of our expulsion itself forced us

Published in German as "Zueignung au Karl Jaspers" in *Sechs Essays*, Heidelberg, 1948. English translation by Robert and Rita Kimber.

* *Lieber Verehrtester* (Dear Most Honored One) is the salutation Hannah Arendt used in almost every letter she wrote to Jaspers from 1946 until his death, in 1969. Though the phrase sounds odd and stiff in English, it is quite natural in German; *Sehr verehrter Herr* (Very Honored Mr., or Sir) was a common salutation. Jaspers was for Arendt both "dear" and "most honored," and this salutation is thus an accurate reflection of the affection and high regard she had for him. —Ed.

at first to look back on our own history, in which expulsion appears not as a unique and unusual phenomenon but as a familiar and repeated one.

This understanding of the present in the light of the past proved, of course, to be illusory. Recent years have taught us things we could in no way document as events that had repeated themselves in our history. Never before had we been faced with a determined effort to eradicate us, and we never seriously considered such a possibility. In view of the annihilation of one-third of the world's Jewish population and almost three-fourths of European Jewry, the catastrophes the Zionists were predicting before Hitler came to power look like tempests in a teapot.

But to say this in no way makes a publication of this kind easier to understand or better understood. It seems clear to me that the majority of both Germans and Jews will find it difficult to regard any Jew who wants to speak to Germans in Germany or, as I am doing in this book, to speak to Europeans as anything but a scoundrel or a fool. This has nothing whatever to do with the question of guilt or responsibility. I speak here only of factual matters as I see them, because one should never stray from the basis of fact without knowing what one is doing and why.

None of the following essays was, I hope, written without awareness of the facts of our time and without awareness of the Jewish fate in our century. But I believe and hope that I have not in any of them taken up a position on the basis of those facts alone, that I have not accepted the world created by those facts as necessary and indestructible. Without your philosophy and without the fact of your existence, both of which became much more vivid to me than ever before in the long years when the madness at loose in the world separated me completely from you, I could never have summoned up such a willed independence of judgment and a conscious distance from all fanaticisms, however attractive these may have seemed and however frightening the isolation, in every sense, that threatened to follow as a consequence of my position.

What I learned from you and what helped me in the ensuing years to find my way around in reality without selling my soul to it the way people in earlier times sold their souls to the devil is that the only thing of importance is not philosophies but the truth, that one has to live and think in the open and not in one's own little shell, no matter how comfortably furnished it is, and that necessity in whatever form is only a will-o'-the-wisp that tries to lure us into playing a role instead of attempting to be a human being. What I have personally never forgotten is your attitude—so difficult to describe—of listening, your tolerance that is constantly ready to offer criticism but is as far removed from skepticism as it is from fanaticism; ultimately, it is simply the realization of the fact that all human beings are rational but that no human being's rationality is infallible.

Back then, I was sometimes tempted to imitate you, even in your manner of speech, because that manner symbolized for me a human being who dealt openly and directly with the world, a human being without ulterior motives. I had little idea at that time how difficult it would be at a later one to find people without ulterior motives, little idea that a time would come when what reason and clear, illuminating attentiveness required of us would appear to be presumptuous, even profligate, optimism. For among the facts of this world we live in today is a fundamental mistrust between peoples and individuals that did not and could not disappear with the Nazis because it is rooted in the overpowering evidence of our experience. It is consequently almost impossible for us Jews today not to ask any German we happen to meet: What did you do in the twelve years from 1933 to 1945? And behind that question lie two unavoidable feelings: a harrowing uneasiness at placing on another human being the inhuman demand to justify his existence and the lurking suspicion that one is face to face with someone who worked in a death factory or who, when he learned something about the monstrous crimes of the government, responded with: You can't make an omelet without breaking eggs. That a person didn't have to be a born murderer to have done the first of these things, or a hired accomplice, indeed, not even a convinced Nazi, to have said the second is precisely the unsettling reality that can so easily tempt us to generalize.

The factual territory onto which both peoples have been driven looks something like this: On the one side is the complicity of the German people, which the Nazis consciously planned and realized. On the other side is the blind hatred, created in the gas chambers, of the entire Jewish people. Unless both peoples decide to leave this factual territory, the individual Jew will no more be able to abandon his fanatical hatred than will the individual German be able to rid himself of the complicity imposed upon him by the Nazis.

The decision to leave this territory completely behind us and to renounce completely the laws that it would impose on our actions is difficult to make. It arises from the insight that something has happened in the past that was not just bad or unjust or cruel, but something that should never under any circumstances have been allowed to happen. That was not the case for as long as the Nazi regime remained within certain limits and as long as a Jew could shape his behavior according to the rules that apply under the conditions of a normal and understood hostility between two peoples. At that time there was still a factual basis on which one could rely without becoming inhuman. One could defend oneself as a Jew because one had been attacked as a Jew. National concepts and national membership still had a meaning; they were still elements of a reality within which one could live and move. In the context of such a world, a world still intact despite all the hostility in it, the possibility of communication between peoples and individuals remains. We are spared that blind and eternal hatred that inevitably seizes us if we accept the consequences of the facts the Nazis created.

But the fabrication of corpses goes beyond hostility and cannot be comprehended by political categories. In Auschwitz, the factual territory opened up an abyss into which everyone is drawn who attempts after the fact to stand on that territory. Here, the reality of the politicians of *Realpolitik*, under whose spell the majority of the peoples always and naturally falls, has become a monster that could only urge us to perpetuate annihilation the way the Nazis continued to produce corpses in Auschwitz.

If the factual territory has become an abyss, then the space one occupies if one pulls back from it is, so to speak, an empty space where there are no longer nations and peoples but only individuals for whom it is now not of much consequence what the majority of peoples, or even the majority of one's own people, happens to think at any given moment. If these individuals who exist today in all the peoples and in all the nations of the world are to reach understanding among themselves, it is essential that they learn not to cling frantically any longer to their own national pasts—pasts that explain nothing anyhow, for Auschwitz can no more be explained from the perspective of German history than from Jewish history—that they don't forget that they are only chance survivors of a deluge that in one form or another can break over us again any day, and that they therefore may be like Noah in his ark; and finally that they must not yield to despair or scorn for humankind but be thankful that there are quite a few Noahs floating around out there on the world's seas trying to bring their arks as close together as they can.

As you said in Geneva, "We live as if we stood knocking at gates that are still closed to us. Today something may perhaps be taking place in the purely personal realm that cannot yet found a world order because it is only given to individuals, but which will perhaps someday found such an order when these individuals have been brought together from their dispersion."

With that hope and with that intent, I feel the publication of this book in Germany is justified. And in any case, your life and your philosophy provide us with a model of how human beings can speak with each other, despite the prevailing conditions of the deluge.

New York, May 1947

Rand School Lecture

[The manuscript of this lecture is marked, in Arendt's hand, "Lecture—Rand School—1948 or 49." From internal evidence it would seem to have been delivered in 1948. The Rand School was a working-class school and a center for New York intellectuals and socialists, many of whom were Arendt's acquaintances; it also provided a forum for lectures. Anti-Stalinism would have been a sensitive issue to many members of the audience, particularly the way Arendt discusses it vis-à-vis their European counterparts.]

ANTI-STALINISM HAS become the creed of those not very large segments of the American left-wing intelligentsia whose honest interest in politics survived the severe shock of disillusion with the Russian Revolution in the thirties, and who out of despair have, in the forties, begun to doubt the fundament of Marxist socialism altogether. Although the term implies no reasoned general political approach to political philosophy, as the older terms socialism, liberalism, and communism did, it is more than a catch-all slogan invented on the spur of the moment to gather together as many people as possible for one specific purpose, people who would otherwise take the most varied stands on political matters. On the contrary, even though anti-Stalinism indicates no political philosophy, not even a definite stand on totalitarianism—one can very well be an anti-Stalinist and still believe in dictatorship, at least, if not in totalitarian rule—it indicates all the more clearly a certain climate, a peculiar atmosphere composed partly of specific American conditions and partly of more generally shared historical and biographical elements. The term points clearly to an experience in the past, common to a certain generation; yet it can hardly be a gauge of the future attitudes of those who have adopted the creed.

The preference for the term anti-Stalinism, as distinguished from anti-Bolshevism or anti-totalitarianism, is significant. No anti-Nazi would have called himself an anti-Hitlerite, because this would have meant he was a participant in the interior struggle of the Nazi party, a colleague of Röhm or Strasser* perhaps, but no enemy of Nazism. Similarly, the term anti-Stalinism originated in the interior struggles of the Bolshevik party, when, in the twenties, one could be for or against Bukharin, for or against Zinoviev, for or against Trotsky,† for or against Stalin. It was the identification of Trotskyism with anti-Stalinism that inflated these struggles within the Russian party into international issues, and this could happen only because radical movements all over the world had long since fallen so deeply under the spell and the power of Moscow that their own political discussions invariably followed specifically Russian inner-party lines. Trotskyism, as it developed after Trotsky's expulsion from the party and exile from Russia, unfortunately perpetuated these inner struggles of the Russian party and dominated the non-conformist elements of the left-wing workers' movements in much the same way as Moscow dominated the Comintern; and this in spite of the fact that by 1930 the actual conflict between Stalin and Trotsky was clearly outdated even in Russia, where the fight against so-called Trotskyism had lost its specific significance and was exclusively used as a means for totalitarian domination. In brief, the term anti-Stalinism does more than gather *de facto* all former opponents of Stalin, regardless of their present political beliefs. What is worse, its very vague-

---

*Ernst Röhm and Gregor Strasser played important roles in the rise of Nazism in Germany. They were liquidated by Hitler in 1934. —Ed.

†Nikolai Bukharin, Grigori Zinoviev, and Leon Trotsky, who played vital roles in the Russian Revolution and the subsequent development of the Soviet Union, became victims of Stalin, in 1938, 1936, and 1940 respectively. —Ed.

ness in specific political convictions, on the one hand, and its concentration of all possible political issues in a single person—which stimulated the justifiable witticism, What will happen to anti-Stalinists when Stalin dies?—on the other, affirms, in a perverse way, Stalin's own loose yet over-specific use of the term Trotskyism, which he, in distinction from his enemies, needs for very practical purposes.

The danger of this terminology is twofold. Its lesser aspect is that people who are genuinely anti-totalitarian seem only to have taken the wrong side within a totalitarian movement and that, because of the existence of real inner-totalitarian opposition, they frequently get mixed up with the wrong kind of friends against the wrong kind of enemies. The point is not just that all former Nazis in Germany are fervent anti-Stalinists today (and I know many anti-Stalinists here who, because of their confused terminology and thinking, are not too sure what attitude to take on the whole issue of denazification), but that Tito, for instance, is doubtless also an anti-Stalinist; and while he may eventually turn out not to be a totalitarian dictator, that issue is by no means yet decided.

The greater danger of the climate of thought inherent in anti-Stalinism lies in the unquestionable petrification of ideas in its approach. Its most conspicuous element for the outsider is the stubbornness with which these intellectuals cling to their past, their basic unwillingness to rethink their political convictions in the light of the political events and historical developments of the last ten years, their helplessness in the face of reality without the spurious support of the political clichés of the twenties—which, to be sure, at that time were certainly not clichés. It was bad enough, in a sense, that the whole radical movement of our time was destroyed through identification with and usurpation by the Russian Revolution; it was worse that the fixation on Russia survived the disillusionment with the revolution itself. And this same approach is certainly no less outmoded when the younger generation, which lacks even the political experience and the sorrows that lie behind our present-day clichés, begins to adopt it for lack of anything else.

The peculiar political unreality and traditionalism among anti-Stalinists seems to be closely connected with the general political situation in this country. All totalitarian movements, but Bolshevism even more today than Nazism a decade ago, are completely absent from the American domestic scene. All that Bolshevism actually means today is a possible menace from abroad, helped by domestic espionage, with the result that anti-Stalinists think more and more exclusively in terms of foreign policy. Since they have no contact with and little lively interest in politics as the realm of the statesman, they have degenerated into armchair strategists who marshal the forces of the world for and against Stalin. The new emphasis on foreign policy is what chiefly distinguishes present-day anti-Stalinism from earlier forms of anti-totalitarianism like Trotskyism or anti-fascism. Although fascist groups in this country were never very strong, they existed nevertheless. The fact, moreover, that totalitarian and partially totalitarian dictatorships of the fascist brand had sometimes been helped to power by the native bourgeoisie (the significance of which was greatly overrated by all Marxists) led American anti-fascists, rightly or wrongly, to believe "it can happen here," which naturally gave them a personal stake in the struggle and revealed to them certain possibilities for action at home. A fascist danger from abroad, on the other hand, was never taken very seriously, not even during the war; as a matter of fact, victory in the war was decided the moment the United States joined it, and Americans, with very few and insignificant exceptions, knew it.

In this respect, the situation in Europe and, indeed, almost all over the world is the very opposite. Bolshevism is not just an outside threat from Russia and her satellites. The danger of a so-called fifth column is much more real than the danger of mere espionage, and the fact is that no Nazi-inspired party, from the anti-Semitic groups in Rumania to the Doriot outfit in France,* could have competed in loyalty, reliability, and efficient supervision with the Moscow-directed Communist parties.

Therefore, mere anti-Stalinism outside the United States has a definite nationalist flavor, and has led many good people, in France, for example, into the De Gaulle movement, for, despite the definite totalitarian potentialities and authoritarian certainties of a De Gaulle government, they prefer, even when they are aware of these dangers, a native dictatorship to a foreign one. On the other hand,

---

*Arendt refers to the pro-Hitler Iron Guard dictatorship of Ion Antonescu in Rumania and to the followers of Jacques Doriot in France. Doriot, who was born in 1898 and assassinated in 1945, was a political extremist all his life, moving from the far left to the far right. Leader of the Parti Populaire Français, he was both an ultra-nationalist and a Nazi collaborator known as "le Führer français." —Ed.

Europeans of distinction and integrity, whose biographical and intellectual backgrounds would very likely make them uncompromising anti-Stalinists in America, have shown an unpleasant inclination to become fellow-travelers and a definite hostility to the American brand of anti-Stalinism.

Sometimes it is useful to look at oneself through foreign eyes. In this instance, it is surprising how Europeans have discovered an underlying, unarticulated element of American anti-Stalinism of which the anti-Stalinists themselves have been only half aware. Behind the stubborn insistence that Stalin is the only enemy worthy of their wrath, and behind the naive assumption that the whole world can be divided into Stalinists and anti-Stalinists, the Europeans perceive an unadmitted and never expressed adherence to the status quo in America. (Needless to say, this suspicion is confirmed when American intellectuals somewhat unimaginatively respond to it by attacking their European friends as backward, immature, and stupid.) Moreover, the anti-Stalinists' preoccupation with foreign affairs makes Europeans fear that this anti-Stalinism is only an ideological, and therefore uninteresting, concomitant of the East-West split, a split which in case of war might well lead to the destruction of the European continent no matter who won. Likewise, the anti-Stalinists' unadmitted adherence to the status quo in America is easily misunderstood and misconstrued as an adherence to the status quo elsewhere, especially because the Marshall Plan has had the inevitable consequence of supporting otherwise tottering governments (especially in France) and leading to a restoration of the status quo in Europe.

It is only natural that the war question should be seen quite differently in Europe; the great political issue of freedom versus total domination is overshadowed by the fear of extinction. Yet, curiously enough, even more decisive in the European estimate of American policy and the attitudes of American intellectuals is a purely historical-intellectual tradition: Long before totalitarianism, and throughout the nineteenth century, eminent historians and statesmen predicted a war between the two great future world powers, the United States and Russia. A well-educated European finds it difficult not to suspect an American radical, whose political convictions are all centered on a possible conflict with Russia, of ulterior nationalist motives, for he tends to think of this conflict as a historical necessity regardless of political regimes. And anti-Stalinism in its present form and terminology, and especially in its present stage of articulateness, is only too likely to fit snugly into typically European ideological approaches to politics. These seem to confirm those attitudes which tend not so much to establish "third forces" as to steer clear of fascism and communism, America and Russia; for the sake of sheer consistency, countries are identified with ideologies and movements (because Russia is communist, America is interpreted as fascist or imperialist) which Europeans believe to be conflicting but not antagonistic. This schematic and abstract way of thinking helps to win an ideologically safe ground for European independence on which, as European with a capital E (whatever that may mean), it would be possible to stand firmly.

The trouble with many European intellectuals in this respect is that now that the long-wished-for European federation is a definite political possibility, new constellations of world powers make it only too easy to apply their former nationalism to a larger structure and become as narrowly and chauvinistically European as they were formerly German, Italian, or French. (And this is true of the best of them, for the others show a definite tendency to use the slogan of a United Europe to claim the leadership of Europe for their respective nations.) What we see today in Europe is a kind of repeat performance of American isolationism; Europeanism frequently is the sign of an isolationist and arrogant mood rather than of true insight into political conditions. (One European who is conspicuously free of this new brand of nationalism is the German philosopher Karl Jaspers; see his article in *Commentary*, November, 1948.)* It is mostly their own new isolationism which makes it difficult for Europeans to understand the fact as well as the full implications of the collapse of American isolationism. If they admit the fact, they misinterpret it as the beginning of American imperialism and fail to understand that export of American money under the Marshall Plan was followed by an all-embracing system of alliances, the Atlantic pact, and not by export of American power and instruments of violence. Those,

---

*"The Axial Age of Human History: A Base for the Unity of Mankind." Arendt wrote to Jaspers that the essay "provides a solid basis for the concept of humanity and reconciles in the best sense of that word. The key thing here, it seems to me, is this element of reconciliation . . ." (*Hannah Arendt–Karl Jaspers Correspondence 1926–1969*, edited by Lotte Kohler and Hans Saner, New York, 1992, Letter 71, July 16, 1948). —Ed.

on the other hand, who are ready to recognize the non-imperialist intentions of America are likely to expect America to give up isolationism for the sake of Europe and tend to include her as a sort of expansion into the new European nationalism. Yet once American isolationism is gone, the geographical location of the United States between the Atlantic and Pacific oceans, the composition of its population (which, no matter what the proportion, counts among its citizens people from every nation on earth), and the specific character of its republican institutions, all point to an all-embracing concept of world politics.

Of the two European suspicions—that American anti-Stalinists are simply more sophisticated and less powerful defenders of the status quo, and that they may be only an ideological "superstructure" for their country's national interests in foreign politics—the one seems to be as well founded as the other is unwarranted. Interminable discussion by anti-Stalinists of the moot question as to whether Soviet Russia is a socialist country has somewhat blurred the fact that anti-Stalinists, along with other Americans, are fundamentally and sincerely opposed to any government that functions with the help of concentration camps and secret police, that aims at the total domination of society and the total humiliation of man. This opposition has nothing to do with a supposed permanent conflict of Russian and American interests; on the contrary, American intellectuals, unlike the Europeans, are blissfully innocent of such considerations. The simple reason is that they know America better than the nineteenth- and twentieth-century professors of history and other prophets who no longer understood the foundations and necessities of this republic; who blindly applied rules concerning the last imperialist stage of European nation-states to a body politic that rested on altogether different conditions.

It is perfectly true that American anti-Stalinism is firmly rooted in adherence to the American form of government, or, to speak in European terms, in affirmation of the status quo. And there is nothing objectionable in this adherence except the reluctance of anti-Stalinists, because of their past, to admit it and their inability to work out their own political philosophy. The American Republic is the only political body based on the great eighteenth-century revolutions that has survived 150 years of industrialization and capitalist development, that has been able to cope with the rise of the bourgeoisie, and that has withstood all temptations, despite strong and ugly racial prejudices in its society, to play the game of nationalist and imperialist politics.

Europeans have great difficulties understanding that this acceptance of the political status quo is neither conformism nor betrayal of earlier radical beliefs; for what is not only tolerable or a lesser evil but also positively full of productive and existing political possibilities in America is intolerable and quite beyond discussion in Europe. To tell the Europeans that even their status quo is much better than what they would be likely to get in case of a Bolshevik revolution is certainly to tell them the truth, but it is a meaningless truth because everybody knows that, short of a miracle, the status quo in certain European countries cannot be preserved. To side with the status quo there can mean to defend an exploitation that frequently does not make the most elementary economic sense, to acquiesce in tremendous injustices, to accept poverty and outright misery for the majority of the population. To cling consistently to anti-Stalinism as the only political criterion may mean to oppose all struggles for higher wages, better food, trade unions, and generally to support the rather outrageous behavior of great parts of Europe's privileged classes. It is out of sheer ignorance that American anti-Stalinists regard European Communist parties as mere groups of Soviet agents. Communist parties are still mass movements or potential mass movements in most parts of the world. Their membership has little in common with the membership of the American branch.

But this difference in the objective roles of the Communist parties is by no means the only cause of misunderstandings. True, American anti-Stalinists will counter the European charge that they are conformists with the suspicion that the European intellectuals' admitted scruples about separating themselves from the masses are due to a weakness of sentiment: a suspicion which can easily be explained by American ignorance of the actually existing relationship between intellectuals and workers in Europe, on the one hand, and their own isolation from all decisive political forces in this country on the other. Behind these banal misunderstandings, however, lie more serious and less easily traceable sources of misunderstanding which concern the structural differences between America and European countries and the different roles of the intelligentsia in them. In certain respects it is not Russia, whose Iron Curtain policy has grown more ruthless in inverse ratio to its effectiveness, but America, with all her eagerness to be understood, which is the least-known country in Europe today.

From a European point of view, the chief difficulty in understanding this country lies in the peculiar relationship of its social and political forces, of society and the body politic. The European visitor simply cannot perceive political realities in the United States, because they are so well hidden by the surface of a society in which publicity and public relations multiply all social factors, as a mirror multiplies light, so that the glaring façade appears to be the overwhelming reality. He cannot imagine that Mr. Jones, who in social matters is obviously the world's greatest conformist and hardly ever speaks about politics, is nevertheless in political matters a most independent creature with a deep feeling of responsibility as a citizen. It is inconceivable to this visitor that a very complicated system of social interrelationships—determined by even more and more heterogeneous groups than one could find in a class system—can underlie the surface composed of all the worst cultural elements of a mass society. Educated more or less by Marxist theories to consider society the tangible reality from which to deduce the working of political forces, the visitor was never prepared for a state of affairs in which social and political forces simply do not match and frequently even contradict each other, or in which political traditions and beliefs are far more stable and permanent than can be judged from social appearances. Who could expect individuals whose personal lives are entirely concentrated on success and the all-pervasive fear of being a "failure" to be thoroughly free of the political success idolatry of the European worshipers of history? The visitor does not understand, in other words, that a twentieth-century (and in some respects a nineteenth-century) society lives and thrives on the solid basis of an eighteenth-century political philosophy.

The trouble with American anti-Stalinists is that they have been reared in the same Marxist theories and therefore, theoretically, cannot believe their eyes, so to speak. Practically, however, they have enough sense not to oppose a form of government that they know is among the few survivors of true political freedom, and among the even fewer guarantors of that minimum of social justice without which citizenship is impossible. This theoretical blindness has had many unfortunate consequences. It is almost a truism that American intellectuals are more isolated from political reality than any other intelligentsia. They are isolated from the political forces in their own country—which Europeans of course are very quick to sense and to point out—not only because American society despises intellectuals in general, but also because they have failed to fulfill their specific intellectual function, of helping in the political self-understanding and self-consciousness of the country as a whole and of criticizing, on a firm ground of political philosophy, the actions of their own government. In addition to their special isolation, American intellectuals share the typical American isolation; they live, as it were, on a happy island and under the dangerous delusion that conditions which exist nowhere else in the world are "normal." Not having experienced totalitarian rule and terror, which is possibly the most crucial political experience of our time, they have done little to bridge the gap between themselves and their friends from other countries by using the one gift which always has been the prerogative of intellectuals, their imagination.

It is mainly because of the theoretical inarticulateness of American intellectuals that Europeans have such an easy time denouncing them as conformists. One thing is true: they are no longer, as they were in the twenties and thirties, in any sense part of a revolutionary movement, and they would be fools if they were. Yet while they appear politically "conformist," they are as non-conformist as ever with respect to the society in which they live. Europeans have seldom grasped the permanent tension in the extreme cultural and social loneliness of people who, as intellectuals, necessarily demand from life more than just a good job, a nice house, and a new car; and who, while they feel themselves solitary, at the same time identify themselves with their country in all political matters. It has been most unfortunate that in their eagerness to explain to European visitors the "progressiveness" of this country's political institutions, they have more often than not neglected to tell them how profoundly they disagree with the present standards of American society, its prevailing conformism, its identification of individuals with their jobs, its murderous concentration on achievement and success, and its fantastic overestimation of publicity—those very social traits which strike the European visitor as potentially totalitarian.

It might help to bridge the present chasm between European and American political thinking if American radicals could get themselves publicly and unashamedly to own up to the American Constitution and begin to interpret it in the light of present events and conditions. Their greatest danger is that because of their inarticulateness and their healthy disdain for political revolutionary gesturing, they might be lured into conforming to American society. This would be bad not only because this society is not exactly a cultural paradise, but also because social non-conformism as such has been and always will be the mark of intellectuals, be they artists, writers, or scholars. Intellectually, non-conformism is almost the *sine qua non* of achievement.

Politically speaking, it should be the task of intellectuals to rescue other Americans from their involuntary isolation, rather than to strengthen it by complacently thinking of the whole world as abnormal and of America as the norm. This would automatically lead to a liquidation of the old terminology—of which the misnomer "anti-Stalinism" is only one example, though possibly the most significant one. It is precisely because the past of American anti-Stalinists has been so closely connected with events in other parts of the world that they are so reluctant to part with it. Yet, if they want to remain contemporary with the rest of humanity they will have to realize that totalitarianism is not just an invention of "evil Mr. Stalin" and that there are more important things to know and worry about in the world today than the inner struggles of the party of the Russian Revolution.

Religion and the Intellectuals

[In 1950 *Partisan Review* asked a number of prominent thinkers and writers, including, in addition to Arendt, W. H. Auden, John Dewey, Robert Graves, Marianne Moore, A. J. Ayer, Sidney Hook, Alfred Kazin, Philip Rahv, Allen Tate, Paul Tillich, Robert Gorham Davis, Jacques Maritain, William Barrett, George Boas, Clement Greenberg, Irving Howe, Dwight Macdonald, and William Phillips, among others, to respond to "the new turn toward religion among intellectuals and the growing disfavor with which secular attitudes and perspectives are now regarded." Five general topics were suggested, corresponding to the paragraph numbers in Arendt's response: 1. the causes of the trend; 2. the change in *convictions* among intellectuals; 3. religion and culture; 4. religion and literature; 5. the separation of religious consciousness from religious beliefs, as in Heidegger and Malraux. Arendt's reply appeared in *Partisan Review*, XVII/2, February 1950.]

1. THE BELIEF THAT "all events have their causes" is not specific for a "naturalistic point of view": naturalism attempts to demonstrate that all events have *natural* causes but takes the principle of causality itself for granted. This is more than a mere quibble, because causality

Partisan Review, XVII/2, February 1950.

has played a very important role in all theological discussions of the past. Medieval arguments, "proving" the existence of God, were frequently based on it, i.e., on the notion that everything that is must have a cause. Genuine atheistic positions, on the other hand, are frequently characterized by the denial of a chain of causality and the assumption of the accidental and coincidental character of all events. If no chain of causality linking one event to the other can be demonstrated, then the conclusion from the existence of *creatura* to the existence of a *creator* is unwarranted.

This same first point, moreover, implies that religion is a kind of—perhaps illusory—"remedy," but this is not a naturalistic interpretation of religion. For the assumption that everything has natural causes is as such quite independent of human needs or social conditions. It pretends to be either true or false.

What I want to point out is that if you take causality as a valid principle, you will always end up with a "demonstration" of the existence of God. The trouble with all such demonstrations is of course that, as Kant showed, one never can prove the existence of a *fact* by logical deduction. By the same token, one can't disprove it. Scientifically speaking, we can't either prove or disprove the existence of God. A "scientific attitude" which believes it can make such statements is the attitude of uncritical superstition.

This impossibility to make valid statements in this matter, however, has a philosophical significance. It seems as though the human condition and the human mind are of such a nature that men have been left in the dark with regard to the most interesting factual information. This in itself is a fact and open to interpretation. Theology may say that without this darkness, there could be no faith and therefore no salvation which is merited. Philosophy may say that without this essential lack of information there could be no human freedom. The chief point with respect to the "scientific attitude" seems to be that it belongs to the very essence of science, which is primarily interested in facts, that our factual information is not only limited but that the answers to the most important factual questions concerning the human condition as well as the existence of Being in general are beyond factual knowledge and experience.

2. I should like to warn you not to overestimate the significance of the present "religious revival." These "puffs of the Zeitgeist" have followed their zigzag line ever since the age of Enlightenment, which was followed so closely by romanticism. If we look at this history from a

purely intellectual point of view and think of it in terms of the history of an idea, we find that every twenty years or so some "naturalistic" (or positivistic, or dialectical-materialistic, or pragmatistic) attitude was followed by a religious revival. This certainly is not surprising. On the contrary, it would be much more surprising if the rapid decline in religious belief which has taken place in Western culture during the last three hundred years were not interrupted by these intellectual memories—memories, after all, of thousands of years of human history and culture.

Historically speaking, not the history of an idea or the history of intellectuals is important, but the history of Western mankind in general. The important historical fact is that an overwhelming majority has ceased to believe in a Last Judgment at the end of time. This, of course, does not mean that this majority has become more scientifically inclined, and one might even doubt that the rise of science during this same period has really caused this development, as is frequently asserted. The same masses, at any rate hardly bothering to think of the old mysteries, like the Incarnation or the Trinity, are quite willing to believe—well, just anything. This is plain superstitiousness and the only connection I can see between this frightful gullibility of modern people and the "scientific attitude" is that the contents of highbrow and lowbrow superstition change even more rapidly than the contents of scientific discoveries.

3 and 4. I must confess that the notion that one can or ought to organize religion as an institution only because one likes to have a culture has always appeared to me as rather funny. The idea of somebody making up his mind to believe in God, follow His Commandments, praying to Him and going regularly to Church, so that poets again may have some inspiration and culture be "integrated," is simply exhilarating. The *catholicisme cérébral* which you mention is one of the surest ways to kill religion—as the Church, by the way, knew well enough when it put its writings on the index. The same is true, of course, with respect to the use of religion as a weapon against totalitarianism or "a safeguard for civilized tradition." Moreover, it seems that all such attempts would be doomed to failure, particularly in the struggle against totalitarianism; recent history has demonstrated how weak and helpless organized religion is when confronted with the new totalitarian forms of government—and this despite the good will and frequent heroism of great parts of the clergy of almost all denominations.

The trouble here, as in all discussions of religion, is that one really cannot escape the question of truth and therefore cannot treat the whole matter as though God had been the notion of some especially clever pragmatist who knew what it is good for . . . and what it is good against. It just is not so. Either God exists and people believe in Him—and this, then, is a more important fact than all of culture and literature; or He does not exist and people do not believe in Him—and no literary or other imagination is likely to change this situation for the benefit of culture and for the sake of the intellectuals.

5. I do not know Malraux's recent writings, but I am quite certain that Heidegger, being a philosopher and, certainly, like the rest of us, without special information on the validity or invalidity of "traditional religious beliefs," never explicitly "rejected" them. On the other hand, I would really like to know who among the great philosophers since Spinoza and Descartes—outside of Catholic philosophy—accepted "traditional religious beliefs."

There has been much discussion of modern attempts "to make viable certain attitudes that were formerly aspects of the religious consciousness." It always has appeared to me to be beside the point. After all, nobody has tried to preach the Christian virtue of humility without the Christian God. On the other hand, it is obvious that as long as Christian faith ruled unchallenged the consciousness of man, all human attitudes were interpreted in religious and specifically Christian terms. If we ourselves had to believe in the specific credo, which was the unquestioned basis of Christian philosophy, in order to understand it, then we should be forced to throw out more than one thousand years of philosophical thought. I must admit I shall be in fullest sympathy with a Zeitgeist that would bring the intellectuals to the point of no longer considering the tremendous body of past philosophy as the "errors of the past."

Social Science Techniques and the Study of Concentration Camps

E VERY SCIENCE IS necessarily based upon a few inarticulate, elementary, and axiomatic assumptions which are exposed and exploded only when confronted with altogether unexpected phenomena which can no longer be understood within the framework of its categories. The social sciences and the techniques which they have developed during the past hundred years are no exception to this rule. It is the contention of this paper that the institution of concentration and extermination camps, that is, the social conditions within them as well their function in the larger terror apparatus to totalitarian regimes, may very likely become that unexpected phenomenon, that stumbling-block on the road toward the proper understanding of contemporary politics and society which must cause social scientists and historical scholars to reconsider their hitherto unquestioned fundamental preconceptions regarding the course of the world and human behavior.

Behind the obvious difficulties of dealing with a subject matter in which the mere enumeration of facts makes one sound "intemperate and unreliable"[1] and on which reports are written by people who during their

Jewish Social Studies, 12/1, 1950.

[1]The notes are at the end of the essay.

very experience were "never wholly successful" in convincing "themselves that this was real, was really happening, and not just a nightmare,"[2] lies the more serious perplexity that within the framework of common-sense judgments neither the institution itself and what went on within its closely guarded barriers nor its political role makes any sense whatsoever. If we assume that most of our actions are of a utilitarian nature and that our evil deeds spring from some "exaggeration" of self-interest, then we are forced to conclude that this particular institution of totalitarianism is beyond human understanding. If, on the other hand, we make an abstraction of every standard we usually live by and consider only the fantastic ideological claims of racism in its logical purity, then the extermination policy of the Nazis makes almost too much sense. Behind its horrors lies the same inflexible logic which is characteristic of certain systems of paranoiacs where everything follows with absolute necessity once the first insane premise is accepted. The insanity of such systems clearly does not lie only in their first premise but in their very logicality, which proceeds regardless of all facts and regardless of reality which teaches us that whatever we do we can't carry through with absolute perfection. In other words, it is not only the non-utilitarian character of the camps themselves—the senselessness of "punishing" completely innocent people, the failure to keep them in a condition so that profitable work might be extorted from them, the superfluousness of frightening a completely subdued population—which gives them their distinctive and disturbing qualities, but their anti-utilitarian function, the fact that not even the supreme emergencies of military activities were allowed to interfere with these "demographic policies." It was as though the Nazis were convinced that it was of greater importance to run extermination factories than to win the war.[3]

It is in this context that the adjective "unprecedented"[4] as applied to totalitarian terror receives full significance. The road to total domination leads through many intermediary stages which are relatively normal and quite comprehensible. It is far from unprecedented to wage aggressive war; massacres of enemy population or even of what one assumes to be a hostile people look like an everyday affair in the bloody record of history; extermination of natives in the process of colonization and the establishment of new settlements has happened in America, Australia, and Africa; slavery is one of the oldest institutions of mankind and forced-labor gangs, employed by the state for the performance of public works, were one of the mainstays of the Roman Empire. Even the claim to world rule, well known from the history of political dreams, is no monopoly of totalitarian governments and can still be explained by a fantastically exaggerated lust for power. All these aspects of totalitarian rule, hideous and criminal as they are, have one thing in common which separates them from the phenomenon with which we are dealing: in distinction from the concentration camps, they have a definite purpose and they benefit the rulers much in the same way as an ordinary burglary benefits the burglar. The motives are clear and the means to achieve the goal are utilitarian in the accepted sense of the term. The extraordinary difficulty which we have in attempting to understand the institution of the concentration camp and to fit it into the record of human history is precisely the absence of such utilitarian criteria, an absence which is more than anything else responsible for the curious air of unreality that surrounds this institution and everything connected with it.

In order to understand more clearly the difference between the comprehensible and the incomprehensible, i.e., between those data which respond to our commonly accepted research techniques and scientific concepts and those which explode this whole framework of reference, it may be useful to recall the various stages in which Nazi anti-Semitism unfolded from the moment of Hitler's rise to power in 1933 up to the establishment of the death factories in the midst of the war. Anti-Semitism by itself has such a long and bloody history that the very fact that the death factories were chiefly fed with Jewish "material" has somewhat obliterated the uniqueness of this "operation." Nazi anti-Semitism, moreover, showed an almost striking lack of originality; it did not contain a single element, either in its ideological expression or propagandistic application, which could not be traced back to earlier movements and which did not already constitute a cliché in the literature of Jew-hatred before the Nazis ever existed. The anti-Jewish legislation in Hitler Germany during the thirties, culminating in the issuance of the Nuremberg laws in 1935, was new in terms of nineteenth- and twentieth-century events; it was neither new as the avowed goal of anti-Semitic parties all over Europe nor new in terms of earlier Jewish history. The ruthless elimination of Jews from the German economy between 1936 and 1938 and the pogroms in November 1938 were still within the framework of what one would expect to happen if an anti-Semitic party seized the monopoly of power in a European country. The next step, the establishment of ghettos in eastern Europe and the concentration of all Jews in them during the first years of the war, could hardly surprise any careful observer. All this appeared hideous and criminal but entirely rational. The anti-Jewish legislation in Germany aimed at satisfying popular demands, the elimination of Jews from the overcrowded professions seemed destined to make place for a seriously underemployed generation of intellectuals; forced emigration, with all its concomitants of plain robbery after 1938, was calculated to spread anti-Semitism throughout the world, as a memo of the German Foreign Office to all officials abroad succinctly pointed out;[5] the herding of the Jews into eastern European ghettos followed by some distribution of their possessions among the native population seemed to be a marvelous political stratagem to win over the large anti-Semitic segments of eastern European peoples, to console them for their loss of political independence and frighten them with the example of a people which suffered so far worse a fate. What could be expected in addition to these measures were starvation diets on the one hand and forced labor on the other during the war; in case of victory, all these measures seemed to be the preparation for the announced project of establishing a Jewish reservation in Madagascar.[6] As a matter of fact, such measures (and not death factories) were expected not only by the outside world and the Jewish people themselves but by the highest German officials in the administration of the Occupied Eastern Territories, by the military authorities, and even by high-ranking officers in the Nazi party hierarchy.[7]

Neither the fate of European Jewry nor the establishment of death factories can be fully explained and grasped in terms of anti-Semitism. Both transcend anti-Semitic reasoning as well as the political, social, and economic motives behind the propaganda of anti-Semitic movements. Anti-Semitism only prepared the ground to make it easier to start the extermination of peoples with the Jewish people. We know now that this extermination program of Hitler's did not stop short of planning the liquidation of large sections of the German people.[8]

The Nazis themselves, or, rather, that part of the Nazi party which, under the inspiration of Himmler and with the help of the SS troops, actually initiated extermination policies, were in no doubt as to the fact that they had entered an altogether different realm of activities, that they were doing something which not even their worst enemies expected them to do. They were quite convinced that one of the best chances for the success of this enterprise lay in the extreme improbability that anybody in the outside world would believe it to be true.[9] For the truth was that while all other anti-Jewish measures made some sense and were likely to benefit their authors in some way, the gas chambers did not benefit anybody. The deportations themselves, during a period of acute shortage of rolling stock, the establishment of costly factories, the manpower employed and badly needed for the war effort, the general demoralizing effect on the German military forces as well as on the population in the occupied territories—all this interfered disastrously with the war in the East, as the military authorities as well as Nazi officials, in protest against the SS troops, pointed out repeatedly.[10] Such considerations, however, were not simply overlooked by those who had put themselves in charge of extermination. Even Himmler knew that in a time of a critical shortage of labor, he was eliminating a large amount of workers who at least could have been worked to death instead of being killed without any productive purpose. And the office of Himmler issued one order after another warning the military commanders as well as the officials of the Nazi hierarchy that no economic or military considerations were to interfere with the extermination program.[11]

The extermination camps appear within the framework of totalitarian terror as the most extreme form of concentration camps. Extermination happens to human beings who for all practical purposes are already "dead." Concentration camps existed long before totalitarianism made them the central institution of government,[12] and it has always been characteristic of them that they were not penal institutions and that their inmates were accused of no crime, but that by and large they were destined to take care of "undesirable elements," i.e., of people who for one reason or another were deprived of their judicial person and their rightful place within the legal framework of the country in which they happened to live. It is interesting to note that totalitarian concentration camps were first established for people who had committed a "crime," i.e., the crime of opposition to the regime in power, but that they increased as political opposition decreased and that they expanded when the reservoir of people genuinely hostile to the regime was exhausted. The early Nazi camps were bad enough, but they were quite comprehensible: they were run by the SA with bestial methods and had the obvious aim to spread terror, kill outstanding politicians, deprive the opposition of their leaders, frighten would-be leaders into obscurity, and to satisfy the SA men's desire to revenge themselves not only upon their immediate opponents but also upon members of the higher classes. In this respect, the SA terror clearly constituted a compromise between the regime, which at that time did not wish to lose its potent industrial protectors, and the movement, which had been led to expect a real revolution. Complete pacification of the anti-Nazi opposition seems to have been achieved by January 1934; this at least was the opinion of the Gestapo itself and of high-ranking Nazi officials.[13] By 1936 the sympathies of the overwhelming majority of the people for the new regime had been won: unemployment had been liquidated, the living standard of the lower classes was steadily rising, and the more potent sources of social resentment had all but dried up. Consequently the population of the concentration camps reached an all-time low for the simple reason that there no longer existed any active or even suspected opponents whom one could take into "protective custody."

It is after 1936, i.e., after the pacification of the country, that the Nazi movement became more radical and more aggressive on the domestic as well as on the international scene. The fewer enemies Nazism encountered within Germany and the more friends it gained abroad the more intolerant and the more extremist became "the revolutionary principle."[14] The concentration camps began their new increase in 1938 with the mass arrests of all male German Jews during the November pogroms; but this development had been announced by Himmler already in 1937 when, during a speech to the higher officer staff of the Reichswehr, he explained that one would have to reckon with a "fourth theater in case of war, internal Germany."[15] No reality whatsoever corresponded to these "fears" and the chief of the German police knew this better than anyone else. When war broke out a year later, he did not even bother to keep up the pretense and use his SS troops for police duties inside Germany but sent them at once to the eastern territories where they arrived when military actions had been successfully concluded in order to take over the occupation of the defeated countries. Later, when the party had decided to bring the whole army under its exclusive control, Himmler did not hesitate to send his SS companies to the front.

The main duty of the SS, however, was and remained even during the war the control and administration of concentration camps, from which the SA was completely eliminated. (Only during the last years of the war did the SA again play some minor role in the camp system, but then the SA troops were under the supervision of the SS.) It is this type of concentration camp rather than its earlier form which strikes us as a new and at first glance incomprehensible phenomenon.

Only a fraction of the inmates of these new camps, usually survivors from earlier years, could be regarded as opponents of the regime. Greater was the percentage of criminals, who were sent to the camps after they had served their normal prison terms, and of the so-called asocial elements, homosexuals, vagabonds, work-shirkers and the like. The overwhelming majority of people who formed the bulk of the camp population was completely innocent from the point of view of the regime, quite harmless in every respect, guilty neither of political convictions nor of criminal actions.

A second characteristic of the camps, such as they were established by Himmler under SS rule, was their permanent character. Compared to Buchenwald, which in 1944 housed more than 80,000 prisoners, all earlier camps lose their significance.[16] Even more obvious is the permanent character of the gas chambers whose costly apparatus made the hunting for new "material" for the fabrication of corpses almost a necessity.

Of great importance for the development of the concentration-camp society was the new type of camp administration. The earlier cruelty of the SA troops, who had been allowed to run wild and kill whomsoever they pleased, was replaced by a regulated death rate[17] and a strictly organized torture, calculated not so much to inflict death as to put the victim into a permanent status of dying. Large parts of the inner administration were given into the hands of the prisoners themselves, who were forced to mistreat their fellow-prisoners in much the same way the SS did. As time went on and the system became more established, torture and mistreatments became more and more the prerogative of the so-called *Kapos*. These measures were not accidental and hardly due to the growing size of the camps. In a number of instances, the SS was expressly ordered to have executions carried out only by prisoners. Similarly, mass-murder, not only in the form of gassing but also in the form of mass-execution in ordinary camps, became as mechanized as possible.[18] The result was that the population in the SS camps lived much longer than in the earlier camps; one has the impression that new waves of terror or deportation to extermination camps occurred only when new supplies were assured.

The administration was given into the hands of the criminals who formed the unchallenged camp aristocracy until, in the early forties, Himmler reluctantly yielded to outside pressure and allowed the camps to be exploited for productive labor. From then on, the political prisoners, mostly old-timers, were promoted to the position of the camp élite, because the SS soon found it impossible to have any work performed under the chaotic conditions of the former aristocracy of criminals. In no instance was the administration given into the hands of the largest and obviously least harmful group of completely innocent inmates. On the contrary, this category always belonged to the lowest level of the internal social hierarchy of the camps, suffered the heaviest losses through deportation, and was most exposed to cruelty. In other words, in a concentration camp it was by far safer to be a murderer or a Communist than simply a Jew, Pole, or Ukrainian.

As to the SS guards themselves, we must unfortunately discard the notion that they constituted a kind of negative élite of criminals, sadists, and half-insane persons—a notion that is largely true for the earlier SA troops who used to volunteer for concentration-camp duty. All evidence points to the fact that the SS men in charge were completely normal; their selection was achieved according to all kinds of fantastic principles,[19] none of which could possibly assure the selection of especially cruel or sadistic men. Moreover, the administration of the camps was run in such a way that it appears to be beyond doubt that within this whole system the prisoners did not fail to fulfill the same "duties" as the guards themselves.

Most difficult to imagine and most gruesome to realize is perhaps the complete isolation which separated the camps from the surrounding world as if they and their inmates were no longer part of the world of the living. This isolation, characteristic already of all earlier forms of concentration camps, but carried to perfection only under totalitarian regimes, can hardly be compared to the isolation of prisons, ghettos, or forced-labor camps. Prisons are never really removed from society, of which they are an important part and to whose laws and controls they are subject. Forced labor as well as other forms of slavery do not involve absolute segregation; laborers by the very fact of their work come constantly in contact with the surrounding world and slaves were never really eliminated from the environment. Ghettos of the Nazi type have the closest similarity to the isolation of concentration camps; but in them families, and not individuals, were segregated so that they constituted a kind of closed society where an appearance of normal life was being carried on and sufficient social relationships existed to create at least an image of being and belonging together.

Nothing of this kind is true for concentration camps. From the moment of his arrest, nobody in the outside world was supposed to hear of the prisoner again; it is as if he had disappeared from the surface of the earth; he was not even pronounced dead. The earlier custom of the SA to inform the family of the death of a concentration-camp inmate by mailing to them the zinc coffin or an urn was abolished and replaced by strict instructions to the effect that "third persons (are to be left) in uncertainty as to the whereabouts of prisoners. . . . This also includes the fact that the relatives may not learn anything when such prisoners die in concentration camps."[20]

The supreme goal of all totalitarian governments is not only the freely admitted, long-range ambition to global rule but also the never-admitted and immediately realized attempt at the total domination of man. The concentration camps are the laboratories in the experiment of total domination, for human nature being what it is, this goal can be achieved only under the extreme circumstances of a human-made hell. Total domination is achieved when the human person, who somehow is always a specific mixture of spontaneity and being conditioned, has been transformed into a completely conditioned being whose reactions can be calculated even when he is led to certain death. This disintegration of personality is carried through in different stages, the first being the moment of arbitrary arrest when the judicial person is being destroyed, not because of the injustice of the arrest but because the arrest stands in no connection whatsoever with the actions or opinions of the person. The second stage of destruction concerns the moral personality and is achieved through the separation of concentration camps from the rest of the world, a separation which makes martyrdom senseless, empty, and ridiculous. The last stage is the destruction of individuality itself and is brought about through the permanence and institutionalizing of torture. The end result is the reduction of human beings to the lowest possible denominator of "identical reactions."

It is with a society of such human beings, each at a different stage on its way to becoming a bundle of reliable reactions, that the social sciences are called upon to deal when they try to investigate the social conditions of the camps. It is in this atmosphere that the amalgamation of criminals, political opponents, and "innocent" people takes place, that ruling classes rise and fall, that interior hierarchies emerge and disappear, that hostility against the SS guards or the camp administration gives way to complicity, that the inmates assimilate themselves to the outlook on life of their persecutors, although the latter rarely attempt to indoctrinate them.[21] The unreality which surrounds the hellish experiment, which is so strongly felt by the inmates themselves and makes the guards, but also the prisoners, forget that murder is being committed when somebody or many are killed, is as strong a handicap for a scientific approach as the non-utilitarian character of the institution. Only people who for one reason or another are no longer ruled by the common motives of self-interest and common sense could indulge in a fanaticism of pseudo-scientific convictions (the laws of life or nature) which for all immediate practical purposes (winning the war or exploitation of labor) was quite obviously self-defeating. "Normal men do not know that everything is possible,"[22] said one of the survivors of Buchenwald. Social scientists, being normal men, will have great difficulties in understanding that limitations which usually are thought to be inherent in the human condition could be transcended, that behavior patterns and motives which usually are identified, not with the psychology of some specific nation or class at some specific moment of its history, but with human psychology in general are abolished or play a quite secondary role, that objective necessities conceived as the ingredients of reality itself, adjustment to which seems a mere question of elementary sanity, could be neglected. Observed from the outside, victim and persecutor look as though they were both insane, and the interior life of the camps reminds the onlooker of nothing so much as an insane asylum. Our common sense, trained in utilitarian thinking for which the good as well as the evil makes sense, is offended by nothing so much as by the complete senselessness of a world where punishment persecutes the innocent more than the criminal, where labor does not result and is not intended to result in products, where crimes do not benefit and are not even calculated to benefit their authors. For a benefit expected to be realized in centuries[23] can hardly be called an incentive, especially not in a situation of great military emergency.

The fact that due to an insane consistency this whole program of extermination and annihilation could be deduced from the premises of racism is even more perplexing, for the ideological supersense, enthroned, as it were, over a world of fabricated senselessness, explains "everything" and therefore nothing. Yet, there is very little doubt that the perpetrators of these unprecedented crimes committed them for the sake of their ideology which they believed to be proved by science, experience, and the laws of life.

Confronted with the numerous reports from survivors which in remarkable monotony always "report but do not communicate"[24] the same horrors and the same reactions, one is almost tempted to draw up a list of phenomena which do not fit into the most general notions we have of human being and behavior. We do not know and can only guess why the criminals withstood the disintegrating influences of camp life longer than other categories and why the innocents in all instances were those who disintegrated most quickly.[25] It seems that in this extreme situation it was more important to an individual that his sufferings could be interpreted as punishment for some real crime or some real defiance against the ruling group than to have a so-called good conscience. The complete absence of even rudimentary regret on the side of the persecutors after the close of the war, however, when some gesture of self-accusation might have been helpful in court, together with the ever-repeated assurances that responsibility for the crimes rested with some superior authorities, seems to indicate that fear of responsibility is not only stronger than conscience but even stronger, under certain circumstances, than fear of death. We know that the object of the concentration camps was to serve as laboratories in training people to become bundles of reactions, in making them behave like Pavlov's dog, in eliminating from the human psychology every trace of spontaneity; but we can only guess how far this is actually possible—and the terrible docility with which all people went to their certain death under camp conditions as well as the surprising small percentage of suicides are frightful indications[26]—and what happens to human social and individual behavior once this process has been carried to the limit of the possible. We know of the general atmosphere of unreality of which the survivors give such uniform accounts; but we can only guess in what forms human life is being lived when it is lived as though it took place on another planet.

While our common sense is perplexed when confronted with actions which are neither passion inspired nor utilitarian, our ethics is unable to cope with crimes which the Ten Commandments did not foresee. It is senseless to hang a man for murder who took part in the fabrication of corpses (although of course we hardly have any other course of action). These were crimes which no punishment seems to fit because all punishment is limited by the death penalty.

The greatest danger for a proper understanding of our recent history is the only too comprehensible tendency of the historian to draw analogies. The point is that Hitler was not like Jenghiz Khan and not worse than some other great criminal but entirely different. The unprecedented is neither the murder itself nor the number of victims and not even "the number of persons who united to perpetrate them."[27] It is much rather the ideological nonsense which caused them, the mechanization of their execution, and the careful and calculated establishment of a world of the dying in which nothing any longer made sense.

NOTES

1. "If I should recite these horrors in words of my own, you would think me intemperate and unreliable," Justice Robert H. Jackson in his opening address at the Nuremberg trials. See *Nazi Conspiracy and Aggression*, Washington, 1946, I, 140.

2. See Bruno Bettelheim's report "On Dachau and Buchenwald" in *Nazi Conspiracy*, VII, 824.

3. Goebbels reports the following in his Diary for March 1943: "The Führer is happy . . . that the Jews have been . . . evacuated from Berlin. He is right in saying that the war has made possible for us the solution of a whole series of problems that could never have been solved in normal times. The Jews will certainly be the losers in this war come what may." *The Goebbels Diaries 1942–1943*, edited by Louis P. Lochner, New York, 1948, 314.

4. Robert H. Jackson, *op. cit.*, II, 3.

5. The Circular letter of January 1939 from the Ministry of Foreign Affairs to all German authorities abroad on "The Jewish Question as a Factor in German Foreign Policy in the Year 1938" stated: "The emigration movement of only about 100,000 Jews has already sufficed to awaken the interest if not the understanding of many countries in the Jewish danger. We can estimate that here the Jewish question will extend to a problem of international politics when large numbers of Jews from Germany, Poland, Hungary, and Rumania are put on the move. . . . Germany is very interested in maintaining the dispersal of Jewry . . . the influx of Jews in all parts of the world invokes the opposition of the native population and thereby forms the best propaganda for the German Jewish policy. . . . The poorer and therefore the more burdensome the immigrating Jew is to the country absorbing him, the stronger this country will react." See *Nazi Conspiracy*, VI, 87ff.

6. This project was propagated by the Nazis at the beginning of the war. Alfred Rosenberg announced in a speech of January 15, 1939, that the Nazis would demand that "those people who are friendly disposed to Jews, above all the Western democracies who have so much space . . . place an area outside of Palestine for the Jews, of course in order to establish a Jewish reserve and not a Jewish State." *Nazi Conspiracy*, VI, 93.

7. It is very interesting to see in the Nazi documents published in *Nazi Conspiracy* and the *Trial of the Major War Criminals* (Nuremberg, 1947) how few people in the Nazi party itself had been prepared for extermination policies. Extermination was always carried out by the SS troops, upon the initiative of Himmler and Hitler, against protests from the civilian and military authorities. Alfred Rosenberg, in charge of the administration of Russian occupied territories, complained in 1942 that "new plenipotentiaries-in-chief [i.e., SS officers] endeavored to carry out direct actions in the occupied eastern territories, overlooking those dignitaries who were appointed by the Führer himself" [i.e., Nazi officials outside of the SS]. (See *Nazi Conspiracy*, IV, 65ff.) Reports about conditions in the Ukraine during the fall of 1942 (*Nazi Conspiracy*, III, 83ff) show clearly that neither the *Wehrmacht* nor Rosenberg was aware of the depopulation plans of Hitler and Himmler. Hans Frank, Governor-General of Poland, dared even in September 1943, when most party officials had been frightened into submission, to say during a meeting of the *Kriegswirtschaftsstabes und des Verteidigungsauschusses*: "Sie kennen ja die törichte Einstellung der Minderwertigkeit der uns unterworfenen Völker, und zwar in einem Augenblick, in welchem die Arbeitskraft dieser Völker eine der wesentlichsten Potenzen unseres Siegringens darstellt." *Trial of the Major War Criminals*, XXIX, 672.

8. During a discussion in Hitler's headquarters about measures to be carried out after the conclusion of the war, Hitler proposed a National Health Bill: "After national X-ray examination, the Führer is to be given a list of sick persons, particularly those with lung and heart diseases. On the basis of the new Reich Health Law . . . these families will no longer be able to remain among the public and can no longer be allowed to produce children. What will happen to these families will be the subject of further orders of the Führer." *Nazi Conspiracy*, VII, 175 (no date).

9. "Imagine only that these occurrences would become known to the other side and exploited by them. Most likely such propaganda would have no effect only because people who hear and read about it simply would not be ready to believe it." From a secret report concerning the killing of 5,000 Jews in June 1943. *Nazi Conspiracy*, I, 1001.

10. It is noteworthy that protests from military authorities were less frequent and less violent than those of old party members. In 1942, Hans Frank stated emphatically that the responsibility for the annihilation of the Jews came from "higher quarters." And he goes on to say: "I was able to prove the other day . . . that [the interruption of a big building program] would not have happened if the many thousands of Jews working at it had not been deported." In 1944, he complains again and adds: "Once we have won the war, then for all I care, mince-meat can be made of the Poles and the Ukrainians and all the others who run around here. . . ." *Nazi Conspiracy*, IV,

902, 917. During an official meeting in Warsaw in January 1943, State Secretary Krüger voiced the concern of the occupying forces: "The Poles say: After the Jews have been destroyed, then they will employ the same methods to get the Poles out of this territory and liquidate them just like the Jews." That this was indeed intended to be the next step is clear from a speech of Himmler in Cracow in March 1942. *Ibidem*, IV, 916, and III, 640ff.

11. That "economic considerations should fundamentally remain unconsidered in the settlement of the [Jewish] problem" had to be repeated from 1941 onward. *Ibidem*, VI, 402.

12. Concentration camps made their first appearance during the Boer War, and the concept of "protective custody" was first used in India and South Africa.

13. In 1934, Reichsminister of the Interior Wilhelm Frick, a party member of old standing, tried to issue a decree "stating that 'on the consideration' of the 'stabilizing of the national situation' and 'to reduce the abuses in connection with the infliction of protective custody,' 'the Reichsminister had decided' to place restrictions upon the exercise of protective custody." See *Nazi Conspiracy*, II, 259; cf. also VII, 1099. This decree was never published and the practice of "protective custody" increased greatly in 1934.

According to a sworn affidavit of Rudolf Diels, former chief of the political police in Berlin and acting chief of the Gestapo in 1933, the political situation had become completely stabilized by January 1934. *Ibid.*, V, 205.

14. In the words of Wilhelm Stuckart, State Secretary of the Ministry of Interior. *Ibidem*, VIII, 738.

15. See Heinrich Himmler, "On Organization and Obligation of the SS and the Police," in *National-politischer Lehrgang der Wehrmacht vom 15.–23. Januar 1937* (restricted for the Armed Forces). Translation in *Nazi Conspiracy*, IV, 616ff.

16. The table on page 246 shows the numerical expansion and the death rate of the concentration camp Buchenwald during the years 1937–1945. It was compiled from several lists, given in *Nazi Conspiracy*, IV, 800ff.

17. The following is an excerpt from a letter of December 1942 from the SS Main Office of Economic Administration to all camp commandants: ". . . a compilation of the current arrivals and departures in all the concentration camps . . . discloses that out of 136,000 arrivals about 70,000 died. With such a high rate of death, the number of the prisoners can never be brought up to the figure that has been ordered by the Reichsführer of the SS. . . . The Reichsführer has ordered that the death rate absolutely must be reduced. . . ." *Ibid.*, IV, Annex II.

18. Ernest Feder in an "Essai sur la Psychologie de la Terreur," in *Synthèses* (Brussels, 1946) reports an order of the SS to kill daily several hundred Russian prisoners of war by shooting through a hole without seeing the victim.

19. Himmler described his selection methods (*op. cit.*) as follows: "I did not accept people under 1.7 m . . . because I know that people who have reached a certain height must possess the desired blood to some degree." He also obtained photographs

YEAR	ARRIVALS	CAMP STRENGTH		DECEASED[2]	SUICIDES
		HIGH	LOW		
1937	2,912	2,561	929	48	—
1938	20,122[1]	18,105	2,633	771	11
1939	9,553	12,775	5,392	1,235	3
1940	2,525	10,956	7,383	1,772	11
1941	5,896	7,911	6,785	1,522	17
1942	14,111[3]	10,075	7,601	2,898	3
1943	42,172	37,319	11,275[4]	3,516	2
1944	97,866	84,505	41,240	8,644	46
1945	42,823[5]	86,232	21,000[6]	13,056	16

[1] These were of course mostly Jews.

[2] The total of deceased is certainly higher and is being estimated at 50,000.

[3] This figure shows the influx from the Eastern Occupied Territories.

[4] The difference between arrivals and camp strength, or between High and Low does no longer indicate liberations, but transports to other camps or to extermination camps.

[5] Only for the first three months of 1945.

[6] Camp strength at moment of liberation.

---

of the applicants, who were asked to trace their ancestry back to 1750, to have no family member of ill political repute, to "acquire black trousers and boots from their own means" and, finally, to appear in person before a race commission.

20. *Nazi Conspiracy*, VII, 84ff. One of the many orders forbidding information on the whereabouts of prisoners gave the following explanation: "The deterrent effect of these measures lies (a) in allowing the disappearance of the accused without a trace, (b) therein that no information whatsoever may be given about their whereabouts and their fate." *Ibid.*, I, 146.

21. Under Himmler's regime, "any kind of instruction on an ideological basis" was expressly prohibited.

22. David Rousset, *The Other Kingdom*, New York, 1947.

23. It was Himmler's specialty to think in centuries. He expected the results of the war to be realized only "centuries later" in the form of "a Germanic World Empire" (see his speech at Kharkov, in April 1943, *Nazi Conspiracy*, IV, 572ff; when confronted with the "deplorable loss of labor" caused by the death of "tens and hundreds" of prisoners, he insisted that this "thinking in terms of generations is not to be regretted." (See his speech at the meeting of the SS Major Generals at Posen, October 1943, *ibidem*, IV, 558ff. The SS troops were trained along similar lines. "Everyday problems do not interest us . . . we are only interested in ideological questions of importance for decades and centuries, so that the man . . . knows he is working for a great task which occurs but once in 2000 years." (See his speech of 1937, *loc. cit.*)

24. See *The Dark Side of the Moon*, New York, 1947, a collection of reports from Polish survivors of Soviet concentration camps.

25. This fact is quite prominent in many published reports. It has been especially remarked and interpreted by Bruno Bettelheim, in his "Behavior in Extreme Situations," in *Journal of Abnormal and Social Psychology*, XXXVIII (1943). Bettelheim speaks of the self-esteem of the criminals and the political prisoners as distinguished from the lack of self-respect in those who have not done anything. The latter "were least able to withstand the initial shock" and were the first to disintegrate. Bettelheim, however, is wrong when he thinks that this is due to the middle-class origin of the "innocents"—at his time mostly Jews; we know from other reports, especially also from the Soviet Union, that lower-class "innocents" disintegrate just as quickly.

26. This aspect is especially stressed in David Rousset, *Les Jours de Notre Mort*, Paris, 1947.

27. Robert H. Jackson, *op. cit.; Nazi Conspiracy*, II, 3.

The Aftermath of Nazi Rule:
Report from Germany

I N LESS THAN six years Germany laid waste the moral structure of Western society, committing crimes that nobody would have
believed possible, while her conquerors buried in rubble the visible
marks of more than a thousand years of German history. Then into this
devastated land, truncated by the Oder-Neisse borderline and hardly
able to sustain its demoralized and exhausted population, streamed millions of people from the Eastern provinces, from the Balkans, and from
Eastern Europe, adding to the general picture of catastrophe the peculiarly modern touches of physical homelessness, social rootlessness,
and political rightlessness. The wisdom of Allied policy in expelling all
German-speaking minorities from non-German countries—as though
there was not enough homelessness in the world already—may be
doubted. But the fact is that European peoples who had experienced the
murderous demographic politics of Germany during the war were seized
with horror, even more than with wrath, at the very idea of having to
live together with Germans in the same territory.

The sight of Germany's destroyed cities and the knowledge of German
concentration and extermination camps have covered Europe with a cloud

Commentary, X/10, 1950.

of melancholy. Together, they have made the memory of the last war more poignant and more persistent, the fear of future wars more actual. Not the "German problem," insofar as it is a national one within the comity of European nations, but the *nightmare* of Germany in its physical, moral, and political ruin has become almost as decisive an element in the general atmosphere of European life as the Communist movements.

But nowhere is this nightmare of destruction and horror less felt and less talked about than in Germany itself. A lack of response is evident everywhere, and it is difficult to say whether this signifies a half-conscious refusal to yield to grief or a genuine inability to feel. Amid the ruins, Germans mail each other picture postcards still showing the cathedrals and market places, the public buildings and bridges that no longer exist. And the indifference with which they walk through the rubble has its exact counterpart in the absence of mourning for the dead, or in the apathy with which they react, or, rather, fail to react, to the fate of the refugees in their midst. This general lack of emotion, at any rate this apparent heartlessness, sometimes covered over with cheap sentimentality, is only the most conspicuous outward symptom of a deep-rooted, stubborn, and at times vicious refusal to face and come to terms with what really happened.

Indifference, and the irritation that comes when indifference is challenged, can be tested on many intellectual levels. The most obvious experiment is to state *expressis verbis* what the other fellow has noticed from the beginning of the conversation, namely, that you are a Jew. This is usually followed by a little embarrassed pause; and then comes—not a personal question, such as "Where did you go after you left Germany?"; no sign of sympathy, such as "What happened to your family?"—but a deluge of stories about how Germans have suffered (true enough, of course, but beside the point); and if the object of this little experiment happens to be educated and intelligent, he will proceed to draw up a balance between German suffering and the suffering of others, the implication being that one side cancels the other and we may as well proceed to a more promising topic of conversation. Similarly evasive is the standard reaction to the ruins. When there is any overt reaction at all, it consists of a sigh followed by the half-rhetorical, half-wistful question, "Why must mankind always wage wars?" The average German looks for the causes of the last war not in the acts of the Nazi regime, but in the events that led to the expulsion of Adam and Eve from Paradise.

Such an escape from reality is also, of course, an escape from responsibility. In this the Germans are not alone; all the peoples of Western Europe have developed the habit of blaming their misfortunes on some force out of their reach: it may be America and the Atlantic Pact today, the legacy of Nazi occupation tomorrow, and history in general every day of the week. But this attitude is more pronounced in Germany, where the temptation to blame everything under the sun on the occupying powers is difficult to resist: In the British zone everything is blamed on British fear of German competition; in the French zone on French nationalism; and in the American zone, where things are better in every respect, on American ignorance of the European mentality. The complaints are only natural, and they all contain a kernel of truth; but behind them is a stubborn unwillingness to make use of the many possibilities left to German initiative. This is perhaps most clearly revealed in the German newspapers, which express all their convictions in a carefully cultivated style of *Schadenfreude*, malicious joy in ruination. It is as though the Germans, denied the power to rule the world, had fallen in love with impotence as such, and now find a positive pleasure in contemplating international tensions and the unavoidable mistakes that occur in the business of governing, regardless of the possible consequences for themselves. Fear of Russian aggression does not necessarily result in an unequivocal pro-American attitude, but often leads to a determined neutrality, as though it were as absurd to take sides in the conflict as it would be to take sides in an earthquake. The awareness that neutrality will not change one's fate makes it in turn impossible to translate this mood into a rational policy, and the mood itself, by its very irrationality, becomes even more bitter.

But, whether faced or evaded, the realities of Nazi crimes, of war and defeat, still visibly dominate the whole fabric of German life, and the Germans have developed various devices for dodging their shocking impact.

The reality of the death factories is transformed into a mere potentiality: Germans did only what others are capable of doing (with many illustrative examples, of course) or what others will do in the near future; therefore, anybody who brings up this topic is *ipso facto* suspected of self-righteousness. In this context, Allied policy in Germany is frequently explained as a campaign of successful revenge, even though it later turns out that the German who offers this interpretation is quite aware that

most of the things he complains of were either the immediate consequence of the lost war or happened outside the will and control of the
Western powers. But the insistence that there must be a careful scheme
of revenge serves as a consoling argument, demonstrating the equal
sinfulness of all men.

The reality of the destruction that surrounds every German is dissolved into a reflective but not very deep-rooted self-pity, easily dissipated
when ugly little one-story structures that might have been imported from
some Main Street in America spring up on some of the great avenues to
conceal fragmentarily the grimness of the landscape, and to offer an
abundance of provincial elegance in super-modern display windows. In
France and Great Britain, people feel a greater sadness about the relatively few landmarks destroyed in the war than the Germans do for all
their lost treasures together. The boastful hope is expressed in Germany
that the country will become the "most modern" in Europe; yet it is
mere talk, and some person who has just voiced that hope will insist a
few minutes later, at another turn in the conversation, that the next
war will do to all European cities what this one did to Germany's—
which of course is possible, but signifies again only the transformation
of reality into potentiality. The undertone of satisfaction that one often
detects in the Germans' talk about the next war expresses no sinister
renewal of German plans of conquest, as so many observers have maintained, but is only another device for escaping reality: in an eventual
equality of destruction, the German situation would lose its acuteness.

But perhaps the most striking and frightening aspect of the German
flight from reality is the habit of treating facts as though they were mere
opinions. For example, the question of who started the last war, by no
means a hotly debated issue, is answered by a surprising variety of
opinions. An otherwise quite normally intelligent woman in Southern
Germany told me that the Russians had begun the war with an attack
on Danzig; this is only the crudest of many examples. Nor is this transformation of facts into opinions restricted to the war question; in all
fields there is a kind of gentlemen's agreement by which everyone has
a right to his ignorance under the pretext that everyone has a right to
his opinion—and behind this is the tacit assumption that opinions really
do not matter. This is a very serious thing, not only because it often
makes discussion so hopeless (one does not ordinarily carry a reference
library along everywhere), but primarily because the average German

honestly believes this free-for-all, this nihilistic relativity about facts, to be the essence of democracy. In fact, of course, it is a legacy of the Nazi regime.

The lies of totalitarian propaganda are distinguished from the normal lying of non-totalitarian regimes in times of emergency by their consistent denial of the importance of facts in general: all facts can be changed and all lies can be made true. The Nazi impress on the German mind consists primarily in a conditioning whereby reality has ceased to be the sum total of hard inescapable facts and has become a conglomeration of ever-changing events and slogans in which a thing can be true today and false tomorrow. This conditioning may be precisely one of the reasons for the surprisingly few traces of any lasting Nazi indoctrination, as well as for an equally surprising lack of interest in the refuting of Nazi doctrines. What one is up against is not indoctrination but the incapacity or un-willingness to distinguish altogether between fact and opinion. A dis-cussion about the events of the Spanish Civil War will be conducted on the same level as a discussion of the theoretical merits and shortcomings of democracy.

Thus the problem at the German universities is not so much to reintroduce freedom to teach as to re-establish honest research, to con-front the student with an unbiased account of what actually happened, and to eliminate the teachers who have become incapable of doing so. The danger to German academic life is not only from those who hold that freedom of speech should be exchanged for a dictatorship in which a single unfounded, irresponsible opinion would acquire a monopoly over all others, but equally from those who ignore facts and reality and es-tablish their private opinions, not necessarily as the only right ones, but as opinions that are as justified as others.

The unreality and irrelevance of most of these opinions, as compared with the grim relevance of the experience of those who hold them, is sharply underlined by their having been formed before 1933. There is an almost instinctive urge to take refuge in the thoughts and ideas one held before anything compromising had happened. The result is that while Germany has changed beyond recognition—physically and psy-chologically—people talk and behave superficially as though absolutely nothing had happened since 1932. The authors of the few really im-portant books written in Germany since 1933 or published since 1945 were already famous twenty and twenty-five years ago. The younger generation seems to be petrified, inarticulate, incapable of consistent thought.

A young German art historian, guiding his audience among the masterpieces of the Berlin Museum, which had been sent on tour through several American cities, pointed to the Ancient Egyptian statue of Nefertiti as the sculpture "for which the whole world envies us," and then proceeded to say (a) that even the Americans had not "dared" to carry this "symbol of the Berlin collections" to the United States, and (b) that because of the "intervention of the Americans," the British did not "dare" to carry the Nefertiti to the British Museum. The two contradictory attitudes to the Americans were separated by only a single sentence: the speaker, devoid of convictions, was merely groping automatically among the clichés with which his mind was furnished to find the one that might fit the occasion. The clichés have more often an old-fashioned nationalistic than an outspoken Nazi tone, but in any case one seeks in vain to discover behind them a consistent point of view, be it even a bad one.

With the downfall of Nazism, the Germans found themselves again exposed to facts and reality. But the experience of totalitarianism has robbed them of all spontaneous speech and comprehension, so that now, having no official line to guide them, they are, as it were, speechless, incapable of articulating thoughts and adequately expressing their feelings. The intellectual atmosphere is clouded with vague pointless generalities, with opinions formed long before the events they are supposed to fit actually happened; one is oppressed by a kind of pervasive public stupidity which cannot be trusted to judge correctly the most elementary events, and which, for example, makes it possible for a newspaper to complain, "The world at large once again deserted us"—a statement comparable for blind self-centeredness to the remark Ernst Jünger in his war diaries (*Strahlungen*, 1949) tells of having overheard in a conversation about Russian prisoners assigned to work near Hannover: "It seems there are scoundrels among them. They steal food from the dogs." As Jünger observes, "One often has the impression that the German middle classes are possessed by the devil."

The rapidity with which, after the currency reform, everyday life in Germany returned to normal and reconstruction began in all fields, has become the talk of Europe. Without a doubt, people nowhere work so hard and long as in Germany. It is a well-known fact that Germans have for generations been overfond of working; and their present industriousness seems at first glance to give substance to the opinion that Germany is still potentially the most dangerous European nation. There are, moreover, many strong incentives for work. Unemployment is rampant and the position of the trade unions is so weak that compensation for overtime is not even demanded by the workers, who frequently refuse to report it to the unions; the housing situation is worse than the many new buildings would seem to indicate: Business and office buildings for the great industrial and insurance companies have an unquestioned priority over dwelling units, and the result is that people prefer going to work on Saturdays and even Sundays to staying at home in overcrowded apartments. In rebuilding, as in almost all areas of German life, everything is done (often in a most spectacular way) to restore a facsimile of pre-war economic and industrial conditions, and very little is done for the welfare of the masses of the people.

Yet none of these facts can explain the atmosphere of feverish busyness on the one hand and the comparatively mediocre production on the other. Beneath the surface, the German attitude to work has undergone a deep change. The old virtue of seeking excellence in the finished product, no matter what the working conditions, has yielded to a mere blind need to keep busy, a greedy craving for something to do every moment of the day. Watching the Germans busily stumble through the ruins of a thousand years of their own history, shrugging their shoulders at the destroyed landmarks or resentful when reminded of the deeds of horror that haunt the whole surrounding world, one comes to realize that busyness has become their chief defense against reality. And one wants to cry out: But this is not real—real are the ruins, real are the past horrors, real are the dead whom you have forgotten. But they are living ghosts, whom speech and argument, the glance of human eyes and the mourning of human hearts, no longer touch.

There are, of course, many Germans whom this description does not fit. Above all, there is Berlin, whose people, in the midst of the most horrible physical destruction, have remained intact. I do not know why this should be so, but customs, manners, speech, approaches to people, are in the smallest details so absolutely different from everything one sees and has to face in the rest of Germany that Berlin is almost like another country. There is hardly any resentment in Berlin against the victors and apparently never was; while the first saturation bombings from England were pulverizing the city, Berliners are reported to have crawled out of their cellars and, seeing one block after another gone, remarked: "Well, if the Tommies mean to keep this up, they'll soon have to bring their own houses with them." There is no embarrassment and no guilt-feeling, but frank and detailed recital of what happened to Berlin's Jews at the beginning of the war. Most important of all, in Berlin the people still actively hate Hitler, and even though they have more reason than other Germans to feel themselves pawns in international politics, they do not feel impotent but are convinced that their attitudes count for something; given half a chance, they will at least sell their lives dear.

The Berliners work just as hard as other people in Germany, but they are less busy, they will take time to show one around the ruins and will somewhat solemnly recite the names of the streets that are gone. It is hard to believe, but it seems there is something in the Berliners' claim that Hitler never entirely succeeded in conquering them. They are remarkably well-informed and have kept their sense of humor and their characteristically ironical friendliness. The only change in the people—apart from their having become somewhat sadder and less ready for laughter—is that "Red Berlin" is now violently anti-Communist. But here again there is an important difference between Berlin and the rest of Germany: only Berliners take the trouble to point out clearly the similarities between Hitler and Stalin, and only Berliners bother to tell you that they are of course not against the Russian people—a sentiment all the more remarkable if one remembers what happened to the Berliners, many of whom had welcomed the Red Army as the true liberator, during the first months of occupation, and what is still happening to them in the Eastern sector.

Berlin is an exception, but unfortunately not a very important one. For the city is hermetically sealed off and has little intercourse with the rest of the country, except that one meets people everywhere who because of the uncertainty there left Berlin for the Western zones and now complain bitterly of their loneliness and disgust. Indeed, there are quite a number of Germans who are "different"; but they use up their energy in efforts to penetrate the stifling atmosphere that surrounds them, and remain completely isolated. In a way these people are today worse off psychologically than in the worst years of Hitler's terror. In the last years of the war, there did exist a vague comradeship of opposition among all who for one reason or another were against the regime. Together they hoped for the day of defeat, and since—apart from the few well-known exceptions—they had no real intention of doing anything to hasten that day, they could enjoy the charm of a half-imaginary rebellion. The very danger involved in even the mere thought of opposition created a sentiment of solidarity all the more consoling because it could express itself only in such intangible gestures of emotion as a glance or a handclasp, which assumed a significance out of all proportion. The emergence from this overheated intimacy of danger into the crude egotism and spreading shallowness of post-war life has been a truly heartbreaking experience for many people. (It may be remarked that today in the Eastern zone, with its police regime, this time almost universally detested by the population, an even stronger atmosphere of comradeship, intimacy, and half-spoken sign language prevails than under the Nazis, so that it is often precisely the best elements in the Eastern zone who find it difficult to make up their minds to move to the West.)

II

Perhaps the saddest part of a sad story is the failure of the three devices used by the Western Allies to solve the moral, economic, and political problem of Germany. Denazification, revival of free enterprise, and federalization are certainly not the cause of present conditions in Germany, but they have helped to conceal and thus to perpetuate moral confusion, economic chaos, social injustice, and political impotence.

Denazification rested on the assumption that there were objective criteria not only for clear-cut distinctions between Nazis and non-Nazis, but for the whole Nazi hierarchy ranging from little sympathizer to war criminal. From the beginning, the whole system, based upon length of party membership, ranks and offices held, date of first entrance, etc., was very complicated, and involved almost everyone. The very few who had been able to keep alive outside the stream of life in Hitler Germany were exempt, and of course rightly so; but they were joined by a number of very different characters who had been lucky or cautious or influential enough to avoid the many annoyances of party membership: men who had actually been prominent in Nazi Germany but now were not required to go through the denazification process. Some of these gentlemen, mostly of the upper middle classes, have by now established open contact with their less fortunate colleagues, jailed for some war crime. This they do partly to seek advice in economic and industrial matters, but also because they have at last become bored with hypocrisy. The injustices of the denazification system were simple and monotonous: the city-employed garbage collector, who under Hitler had to become a party member or look for another job, was caught in the denazification net, while his superiors either went scot-free because they knew how to manage these matters, or else suffered the same penalty as he—to them, of course, a much less serious matter.

Worse than these daily injustices was the fact that the system, devised to draw clear moral and political distinctions in the chaos of a completely disorganized people, actually tended to blur even the few genuine distinctions that had survived the Nazi regime. Active opponents of the regime naturally had to enter a Nazi organization in order to camouflage their illegal activities, and those members of any such resistance movement as had existed in Germany were caught in the same net as their enemies, to the great pleasure of the latter. In theory, it was possible to present proofs of anti-Nazi activity; but not only was it difficult to convince occupation officers without the slightest experience of the intricacies of a terror regime; there was also the danger that the applicant might compromise himself in the eyes of the authorities, who were, after all, primarily interested in peace and order, by showing too convincingly that he had been capable of independent thought and rebellious action.

It is doubtful, however, that the denazification program has stifled new political formations in Germany that might conceivably have grown out of the resistance to Nazism, since the resistance movement itself had so very little vitality in the first place. But there is no doubt that denazification has created an unwholesome new community of interest among the more-or-less compromised, those who for opportunistic reasons had become more-or-less convinced Nazis. This powerful group of slightly dubious characters excludes both those who kept their integrity and those who participated in any resounding way in the Nazi movement. It would be inaccurate in either case to think of exclusion as based on specific political convictions: the elimination of confirmed anti-Nazis does not prove the others to be confirmed Nazis, and the elimination of "famous" Nazis does not mean that the others hate Nazism. It is simply that the denazification program has been a direct threat to livelihood and existence, and the majority have tried to relieve the pressure by a system of mutual assurance that the whole thing need not be taken too seriously. Such assurance can be gained only from those who are as much and as little compromised as oneself. Those who became Nazis out of conviction as well as those who kept their integrity are felt to constitute an alien and threatening element, partly because they cannot be frightened by their past, but also because their very existence is living testimony that something really serious happened, that some decisive act was committed. Thus it has come about that not only the active Nazis but the convinced anti-Nazis are excluded from positions of power and influence in Germany today; this is the most significant symptom of the German intelligentsia's unwillingness to take its own past seriously or to shoulder the burden of responsibility bequeathed to it by the Hitler regime.

The community of interest that exists among the more-or-less compromised is further strengthened by the general German—but not only German!—attitude to official questionnaires. In contrast to Anglo-Saxon and American habits, Europeans do not always believe in telling the absolute truth when an official body asks embarrassing questions. In countries whose legal system does not allow one to give testimony in one's own cause, lying is considered no great sin if the truth happens to prejudice one's chances. Thus for many Germans there is a discrepancy between their answers to military government questionnaires and the truth as known to their neighbors; and so the bonds of duplicity are strengthened.

Yet it was not even conscious dishonesty that defeated the denazification program. A great number of Germans, especially among the more educated, apparently are no longer capable of telling the truth even if they want to. All those who became Nazis after 1933 yielded to some kind of pressure, which ranged from the crude threat to life and livelihood, to various considerations of career, to reflections about the "irresistible stream of history." In the cases of physical or economic pressure, there should have been the possibility of mental reservation, of acquiring with cynicism that absolutely necessary membership card. But, curiously, it seems that very few Germans were capable of such healthy cynicism; what bothered them was not the membership card but the mental reservation, so that they often ended by adding to their enforced enrollment the necessary convictions, in order to shed the burden of duplicity. Today, they have a certain inclination to remember only the initial pressure, which was real enough; from their belated inner adjustment to Nazi doctrines, dictated by conscience, they have drawn the half-conscious conclusion that it was their conscience itself that betrayed them—an experience that does not exactly promote moral improvement.

Certainly the impact of an everyday life wholly permeated by Nazi doctrines and practices was not easy to resist. The position of an anti-Nazi resembled that of a normal person who happens to be thrown into an insane asylum where all the inmates have exactly the same delusion: It becomes difficult under such circumstances to trust one's own senses. And there was the continual added strain of behaving according to the rules of the insane environment, which after all was the only tangible reality, in which a man could never afford to lose his sense of direction. This demanded an ever-present awareness of one's whole existence, an attention that could never relax into the automatic reactions we all use to cope with many daily situations. The absence of such automatic reactions is the chief element in the anxiety of maladjustment; and although, objectively speaking, maladjustment in Nazi society signified mental normality, the strain of maladjustment on the individual was just as great as in a normal society.

The deep moral confusion in Germany today, which has grown out of this Nazi-fabricated confusion of truth with reality, is more than amorality and has deeper causes than mere wickedness. The so-called good Germans are often as misled in their moral judgments of themselves and others as those who simply refuse to recognize that anything wrong or out of the ordinary was done by Germany at all. Quite a number of Germans who are even somewhat overemphatic about German guilt in general and their own guilt in particular become curiously confused if they are forced to articulate their opinions; they may make a mountain out of some irrelevant molehill, while some real enormity escapes their notice altogether. One variation of this confusion is that Germans who confess their own guilt are in many cases altogether innocent in the ordinary, down-to-earth sense, whereas those who are guilty of something real have the calmest consciences in the world. The recently published post-war diary of Knut Hamsun, which has found a large and enthusiastic audience in Germany, gives testimony on the highest level to this horrible innocence that transforms itself into a persecution complex when confronted with the judgment of a morally intact world.

Ernst Jünger's war diaries offer perhaps the best and most honest evidence of the tremendous difficulties the individual encounters in keeping himself and his standards of truth and morality intact in a world where truth and morality have lost all visible expression. Despite the undeniable influence of Jünger's earlier writings on certain members of the Nazi intelligentsia, he was an active anti-Nazi from the first to the last day of the regime, proving that the somewhat old-fashioned notion of honor, once current in the Prussian officer corps, was quite sufficient for individual resistance. Yet even this unquestionable integrity has a hollow ring; it is as though morality had ceased to work and had become an empty shell into which the person who has to live, function, and survive all day long, retires for the night and solitude only. Day and night become nightmares of each other. The moral judgment, reserved for the night, is a nightmare of fear of being discovered by day; and the life of the day is a nightmare of horror in the betrayal of the intact conscience that functions only by night.

In view of the very complicated moral situation of the country at the close of the war, it is not surprising that the gravest single error in the American denazification policy occurred in its initial effort to arouse the conscience of the German people to the enormity of the crimes committed in their name and under conditions of organized complicity. In the early days of occupation, posters appeared everywhere showing the photographed horrors of Buchenwald with a finger pointing at the spectator, and the text: "You are guilty." For a majority of the population these pictures were the first authentic knowledge of what had been done in their name. How could they feel guilty if they had not even known? All they saw was the pointed finger, clearly indicating the wrong person. From this error they concluded that the whole poster was a propaganda lie.

Thus, at least, runs the story one hears time and again in Germany. The story is true enough so far as it goes; yet it does not explain the very violent reaction to these posters, which even today has not died down, and it does not explain the affronting neglect of the content of the photographs. Both the violence and the neglect are called forth by the hidden truth of the poster rather than by its obvious error. For while the German people were not informed of all Nazi crimes and were even deliberately kept ignorant of their exact nature, the Nazis had seen to it that every German knew some horrible story to be true, and he did not need a detailed knowledge of all the horrors committed in his name to realize that he had been made accomplice to unspeakable crimes.

This is a sad story which is not made less sad by the realization that, under the circumstances, the Allied powers had very little choice. The only conceivable alternative to the denazification program would have been a revolution—the outbreak of the German people's spontaneous wrath against all those they knew to be prominent members of the Nazi regime. Uncontrolled and bloody as such an uprising might have been, it certainly would have followed better standards of justice than a paper procedure. But the revolution did not come to pass, and not primarily because it was difficult to organize under the eyes of four foreign armies. It is only too likely that not a single soldier, German or foreign, would have been needed to shield the real culprits from the wrath of the people. This wrath does not exist today, and apparently it has never existed.

Not only was the denazification program inadequate to the moral and political situation at the end of the war; it quickly came into conflict with American plans for the reconstruction and re-education of Germany. To rebuild the German economy along lines of free enterprise seemed a plausible enough anti-Nazi measure, since the Nazi economy had been a clearly planned economy, although it had not—or perhaps not yet—touched property conditions in the country. But the factory owners as a class had been good Nazis, or at least strong supporters of a regime that had offered, in exchange for some relinquishment of private control, to bring the whole European trade and industrial system into German hands. In this, German businessmen behaved no differently from businessmen in other countries in the imperialist era: the imperialist-minded businessman is no believer in free enterprise—on the contrary, he sees state intervention as the only guarantee of safe returns from his far-flung enterprises. It is true enough that the German businessmen, unlike the old-style imperialists, did not control the state but were used by the party for party interests. But this difference, decisive as it might have become in the long run, had not yet appeared in its full force.

In exchange for state-guaranteed expansion, the German business class had been ready enough to liquidate some of its more conspicuous positions of power, especially over the working class. A controlled economic system, with greater safeguards for workers' interests, had therefore come to be the strongest single attraction of the Nazi regime for both working class and upper middle class. Here again, the development did not run its course, and state-owned, or, rather, party-owned, slavery as we know it in Russia had not yet become a threat to German workers (though of course it had been the chief threat to the working classes of all other European countries during the war). The result has been that planned economy in Germany, with no Communist connotations, is remembered as the only safeguard against unemployment and overexploitation.

The reintroduction of truly free enterprise meant handing over the factories and the control of economic life to those who, even if a little wrong about the ultimate consequences of Nazism, had been staunch supporters of the regime for all practical purposes. If they had not had much real power under the Nazis, they had enjoyed all the pleasures of status, and this regardless of actual membership in the party. And since the end of the war, together with almost unlimited power over economic life, they have regained their old power over the working class—that is, the only class in Germany which, though it had welcomed state intervention as insurance against unemployment, had never been wholeheartedly Nazi. In other words, at the time when denazification was the official watchword of Allied policy in Germany, power was returned to people whose Nazi sympathies were a matter of record, and power was taken away from those whose untrustworthiness with regard to the Nazis had been the only somewhat established fact in an otherwise fluctuating situation.

To make things worse, the power returned to the industrialists was freed even of the feeble controls that had existed under the Weimar Republic. The trade unions which the Nazis had wiped out were not reinstated to their former position—partly because they lacked competent personnel and partly because they were suspected of anti-capitalist convictions—and the efforts of the unions to regain their former influence over the workers failed badly, with the result that by now they have lost the little confidence they may have inherited from memories of former times.

The socialists' stubborn attack on the Schuman plan* may look foolish to the outside world. This attack, however, can be properly understood (though hardly excused) only if one bears in mind that, under present circumstances, the combination of the Rhine-Ruhr industry with French industry might very well mean an even more concerted and better supported assault on the workers' standard of living. The mere fact that the Bonn government, frequently considered a mere façade for the interests of the industrialists, has supported the plan so heartily seems reason enough for suspicion. For, unfortunately, the German upper middle classes have neither learned from nor forgotten the past; they still believe, despite a wealth of experience to the contrary, that a large "labor reserve"—that is, considerable unemployment—is a healthy economic sign, and they are satisfied if they can keep wages down in this way.

The economic issue is considerably sharpened by the problem of the refugees, which is the greatest economic and social problem of present-day Germany. So long as these people are not resettled, they will constitute a grave political danger, precisely because they have been driven into a political vacuum. In common with the comparatively few convinced Nazis who are still left in Germany and who almost without exception were former members of the SS, the expellees have a clear-cut political program and can rely upon a certain group solidarity, two elements conspicuously absent in all other strata of the population. Their program is the re-establishment of a powerful Germany which would make it possible for them to return to their former homes in the East and take their revenge on the populations that expelled them. In the meantime, they are busy hating and despising the native German population, which received them with something less than fraternal sentiments.

As distinguished from the problem posed by the remnants of the Nazi movement, the refugee problem could be solved by energetic and intelligent economic measures. That, failing such measures, the refugees have been driven into a position where they had virtually no choice but to establish a party of their own if they wanted their interests to be

*Robert Schuman, French Foreign Minister, proposed a plan for European industrial co-operation that was realized in 1952 as the European Community of Coal and Steel (ECCS). It was the beginning of the European Economic Community (EEC). —Ed.

represented at all is in no small part the fault of the present regime, and more specifically of the influence of the free-enterprise slogan as it has been understood or misunderstood by Germans. Public funds are used for credit to big enterprises; encouragement of small enterprises (many of the refugees are skilled workers and craftsmen), especially in the form of co-operatives, has been almost completely neglected. The amount of money spent for the benefit of the refugees varies from one Land (state) to the other, but the amounts are nearly always hopelessly inadequate, not only in terms of absolute help but also in proportion to the general state budget. Recent proposals by the Bonn government to reduce business taxes—a clear index to the government's economic policy—would have decreased the available funds for refugees even more sharply. The fact that the occupation authorities vetoed this measure may offer some hope that the American authorities are coming to understand that the free-enterprise slogan has different connotations in Germany, and in Europe in general, from those that surround it in the United States.

It is indeed one of the chief handicaps of American policy in Europe that this difference is not clearly understood. The American system, where the power of industrial management is strongly counterbalanced by the power of organized labor, would hardly seem acceptable to the European believer in free enterprise; in Europe, the trade unions even in their best days were never among the established powers, but always led the uncertain existence of a mildly rebellious force operating with varying success in an everlasting battle against the employers. In America, moreover, there is a certain reluctance, shared by employers and workers, to resort to state intervention; sometimes the mere threat of state arbitration may bring the disputing parties back to bilateral negotiations. In Germany, both workers and employers have only one idea in their heads: that the state must throw its full weight on the side of their interests. With the possible exception of the Scandinavians, no European citizenry has the political maturity of Americans, for whom a certain amount of responsibility, i.e., of moderation in the pursuit of self-interest, is almost a matter of course. Furthermore, this is still a country of abundance and of opportunity, so that the talk of free initiative has not yet become meaningless; and the very dimensions of the American economy tend to defeat over-all planning. But in European countries, where national territories have continually shrunk in proportion to industrial capacity, most people are firmly convinced that even the present standard of living can be guaranteed only if there is some measure of planning to assure everyone a just share in the national income.

Behind the loose and wholly unjustified talk of American "imperialism" in Europe looms the not so unjustified fear that the introduction of the American economic system into Europe, or, rather, American support of the economic *status quo*, can only result in a miserably low standard of living for the masses. The social and political stability of the Scandinavian countries results partly from strong trade unions, partly from the role of co-operatives in economic life, and partly from a wisely exerted state intervention. These factors indicate at least the general direction that the solution of European economic and social problems might take if unsolved political problems did not interfere and if the general world situation allowed enough time. In Germany, at any rate, the system of free enterprise has led quickly to cut-throat practices, monopolization, and trustification, regardless of all efforts of the American authorities to prevent these developments.

Politically, the most serious aspect of the situation is not, as might be expected, the rising dissatisfaction of the working classes. The tragic history of the German socialist parties seems to have exhausted their vitality; never before has the German working class been in a less revolutionary mood. There is a certain embittered resignation to a system that is "sold" to them under the trade name of democracy, but this resentment will hardly cause any trouble; on the contrary, it is almost a guarantee that any regime, however good or bad, will be acceptable, as a matter of indifference. An altogether different and really dangerous side of the matter is that since the situation of the workers has become more hopeless, more insecure, and more miserable than before, the old fear of "proletarianization" has received new and powerful motivation.

This fear especially grips the middle classes, who once again lost their money through the currency reform, in contrast to the industrialists, whose fortunes were secure in real properties. The financial status of the middle-class Germans, especially if they lost their belongings in the bombings or are refugees, differs in no way from that of the ordinary worker's family. But the idea of having to share the worker's lot for a lifetime is forbidding indeed.

To avoid this, the younger people therefore try desperately to scrape together a few marks to enter one of the many universities—all of them overcrowded. It is their only chance to keep their middle-class status and to escape the misery of a proletarianized life. Everywhere in Germany one is told that in a few years there will be enough lawyers, physicians, teachers, art historians, philosophers, and theologians to form a breadline stretching over all the highways. And most of these potentially unemployed academicians will have earned their degrees at the price of appalling sacrifices; many students live on a monthly income of sixty or seventy marks, which means chronic undernourishment and complete abstention from even the most modest pleasures, such as a glass of wine or an evening at the movies. Academic requirements in general are not much lower than they used to be, so that the fanatic devotion of these young people to their studies, prompted as it may be by quite non-intellectual motives, is interrupted only by recurring spells of hard manual labor to earn a little extra money.

Nobody in Germany seems to doubt that the tremendous sacrifices of the student generation can only end in severe disappointment, and nobody seems to give this problem much serious thought. The only solution would be the closing of a number of German universities, combined with a pitiless screening of the high-school graduates, perhaps even the introduction of the otherwise questionable French system of competitive examinations in which the number of successful candidates is determined beforehand by the number of available places. Instead of a discussion along these or other lines, the Bavarian government only recently opened one more (the fourth) university in Bavaria, and the French occupation authorities, in some ill-advised urge to improve German culture, have actually opened a brand-new university in Mainz—which means that six thousand students have come to aggravate the already quite hopeless housing situation in a city almost completely destroyed. And indeed a rather desperate courage would be required under present conditions to take measures that would forcibly empty the universities; it would be like depriving a despairing man of his last chance, even though this chance had become a gambler's chance. What course political development will take in Germany when a whole class of frustrated and starving intellectuals is let loose on an indifferent and sullen population is anybody's guess.

Even those observers of Allied policy in Germany who viewed denazification with misgivings and saw that a system of free enterprise could lead only to the aggrandizement of politically undesirable elements placed considerable hope on the federalization program, under which Germany was divided into Länder (states) with extensive powers of local self-government. It seemed indisputably right in so many ways: It would act as a safeguard against accumulation of power, and thus appease the understandable if exaggerated fears of Germany's neighbors; it would prepare the German people for the hoped-for federalization of Europe; it would teach grass-roots democracy in the field of communal or local affairs where people had their immediate interests and were supposed to know the ropes, and thus might counteract the Nazi megalomania which had taught Germans to think in continents and plan in centuries.

But the failure of the Länder governments is already almost a matter of record. It is a failure in the only political field where the Germans have been left alone almost from the beginning of the occupation, and where success or failure was independent of Germany's status on the international scene. To some extent, of course, the failure of the local governments can be blamed upon the general climate of German life created by denazification and the social consequences of a ruthless economic policy; but this explanation sounds valid only if one willfully ignores the great degree of freedom that was granted to the Germans in the Länder governments. The truth is that centralization, as it was accomplished by nation-states and as it was established in Germany, not by Hitler but by Bismarck, succeeded in destroying all authentic desire for local autonomy and in undermining the political vitality of all provincial or municipal bodies. Whatever is left of such traditions has assumed a hopelessly reactionary character and has petrified into the cheapest kind of folklore. Local government in most instances has liberated the most vicious local conflicts, creating chaos everywhere because there is no power great enough to overawe conflicting factions. The element of public responsibility and even of national interest being conspicuously absent, local politics tends to deteriorate quickly into the lowest possible form of plain corruption. The dubious political past of everybody who is experienced (and the "inexperienced" elements have by now been rather ruthlessly eliminated) and the low salaries paid to the civil servants together open the door to all kinds of mismanagement: many public officials can easily be blackmailed, and many more find it very difficult to resist the temptation to augment their salaries by accepting bribes.

The Bonn government has little direct connection with the Länder governments: it is neither controlled by them nor does it exercise any noticeable control over them. The only functioning links between Bonn and the Länder governments are the party machines, which rule supreme in all questions of personnel and administration, and which, in sharp contrast to the "small state" structure of the country, are more centralized than ever and therefore represent the only visible power.

This is a dangerous situation, but in itself it is not necessarily the worst that could have happened. The real trouble comes from the nature of the party machines themselves. The present parties are continuations of the pre-Hitler parties—that is, of the parties that Hitler found it so surprisingly easy to destroy. They are in many cases run by the same people and are dominated by the old ideologies and the old tactics. However, only the tactics have somehow preserved their vitality; the ideologies are carried along simply for tradition's sake and because a German party cannot very well exist without a *Weltanschauung*. One cannot even say that the ideologies have survived for want of something better; it is rather as though the Germans, after their experience with Nazi ideology, have become convinced that just about anything will do. The party machines are primarily interested in providing jobs and favors for their members, and they are all-powerful to do so. This means that they tend to attract the most opportunistic elements of the population. Far from encouraging initiative of any kind, they are afraid of young people with new ideas. In short, they have been reborn in senility. Consequently, what little there is of political interest and discussion occurs in small circles outside the parties and outside the public institutions. Each of these small groups, because of the political vacuum and the general corruption of public life around them, is the potential nucleus for a new movement; for the parties have not only failed to enlist the support of the German intelligentsia, they have also convinced the masses that they do not represent their interests.

The melancholy story of post-war Germany is not one of missed opportunities. In our eagerness to find a definite culprit and definable mistakes we tend to overlook the more fundamental lessons this story may teach us. When all is said, the twofold question remains: What could one reasonably expect from a people after twelve years of totalitarian rule? What could one reasonably expect from an occupation confronted with the impossible task of putting back on its feet a people that had lost the ground from under it?

But it would be well to remember and try to understand the experience of the occupation of Germany, for we are all too likely to see it
repeated in our lifetime on a gigantic scale. Unfortunately, the liberation
of a people from totalitarianism is not likely to come to pass merely
through "the breakdown of communications and centralized control
[which] might well enable the brave Russian peoples to free themselves
from a tyranny far worse than that of the Czars," as Churchill put it
in his recent speech to the Assembly of the Council of Europe. The
German example shows that help from the outside is not likely to set
free indigenous forces of self-help, and that totalitarian rule is something
more than merely the worst kind of tyranny. Totalitarianism kills the
roots.

Politically speaking, the present conditions of German life have a
greater significance as an object lesson for the consequences of totalitarianism than as a demonstration of the so-called German problem in
itself. This problem, like all other European problems, could be solved
only in a federated Europe; but even such a solution seems of little
relevance in view of the imminent political crisis of these coming years.
Neither a regenerated nor an unregenerated Germany is likely to play a
great role in it. And this knowledge of the ultimate futility of any political
initiative on their part in the present struggle is not the least potent
factor in the Germans' reluctance to face the reality of their destroyed
country.

The Eggs Speak Up

"There set out, slowly, for a Different World,

At four, on winter mornings, different legs . . .

You can't break eggs without making an omelette

— That's what they tell the eggs."

         — Randall Jarrell, "A War"

S INCE THE DEFEAT of Nazi Germany, the word "totalitarianism" has been more and more identified with Communism,
and the fight against it has become increasingly popular. This
popularity is suspect because it occurs in a country where no danger of
totalitarian movements exists, and for which the totalitarian threat is
almost exclusively an issue, the gravest issue, of foreign politics. Popularity is even more suspect at a moment when the public authorities—the State Department, on one hand; the FBI, on the other—have
become fully aware of all its external and internal implications. This,
certainly, could not and should not absolve intellectuals from trying to
understand ever better and deeper the nature of totalitarian government
and the causes of totalitarian movements. Yet the fact that the public
authorities are aware seems to make denunciations born of sheer fighting
spirit, and the concomitant unqualified and often inarticulate praise of
"democracy," rather superfluous. It is strange to watch how a whole
generation of people who once had tried to break their heads in rebellion

The manuscript of this unpublished essay, probably delivered as an address, is marked
"Circa 1950." From internal evidence it would appear that it was not written before
1951.

270

against the most solid and unyielding walls of society now spends its energies in the violent opening of open doors; and, not content like other citizens quietly to support their government, fight for more power for the powers-that-be as though these powers were threatened by a domestic conspiracy, which, however, stubbornly fails to materialize.

The one excellent reason for this strange behavior is the insight that, independent of totalitarian movements in any given country, totalitarianism as such constitutes the central political issue of our time. And it is unfortunately true that this country, which in many respects looks like a happy island to a world in turmoil, would spiritually be even more isolated without this "anti-totalitarianism"—even though the insistence of our fighters on the unqualified happiness of the happy island does not exactly form the best of all possible bridges. The point is that to state that totalitarianism is the central political issue of our time makes sense only if one also admits that all other evils of the century show a tendency eventually to crystallize into that one supreme and radical evil we call totalitarian government. All these other evils, to be sure, are lesser evils if compared with totalitarianism: be they tyrannies and dictatorships, or misery and shameless exploitation of man by man, or the imperialist type of oppression of foreign peoples, or the bureaucratization and corruption of democratic governments. Yet this statement is meaningless, because this may well be true of all evils in our entire history. The trouble begins whenever one comes to the conclusion that no other "lesser" evil is worth fighting. Some anti-totalitarians have already started even to praise certain "lesser evils" because the not-so-far-away time when these evils ruled in a world still ignorant of the worst of all evils looks like the good old days by comparison. Yet all historical and political evidence clearly points to the more-than-intimate connection between the lesser and the greater evil. If homelessness, rootlessness, and the disintegration of political bodies and social classes do not directly produce totalitarianism, they at least produce almost all of the elements that eventually go into its formation. Even old-fashioned dictators and tyrants have become more dangerous since totalitarian dictators have shown them new and unexpected techniques for seizing and retaining power. The natural conclusion from true insight into a century so fraught with danger of the greatest evil should be a radical negation of the whole concept of the lesser evil in politics, because far from protecting us against the greater ones, the lesser evils have invariably led us into them. The greatest danger of recognizing totalitarianism as the curse of the century would be an obsession with it to the extent of becoming blind to the numerous small and not so small evils with which the road to hell is paved.

One of the minor reasons why this natural conclusion is so rarely drawn is that it comes into conflict with an even more natural attitude: the tendency to escape from reality and the real discomforts of political struggles. It is more pleasant, less boring, and even more flattering to oneself, if one lives in this century, to be an enemy of Stalin in Moscow than a foe of Joseph McCarthy in Washington. One of the major reasons arises from the role played by the ex-Communists who have recently joined the fight against totalitarianism and transformed it, sometimes for excellent political and sometimes for not less weighty biographical reasons, into a fight against Stalin. The reasons these people have achieved such prominence in our common fight again seem to be excellent. Who would know better the methods and aims of the enemy than those who have just escaped from the enemy's camp? (True, when we were still fighting totalitarianism in the form of Nazism, we hardly looked for ex-Nazis to lead us; but then, there weren't any, and it is difficult to imagine now how we would have received them if there had been. Rauschning was a different case; he had been a Nazi by mistake, and Otto Strasser was never quite trusted.*) This knowledge, however, becomes daily less the monopoly of the initiated few; the technical means of totalitarian organization may be complicated and difficult to grasp, but they are certainly no mystery. And, moreover, what is not so sure is that these ex-Communists know our own methods and our own aims.

There exists another, a much better, though perhaps less plausible, reason for welcoming former members of totalitarian movements back into the political and cultural life of the non-totalitarian world, but— and this indeed illuminates the present situation—this reason is almost never advanced, least of all by the concerned parties themselves. These people, after all, have proved by the very decision which they today consider their worst mistake that they might be more closely connected

---

*Hermann Rauschning, political ally and confidant of Hitler before breaking with him in the early thirties, wrote *The Revolution of Nihilism* (New York, 1939) and *The Voice of Destruction* (New York, 1940), among other works. Otto Strasser, an early follower of Hitler, was expelled from the Nazi party in 1930. (His brother Gregor was executed in 1934 in connection with the so-called Röhm plot.) —Ed.

with and more deeply touched by the central predicaments of this century than the normally happy philistines around them. Those very things which, as we now know, led to pure and unmitigated catastrophe, once appealed to them in much the same way they still appeal, not only to misguided masses, but to a great many intellectuals all over the world. This would of course apply only to a certain type of Communist, to the "revolutionaries," rather than to the "apparatchiks," and it would then also be true for certain types of former Nazis, if it is valid at all. Coming back or having escaped from the totalitarian world (for our purposes it would make little difference if this world were represented by a government in power or a movement fighting for power) seems to give these ex-revolutionaries an indisputable advantage over all those who have never left the smug and comfortable four walls of established institutions, never questioned the values of a world whose institutions almost everywhere are being undermined from within. The advantage would be real, however, only if they turned their backs in full and continued knowledge of the "cause" in which they once believed, including knowledge of the pre-totalitarian conditions which eventually led to the rise of totalitarianism as well as of totalitarian ideology itself. The advantage would be entirely illusory if, for whatever reasons, they had forgotten in the meantime why they once had been able to summon up the courage to leave the spiritual comforts of respectable liberalism or conservatism or even socialism to rebel against social and political conditions which were both hidden and represented by these typically nineteenth-century ideologies.

The chief trouble is, of course, that only for a few has this ever been a matter of conscious courage. Among the numerous recent defections from the Communist parties, there are many for whom the movement was little more than one powerful organization among others in which careers were still open. There are all the little boastful self-confessed Soviet spies or GPU agents who have "turned professional informers," as Joseph Alsop "in plain blunt language" recently put it in *Commonweal*. The old game has become a little too dangerous; they are looking for new masters and are very disappointed when the democratic world refuses to believe in their past importance and help them into new prominence. This trouble should never have become a trouble at all, and the inevitable rise of a popular infatuation with the "I also was a Communist" line, as with anything new, is less its cause than the amazing lack of discrimination in large parts of the politically most interested audience.

The highly respectable former Communists are those who as party members had done everything in their power to steer clear of the spy apparatus within the party, and who had nothing but contempt for those who had made it their business to inform on the many "deviations" from the party line with which good people caught in a bad cause tried to put their consciences to rest. Much of the present confusion could have been avoided if only a few of these respectable former Communists had resisted the temptation of an ill-inspired solidarity and had protested against being thrown into the same pot with the less reputable characters who, for altogether different reasons, left the movement at the same time.

II

Yet more than lack of prudence and need for comradeship accounts for the present unhappy situation. These ex-Communists, no matter what their past careers in the party and no matter when they decided to break with it, all find themselves in the same predicament today: They have to explain to their new non-totalitarian friends why they did not break earlier than they did. And since their consciences are troubled exactly by this particular point, they tend to become very bitter about any of their former colleagues who happened to stick it out a little longer. This intolerance becomes especially irritating when directed toward people who were never members of the party but, for one reason or another, and sometimes for excellent ones, had shown some sympathy for what they still thought might be the "great new experiment in Soviet Russia," even when these ex-Communists had already raised their first warning cries. Among these sympathizers are comparatively few who could be called fellow-travelers in any strict sense of the word. Far from being involved in any kind of "conspiracy," they were more or less articulately aware of the general critical political situation on an international level and, consequently, of the positive, objective possibilities of the October Revolution. Yet they were not sufficiently informed and up to date about the intricate developments in the Soviet Union, and about the even more complicated history of the Communist parties.

What the ex-Communists hardly ever mention today and what, nevertheless, probably troubles their consciences more than anything else is that there was something fundamentally wrong with the party from the beginning. This "wrong" was most strongly denounced, not by the normal, non-Communist world, but by the early protests and warnings of Rosa Luxemburg against the suppression of inner-party democracy. It is worth noting and remembering that one did not need the standards of "normal" society—standards which a revolutionary party naturally cannot accept indiscriminately—in order to detect and judge quite early the first germs, not of totalitarianism, but of tyranny; one needed only to look at the revolutionary past of the party itself. Things went from bad to worse right after Lenin's death, until they became downright intolerable for any freedom-loving individual, even before Stalin liquidated the right- and left-wing deviations in 1930. These things were known only to party members or very close fellow-travelers, hardly ever to outsiders. In a largely moral, but not only moral, sense one might say that it is still the ghost of Rosa Luxemburg who haunts the consciences of the ex-Communists of the older generation.

However that may be, it is certain that, from roughly 1930 on, the question of membership in the Communist party could no longer be debated on political or revolutionary grounds alone. It became a question involving the moral integrity and the private life of each individual. With all the wisdom of hindsight, it is easy to pinpoint this particular moment today; but in all justice to those concerned, one must admit that it was not so easy to judge the situation then. Manners and morals within all groups and factions of the Communist parties, those which were in opposition to Stalin no less than those which supported him, had deteriorated since Rosa Luxemburg's early warnings to a point where all kinds of personal treachery had become commonplace. Stalin, moreover, introduced his new party line without fanfare, and although in practice they were of tremendous consequence, his changes were deceptively small in words and in terms of theory—in precisely those terms, that is, in which these people, because of the scholastic deformation of all party theory, could alone think and orient themselves.

Again with the wisdom of hindsight, it is easy today to formulate what Stalin actually did: He changed the old political and especially revolutionary belief expressed popularly in the proverb "You can't make an omelette without breaking eggs" into a veritable dogma: "You can't break eggs without making an omelette." This, as a matter of fact, is the practical consequence of Stalin's only original contribution to socialist theory. Reinterpreting Marxist doctrine, he proclaimed that the "socialist state" first must grow stronger and stronger and stronger, until it suddenly, in some distant future, "withers away"—just as if the breaking and breaking and breaking of eggs were suddenly and automatically to produce the desired omelette.

It would be naive to assume that well-trained and informed Communists in Western countries had not been aware of the existence of concentration camps and of a singularly "simplified" procedure of justice in the Soviet Union even before 1930. But it would be unjust and unjustified to conclude that they were not bothered by this state of affairs. It was as easy then as it is today to console oneself for concrete instances of breaches of faith and outrages against justice with some historical and wise-sounding generalities, such as that "revolutions always tend to devour their own children." As Marxists, moreover, and convinced adherents of the theory of class struggle, they never doubted the validity of the concept of "objective guilt." This alone sufficed to make them swallow an indefinite number of very unpleasant and morally aggravating occurrences which involved "subjectively" innocent victims.*

In all predicaments they had salved their consciences with the sincere and firm belief that a socialist and classless society—and this still signified for them some realization of justice on earth—can be built only with the greatest sacrifices in human lives. This belief appeared self-evident because it actually was only a more emphatic application of general historical theories, shared in a popular or learned form by everybody, according to which world history, insofar as it aspires to greatness, has always demanded and received great sacrifices. No matter how grandiose this greatness might appear to those who were drunk with History, its practical application coincided uncannily with the pseudo-wisdom of popular proverbs in all Western languages, such as "From planing come shavings"† and "You can't make an omelette without breaking eggs." Nor is this coincidence a mere accident of vulgarization; the "wisdom"

---

*Merely belonging to a "dying" class made one "objectively" guilty, without having "subjectively" committed any crime whatsoever. —Ed.

†Here and later in this essay Arendt wrote "from chipping come chips," which lacks resonance in English. She most likely had in mind the German proverb "Wo gehobelt wird, da fallen Späne," which refers to a carpenter's plane and the shavings resulting from its use. —Ed.

of truly popular proverbs is usually the crystallized result of a long line of authentic philosophical or theological thought.

Against this background of generally shared beliefs about the nature of History and of popularly accepted standards for political activity, the intellectual difficulties of an early moral resistance to totalitarian practices can best be seen. The great personal shock resulted when it became clear to the members of Communist parties and especially to the members of the Bolshevik party in Russia that from now on the "breaking of eggs" had ceased to be an impersonal affair in which History was supposed to do all the breaking. On the contrary, those who had proclaimed themselves the protagonists of History were ordered to do it themselves. Yet great as this shock proved to be for many of them, the experience itself, though frequently analyzed and thought of in terms of personal tragedy, did not penetrate the ideological walls of Marxist doctrine and was therefore hardly ever met on its own moral or political terms. Those among the Marxist-history makers who felt an insurmountable aversion to their new role suspected themselves of moral cowardice and an indecent desire to keep their hands clean and their personalities intact. Trusted party members—who up to this time had owed their reputations to their single-minded devotion (beyond all private concerns) to the "cause," and who in a case of conflicting loyalties would always have thought it a matter of course to care more for the establishment of socialism than for loyalty to their friends or love of their families—were curiously helpless and lacking in arguments when Stalin or, as they thought, History entrusted them with the breaking of eggs by ordering that one "must prove loyalty by delivering a close comrade into [the OGPU's] clutches." A few years later, during the great purges, "there was only one passport across [the] frontier [that separated the old Bolshevik party from the new]. You had to present Stalin and his OGPU with the required quota of victims."* How could those who had always believed that "from planing come shavings" refuse to help in the planing? The result was, and was meant to be, that from now on every party member had to look upon everybody he knew, including himself, as a potential shaving.

It seems only natural, though this does not make things easier today, that under such circumstances the moment when a person decided to

*W. G. Krivitsky, *In Stalin's Secret Services*, New York, 1939, xii, 39.

get out and to stop "breaking eggs" was almost entirely arbitrary. Seen from the inside—though this is difficult to grasp for us on the outside—it did not make much difference whether someone quit because he could not stand the amount of disloyalty and bad faith demanded during the Moscow Trials, when he was asked to sacrifice members of the Old Guard who had been the friends of his manhood or the heroes of his youth (was the consent of the Old Guard to its own sacrifice not obvious enough?), or whether he left the party because of the Hitler-Stalin pact, when he was asked either to make his peace with his worst enemies and the murderers of many of his best comrades or, if a Jew, to regard his whole people as eggs broken for the greater glory of the socialist omelette. It did not make such a tremendous difference because in either case he already had such a long career of egg-breaking behind him that only a great human effort could save him from becoming a broken man.

In this, as in many other respects, it is unfortunately true that totalitarian politicians are only the most extreme and consistent appliers of generally shared, deep-rooted modern political prejudices. The vulgarity and wickedness of these prejudices have been made emphatic beyond endurance, but they arose out of other, more respectable traditions and have acquired new pertinence since our confrontation with the problems of mass-men and mass-society. The ex-Communists had, and still have, to explain the circumstances surrounding their former membership in and eventual break with the party to a world which, at least intellectually, contains many of the very elements which the totalitarians have driven to their logical and bloody consequences. It is doubtless wiser not to insist on the moral side of the question, even though moral motives account for the overwhelming majority of recent defections from the Communist parties. Instead of complaining about breaking eggs, a complaint which could be easily dismissed as sheer sentimentality, the ex-Communists have complained about the omelette, and then launched on endless discussions and "scientific" quibbles about whether or not socialism was being built in Soviet Russia. They have not, at least not consciously and articulately, lost their faith in History and its bloody and grandiose demands upon mankind, but have told the world only that there is no omelette and little likelihood that an omelette will ever develop from so many broken eggs. More recently, the tone has changed and the complaint has been transformed into the stern warning that the omelette has turned out to be a witch's brew.

III

The more or less opportunistic reluctance to come to terms with a genuine moral-political shock plus the tendency to present a tragedy in pseudo-scientific terminology have resulted in some serious consequences. Striking among them is the peculiar barrenness and flatness of the relevant literature with respect to both moral passion and philosophical consideration. The triteness of the human response is surprising, especially when the authors are otherwise sophisticated and articulate people. Even Margarete Buber's recent report on the Soviet and Nazi concentration camps,* which is in every other respect outstanding in this whole genre of literature, has practically nothing of greater general significance to remark than "Will we ever be so close to human beings again as we were in Ravensbrück?" The point is that opportunism, the understandable fear to utter any thought that another might judge to be "sentimental" or "emotional," sometimes appears like a screen which hides . . . nothing. The situation seems to be summed up in drastic simplicity in a story which Silone once told and with which he meant to describe the culminating experience of a whole generation: "One of these revolutionaries—whom wars, revolutions and fascism have broken to such an extent that I am surprised they are not already dead or in an insane asylum—recently came to see me and, with a fervor and an intensity which would be fitting for an important discovery, said to me: 'One always should act towards others as one wants them to act towards himself.' "† At this point, I think one may begin to understand the true predicament underlying all difficulties and all irritations. If those who

*Margarete Buber-Neumann, *Under Two Dictators*, New York, 1951. —Ed.

†The source for this story has not been found, and it may simply have been told to Arendt, who knew Ignazio Silone. In any case, it comports well with remarks Silone made in "An Interview with Ignazio Silone," *Partisan Review*, Fall 1939. Silone was the antifascist Italian author of *Bread and Wine*, *Fontamara*, and *School for Dictators*, among other works. —Ed.

escaped from the totalitarian hell have brought back nothing from their experience but the very truisms, moral or otherwise, from which they escaped twenty or thirty years ago—escaped for the very good reason that they had found them no longer sufficient either to explain the world we live in or to offer a guide for action within it—then we may, morally speaking, indeed be caught between pious banalities which have lost their meaning and in which nobody believes any longer and the vulgar banality of *homo homini lupus*,* which as a guide for human action is also utterly meaningless even though quite a number of people do believe in it as they have always believed in it.

What is frightening, in other words, in the ex-Communists' return to the "normal" world is their easy and unconsidered acceptance of its normalcy in its most banal aspects. It is as though they tell us every day that we have no other choice but that between the totalitarian hell and philistinism. This is made emphatically clear by the peculiar "fervor" on which Silone rightly insists in telling his story, the enthusiasm with which the banalities of philistinism are offered to us. Fighting for the values of philistinism is new indeed, and one can hardly be surprised that it is warmly welcomed. This does not mean that these ex-totalitarians who have discovered their love of respectability are philistines themselves. Their very fervor indicates only too clearly that they are really idealistic extremists who, having lost their "ideal," are on the lookout for substitutes and so carry their extremism into Catholicism, liberalism, conservatism, and whatnot.

Annoying as this fervor may be, it certainly is not dangerous. It becomes dangerous only if applied to existing political institutions or bodies politic, verbally transforming them into a "cause" whose realization, by definition, lies in the future. In the style of extreme idealists, such a "cause" has to be treated as an end which justifies a great many otherwise disreputable means. Such solidly established, firmly rooted political bodies as, for instance, the Republic of the United States need for their continued existence the spirit and the vigilance of their citizenry, but deeds of an idealistic nature are required and useful only in times of "clear and present danger"; at all other times they are only too likely to spoil the manners and customs of democracy. Democratic society as a living reality is threatened at the very moment that democracy

*"Man is a wolf to his fellow man." —Ed.

becomes a "cause," because then actions are likely to be judged and opinions evaluated in terms of ultimate ends and not on their inherent merits. The democratic way of life can be threatened only by people who see everything as a means to an end, i.e., in some necessary chain of motives and consequences, and who are prone to judge actions "objectively," independent of the conscious motives of the doer, or to deduce certain consequences from opinions of which the holder is unaware. In the simplicity of everyday life one rule reigns supreme: Each good action, even for a "bad cause," adds some real goodness to the world; each bad action even for the most beautiful of all ideals makes our common world a little worse. Extreme seriousness can become a real threat to the ease which so primarily characterizes all free societies, in which utterances, as long as they remain in the realm of mere opinion, do not even aim at truth; nor, of course, is social talk very likely ever to produce it. All grace and all good faith in social gatherings are lost if analysis of ulterior motives or the search for possible sinister consequences is permitted to terrorize the free, and therefore sometimes playful and even irresponsible, minds of free men.

IV

It would be good if one could let the matter rest here, and it would be possible if the picture we used for argument's sake of a more or less intact democratic society, to which the ex-Communists have returned in a spirit of conversion, were actually true. This, unfortunately, is not the case. This is still the same world against whose complacency, injustice, and hypocrisy these same men once raised a radical protest, and the tragedy is that everybody today seems to understand this protest better than they do. It is the same world—and not some landscape on the moon—where the elements which eventually crystallized, and have never ceased to crystallize, into totalitarianism are to be found. Their rediscovery of the good old clichés of liberalism, conservativism, and so forth is not only bad because of misplaced fanaticism, and not only harmful because of inherent meaninglessness for the necessary fight against totalitarianism on an intellectual level. It also stands in the way of every serious attempt to form new concepts in political philosophy as well as new solutions to our political predicaments, because it artificially endows with a semblance of life all that, for better or worse, is dead.

Liberalism, the only ideology that ever tried to articulate and interpret the genuinely sound elements of free societies, has demonstrated its inability to resist totalitarianism so often that its failure may already be counted among the historical facts of our century. Wherever free bodies politic and free societies still exist and function, reasonably free from immediate danger—and where do they function except in the United States and possibly Great Britain?—they owe their existence to the customs, habits, and institutions formed in a great past and cultivated through a great tradition. Yet whenever people of good will and sometimes of great intelligence have tried to stem the tide of totalitarianism with them, the great past and the great tradition have remained singularly silent and uninspiring.

It is one thing to love the past and to revere the dead; it is another to pretend that the past is alive in the sense that it is in our power to return to it, that all we have to do is to listen to the voices of the dead. But there is a threatening silence of all good things in our political and social life, even of those many good things which are very much alive. It is easy, at least in times of such comparative normalcy as the last five years in this country, to overshout this silence and to act as though everything were for the best in this best of all worlds. Or, to put it more correctly, it is much harder not to lose one's head in our century during the periods of quiet and seeming normalcy than to keep one's head during the panic of the catastrophes. The recent revivals of conservativism, often affirmed or proclaimed by converted ex-radicals or ex-Communists, are such attempts to overshout the threatening silence that reveals itself the very moment we look to the past for advice in our present situation. These neo-conservatives pretend not to be bothered about this silence because conservativism itself has always maintained the superiority of silent customs and inarticulate traditions in political life over programs, ideas, and formulae. Whether or not this superiority exists is of theoretical interest only; the historical truth of the matter is that conservativism, one ideology of the nineteenth century among others, came into existence only when (during and especially after the French Revolution) traditions and customs began to crumble away and Western mankind actually was confronted with the necessity of change. It is evident that a conscious effort to return to some ideologically defined paradise in some arbitrarily selected past would involve the same elements of man-made change as any other revolution. As an ideology, conservativism, like liberalism, has had ample time and opportunity to reveal its inability to withstand the superior dynamism of totalitarian ideologies, and this even before Hitler demonstrated very specifically and concretely that all ideologies could equally well be used and abused for the purposes of a totalitarian amalgamation.

To return to our specific example: proverbs like "You can't make an omelette without breaking eggs" owe their general common-sense appeal to the fact that they represent, albeit in a vulgar form, some quintessence of Western philosophical thought. Their wisdom, like their imagery, stems from Western mankind's experience of fabrication: You can't make a table without killing a tree. Their wisdom becomes very dubious even when applied in general to the interaction between man and nature; it can result, and has often enough, in the misrepresentation of all naturally given things as mere material for the human artifice—as though trees were nothing but potential wood, material for tables. The element of destruction inherent in all purely technical activity becomes preeminent, however, as soon as its imagery and its line of thinking is applied to political activity, action, or historical events, or any other interaction between man and man. Its current application to politics, by no means a monopoly of totalitarian thinking, indicates a profound crisis in applying our usual standards of right and wrong. Totalitarianism, in this as in most other respects, only draws the final, most unfettered consequences from certain heritages that have become predicaments. There are excellent reasons why this is so, why the only movements that discovered new devices for the organization of the homeless and rootless masses of our times should also be the ones which insisted without compromise on the technical and destructive elements in our political thought. Unfortunately, and this is perhaps even more serious, there are very good reasons why all arguments which fall back on this tradition of human handiwork, and use its images, exert so strong an appeal in the non-totalitarian world as well. The moment man defines himself no longer as *creatura Dei*, he will find it very difficult not to think of himself, consciously or unconsciously, as *homo faber*.

There is indeed only one principle which announces, with the same uncompromising clarity as the principle that "you can't make an omelette without breaking eggs," the diametrically opposite maxim for political action. It was expressed almost incidentally in a lonely phrase of one of the loneliest men of the last generation, Georges Clemenceau, when he suddenly exclaimed during his fight in the Dreyfus Affair: "*L'Affaire d'un seul est l'affaire de tous*" ("The concern of one is the concern of all").

At Table with Hitler

HITLER'S TABLE TALK*: This more misleading than revealing document from recent history appears to be the first
publication commissioned by the German Institute for the
History of the National Socialist Period in Munich. The selection of the
subject and the form of the publication could hardly have been less
fortunate. The title alone, with its embarrassing allusion to Luther's
Table Talk, an allusion underscored by Professor Ritter in his introduction, suggests a tendency to glorify the "great man," in whose features
Mr. Picker perceives the eternal essence of all dictators and the "tremendous possibilities revolutionary men of action represent for the development of humanity." Equivocal and implicit as this tendency may
remain in the two editors, it becomes utterly explicit in a reading of this
book. Professor Ritter's asseveration that Hitler was guilty of "numerous
errors, exaggerations, and falsifications of historical truth" probably
would not have made the reader more wary than he would be anyway

Published in German as "Bei Hitler zu Tisch," Der Monat, IV/37, 1951–1952.
English translation by Robert and Rita Kimber.

*Henry Picker, Hitler's Tischgespräche, edited, introduced, and published by Gerhard
Ritter, Bonn, 1951.

had it appeared in a more prominent place than in an afterword set in the smallest of type. Because there is no commentary whatsoever, Hitler is allowed, as he was when he was alive, to speak freely and unrefuted. The result, of course, could be nothing other than propaganda for Hitler, a boost for German neo-Nazism that Professor Ritter and the commissioning institute have presumably provided unwittingly but that is probably a not-so-unexpected by-product for Mr. Picker, on whose transcriptions the publication is primarily based.

The main reason why this publication is not likely to bring "the truth or at least a significant portion of it to light" lies in the nature of the company in which these conversations were conducted. It consisted of Hitler's military advisers, with whom he took his meals in headquarters from July 1941 (i.e., shortly after the attack on the Soviet Union) until August 1942 (i.e., until the beginning of the battle for Stalingrad). After that date, "the question of who bore responsibility for the double offensive Stalingrad/Caucasus" bred between Hitler and the army "dissension that would never again be resolved." That marked the end of the shared meals.

What we have here then are not Hitler's genuine opinions and presentations of his plans, which he expressed often enough in other circles, but, instead, speeches specifically tailored for the ears of the military men, speeches with which he hoped to convince them of his national goals and cautiously prepare them for his actual plans. In other words, these "Table Talks" were propaganda from the outset and, on top of that, nationalistic propaganda designed to dupe the nationalistically inclined elements of the population. This intention to mislead is blatantly evident because the plans and opinions expressed in the talks stand in blatant contradiction to the actions carried out at the same time on Hitler's orders. It would have been the task of a commentator not so much to correct the actually always rather insignificant errors, but to show, by means of a running comparison with the Führer's orders and with records of other discussions held in the headquarters at the same time, the deliberately duplicitous nature of these talks. Such a commentary would not only have avoided the perpetuation of Hitler's misleading nationalistic propaganda, but would also have provided a genuine source book for recent history.

It is, of course, not the task of a review to supply such commentary after the fact. The discrepancy between Hitler's propaganda *ad usum* *delphini* and the policies he was actually pursuing is, as was to be expected, most striking in the question of the "eradication" of the Jews and of the Eastern European peoples. As late as 1942 Hitler spoke of his plan to resettle the Jews in Madagascar or (in a new version) in Lappland or Siberia, even though since the beginning of the Russian campaign, that is, since spring of 1941, the elimination of Jewry had been decided upon and was being carried out. The units assigned to "eradication work" were formed four weeks before the launching of the attack on Russia, and we know from the sworn testimony of the commanders of these units that in the summer of 1941 more than 300,000 Jews died in mass shootings.* It had already become clear at that time that pogroms, staged with the help of the "reliable population" in the eastern regions, would not suffice for the "total annihilation of the Jews." As early as the fall of 1941, the architect and SS-Standartenführer Blobel had been ordered to provide a plan for constructing gas ovens. While Hitler chatted with his generals about suitable settlement areas for the Jews and about the possibility that even Jews could be decent human beings, this plan was presented to him and "immediately approved" by him.† The first mobile gas chambers were ready in the spring of 1942 and were used from then on until the end of the war.**

Whether Hitler relied more on the "fascination" he exerted over others or on his actual ability to shield himself from confrontation with facts can remain an open question. The uncritical publication of his propaganda talks at the table will in any case provide support for that historically completely unfounded fairy tale of the "good" Hitler who knew nothing of the deeds of the "evil" Himmler. That fairy tale owes its existence to those old party friends of Hitler's (Wilhelm Frick, for example, but also Alfred Rosenberg) who tried to protest against Himmler's "new direction."‡ Hitler himself counted these old comrades among those who "couldn't adapt" and shrank back "once the party's work had gone far beyond what they could understand or had pictured it as being." Innumerable documents refute this old fairy tale unequivocally. Certain subheadings in the present publication seem to suggest

---

*Cf. *Nazi Conspiracy and Aggression*, II, 265ff. and III, 783ff., Document PS-1104.

†Cf. *ibid.*, V, 322ff., Document PS-2605.

**Cf. *ibid.*, II, 275; III, 418ff., Document PS-501.

‡Cf., for example, Frick's sworn statement, *ibid.*, V, Document PS-3043.

that the editors are unfamiliar with these documents; for example, the one on page 66: "Himmler's Policy of Casting Nets for the Racially Pure: No." This subheading, which attempts to establish a difference between Hitler and Himmler, is all the more suspect because it is contradicted by a passage on page 122 in the text itself. Under the subheading "Germanic Gathering," Hitler himself says: "We should draw out from the Germanic peoples the best as with a magnet—that element of humanity with iron in it, as it were. . . ."

The magnet in these cases could of course only be the SS troops under Himmler's command. The "humanity with iron in it" consisted of blue-eyed and blond-haired children that the Nazis meant to steal from their parents and raise in Germany. Himmler organized this on Hitler's command. And finally it is high time to remind people most emphatically that the initial step in this whole process of mass murder was a personal order of Hitler's. Issued on September 1, 1939, it instructed the Reichsleiter Bouhler and the physician Brandt to kill all the "incurably ill" (not, by any means, just the mentally ill!).* The mass murders initiated by Hitler and organized by Himmler were not a "revolutionary excess" carried out by one sector of the party, but the logical consequence of its ideology.

Among the many concessions that Hitler made in his conversations with his officers to the "bourgeois prejudices" of still-halfway respectable people in general and to the army's "code of honor" in particular, his remarks about "decent Jews" and "unavoidable hardships" for the individual are the most striking only because he so often ridiculed these phrases and the lack of "logical" thinking inherent in them. His protestations that he could not bear spying and police snooping are amusing, too, if one recalls how much his career owed to successful spying right after World War I, and though history probably will not grant him status as a "great man," he will perhaps be regarded by posterity as the creator of one of the world's greatest spy systems. But then, his partners at table would, it seems, swallow just about anything. Flattering remarks were accepted at face value even when they were grossly at odds with their everyday experiences: In some comments about executive power in the state, Hitler placed the army at the head of the executive branch, and this at a time when almost every one of his generals was sadly complaining

*Cf. *ibid.*, III, Document PS-630.

that supreme command obviously always lay with the security service and its police force. Then, too, in his discussions of spy activity Hitler once let down his guard and even in these table conversations said what he really meant:

"The real task of the Foreign Office is to find out what solutions England will turn to now [i.e., in the summer of 1942]. But it will hardly be possible to learn what they are except by means of a love affair with Churchill's daughter, and the Foreign Office, which is to say its diplomats, no doubt had too many scruples to initiate such an affair at the appropriate time."

That "spontaneous outbursts" are not exactly characteristic of these talks (as Mr. Picker says; is that what he really thinks?) becomes obvious when Hitler speaks about the Reichstag fire. He serenely rolls out the old propaganda lie about the Communists starting the fire even though on the day after the fire all of Berlin knew what had actually happened. A month later, all of Germany knew, and a year later, the whole world knew. Göring, who was not one to be troubled by scruples in such matters, touched on a fact known to everyone when he said in December 1934 that the Nazis had not needed the Reichstag fire to dispose of the Communists. He did not of course say what they did need it for. That becomes clear from the minutes of the Reich cabinet meetings of January 30 and March 15, 1933, which are now available. The great concern was how to bring about the two-thirds majority needed in the Reichstag itself to pass the Enabling Act by which the Weimar constitution could be circumvented and the legislative function transferred from the Reichstag to the Reich cabinet. The Communist votes had to be eliminated. Was Hitler, who on the night of the fire was in the editorial offices of the *Völkischer Beobachter* by two in the morning to see that the report was properly edited, supposed to be the only person who knew nothing of all this?

More revealing of Hitler's real plans and ideas than the *Table Talk* is the November 1937 "Secret Speech before the Future Political Leaders at the Castle of the Teutonic Order at Sonthofen," contained in the appendix. Here Hitler is speaking to Nazis and not to reactionary military men, for whose feelings he had to make all due allowance. A careful comparison of this speech with the chitchat at the table reveals crucial and obvious discrepancies in Hitler's basic position, discrepancies which have unfortunately evaded Professor Ritter, because he is so overwhelmed by this "mixture of good and evil motives, of the noble with the debased . . ." and because he can imagine all too well how "powerfully [this speech] must have affected these young people." (Can Ritter still really not know of what altogether special breed these "young people" were, from among whom Himmler would later recruit his most reliable troops?) While the *Table Talk* always stresses the importance of the state, the speech says that the Nazis do not consider "the idea of the state of fundamental importance but rather the united folk community." While the *Table Talk* never envisions extending Germany's plans for conquest beyond Europe, the speech refers explicitly to a "world empire." And while the "concept of nation," of which Hitler had taken a totally negative view in *Mein Kampf*, occupies a prominent position in the *Table Talk*, the speech speaks only of an "understanding of the importance of blood and race." How consciously even the lower levels of Nazi leadership did away with reference to things "national" is evident in the minutes of a conference held in SS headquarters in Berlin in January 1943, in which it was suggested that because of its liberal overtones the word "nation" should not be used anymore.*

If we see the table talk as we must see it, that is, essentially as Hitler's propaganda aimed at the army, it becomes clear why, in the thick of a war and of an unprecedented eradication effort, he presents himself here in a much more conciliatory way than he did in his peacetime talks for members of the Wehrmacht. He obviously had more pressing need of the army and its generals in time of war than in peace, and his verbal concessions became all the more necessary the more his actions contradicted them. This explains why, for example, we find in Hitler's speech of November 1937 before Blomberg, Fritsch, Raeder, Neurath, Göring, and Hossbach much better clues to the policy the Nazis would later pursue during the war than we find in the chatter he delivered himself of when these policies were in full swing. In this speech, Hitler stresses repeatedly that Germany's goal was not the conquest of foreign peoples but the acquisition of land without populations. And he adds that there was no such thing as unpeopled land and that a conquerer would always encounter someone in possession. The logical conclusion from this line of reasoning was that the task of the German army would be radically and totally to depopulate populated areas. It would not, of

*Cf. *ibid.*, III, 515, Document PS-705.

course, devolve upon the Wehrmacht to devise methods for this depopulation. That would be left to other and more important agencies of executive power.

This is, then, in many respects a peculiar book. It is published by an editor who does not want either "to accuse or defend, to condemn or glorify" a man proved to be a mass murderer; who does not know that the content of a historical and political source is determined by the moment in which certain things are said to a certain audience; who does not consider it necessary to document discrepancies carefully in footnotes in order to discover what in fact it is that the source conveys; who, after he has hidden all the facts and all the actions behind a cloak of truly extraordinary brotherly love, then claims he wanted "to show things as they actually were"; who then further, in the smallest of type, which hardly anyone will ever bother to read, apologizes for not having corrected "errors" because that would have required too much space; who, however, then allows a co-editor enough space to babble about Hitler's sixth sense and to express his admiration for Eva Braun; and who, finally, has room left for nothing other than rescuing the honor of—Hjalmar Schacht.

If, however, one does read this book with the eyes of a historian, it offers in one respect source material of inestimable value: It shows with utmost clarity Hitler's unquestionable superiority over those around him and the particular quality "of the uncanny charisma Hitler emanated in such a commanding way" that even his editors were unable to escape its influence.

The problem of Hitler's charisma is relatively easy to solve. It was to a great extent identical with what Professor Ritter calls the "fanatical faith this man had in himself," and it rested on the well-known experiential fact that Hitler must have realized early in his life, namely, that modern society in its desperate inability to form judgments will take every individual for what he considers himself and professes himself to be and will judge him on that basis. Extraordinary self-confidence and displays of self-confidence therefore inspire confidence in others; pretensions to genius waken the conviction in others that they are indeed dealing with a genius. This is merely the perversion of an old and justified rule of all good society according to which everyone has to be capable of showing what he is and of presenting himself in the proper light. The perversion occurs when the social role becomes, as it were, arbitrary, when it is completely separated from the actual human substance, indeed, when a role consistently played is unquestioningly accepted as the substance itself. In such an atmosphere any kind of fraud becomes possible because there appears to be no one at all left for whom the difference between fraud and authenticity matters in the least. People therefore fall prey to judgments apodictically expressed because the apodictic tone frees them from the chaos of an infinite number of totally arbitrary judgments. The crucial point is that not only is the apodictic quality of tone more convincing than the content of the judgment but also the content of the judgment, the object judged, becomes irrelevant. Hitler's tirades about the evils of smoking seem to have had a no less fascinating effect on his listeners than his speeches about Napoleon I or his views on world history. To assess correctly this phenomenon of charisma in Hitler's case we have to remind ourselves that in present-day society it is not really all that difficult to create an aura about oneself that will fool everyone—or just about everyone—who comes under its influence. In this respect Hitler behaved no differently than have many less talented charlatans. It goes without saying that under these conditions the rule of a good upbringing that says one must not blow one's own horn has to be ruthlessly put aside. The more that the vulgar practice of unbridled self-praise spreads in a society which for the most part still adheres to the rules of good upbringing, the more powerful its effect will be and the more easily that society can be convinced that only a truly "great man" who cannot be judged by normal standards could summon the courage to break rules as sacrosanct as those of good breeding. In other words, Hitler held a far greater fascination for generals and other members of good society than he did for the "old fighters" who, like him, came from the mob strata of society.

In the prevailing chaos that inability to form judgments created, however, Hitler's superiority went considerably beyond the fascination, the mere "charisma," that any charlatan can emanate. The awareness of the social possibilities that the modern inability to judge offered, and the ability to exploit them, were supported by the vastly more telling insight that in the modern world's chaos of opinion the normal mortal is yanked about from one opinion to another without the slightest understanding of what distinguishes the one from the other. Hitler knew from his own most personal experience what the maelstrom was like into which modern man is drawn and in which he changes his political or other "philosophy" from day to day on the basis of whatever options are offered him as he whirls helplessly about. He is himself that newspaper reader of whom he says that "in a city [in which] twelve newspapers each report the same event differently . . . he will finally come to the conclusion that it is all nonsense." What distinguished Hitler from this newspaper reader and his desperation was simply that he had discovered one fine day that if you really hang onto any one of the current opinions and develop it with (as he was fond of saying) "ice-cold" consistency, then everything would somehow fall back into place again. Hitler's real superiority consisted in the fact that under any and all circumstances he had an opinion and that his opinion always fit perfectly into his over-all "philosophy." In this social context (and only in this context) superiority is indeed increased by fanaticism because obvious and de-monstrable errors can no longer undermine it. What immediately reas-serts itself after any demonstrated error is the fact that one not only has an opinion but also embraces that opinion and is therefore capable of judgment. And in politics, where one constantly has to act and therefore constantly has to make judgments, it is indeed altogether correct in a practical sense and more advantageous to reach any judgment and to pursue any course of action than not to judge and not to act at all.

Not to judge and not to act at all is a condition devoutly desired by many in the modern world. Nevertheless, Hitler's argument that "a man in some little village [cannot] assess the vital questions that concern entire continents," like the argument that one can no more expect po-litical decisions and insights from such a man than one can put someone who doesn't know how to drive behind the steering wheel of a car, had a greater impact in Germany, was more convincing there, than in other countries. This old standard argument of the opponents of democracy was supported there by an unusually strong tradition of political passivity and by a no less unusually strong tradition of work and pure production. Taken together, these traditions made appear quite plausible a curious equating of purely technical capability with purely human activity, the latter of which has always had to do with questions of right and wrong. Once the moral basis of the knowledge of right and wrong, unarticulated as it was, began to crumble, the next step was to measure social and political actions by technical and work-oriented standards that were inherently alien to these larger spheres of human activity.

Along with these insights, which came all too naturally to European mob leaders since Napoleon III, and along with an extraordinary skill in making use of them, Hitler also had an above-average and keen intelligence and a genuine, if very limited, faculty of judgment, which functioned well within its limits. Hitler's assessments of international relationships in Europe were almost always correct. His comments on European history were often truly excellent—especially his comments on the mistakes of Napoleon I, who ought never to have exchanged the title first consul for that of emperor, nor mixed family matters with politics. His judgments of people were often perceptive and amusing, but his judgment failed completely where the Anglo-Saxon countries were concerned. There he misunderstood every event and every situation. His views of America were so unrealistic that they caused him to slap his hand on his knee with pleasure when he heard that America had entered the war. He did not even understand the most primitive power relationships. How could he have understood that for Anglo-Saxon peoples treaties are by no means mere scraps of paper?

Since its emergence in the early eighteenth century, racism had always been so closely linked with contempt for one's own people that it is not astonishing to come across Hitler's remark that as far as he was concerned the German people might as well perish if they failed to win his war for him. More astonishing is his undisguised contempt for the the great cultural accomplishments of the Teutons. With the aid of the whole folk-oriented archaeological establishment, these accomplishments were at the time being hauled to the light of day by hook or by crook and falsifications. It is quite clear that he was no longer satisfied with the "Teuton" concept (no more than he was before with the concepts "German" and "nation"), and he was then on the verge of becoming serious with his talk of the "Aryans," under which the Greeks, too, could confidently be subsumed. Whenever he spoke positively of the Teutons, it was characteristically at the cost of the Germans. His intent was probably slowly to rid his listeners—already accustomed to hearing folkish language but still burdened with "patriotic and national prejudices"—of their narrow-minded nationalism.

If logic is defined as the capability to press on to conclusions with a total disregard for all reality and all experience, then Hitler's greatest gift—the gift to which he owed his success and which brought about his downfall—was one of pure logic. When he says, for instance: "Thinking exists only in the giving or in the execution of an order," he is with that one statement drawing the last, valid conclusion that follows not so much from all philosophies of power as from the opinion that rules in the chaos of opinion, namely, that everything is "nonsense." His listeners, fascinated as they were by the seamless coherence of this world view, no doubt had only in the rarest of cases enough practical imagination to grasp the true meaning of this unswerving logic. Only in the rarest cases would they have understood that Hitler was providing what was in his view an altogether adequate justification for organized murder when he claimed "that nature had modeled everything, and therefore the most correct thing to do was always to adopt her laws"; and when he added that "for example, monkeys trample outsiders to death because they are alien to the society." And when he said still further that "what was right for the monkeys was right in still higher degree for human beings," then he had every right to assume he had been properly understood. Anyone who allowed him his premise of the omnipotence of nature but then did not draw the logical conclusion that called for the "eradication" of all who were not "viable" or were "alien to the community"—anyone with such scruples belonged among those weaklings or blockheads who "denying the force of logic, shrank back from saying B and C after they had said A." There were of course, both within the party and outside it, weaklings of this sort with their moral scruples, just as there were idiots who translated into practice the "totally mad plan" of zeppelins, even though "nature had not provided a single bird with a balloon."

In terms of politics, nature had taught Hitler only two "laws." One was the "trampling to death" of alien species "to maintain [one's own] species." The other was "not to value the individual life too highly," that is, it was all right to trample to death individuals of one's own species. The latter principle he even considered a "divine law," the only one in which he was inclined to believe. He demonstrated the dispensation of God with the example of—flies.

Interesting details alter little in the character of the book. In view of the growing neo-Nazism in Germany and in view of the even more blatant lack of enlightenment among the German people about the events of their recent history, one wonders whether the German Institute for the History of the National-Socialist Period will learn something from this misstep and from the suspect popularity of this "source," a pre-publication version of which it managed to place in an illustrated magazine. Will it, for example, as its next publication prepare a collection including all the statements made under oath by the commanders of the eradication units, the Führer's secret orders, and the minutes of the party discussions in Hitler's headquarters? Those are documents from which, if one cared to, one could indeed see "things as they actually were."

Mankind and Terror

HISTORY TEACHES US that terror as a means of frightening people into submission can appear in an extraordinary variety of forms and can be closely linked with a large number of political and party systems that have become familiar to us. The terror of tyrants, despots, and dictators is documented from ancient times on, the terror of revolutions and counter-revolutions, of majorities against minorities and of minorities against the majority of humanity, the terror of plebiscitary democracies and of modern one-party systems, the terror of revolutionary movements and the terror of small groups of conspirators. Political science cannot content itself with simply establishing the fact that terror has been used to intimidate people. Rather, it must separate out and clarify the differences between all these forms of terror regimes, forms that assign quite different functions to terror in each specific regime.

In what follows here, we will deal only with totalitarian terror as it appears in the two totalitarian political systems most familiar to us: Nazi Germany after 1938 and Soviet Russia after 1930. The key difference

Speech, in German, for RIAS Radio University, March 23, 1953. English translation by Robert and Rita Kimber.

between totalitarian terror and all other forms of terror we know of is not that it existed on a quantitatively larger scale and claimed a larger number of victims. Who would dare to measure and compare the fears human beings experienced? And who has not wondered whether the number of the victims and the increasing indifference of others toward them are not linked closely to an increase in population that has bred in all modern mass states a kind of Asiatic indifference to the value of human life and a conviction, no longer even concealed, of the superfluity of human beings?

Wherever we find terror in the past, it is rooted in the use of force that originates outside the law and in many cases is consciously applied to tear down the fences of law that protect human freedom and guarantee citizens' freedoms and rights. From history, we are familiar with the mass terror of revolutions in whose furor the guilty and the innocent die, until the bloodbath of the counter-revolution suffocates the furor in apathy or until a new reign of law puts an end to the terror. If we single out the two forms of terror that have been historically the most effective and politically the bloodiest—the terror of tyranny and the terror of revolution—we soon see that they are directed toward an end and find an end. The terror of tyranny reaches an end once it has paralyzed or even totally dispensed with all public life and made private individuals out of all citizens, stripping them of interest in and a connection with public affairs. And public affairs are concerned, of course, with much more than we generally circumscribe with the term "politics." Tyrannical terror has come to an end when it has imposed a graveyard peace on a country. The end of a revolution is a new code of laws—or counter-revolution. The terror finds its end when the opposition is destroyed, when nobody dares lift a finger, or when the revolution has exhausted all reserves of strength.

Totalitarian terror is so often confused with the intimidation measures of tyranny or the terror of civil wars and revolutions because the totalitarian regimes we are familiar with developed directly out of civil wars and one-party dictatorships and in their beginnings, before they became totalitarian, used terror in precisely the same way as other despotic regimes we know of from history. The turning point that decides whether a one-party system will remain a dictatorship or develop into a form of totalitarian rule always comes when every last trace of active or passive opposition in the country has been drowned in blood and terror.

Genuinely totalitarian terror, however, sets in only when the regime has no more enemies who can be arrested and tortured to death and when even the different classes of suspects are eliminated and can no longer be taken into "protective custody."

From this first characteristic of totalitarian terror—that it does not shrink but grows as the opposition is reduced—follow the next two key features. Terror that is directed against neither suspects nor enemies of the regime can turn only to absolutely innocent people who have done nothing wrong and in the literal sense of the word do not know why they are being arrested, sent to concentration camps, or liquidated. The second key factor follows from this, namely, that the graveyard peace that spreads over the land under pure tyranny as well as under the despotic rule of victorious revolutions, and during which the country can recover, is never granted to a country under totalitarian rule. There is no end to the terror, and it is a matter of principle with such regimes that there can be no peace. As totalitarian movements promise their adherents before they come to power, everything will remain in permanent flux. Trotsky, who first coined the phrase "permanent revolution," no more understood what that really meant than Mussolini, to whom we owe the term "total state," knew what totalitarianism meant.

This is clear both in Russia and in Germany. In Russia, the concentration camps that were originally built for enemies of the Soviet regime began to grow enormously after 1930, that is, at a time not only when the armed resistance of the civil-war period had been crushed but also when Stalin had liquidated the opposition groups within the party. During the first years of Nazi dictatorship in Germany there were at most ten camps, with no more than 10,000 inmates. By about 1936 all effective resistance to the regime had died out, partly because the preceding and extraordinarily bloody and brutal terror had destroyed all the active forces (the number of deaths in the first concentration camps and in the Gestapo cellars was extremely high) and partly because the apparent solution of the unemployment problem had won over many working-class people who had originally opposed the Nazis. It was at this very time, in the first months of 1937, that Himmler gave his famous speech to the Wehrmacht in which he expressed the need for major enlargement of the concentration camps and announced that it would be undertaken in the near future. By the time war broke out there were already more than 100 concentration camps that from 1940 on must have collectively had an average constant population of a million inmates. The corresponding numbers for the Soviet Union are vastly higher. There are different estimates, the lowest being about 10 million people, the highest, about 25 million.

The fact that terror becomes totalitarian after the liquidation of the political opposition does not mean that the totalitarian regime then fully renounces acts of intimidation. The initial terror is replaced by draconian legislation that establishes in law what will be considered "transgressions"—interracial sexual relations or arriving late for work, i.e., insufficient grasp of the Bolshevist system, in which the worker belongs body and soul to a production process guided by principles of political terror—and so retroactively legalizes the initial reign of terror. This retroactive legalization of conditions created by revolutionary terror is a natural step in revolutionary legislation. The new draconian measures were supposed to put an end to the extra-legal terror and establish the new law of the revolution. What is characteristic of totalitarian regimes is not that they too pass new laws of this kind, such as the Nuremberg laws, but that they do not stop there. Instead, they retain terror as a power functioning outside the law. Consequently, totalitarian terror pays no more attention to the laws decreed by the totalitarian regime than it does to those in effect before the regime's assumption of power. All laws, including the Bolshevist and Nazi laws, become a façade whose purpose is to keep the population constantly aware that the laws, no matter what their nature or origin, do not really matter. This becomes all too clear in documents from the Third Reich that show Nazi judges and often even party agencies desperately trying to judge crimes according to a specific code and to protect duly sentenced people from the "excesses" of terror. To cite only one example from many: We know that people who were convicted of racial violations after 1936 and were sentenced to prison by normal legal procedures were then sent to concentration camps after already having served their prison terms.

Because of its racial ideology, Nazi Germany could fill its concentration camps with a majority of innocent people far more easily than the Soviet Union could. It could maintain some sense of order without having to adhere to any criteria of guilt or innocence simply by arresting certain racial groups on no other grounds than race: first, after 1938, the Jews; then later, indiscriminately, members of Eastern European ethnic groups. Because the Nazis had declared these non-Germanic ethnic groups enemies of the regime, it could uphold the pretense of their "guilt." Hitler, who in this matter as in all others always contemplated the most radical and far-reaching measures, saw a time coming after the war when these groups would have been eradicated and a need for new categories would arise. In a 1943 draft for a comprehensive Reich health law, he therefore suggested that after the war all Germans should be X-rayed and that all families in which anyone suffered from a lung or heart disease should be incarcerated in camps. If this measure had been carried out—and there is little doubt that if the war had been won it would have been one of the first measures on the post-war agenda—then the Hitler dictatorship would have decimated the German people just as the Bolshevist regime did the Russian people. (We know, of course, that systematic decimations of this kind are far more effective than even the bloodiest wars. In the years of the artificially imposed famine in the Ukraine and of the so-called de-Kulakization of that region, more people died each year than in the extremely ruthless and bloody war fought in Eastern Europe.)

In Russia, too, in periods that permit such actions, the category of the innocently condemned is determined by certain criteria. Thus, not just Poles who fled to Russia but also Russians of Polish, German, or Baltic ancestry all wound up in huge numbers in the concentration camps during the war and died in them. It is a matter of course, too, that the people who are liquidated, deported, or incarcerated in camps either are labeled members of so-called "dying classes"—such as the Kulaks or the petit bourgeoisie—or are declared adherents of one of the currently alleged conspiracies against the regime—Trotskyites, Titoites, agents of Wall Street, cosmopolitans, Zionists, etc. Whether these conspiracies exist or not, the liquidated groups have nothing whatever to do with them, and the regime knows that very well. Granted, we have no documentation, such as we now have for the Nazi regime in depressing abundance, but we do have enough information to know that arrests are centrally regulated with certain percentages required for every part of the Soviet Union. This makes for much more arbitrary arrest than in Nazi Germany. It is, for example, typical that if some prisoners in a marching column fall down and lie dying on the roadside, the soldier in charge will arrest any people he happens to find along the way and force them into the column to maintain his quota.

Closely linked to the increase in totalitarian terror as political opposition shrinks and to the resulting massive increase in innocent victims is a final characteristic that has far-reaching consequences for the completely altered mission and goals of the secret police in totalitarian governments. This feature is a modern form of mind control that is not so much interested in what is actually going on in the mind of the prisoner as it is in forcing him to confess crimes that he never committed. This is also the reason why provocation plays practically no role at all in the totalitarian police system. Who the person to be arrested and liquidated is, what he is thinking or planning—that is already determined by the government in advance. Once he is arrested, his actual thoughts and plans are of no consequence whatever. His crime is objectively determined, without the help of any "subjective" factors. If he is a Jew, he is a member of the conspiracy of the Elders of Zion; if he has heart disease, he is a parasite on the healthy body of the Germanic people; if he is arrested in Russia when an anti-Israeli and pro-Arab foreign policy is in force, then he is a Zionist; if the government is intent on eradicating the memory of Trotsky, he is a Trotskyite. And so on.

Among the great difficulties in the way of understanding this newest form of domination—difficulties that are at the same time proof we are indeed up against something new and not just a variant of tyranny—is that not only are all our political concepts and definitions insufficient for an understanding of totalitarian phenomena, but also all our categories of thought and standards for judgment seem to explode in our hands the instant we try to apply them here. If, for example, we apply to the phenomenon of totalitarian terror the category of means and ends, by which terror would be a means to retain power, to intimidate people, to make them afraid, and so in this way to cause them to behave in certain ways and not in others, it becomes clear that totalitarian terror will be less effective than any other form of terror in achieving that end. Fear cannot possibly be a reliable guide if what I am constantly afraid of can happen to me regardless of anything I do. Totalitarian terror can be given a free hand only at that point when the regime has assured itself by means of a wave of the most extreme terror that opposition has indeed become impossible. One can of course say, and it has often been said, that in this case the means have become the ends. But this is not really an explanation. It is only a confession, disguised as a paradox, that the category of means and ends no longer works; that terror is apparently without an end; that millions of people are being senselessly sacrificed; that, as in the case of the mass murders during the war, the measures actually run counter to the perpetrator's real interests. If the means have become the ends, if terror is not just a means to subjugate people by fear but is an end for the sake of which people are sacrificed, then the question of the meaning of terror in totalitarian systems has to be put differently and answered outside the category of means and ends.

To understand the meaning of totalitarian terror, we have to turn our attention to two noteworthy facts that would appear to be completely unrelated. The first of these is the extreme care that both Nazis and Bolshevists take to isolate concentration camps from the outside world and to treat those who have disappeared into them as if they were already dead. The facts are too well known to require further elaboration. The authorities behaved identically in both the cases of totalitarian rule we know of. Not even word of deaths is released. Every effort is made to create the impression not only that the person in question has died but also that he never existed at all. Any efforts to learn anything about his fate thus become utterly pointless. The often maintained view that the Bolshevist concentration camps are a modern form of slavery and are therefore fundamentally different from the Nazi death camps, which were operated like factories, is therefore mistaken on two counts. No slaveholders in history ever used up their slaves with such incredible speed. Different from other forms of enforced labor, too, is a mode of arrest and deportation that cuts off its victims from the world of the living and sees that they "die off" under the pretext that they belong to a dying class; that is, exterminating them is justified because their death, though perhaps by other means, is foreordained anyhow.

The second fact is the striking one repeatedly verified, particularly in the Bolshevist regime, that no one except for the leader in power at the moment is immune from terror, that the people who are the executioners today can easily be transformed into the victims of tomorrow. The observation that revolution devours its own children has often been cited to account for this phenomenon. However, this observation, which originated in the French Revolution, proved meaningless once the terror continued after the Revolution had already devoured all its own children, the factions from right to left, and the remaining centers of power in the army and the police. The so-called purges are obviously one of the most striking and permanent institutions of the Bolshevist regime. They no longer devour the children of the Revolution, because those children are already dead. They devour, instead, the party and police bureaucracies, even at their highest levels.

The millions imprisoned in the concentration camps have to submit to the first of these measures because there is no way to defend oneself against total terror. The party and police functionaries submit to the second because, schooled in the logic of totalitarian ideology, they are as well suited to be the regime's victims as its executioners. These two factors, these ever recurring features of totalitarian governmental systems, are closely related. Both mean to make human beings in their infinite variety and their unique individuality superfluous. David Rousset has called concentration camps the "most totalitarian society," and it is true that the camps serve, among other purposes, as laboratories in which human beings of the most varied kinds are reduced to an always constant collection of reactions and reflexes. This process is carried so far that any one of these bundles of reactions can be exchanged for any other and so far that no specific person is killed, no one with a name, an unmistakable identity, a life of one particular cast or another and with certain attitudes and impulses, but, rather, a completely undistinguishable and undefinable specimen of the species *homo sapiens*. The concentration camps not only eradicate people; they also further the monstrous experiment, under scientifically exacting conditions, of destroying spontaneity as an element of human behavior and of transforming people into something that is even less than animal, namely, a bundle of reactions that, given the same set of conditions, will always react in the same way. Pavlov's dog, trained to eat not when it was hungry but when it heard a bell ring, was a perverted animal. For a totalitarian government to achieve its goal of total control over the governed, people have to be deprived not only of their freedom but also of their instincts and drives, which are not programmed to produce identical reactions in all of us but always move different individuals to different acts. Totalitarian government's failure or success therefore ultimately depends on its ability to transform human beings into perverted animals. Ordinarily this is never altogether possible, even under the conditions of totalitarian terror. Spontaneity can never be entirely eradicated, because life as such, and surely human life, is dependent on it. In concentration camps, however, spontaneity can be eradicated to a great extent; or, at any rate, the most careful attention and effort is expended there on experiments for that purpose. If that is to be accomplished, people obviously have to be robbed of the last traces of their individuality and transformed into collections of identical reactions; they have to be cut off from everything that made them unique, identifiable individuals within human society. The purity of the experiment would be compromised if one admitted even as a remote possibility that these specimens of the species *homo sapiens* had ever existed as real human beings.

At the other extreme from these measures and the experiments connected with them are the purges, which recur at regular intervals and make tomorrow's victims of today's executioners. It is crucial to a purge that its victims offer no resistance, willingly accept their new fate, and cooperate in the widely publicized show trials in which they wipe out and defame their past lives. By confessing to crimes that they never committed and in most cases never could have committed, they publicly proclaim that the people whom we thought we were seeing for so many years really never existed at all. These purges, too, are a kind of experiment. They test whether the government can actually depend on the ideological training of its bureaucracy, whether the internal coercion created by indoctrination corresponds to the external coercion of terror by forcing the individual to participate unquestioningly in the show trials and thus to fall completely in line with the regime no matter what monstrosities it commits. A purge that instantaneously transforms the accuser into the accused, the hangman into the hanged, the executioner into the victim puts people to that test. The so-called convinced Communists who quietly disappeared by the thousands in Stalin's concentration camps because they refused to make confessions did not pass this test, and only someone who can pass it truly belongs to the totalitarian system. The purges also serve the purpose, among others, of ferreting out, as it were, those "convinced" adherents of the government. Someone who supports a cause of his own volition can change his mind tomorrow. He is not a reliable member of the totalitarian team. The only reliable people are those who not only know enough or are well trained enough not to have an opinion, but also don't even know any more what it means to be convinced. The experiments of the purges have shown that the ideal type of the totalitarian functionary is the one who functions no matter what, who has no life outside his function.

Totalitarian terror, then, is no longer a means to an end; it is the very essence of such a government. Its ultimate political goal is to form and maintain a society, whether one dominated by a particular race or one in which classes and nations no longer exist, in which every individual would be nothing other than a specimen of the species. Totalitarian ideology conceives of this species of the human race as the embodiment of an all-pervasive, all-powerful law. Whether it is seen as a law of nature or a law of history, this law is actually the law of a movement that rages through mankind, that finds its embodiment in humankind, and is constantly put into action by totalitarian leaders. Dying classes or decadent races on which history and nature have in any case passed judgment will be the first to be handed over to the destruction already decreed for them. The ideologies that are carried out by totalitarian governments with unswerving and unprecedented consistency are not inherently totalitarian and are much older than the systems in which they have found their full expression. From within their own camps, Hitler and Stalin have often been accused of mediocrity because neither of them has enriched his ideology by even a single iota of new nonsense. But this overlooks the fact that these politicians, in following the prescriptions of their ideologies, could not help but discover the true essence of the laws of motion in nature and history, whose movement it was their task to accelerate. If it is the law of nature to eliminate what is harmful and unfit for life, a logically consistent racial politics cannot be well served by one-time terrorist eradications of certain races, for if no new categories of parasitic and unfit lives can be found, that would mean the end of nature altogether—or at least the end of a racial politics that seeks to serve such a law of motion in nature. Or if it is the law of motion in history that in a war between the classes certain classes will "die off," then it would mean the end of human history if no new classes could be discovered for the totalitarian government to bring to the point of dying off. In other words, the law of killing, the law by which totalitarian movements come to power, remains in effect as the law of the movements themselves; and it would not change if the utterly improbable should come to pass, namely, if they achieved their goal of bringing all of humanity under their sway.

Understanding and Politics
(The Difficulties of Understanding)

["Understanding and Politics" was published in *Partisan Review*, XX/4, 1954. Arendt had originally called it "The Difficulties of Understanding"; some material deleted from that first version has been reinstated here. The essay is based on the earlier sections of a long manuscript called "On the Nature of Totalitarianism: An Essay in Understanding," and additional material from those sections is given here in the notes at the end. The later sections of the manuscript are in the next essay. The Introduction to this volume contains further explanation.]

Es ist schwer, die Wahrheit zu sagen, denn es gibt zwar nur eine;

aber sie ist lebendig und hat daher ein lebendig wechselndes Gesicht. — Franz Kafka

MANY PEOPLE SAY that one cannot fight totalitarianism without understanding it.[1] Fortunately this is not true; if it were, our case would be hopeless. Understanding, as distinguished from having correct information and scientific knowledge, is a complicated process which never produces unequivocal results. It is an

[1] The notes are at the end of the essay.

unending activity by which, in constant change and variation, we come to terms with and reconcile ourselves to reality, that is, try to be at home in the world.

The fact that reconciliation is inherent in understanding has given rise to the popular misrepresentation *tout comprendre c'est tout pardonner.* Yet forgiving has so little to do with understanding that it is neither its condition nor its consequence. Forgiving (certainly one of the greatest human capacities and perhaps the boldest of human actions insofar as it tries the seemingly impossible, to undo what has been done, and succeeds in making a new beginning where everything seemed to have come to an end) is a single action and culminates in a single act. Understanding is unending and therefore cannot produce final results. It is the specifically human way of being alive; for every single person needs to be reconciled to a world into which he was born a stranger and in which, to the extent of his distinct uniqueness, he always remains a stranger. Understanding begins with birth and ends with death. To the extent that the rise of totalitarian governments is the central event of our world, to understand totalitarianism is not to condone anything, but to reconcile ourselves to a world in which such things are possible at all.

Many well-meaning people want to cut this process short in order to educate others and elevate public opinion. They think that books can be weapons and that one can fight with words. But weapons and fighting belong in the realm of violence, and violence, as distinguished from power, is mute; violence begins where speech ends. Words used for the purpose of fighting lose their quality of speech; they become clichés. The extent to which clichés have crept into our everyday language and discussions may well indicate the degree to which we not only have deprived ourselves of the faculty of speech, but are ready to use more effective means of violence than bad books (and only bad books can be good weapons) with which to settle our arguments.

The result of all such attempts is indoctrination. As an attempt to understand, it transcends the comparatively solid realm of facts and figures, from whose infinity it seeks to escape; as a short-cut in the transcending process itself, which it arbitrarily interrupts by pronouncing apodictic statements as though they had the reliability of facts and figures, it destroys the activity of understanding altogether. Indoctrination is dangerous because it springs primarily from a perversion, not of knowledge, but of understanding. The result of understanding is meaning, which we originate in the very process of living insofar as we try to reconcile ourselves to what we do and what we suffer.

Indoctrination can only further the totalitarian fight against understanding, and, in any case, it introduces the element of violence into the whole realm of politics. A free country will make a very poor job of it compared with totalitarian propaganda and education; by employing and training its own "experts," who pretend to "understand" factual information by adding a non-scientific "evaluation" to research results, it can only advance those elements of totalitarian thinking which exist today in all free societies.[2]

This is, however, but one side of the matter. We cannot delay our fight against totalitarianism until we have "understood" it, because we do not, and cannot expect to understand it definitively as long as it has not definitively been defeated. The understanding of political and historical matters, since they are so profoundly and fundamentally human, has something in common with the understanding of people: who somebody essentially *is*, we know only after he is dead. This is the truth of the ancient *nemo ante mortem beatus esse dici potest*. For mortals, the final and eternal begins only after death.

The most obvious escape from this predicament is the equation of totalitarian government with some well-known evil of the past, such as aggression, tyranny, conspiracy. Here, it seems, we are on solid ground; for together with its evils, we think we have inherited the wisdom of the past to guide us through them. But the trouble with the wisdom of the past is that it dies, so to speak, in our hands as soon as we try to apply it honestly to the central political experiences of our own time.[3] Everything we know of totalitarianism demonstrates a horrible originality which no farfetched historical parallels can alleviate. We can escape from its impact only if we decide not to focus on its very nature, but to let our attention wander into the interminable connections and similarities which certain tenets of totalitarian doctrine necessarily show with familiar theories of occidental thought. Such similarities are inescapable. In the realm of pure theory and isolated concepts, there can be nothing new under the sun; but such similarities disappear completely as soon as one neglects theoretical formulations and concentrates on their practical application. The originality of totalitarianism is horrible, not because some new "idea" came into the world, but because its very actions constitute a break with all our traditions; they have clearly exploded our categories of political thought and our standards for moral judgment.

In other words, the very event, the phenomenon, which we try—and must try—to understand has deprived us of our traditional tools of understanding. Nowhere was this perplexing condition more clearly revealed than in the abysmal failure of the Nuremberg Trials. The attempt to reduce the Nazi demographic policies to the criminal concepts of murder and persecution had the result, on the one hand, that the very enormity of the crimes rendered any conceivable punishment ridiculous; and, on the other, that no punishment could even be accepted as "legal," since it presupposed, together with obedience to the command "Thou shalt not kill," a possible range of motives, of qualities which cause men to become murderers and make them murderers, which quite obviously were completely absent in the accused.

Understanding, while it cannot be expected to provide results which are specifically helpful or inspiring in the fight against totalitarianism, must accompany this fight if it is to be more than a mere fight for survival. Insofar as totalitarian movements have sprung up in the non-totalitarian world (crystallizing elements found in that world, since totalitarian governments have not been imported from the moon), the process of understanding is clearly, and perhaps primarily, also a process of self-understanding. For, although we merely know, but do not yet understand, what we are fighting against, we know and understand even less what we are fighting for. And the resignation, so characteristic of Europe during the last war and so precisely formulated by an English poet who said that "we who lived by noble dreams / defend the bad against the worse,"* will no longer suffice. In this sense, the activity of understanding is necessary; while it can never directly inspire the fight or provide otherwise missing objectives, it alone can make it meaningful and prepare a new resourcefulness of the human mind and heart which perhaps will come into free play only after the battle is won.[4]

Knowledge and understanding are not the same, but they are interrelated. Understanding is based on knowledge and knowledge cannot proceed without a preliminary, inarticulate understanding. Preliminary understanding denounces totalitarianism as tyranny and has decided that our fight against it is a fight for freedom. It is true that whoever cannot

*C. Day Lewis, "Where Are the War Poets?" Lewis wrote "honest dreams." —Ed.

be mobilized on these grounds will probably not be mobilized at all. But many other forms of government have denied freedom, albeit never so radically as the totalitarian regimes, so that this denial is not the primary key to understanding totalitarianism. Preliminary understanding, however, no matter how rudimentary and even irrelevant it may ultimately prove to be, will certainly more effectively prevent people from joining a totalitarian movement than the most reliable information, the most perceptive political analysis, or the most comprehensive accumulated knowledge.[5]

Understanding precedes and succeeds knowledge. Preliminary understanding, which is at the basis of all knowledge, and true understanding, which transcends it, have this in common: They make knowledge meaningful. Historical description and political analysis[6] can never prove that there is such a thing as the *nature* or the *essence* of totalitarian government, simply because there is a *nature* to monarchical, republican, tyrannical, or despotic government. This specific nature is taken for granted by the preliminary understanding on which the sciences base themselves, and this preliminary understanding permeates as a matter of course, but not with critical insight, their whole terminology and vocabulary. True understanding always returns to the judgments and prejudices which preceded and guided the strictly scientific inquiry. The sciences can only illuminate, but neither prove nor disprove, the uncritical preliminary understanding from which they start. If the scientist, misguided by the very labor of his inquiry, begins to pose as an expert in politics and to despise the popular understanding from which he started, he loses immediately the Ariadne thread of common sense which alone will guide him securely through the labyrinth of his own results. If, on the other hand, the scholar wants to transcend his own knowledge—and there is no other way to make knowledge meaningful except by transcending it—he must become very humble again and listen closely to the popular language, in which words like "totalitarianism" are daily used as political clichés and misused as catchwords, in order to re-establish contact between knowledge and understanding.

The popular use of the word "totalitarianism" for the purpose of denouncing some supreme political evil is not much more than about five years old. Up to the end of the Second World War, and even during the first postwar years, the catchword for political evil was "imperialism." As such, it was generally used to denote aggression in foreign politics;

this identification was so thorough that the two terms could easily be exchanged one for the other. Similarly, totalitarianism is used today to denote lust for power, the will to dominate, terror, and a so-called monolithic state structure. The change itself is noteworthy. Imperialism remained a popular catchword long after the rise of Bolshevism, Fascism, and Nazism; obviously people had not yet caught up with events or did not believe that these new movements would eventually dominate the whole historical period. Not even a war with a totalitarian power, but only the actual downfall of imperialism (which was accepted after the liquidation of the British Empire and the reception of India into the British Commonwealth) marked the moment when the new phenomenon, totalitarianism, was admitted to have taken the place of imperialism as the central political issue of the era.

Yet while popular language thus recognizes a new event by accepting a new word, it invariably uses such concepts as synonyms for others signifying old and familiar evils—aggression and lust for conquest in the case of imperialism, terror and lust for power in the case of totalitarianism. The choice of the new word indicates that everybody knows that something new and decisive has happened, whereas its ensuing use, the identification of the new and specific phenomenon with something familiar and rather general, indicates unwillingness to admit that anything out of the ordinary has happened at all. It is as though with the first step, finding a new name for the new force which will determine our political destinies, we orient ourselves toward new and specific conditions, whereas with the second step (and, as it were, on second thought) we regret our boldness and console ourselves that nothing worse or less familiar will take place than general human sinfulness.

Popular language, as it expresses preliminary understanding, thus starts the process of true understanding.[7] Its discovery must always remain the content of true understanding, if it is not to lose itself in the clouds of mere speculation—a danger always present. It was the common uncritical understanding on the part of the people more than anything else that induced a whole generation of historians, economists, and political scientists to devote their best efforts to the investigation of the causes and consequences of imperialism, and, at the same time, to misrepresent it as "empire-building" in the Assyrian or Egyptian or Roman fashion and misunderstand its underlying motives as "lust for conquest," describing Cecil Rhodes as a second Napoleon and Napoleon as a second

Julius Caesar. Totalitarianism, similarly, has become a current topic of study only since preliminary understanding recognized it as the central issue and the most significant danger of the time. Again, the current interpretations even on the highest scholarly level let themselves be guided further by the design of preliminary understanding: they equate totalitarian domination with tyranny or one-party dictatorship, when they do not explain the whole thing away by reducing it to historical, social, or psychological causes relevant for only one country, Germany or Russia. It is evident that such methods do not advance efforts to understand, because they submerge whatever is unfamiliar and needs to be understood in a welter of familiarities and plausibilities.[8] It lies, as Nietzsche once remarked, in the province of the "development of science" to "dissolve the 'known' into the unknown:—but science *wants* to do the *opposite* and is inspired by the instinct to reduce the unknown to something which is known" (*Will to Power*, No. 608).

Yet has not the task of understanding become hopeless if it is true that we are confronted with something which has destroyed our categories of thought and standards of judgment? How can we measure length if we do not have a yardstick, how could we count things without the notion of numbers? Maybe it is preposterous even to think that anything can ever happen which our categories are not equipped to understand. Maybe we should resign ourselves to the preliminary understanding, which at once ranges the new among the old, and with the scientific approach, which follows it and deduces methodically the unprecedented from precedents, even though such a description of the new phenomena may be demonstrably at variance with the reality. Is not understanding so closely related to and inter-related with judging that one must describe both as the subsumption (of something particular under a universal rule) which according to Kant is the very definition of judgment, whose absence he so magnificently defined as "stupidity," an "infirmity beyond remedy" (*Critique of Pure Reason*, B 172–73)?

These questions are all the more pertinent because they are not restricted to our perplexity in understanding totalitarianism. The paradox of the modern situation seems to be that our need to transcend both preliminary understanding and the strictly scientific approach springs from the fact that we have lost our tools of understanding. Our quest for meaning is at the same time prompted and frustrated by our inability to originate meaning. Kant's definition of stupidity is by no means beside the point. Since the beginning of this century, the growth of meaninglessness has been accompanied by loss of common sense. In many respects, this has appeared simply as an increasing stupidity. We know of no civilization before ours in which people were gullible enough to form their buying habits in accordance with the maxim that "self-praise is the highest recommendation," the assumption of all advertising. Nor is it likely that any century before ours could have been persuaded to take seriously a therapy which is said to help only if the patients pay a lot of money to those who administer it—unless, of course, there exists a primitive society where the handing over of money itself possesses magical power.

What has happened to the clever little rules of self-interest has happened on a much larger scale to all the spheres of ordinary life which, because they are ordinary, need to be regulated by customs. Totalitarian phenomena which can no longer be understood in terms of common sense and which defy all rules of "normal," that is, chiefly utilitarian, judgment are only the most spectacular instances of the breakdown of our common inherited wisdom. From the point of view of common sense, we did not need the rise of totalitarianism to show us that we are living in a topsy-turvy world, a world where we cannot find our way by abiding by the rules of what once was common sense. In this situation, stupidity in the Kantian sense has become the infirmity of everybody, and therefore can no longer be regarded as "beyond remedy." Stupidity has become as common as common sense was before; and this does not mean that it is a symptom of mass society or that "intelligent" people are exempt from it. The only difference is that stupidity remains blissfully inarticulate among the non-intellectuals and becomes unbearably offensive among "intelligent" people. Within the intelligentsia, one may even say that the more intelligent an individual happens to be, the more irritating is the stupidity which he has in common with all.

It seems like historical justice that Paul Valéry, the most lucid mind among the French, the classical people of *bon sens*, was the first to detect the bankruptcy of common sense in the modern world, where the most commonly accepted ideas have been "attacked, refuted, surprised and dissolved by *facts*," and where therefore we witness a "kind of insolvency of imagination and bankruptcy of understanding" (*Regards sur le monde actuel*). Much more surprising is that as early as the eighteenth century Montesquieu was convinced that only customs—which, being mores, quite literally constitute the morality of every civilization—prevented a spectacular moral and spiritual breakdown of occidental culture. He certainly cannot be counted among the prophets of doom, but his cold and sober courage has hardly been matched by any of the famous historical pessimists of the nineteenth century.

The life of peoples, according to Montesquieu, is ruled by laws and customs; the two are distinguished in that "laws govern the actions of the citizen and customs govern the actions of man" (*L'Esprit des Lois*, Book XIX, ch. 16). Laws establish the realm of public political life, and customs establish the realm of society. The downfall of nations begins with the undermining of lawfulness, whether the laws are abused by the government in power, or the authority of their source becomes doubtful and questionable. In both instances, laws are no longer held valid. The result is that the nation, together with its "belief" in its own laws, loses its capacity for responsible political action; the people cease to be citizens in the full sense of the word. What then still remains (and incidentally explains the frequent longevity of political bodies whose lifeblood has ebbed away) are the customs and traditions of society. So long as they are intact, men as private individuals continue to behave according to certain patterns of morality. But this morality has lost its foundation. Tradition can be trusted to prevent the worst only for a limited time. Every incident can destroy customs and morality which no longer have their foundation in lawfulness; every contingency must threaten a society which is no longer guaranteed by citizens.

For his own time and its immediate prospects, Montesquieu had this to say: "The majority of the nations of Europe are still ruled by customs. But if through a long abuse of power, if through some large conquest, despotism should establish itself at a given point, there would be neither customs nor climate to resist; and in this beautiful part of the world, human nature would suffer, at least for a time, the insults which have been inflicted on it in the three others" (*L'Esprit des Lois*, Book VIII, ch. 8). In this passage, Montesquieu outlines the political dangers to a political body which is held together only by customs and traditions, that is, by the mere binding force of morality. The dangers could appear from within, as misuse of power, or from without, as aggression. The factor that was eventually to bring about the downfall of customs in the early nineteenth century, he could not foresee. It came from that radical change in the world which we call the Industrial Revolution, certainly the greatest revolution in the shortest span of time mankind has ever witnessed; in a few decades it changed our whole globe more radically than all the three thousand years of recorded history before it. Reconsidering Montesquieu's fears, which were voiced almost one hundred years before this revolution developed its full force, it is tempting to reflect on the probable course of European civilization without the impact of this one, all-overriding factor. One conclusion seems inescapable: the great change took place within a political framework whose foundations were no longer secure and therefore overtook a society which, although it was still able to understand and to judge, could no longer give an account of its categories of understanding and standards of judgment when they were seriously challenged. In other words, Montesquieu's fears, which sounded so strange in the eighteenth century and would have sounded so commonplace in the nineteenth, may at least give us a hint of the explanation, not of totalitarianism or any other specific modern event, but of the disturbing fact that our great tradition has remained so peculiarly silent, so obviously wanting in productive replies, when challenged by the "moral" and political questions of our own time. The very sources from which such answers should have sprung had dried up. The very framework within which understanding and judging could arise is gone.

However, Montesquieu's fears go even further, and therefore come even closer to our present perplexity than the passage quoted above would indicate.[9] His main fear, which he puts at the head of his whole work, concerns more than the welfare of the European nations and the continued existence of political freedom. It concerns human nature itself: "Man, this flexible being, who bends himself in society to the thoughts and impressions of others, is equally capable of knowing his own nature when it is shown to him and of losing the very sense of it (*d'en perdre jusqu'au sentiment*) when he is being robbed of it" (*L'Esprit des Lois*, "Preface"). To us, who are confronted with the very realistic totalitarian attempt to rob man of his nature under the pretext of changing it, the courage of these words is like the boldness of youth, which may risk everything in imagination because nothing has yet happened to give the imagined dangers their horrible concreteness. What is envisaged here is more than loss of the capacity for political action, which is the central condition of tyranny, and more than growth of meaninglessness and loss of common sense (and common sense is only that part of our mind and that portion of inherited wisdom which all men have in common in any given civilization); it is the loss of the quest for meaning and need for understanding. We know how very close the people under totalitarian domination have been brought to this condition of meaninglessness, by means of terror combined with training in ideological thinking, although they no longer experience it as such.[10]

In our context, the peculiar and ingenious replacement of common sense with stringent logicality, which is characteristic of totalitarian thinking, is particularly noteworthy. Logicality is not identical with ideological reasoning, but indicates the totalitarian transformation of the respective ideologies. If it was the peculiarity of the ideologies themselves to treat a scientific hypothesis, like "the survival of the fittest" in biology or "the survival of the most progressive class" in history, as an "idea" which could be applied to the whole course of events, then it is the peculiarity of their totalitarian transformation to pervert the "idea" into a premise in the logical sense, that is, into some self-evident statement from which everything else can be deduced in stringent logical consistency. (Here truth becomes indeed what some logicians pretend it is, namely, consistency, except that this equation actually implies the negation of the existence of truth insofar as truth is always supposed to reveal something, whereas consistency is only a mode of fitting statements together, and as such lacks the power of revelation. The new logical movement in philosophy, which grew out of pragmatism, has a frightening affinity with the totalitarian transformation of the pragmatic elements inherent in all ideologies into logicality, which severs its ties to reality and experience altogether.* Of course, totalitarianism proceeds

---

*At a conference held the year this essay was published, Arendt further distinguished totalitarianism from pragmatism. "Totalitarianism is distinguished from pragmatism in that it no longer believes that reality as such can teach anything and, consequently, has lost the earlier Marxist respect for facts. Pragmatism, even in the Leninist version, still assumes with the tradition of occidental thought that reality reveals truth to man, although it asserts that not contemplation, but action is the proper truth-revealing attitude. . . . Pragmatism always assumes the validity of experience and 'acts' accordingly; totalitarianism assumes only the validity of the law of a moving History or Nature. Whoever acts in accordance with this law no longer needs particular experiences." *Totalitarianism: Proceedings of a Conference Held at the American Academy of Arts and Sciences, March 1953*, edited, with an introduction, by C. J. Friedrich, Cambridge, MA, 1954, 228. —Ed.

in a cruder fashion, which unfortunately, by the same token, is also more effective.)

The chief political distinction between common sense and logic is that common sense presupposes a common world into which we all fit, where we can live together because we possess one sense which controls and adjusts all strictly particular sense data to those of all others; whereas logic and all self-evidence from which logical reasoning proceeds can claim a reliability altogether independent of the world and the existence of other people. It has often been observed that the validity of the statement $2 + 2 = 4$ is independent of the human condition, that it is equally valid for God and man. In other words, wherever common sense, the political sense par excellence, fails us in our need for understanding, we are all too likely to accept logicality as its substitute, because the capacity for logical reasoning itself is also common to us all. But this common human capacity which functions even under conditions of complete separation from world and experience and which is strictly "within" us, without any bond to something "given," is unable to understand anything and, left to itself, utterly sterile. Only under conditions where the common realm *between* men is destroyed and the only reliability left consists in the meaningless tautologies of the self-evident can this capacity become "productive," develop its own lines of thought, whose chief political characteristic is that they always carry with them a compulsory power of persuasion. To equate thought and understanding with these logical operations means to level the capacity for thought, which for thousands of years has been deemed to be the highest capacity of man, to its lowest common denominator, where no differences in actual existence count any longer, not even the qualitative difference between the essence of God and men.

For those engaged in the quest for meaning and understanding, what is frightening in the rise of totalitarianism is not that it is something new, but that it has brought to light the ruin of our categories of thought and standards of judgment. Newness is the realm of the historian, who—unlike the natural scientist, who is concerned with ever-recurring happenings—deals with events which always occur only once. This newness can be manipulated if the historian insists on causality and pretends to be able to explain events by a chain of causes which eventually led up to them. He then, indeed, poses as the "prophet turned backward" (F. von Schlegel, *Athenaeum*, Frag. 80), and all that separates him from the gifts of real prophecy seems to be the deplorable physical limitations of the human brain, which unfortunately cannot contain and combine correctly all causes operating at the same time. Causality, however, is an altogether alien and falsifying category in the historical sciences. Not only does the actual meaning of every event always transcend any number of past "causes" which we may assign to it (one has only to think of the grotesque disparity between "cause" and "effect" in an event like the First World War[11]), but this past itself comes into being only with the event itself. Only when something irrevocable has happened can we even try to trace its history backward. The event illuminates its own past; it can never be deduced from it.[12]

Whenever an event occurs that is great enough to illuminate its own past, history comes into being. Only then does the chaotic maze of past happenings emerge as a story which can be told, because it has a beginning and an end. Herodotus is not merely the first historiographer: in the words of Karl Reinhardt, "history exists since Herodotus" ("Herodotus Persergeschichten," *Von Werken und Formen*, 1948)—that is, the Greek past became history through the light shed on it by the Persian Wars. What the illuminating event reveals is a beginning in the past which had hitherto been hidden; to the eye of the historian, the illuminating event cannot but appear as an end of this newly discovered beginning. Only when in future history a new event occurs will this "end" reveal itself as a beginning to the eye of future historians. And the eye of the historian is only the scientifically trained gaze of human understanding; we can *understand* an event only as the end and the culmination of everything that happened before, as "fulfillment of the times"; only in action will we proceed, as a matter of course, from the changed set of circumstances that the event has created, that is, treat it as a beginning.

Whoever in the historical sciences honestly believes in causality actually denies the subject matter of his own science.[13] Such a belief can be concealed in the application of general categories to the whole course of happenings, such as challenge and response, or in the search for general trends which supposedly are the "deeper" strata from which events spring and whose accessory symptoms they are. Such generalizations and categorizations extinguish the "natural" light history itself offers and, by the same token, destroy the actual story, with its unique distinction and its eternal meaning, that each historical period has to tell us. Within the framework of preconceived categories, the crudest of which is causality, events in the sense of something irrevocably new can never happen; history without events becomes the dead monotony of sameness, unfolded in time—Lucretius's *eadem sunt omnia semper*.[14]

Just as in our personal lives our worst fears and best hopes will never adequately prepare us for what actually happens—because the moment even a foreseen event takes place, everything changes, and we can never be prepared for the inexhaustible literalness of this "everything"—so each event in human history reveals an unexpected landscape of human deeds, sufferings, and new possibilities which together transcend the sum total of all willed intentions and the significance of all origins. It is the task of the historian to detect this unexpected *new* with all its implications in any given period and to bring out the full power of its significance. He must know that, though his story has a beginning and an end, it occurs within a larger frame, history itself.[15] And history is a story which has many beginnings but no end. The end in any strict and final sense of the word could only be the disappearance of man from the earth. For whatever the historian calls an end, the end of a period or a tradition or a whole civilization, is a new beginning for those who are alive.[16] The fallacy of all prophecies of doom lies in the disregard of this simple but fundamental fact.

For the historian, to remain aware of this fact will be of no greater importance than to check what the French would call his *déformation professionelle*. Since he is concerned with the past, that is, with certain movements which could not even be grasped by the mind if they had not come to some kind of end, he has only to generalize in order to see an end (and doom) everywhere. It is only natural for him to see in history a story with many ends and no beginning; and this inclination becomes really dangerous only when—for whatever reasons—people begin to make a philosophy out of history as it presents itself to the professional eyes of the historian. Nearly all modern explications of the so-called historicity of man have been distorted by categories which, at best, are working hypotheses for arranging the material of the past.[17]

Fortunately, the situation of the political sciences, which in the highest sense are called upon to pursue the quest for meaning and to answer the need for true understanding of political data, is quite different. The great consequence which the concept of beginning and origin has for all strictly political questions comes from the simple fact that political action, like all action, is essentially always the beginning of something new; as such, it is, in terms of political science, the very essence of human freedom. The central position which the concept of beginning and origin must have in all political thought has been lost only since the historical sciences have been permitted to supply the field of politics with their methods and categories. The centrality of origin was indicated, as a matter of course, for Greek thought in the fact that the Greek word *archē* means both beginning and rule. It is still fully alive, though generally overlooked by modern interpreters, in Machiavelli's theory of political power, according to which the act of foundation itself—that is, the conscious beginning of something new—requires and justifies the use of violence. In its full significance, however, the importance of beginnings was discovered by the one great thinker who lived in a period which, in some respects, resembled our own more than any other in recorded history, and who in addition wrote under the full impact of a catastrophic end which perhaps resembles the end to which we have come. Augustine, in his *Civitas Dei* (Book XII, ch. 20), said: *"Initium ergo ut esset, creatus est homo, ante quem nullus fuit"* ("That there might be a beginning, man was created before whom nobody was"). According to Augustine, who might rightly be called the father of all Western philosophy of history, man not only has the capacity of beginning, but is this beginning himself.[18] If the creation of man coincides with the creation of a beginning in the universe (and what else does this mean but the creation of freedom?), then the birth of individual men, being new beginnings, re-affirms the *original* character of man in such a way that origin can never become entirely a thing of the past; the very fact of the memorable continuity of these beginnings in the sequence of generations guarantees a history which can never end because it is the history of beings whose essence is beginning.

In light of these reflections, our endeavoring to understand something which has ruined our categories of thought and our standards of judgment appears less frightening. Even though we have lost yardsticks by which to measure, and rules under which to subsume the particular, a being whose essence is beginning may have enough of origin within himself to understand without preconceived categories and to judge without the set of customary rules which is morality. If the essence of all, and in particular of political, action is to make a new beginning, then understanding becomes the other side of action, namely, that form of cognition, distinct from many others, by which acting men (and not men who are engaged in contemplating some progressive or doomed course of history) eventually can come to terms with what irrevocably happened and be reconciled with what unavoidably exists.

As such, understanding is a strange enterprise. In the end, it may do no more than articulate and confirm what preliminary understanding, which always consciously or unconsciously is directly engaged in action, sensed to begin with.[19] It will not shy away from this circle but, on the contrary, will be aware that any other results would be so far removed from action, of which understanding is only the other side, that they could not possibly be true. Nor will the process itself avoid the circle the logicians call "vicious"; it may in this respect even somewhat resemble philosophy, in which great thoughts always turn in circles, engaging the human mind in nothing less than an interminable dialogue between itself and the essence of everything that is.[20]

In this sense the old prayer which King Solomon, who certainly knew something of political action, addressed to God—for the gift of an "understanding heart" as the greatest gift a man could receive and desire—might still hold for us. As far removed from sentimentality as it is from paperwork, the human heart is the only thing in the world that will take upon itself the burden that the divine gift of action, of being a beginning and therefore being able to make a beginning, has placed upon us. Solomon prayed for this particular gift because he was a king and knew that only an "understanding heart," and not mere reflection or mere feeling, makes it bearable for us to live with other people, strangers forever, in the same world, and makes it possible for them to bear with us.[21]

If we wish to translate the biblical language into terms that are closer to our speech (though hardly more accurate), we may call the faculty of imagination the gift of the "understanding heart." In distinction from fantasy, which dreams something, imagination is concerned with the particular darkness of the human heart and the peculiar density which surrounds everything that is real. Whenever we talk of the "nature" or "essence" of a thing, we actually mean this innermost kernel, of whose existence we can never be so sure as we are of darkness and density. True understanding does not tire of interminable dialogue and "vicious circles," because it trusts that imagination eventually will catch at least a glimpse of the always frightening light of truth. To distinguish imagination from fancy and to mobilize its power does not mean that understanding of human affairs becomes "irrational." On the contrary, imagination, as Wordsworth said, "is but another name for . . . clearest insight, amplitude of mind, / And Reason in her most exalted mood" (*The Prelude*, Book XIV, 190–92).

Imagination alone enables us to see things in their proper perspective, to be strong enough to put that which is too close at a certain distance so that we can see and understand it without bias and prejudice, to be generous enough to bridge abysses of remoteness until we can see and understand everything that is too far away from us as though it were our own affair. This distancing of some things and bridging the abysses to others is part of the dialogue of understanding, for whose purposes direct experience establishes too close a contact and mere knowledge erects artificial barriers.

Without this kind of imagination, which actually is understanding,[22] we would never be able to take our bearings in the world. It is the only inner compass we have. We are contemporaries only so far as our understanding reaches. If we want to be at home on this earth, even at the price of being at home in this century, we must try to take part in the interminable dialogue with the essence of totalitarianism.

NOTES

1. Additional material from the manuscript: From this they conclude that in light of the complex structure of the phenomenon, only organized research, that is, the combined efforts of the historical, economic, social, and psychological sciences, can produce understanding. This, I think, is as wrong as it sounds plausible. Information contained in every newspaper in the free world and experience suffered every day in the totalitarian world are enough to launch the fight against totalitarianism. But neither of these, together or alone, promotes any true understanding of its nature. Nor will understanding ever be the product of questionnaires, interviews, statistics, or the scientific evaluation of these data.

2. Facts must be enough; they can only lose their weight and poignancy through evaluation or moral preaching. There no longer exists any accepted morality upon which sermons can be based and there does not yet exist any rule which would promote non-arbitrary evaluation. The actual fight against totalitarianism needs no more than a steady flow of reliable information. If from these facts an appeal emerges, an appeal to Freedom and Justice, to mobilize people for the fight, then this appeal will not be a piece of abstract rhetoric.

3. To understand the nature of totalitarianism—which can be understood only after its origins and structures have been analyzed and described—is, therefore, almost identical with understanding the very heart of our own century. And this performance is probably only a little less difficult to achieve than the proverbial jump over one's own shadow. Its practical political value is even more doubtful than the efforts of the historians, whose results can at least be used for long-range, though hardly for immediate, political purposes.

4. Only after victory is won does it become necessary for practical political purposes to transcend the limitations of facts and information and to develop some comprehension of the elements, the crystallization of which brought about totalitarianism. For these elements do not cease to exist with the defeat of one or all totalitarian governments. It was, for instance, the presence of the very elements of Nazism that made the Nazis' victory in Europe not only possible but also so shamefully easy. Had the extra-European powers of the world, which required six years to defeat Hitler's Germany, comprehended these elements, they would not have supported the restoration of the status quo in Europe—complete with the old political, class, and party systems which, as though nothing had happened, continue to disintegrate and prepare the soil for totalitarian movements—and they would have given their full attention to the continued growth of the refugee population and the spread of statelessness.

5. For it seems quite doubtful that this kind of comprehensive knowledge, which is not yet understanding and does not deal with the essence of totalitarianism, can be produced by organized research. The chances are great that the relevant data will get buried in an avalanche of statistics or observations on the one hand and evaluation on the other, neither of which tells us anything about historical conditions and political aspirations. Only the sources themselves talk—documents, speeches, reports, and the like—and this material is readily accessible and need not be organized and institutionalized. These sources make sense to the historians and the political scientists; they become unintelligible only if asked to yield information about the superego, the father image, the wrong way of swaddling babies, or if approached with fixed stereotypes in mind, such as the lower middle classes, the bureaucracy, the intellectuals, and so forth. Obviously, the categories of the social sciences, stereotyped as they may have become, are more likely to produce some insights into this matter than those of the psychologists, if only because they are abstracted from the real world and not from a dream world. In actual fact, unfortunately, it makes little difference. Since the father image invaded the social sciences and the lower middle classes the psychological sciences, the differences between the two have become negligible.

6. based as they are on only a preliminary understanding, must already have yielded enough results and covered enough ground to give the dialogue of understanding its concrete and specific content.

7. Popular language which expresses popular understanding thus at the same time presents our effort of understanding with its chief discovery and its greatest danger.

8. The same need for orientation in a world changed through a new event that prompts popular understanding should also be the guide of true understanding, lest we lose ourselves in the labyrinths of facts and figures erected by the unquenchable curiosity of scholars. True understanding is distinguished from public opinion in both its popular and scientific forms only by its refusal to relinquish the original intuition. To put it in a schematic and therefore necessarily inadequate way, it is as though, whenever we are confronted with something frighteningly new, our first impulse is to recognize it in a blind and uncontrolled reaction strong enough to coin a new word; our second impulse seems to be to regain control by denying that we saw anything new at all, by pretending that something similar is already known to us; only a third impulse can lead us back to what we saw and knew in the beginning. It is here that the effort of true understanding begins.

9. He had given too much thought to the evil of tyranny on the one side, and to the conditions of human freedom on the other, not to be driven to some ultimate conclusions.

10. If we have a chance to save anything from the conflagration in which we are caught, then certainly it can be only those essentials which are even more basic than the fundaments of law and the texture of tradition and morality which is woven about them. These essentials can say no more than that Freedom is the quintessence of the human condition and that Justice is the quintessence of man's social condition, or, in other words, that Freedom is the essence of the human individual and Justice the essence of men's living together. Both can disappear from the earth only with the physical disappearance of the human race.

11. One of the chief problems which the event by its very nature presents to the historian is that its significance seems always not only different from, but also so much greater than that of the elements which comprise it and of the intentions which bring about the crystallization. Who could doubt that the historical significance of the First World War transcended whatever latent elements of conflict broke out in it as well as whatever good or evil the statesmen concerned may have intended? In this particular instance, even the factor of freedom which eventually caused the crystallization of these elements and caused the war is dwarfed into ridicule.

12. The elements of totalitarianism comprise its origins, if by origins we do not understand "causes." Elements by themselves never cause anything. They become origins of events if and when they suddenly crystallize into fixed and definite forms. It is the light of the event itself which permits us to distinguish its own concrete elements from an infinite number of abstract possibilities, and it is still this same light that must guide us backward into the always dim and equivocal past of these elements themselves. In this sense, it is legitimate to talk of the origins of totalitarianism, or of any other event in history.

13. He denies by the same token the very existence of events which, always suddenly and unpredictably, change the whole physiognomy of a given era. Belief in causality, in other words, is the historian's way of denying human freedom which, in terms of the political and historical sciences, is the human capacity for making a new beginning.

14. That the discrepancy between "cause and effect" should reach such proportions as to become eventually comical has become one of the hallmarks of modern history and politics—and, incidentally, is one of the main reasons modern historians and ideologists have been so tempted by some notion of objective causality or some superstitious belief in necessity, be this a necessity of doom or of salvation. Yet some discrepancy between objective elements and free human action, on one hand, and the event—in its majestic irrevocability, originality, and abundance of meaning—on the other, is always present and permeates the whole of human reality. This is also the reason we know of no historical event which does not depend upon a great number of coincidences or for which we could not imagine one or more alternatives. The necessity which all causal historiography consciously or unconsciously presupposes does not exist in history. What really exists is the irrevocability of the events themselves, whose poignant effectiveness in the field of political action does not mean that certain elements of the past have received their final, definite form, but that something inescapably new was born. From this irrevocability we can escape only through submission to the mechanical sequence of mere time, without events and without meaning.

15. He must have a sense for reality, not necessarily in the sense of being practical and realistic, but in the sense of having experienced the very power of all things real, which is the power of overcoming and surpassing all our expectations and calculations. And since this overpowering quality of reality quite obviously is connected with the fact that men, no matter how well or how badly they are integrated into the fellowship of their equals, always remain individuals whom some hazard or providence threw into the adventure of life on earth, the historian would do well to remember that it is always one man alone who is confronted with, has to adjust to, and tries to act into what all men together have done and suffered.

16. An event belongs to the past, marks an end, insofar as elements with their origins in the past are gathered together in its sudden crystallization; but an event belongs to the future, marks a beginning, insofar as this crystallization itself can never be deduced from its own elements, but is caused invariably by some factor which lies in the realm of human freedom.

17. The task of the historian is to analyze and describe the new structure which emerges after the event takes place as well as its elements and origins. He does this with the help of the light which the event itself provides, but this does not mean that he must or can understand the nature of this light itself. The quest for the *nature* of totalitarianism is no longer a historical (and certainly not a sociological or psychological) undertaking; it is, strictly speaking, a question for political science, which, if it understands itself, is the true guardian of the keys which open the doors to the problems and uncertainties of the philosophy of history.

18. The so-called chain of happenings—a chain of events is, strictly speaking, a contradiction in terms—is interrupted every minute by the birth of a new human being bringing a new beginning into the world.

19. for example, that totalitarian governments deny human freedom radically.

20. of things and events.

21. Only in the patient endurance of the non-vicious circle of understanding do all complacencies and all notions of "know-better" melt away.

22. Without this kind of imagination, and the understanding which springs from it, we would never be able to take our bearings in the world.

On the Nature of Totalitarianism:
An Essay in Understanding

I N   O R D E R   T O fight totalitarianism, one need understand only one thing: Totalitarianism is the most radical denial of freedom. Yet this denial of freedom is common to all tyrannies and is of no primary importance for understanding the peculiar nature of totalitarianism. Nonetheless, whoever cannot be mobilized when freedom is threatened will not be mobilized at all. Even moral admonitions, the outcry against crimes unprecedented in history and not foreseen in the Ten Commandments will remain of little avail. The very existence of totalitarian movements in the non-totalitarian world, that is, the appeal totalitarianism exerts on those who have all the information before them and who are warned against it day in and day out, bears eloquent witness to the breakdown of the whole structure of morality, the whole body of commands and prohibitions which had traditionally translated and embodied the fundamental ideas of freedom and justice into terms of social relationships and political institutions.

Still, many people doubt that this breakdown is a reality. They are inclined to think some accident has happened after which one's duty is

See the headnote to the preceding essay and the Introduction to this volume for information on this essay.

to restore the old order, appeal to the old knowledge of right and wrong, mobilize the old instincts for order and safety. They label anyone who thinks and speaks otherwise a "prophet of doom" whose gloominess threatens to darken the sun rising over good and evil for all of eternity.

The fact of the matter is that the "prophets of doom," the historical pessimists of the late nineteenth and early twentieth centuries, from Burckhard to Spengler, were put out of business by the actuality of catastrophes the size and horror of which no one ever foresaw. Certain developments, however, apparently could have been and were predicted. Though these predictions hardly ever occurred in the nineteenth century, they can be found in the eighteenth century, and were overlooked because nothing seemed to justify them. It is worthwhile, for instance, to learn what Kant, in 1793, had to say about the "balance of power" as a solution to the conflicts rising from the European nation-state system: "The so-called balance of powers in Europe is like Swift's house which was built in such perfect harmony with all laws of equilibrium that, when a bird sat down on it, it immediately collapsed—a mere phantasm."* The balance achieved by the system of nation-states was not a mere phantasm, but it did collapse exactly as Kant predicted. In the words of a modern historian: "The iron test of the balance of power lies in the very thing it is designed to stave off—war" (Hajo Holborn, *The Political Collapse of Europe*, 1951).

More sweeping in outlook and yet closer to reality is another eighteenth-century author, who is usually not counted among the "prophets of doom" and who is as serene, as sober, and even less disturbed (the French Revolution had not yet taken place) than Kant. There is hardly an event of any importance in our recent history that would not fit into the scheme of Montesquieu's apprehensions.

Montesquieu was the last to inquire into the nature of government; that is, to ask what makes it what it is ("sa nature est ce qui le fait être tel," *L'Esprit des Lois*, Book III, ch. 1). But Montesquieu added to this a second and entirely original question: What makes a government act as it acts? He thus discovered that each government has not only its "particular structure" but also a particular "principle" which sets it in motion. Political science has now discarded both questions because they

On the Common Saying: That may be true in theory but does not apply to practice.
—Ed.

are, in a way, pre-scientific. They refer to preliminary understanding which expresses itself only in giving names: this is a republic, this is a monarchy, this is a tyranny. Still, they start the dialogue of true understanding by asking, What is it that makes a state recognizable as a republic, a monarchy, or a tyranny? After giving the traditional answer to the traditional question—affirming that a republic is a constitutional government with the sovereign power in the hands of the people; a monarchy, a lawful government with sovereign power in the hands of one man; and a tyranny, a lawless government where power is exercised by one man according to his arbitrary will—Montesquieu adds that in a republic the principle of action is virtue, which, psychologically, he equates with love of equality; in a monarchy, the principle of action is honor, whose psychological expression is a passion for distinction; and in a tyranny, the principle of action is fear.

It is striking and strange that Montesquieu, who is famous chiefly for his discovery and articulation of the division of powers into the executive, legislative, and judiciary, defines governments as though power is necessarily sovereign and indivisible. Curiously enough, it was Kant, and not Montesquieu, who redefined the structure of governments according to Montesquieu's own principles.

In his *Perpetual Peace*, Kant introduces a distinction between "forms of domination" (*Formen der Beherrschung*) and forms of government. The forms of domination are distinguished solely according to the locus of power: All states in which the prince has undivided sovereign power are called autocracies; if the power is in the hands of the nobility, the form of domination is aristocracy; and if the people wield absolute power, domination comes about in the form of democracy. Kant's point is that all these forms of domination (as the word "domination" itself indicates) are, strictly speaking, illegal. Constitutional or lawful government is established through the division of power so that the same body (or man) does not make the laws, execute them, and then sit in judgment on itself. According to this new principle, which comes from Montesquieu and which found unequivocal expression in the Constitution of the United States, Kant indicated two basic structures of government: republican government, based on the division of powers, even if a prince is at the head of the state; and despotic government, where the powers of legislation, execution, and judgment are not separated. In the concrete political sense, power is needed and incorporated in the possession of the means of violence for the execution of laws. Where, therefore, the executive power is not separated from and controlled by legislative and judicial powers, the source of law can no longer be reason and consideration, but becomes power itself. That form of government for which the dictum "Might Is Right" rings true is despotic—and this holds regardless of all other circumstances: a democracy ruled by majority decisions but unchecked by law is just as despotic as an autocracy.

It is true that even Kant's distinction is no longer quite satisfactory. Its chief weakness is that behind the relationship of law and power lies the assumption that the source of law is human reason (still in the sense of the *lumen naturale*) and the source of power is human will. Both assumptions are questionable on historical as well as philosophical grounds. We cannot discuss these difficulties here, nor do we need to. For our purpose, which is to isolate the nature of a new and unprecedented form of government, it may be wise to appeal first to the traditional—though no longer traditionally accepted—criteria. In searching for the nature of totalitarian government, its "structure," in Montesquieu's words, we shall also use Kant's distinction between forms of domination and forms of government, as well as between constitutional (in his words, "republican") and despotic government.

Montesquieu's discovery that each form of government has its own innate principle which sets it into motion and guides all its actions is of great relevance. Not only was this motivating principle closely connected to historical experience (honor obviously being the principle of medieval monarchy, based on nobility, as virtue was the principle of the Roman Republic), but as a principle of motion it introduced history and historical process into structures of government which, as the Greeks had originally discovered and defined them, were conceived as unmoved and unmovable. Before Montesquieu's discovery, the only principle of change connected with forms of government was change for the worse, the perversion that would transform an aristocracy (the government of the best) into an oligarchy (the government of a clique for the interest of the clique), or overturn a democracy that had degenerated into ochlocracy (mob rule) into tyranny.

Montesquieu's moving and guiding principles—virtue, honor, fear —are principles insofar as they rule both the actions of the government and the actions of the governed. Fear in a tyranny is not only the subjects' fear of the tyrant, but the tyrant's fear of his subjects as well. Fear, honor, and virtue are not merely psychological motives, but the very criteria according to which all public life is led and judged. Just as it is the pride of a citizen in a republic not to dominate his fellow-citizens in public matters, so it is the pride of a subject in a monarchy to distinguish himself and be publicly honored. In establishing these principles, Montesquieu was not suggesting that all people behave at all times according to the principles of the government under which they happen to live, or that people in republics do not know what honor is, or people in a monarchy what virtue is. Nor does he speak of "ideal types." He analyzes the public life of citizens, not people's private lives, and discovers that in this public life—that is, in the sphere where all men act together concerning things that are of equal concern to each—action is determined by certain principles. If these principles are no longer heeded and the specific criteria of behavior are no longer held valid, the political institutions themselves are jeopardized.

Beneath Montesquieu's distinction between the nature of government (that which makes it what it is) and its moving or guiding principle (that which sets it into motion through actions) lies another difference, a problem which has plagued political thought since its beginning, and which Montesquieu indicates, but does not solve, by his distinction between man as a citizen (a member of a public order) and man insofar as he is an individual. In case of conquest, for instance, "the citizen may perish and the man survive" ("*le citoyen peut périr, et l'homme rester,*" *L'Esprit des Lois*, Book X, ch. 3.). This problem is usually dealt with in modern political thought as the distinction between public and private life, or the sphere of politics and the sphere of society; and its troublesome aspect is conventionally found in a pretended double standard of morality.

In modern political thought—insofar as its central predicaments are dictated by Machiavelli's discovery of power as the center of all political life, and of power-relations as the supreme laws of political action—the problem of the individual and the citizen has been complicated and overshadowed by the dilemma between legality as the center of domestic constitutional government and arbitrary sovereignty as the natural condition in the field of international relations. It seems, then, that we are confronted with two sets of duplicity in judging right or wrong in actions—the double standard originating in the simultaneous status of man as both citizen and individual, and the double standard originating in the differentiation between foreign and domestic politics. Both problems are pertinent to our effort to understand the nature of totalitarianism, since totalitarian governments claim to have solved them both. The distinction between and the dilemma of foreign and domestic politics are solved by the claim to global rule. This claim is then substantiated by treating each conquered country, in complete disregard of its own law, as an erstwhile transgressor of totalitarian law and by punishing its inhabitants according to laws administered retroactively. In other words, the claim to global rule is identical to the claim establishing a new and universally valid law on earth. In consequence, all foreign politics are, to the totalitarian mind, disguised domestic politics, and all foreign wars are, in fact, civil wars. The distinction between and the dilemma of citizen and individual, meanwhile, with the concomitant perplexities of the dichotomy between public and personal life, are eliminated by the totalitarian claim to the total domination of man.

To Montesquieu, only the dilemma of the citizen and the individual was a real political problem. The conflict between domestic and foreign politics, as a conflict between law and power, exists only so long as one maintains that power is indivisible and sovereign. Montesquieu as well as Kant held that only division of powers can guarantee the rule of law, and that a world federation would eventually solve the conflicts of sovereignty. An eminently practical step toward the identification of foreign and domestic politics was taken in Article VI of the United States Constitution, which, in perfect spiritual agreement with Montesquieu, provides that, together with the Constitution and constitutionally enacted laws, "all treaties made . . . under authority of the United States, shall be the supreme law of the land."

The distinction between the citizen and the individual becomes a problem as soon as we become aware of the discrepancy between public life, in which I am a citizen like all other citizens, and personal life, in which I am an individual unlike anybody else. Equality before the law is not only the distinguishing feature of modern republics, but also, in a deeper sense, prevails in constitutional governments as such, in that all people living under a constitution must equally receive from it what is rightfully theirs. The law in all constitutional forms of government determines and provides *suum cuique*: through it everybody comes into his own.

The rule of *suum cuique*, however, never extends to all spheres of life. There is no *suum cuique* which could be determined and handed to individuals in their personal lives. The very fact that in all free societies everything is permitted which is not explicitly prohibited reveals the situation clearly: The law defines the boundaries of personal life but cannot touch what goes on within them. In this respect, the law fulfills two functions: it regulates the public-political sphere in which men act in concert as equals and where they have a common destiny, while, at the same time, it circumscribes the space in which our individual destinies unfold—destinies which are so dissimilar that no two biographies will ever read alike. The law in its sublime generality can never foresee and provide the *suum* which everybody receives in his irrevocable uniqueness. Laws, once they are established, are always applied according to precedents; the trouble with the deeds and events of personal life is that this life is destroyed in its very essence as soon as it is judged by standards of comparison or in light of precedents. One could define philistinism, and explain its deadening effect upon the creativity of human life, as the attempt, through a moralizing transformation of customs into general "laws" of behavior equally valid for all, to judge by precedents what by definition defies all precedent.

The trouble, obviously, with this discrepancy between public and personal life, between man as citizen and man as individual, is not only that laws can never be used to guide and judge actions in personal life, but also that the very standards of right and wrong in the two spheres are not the same and are often even in conflict. That such conflicts— ranging from the man who breaks traffic laws because his wife is dying to the central theme of *Antigone*—are always regarded as insoluble, and that such "lawbreakers" are almost invariably depicted by the great tragedians as acting according to a "higher law," reveals the depth of Western man's experience of the calamity of citizenship even in the best body politic. Strangely enough, even his philosophers have deserted him in this particular experience and done their best to evade the issue by elevating civil law to a level of unambiguous universality which it never in fact possesses. Kant's famous categorical imperative—"Act in such a way that the maxim of your action could become a universal law"— indeed strikes to the root of the matter in that it is the quintessence of the claim that the law makes upon us. This rigid morality, however, disregards sympathy and inclination; moreover, it becomes a real source for wrongdoing in all cases where no universal law, not even the imagined law of pure reason, can determine what is right in a particular case.

Even in the personal sphere, where no universal laws can ever determine unequivocally what is right and what is wrong, man's actions are not completely arbitrary. Here he is guided not by laws, under which cases can be subsumed, but by principles—such as loyalty, honor, virtue, faith—which, as it were, map out certain directions. Montesquieu never asked himself if these principles might not have, in themselves, some cognitive power of judging or even creating what is right and wrong. But what he discovered when he added to the traditionally defined structure of government a moving principle which alone makes men act, rulers and ruled alike, was that law and power-relations in any given form of polity can define only the boundaries within which an entirely different, non-public, sphere of life exists. And it is this non-public sphere from which the sources of action and motion, as distinguished from the stabilizing, structural forces of law and power, spring. Hedged in by law and power, and occasionally overwhelming them, lie the origins of motion and action.

Montesquieu saw, as others had before him, that these principles of action and their standards of right and wrong varied widely in different countries at different times. More important, he discovered that each structure of government, manifesting itself in law and power, had its own correlative principle according to which men living within that structure would act. Only this, incidentally, gave him, and those historians who came after him, the tools to describe the peculiar unity of each culture. Since there was an obvious, historically patent correspondence between the principle of honor and the structure of monarchy, between virtue and republicanism, and between fear (understood not as a psychological emotion but as a principle of action) and tyranny, then there must be some underlying ground from which both man as an individual and man as a citizen sprang. In other words, Montesquieu found that there was more to the dilemma of the personal and the public spheres than discrepancy and conflict, even though they might conflict.

The phenomenon of correspondence between the different spheres of life and the miracle of the unities of cultures and periods despite discrepancies and contingencies indicates that at the bottom of each cultural or historical entity lies a common ground which is both fundament and source, basis and origin. Montesquieu defines the common ground in which the laws of a monarchy are rooted, and from which the actions of its subjects spring, as distinction; and he identifies honor, the supreme guiding principle in a monarchy, with a corresponding love of distinction. The fundamental experience upon which monarchies and, we may add, all hierarchical forms of government are founded is the experience, inherent in the human condition, that men are distinguished, that is, different from each other by birth. Yet we all know that directly opposing this and with no less insistent validity rises the opposite experience, the experience of the inherent equality of all men, "born equal" and distinguished only by social status. This equality—insofar as it is not an equality before God, an infinitely superior Being before whom all distinctions and differences become negligible—has always meant not only that all men, regardless of their differences, are equally valuable, but also that nature has granted to each an equal amount of power. The fundamental experience upon which republican laws are founded and from which the action of its citizens springs is the experience of living together with and belonging to a group of equally powerful men. The laws which regulate the lives of republican citizens do not serve distinction, but, rather, restrict the power of each that room may remain for the power of his fellow. The common ground of republican law and action is thus the insight that human power is not primarily limited by some superior power, God or Nature, but by the powers of one's equals. And the joy that springs from that insight, the "love of equality" which is virtue, comes from the experience that only because this is so, only because there is equality of power, is man not alone. For to be alone means to be without equals: "One is one and all alone and ever more shall be so," runs the old English nursery rhyme, daring to suggest what to the human mind can only be the supreme tragedy of God.

Montesquieu failed to indicate the common ground of structure and action in tyrannies; we may therefore be permitted to fill in this gap in light of his own discoveries. Fear, the inspiring principle of action in tyranny, is fundamentally connected to that anxiety which we experience in situations of complete loneliness. This anxiety reveals the other side of equality and corresponds to the joy of sharing the world with our equals. The dependence and interdependence which we need in order to realize our power (the amount of strength which is strictly our own) becomes a source of despair whenever, in complete loneliness, we realize that one man alone has no power at all but is always overwhelmed and defeated by superior power. If one man alone had sufficient strength to match his power with the power of nature and circumstance, he would not be in need of company. Virtue is happy to pay the price of limited power for the blessing of being together with other men; fear is the despair over the individual impotence of those who, for whatever reason, have refused to "act in concert." There is no virtue, no love of equality of power, which has not to overcome this anxiety of helplessness, for there is no human life which is not vulnerable to utter helplessness, without recourse to action, if only in the face of death. Fear as a principle of action is in some sense a contradiction in terms, because fear is precisely despair over the impossibility of action. Fear, as distinct from the principles of virtue and honor, has no self-transcending power and is therefore truly anti-political. Fear as a principle of action can only be destructive or, in the words of Montesquieu, "self-corrupting." Tyranny is therefore the only form of government which bears germs of its destruction within itself. External circumstances cause the decline of other forms of government; tyrannies, on the contrary, owe their existence and survival to such external circumstances as prevent their self-corruption (*L'Esprit des Lois*, Book VIII, ch. 10).

Thus the common ground upon which lawlessness can be erected and from which fear springs is the impotence all men feel who are radically isolated. One man against all others does not experience equality of power among men, but only the overwhelming, combined power of all others against his own. It is the great advantage of monarchy, or of any hierarchical government, that individuals whose "distinction" defines their social and political status never confront an undistinguished and undistinguishable "all others" against whom they can only summon their own absolute minority of one. It is the specific danger of all forms of government based on equality that the moment the structure of lawfulness—within whose framework the experience of equal power receives its meaning and direction—breaks down or is transformed, the powers among equal men cancel each other out and what is left is the experience of absolute impotence. Out of the conviction of one's own impotence and the fear of the power of all others comes the will to dominate, which is the will of the tyrant. Just as virtue is love of the equality of power, so fear is actually the will to, or, in its perverted form, lust for, power. Concretely and politically speaking, there is no other will to power but the will to dominate. For power itself in its true sense can never be possessed by one man alone; power comes, as it were, mysteriously into being whenever men act "in concert" and disappears, not less mysteriously, whenever one man is all by himself. Tyranny, based on the essential impotence of all men who are alone, is the hubristic attempt to be like God, invested with power individually, in complete solitude.

These three forms of government—monarchy, republicanism, and tyranny—are authentic because the grounds on which their structures are built (the distinction of each, equality of all, and impotence) and from which their principles of motion spring are authentic elements of the human condition and are reflected in primary human experiences. The question with which we shall now approach totalitarianism is whether or not this unprecedented form of government can lay claim to an equally authentic, albeit until now hidden, ground of the human condition on earth, a ground which may reveal itself only under circumstances of a global unity of humanity—circumstances certainly as unprecedented as totalitarianism itself.

II

Before we proceed, it may be well to admit that we are at least aware of a basic difficulty in this approach. To the modern mind there is perhaps nothing more baffling in Montesquieu's definitions than that he takes at face value the self-interpretations and self-understandings of the governments themselves. That he does not seek ulterior motives behind the confirmations of virtue in a republic, honor in a monarchy, or fear in a tyranny seems all the more surprising in an author who admittedly was the first to observe the great influence of "objective" factors, such as climatic, social, and other circumstances, on the formation of strictly political institutions.

However, in this as in other matters, true understanding has hardly any choice. The sources talk and what they reveal is the self-understanding as well as the self-interpretation of people who act and who believe they know what they are doing. If we deny them this capacity and pretend that we know better and can tell them what their real "motives" are or which real "trends" they objectively represent—no matter what they themselves think—we have robbed them of the very faculty of speech, insofar as speech makes sense. If, for instance, Hitler time and again called Jews the negative center of world history, and in support of his opinion designed factories to liquidate all people of Jewish origin, it is nonsensical to declare that anti-Semitism was not greatly relevant to the construction of his totalitarian regime, or that he merely suffered an unfortunate prejudice. The task of the social scientist is to find the historical and political background of anti-Semitism, but under no circumstances to conclude that Jews are only stand-ins for the petite bourgeoisie or that anti-Semitism is a surrogate for an Oedipus complex, or whatnot. Cases in which people consciously tell lies and, to remain with our example, pretend to hate Jews while in fact they want to murder the bourgeoisie, are very rare and easily detectable. In all other cases, self-understanding and self-interpretation are the very foundation of all analysis and understanding.

Therefore, in trying to understand the nature of totalitarianism, we shall ask in good faith the traditional questions regarding the nature of this form of government and the principle which sets it in motion. Since the rise of the scientific approach in the humanities, that is, with the development of modern historicism, sociology, and economics, such questions have no longer been considered likely to further understanding; Kant, in fact, was the last to think along these lines of traditional political philosophy. Yet while our standards for scientific accuracy have constantly grown and are higher today than at any previous time, our standards and criteria for true understanding seem to have no less constantly declined. With the introduction of completely alien and frequently nonsensical categories of evaluation into the social sciences, they have reached an all-time low. Scientific accuracy does not permit any understanding which goes beyond the narrow limits of sheer factuality, and it has paid a heavy price for this arrogance, since the wild superstitions of the twentieth century, clothed in humbug scientism, began to supplement its deficiencies. Today the need to understand has grown desperate and plays havoc with the standards not only of understanding, but of pure scientific accuracy and intellectual honesty as well.

Totalitarian government is unprecedented because it defies comparison. It has exploded the very alternative on which definitions of the nature of government have relied since the beginning of Western political thought—the alternative between lawful, constitutional or republican government, on the one hand, and lawless, arbitrary, or tyrannical government on the other. Totalitarian rule is "lawless" insofar as it defies positive law; yet it is not arbitrary insofar as it obeys with strict logic and executes with precise compulsion the laws of History or Nature. It is the monstrous, yet seemingly unanswerable claim of totalitarian rule that, far from being "lawless," it goes straight to the sources of authority from which all positive laws—based on "natural law," or on customs and tradition, or on the historical event of divine revelation—receive their ultimate legitimation. What appears lawless to the non-totalitarian world would, on the strength of being inspired by the sources themselves, constitute a higher form of legitimacy, one that can do away with the petty legality of positive laws which can never produce justice in any single, concrete, and therefore unpredictable case, but can only prevent injustice. Totalitarian lawfulness, executing the laws of Nature or History, does not bother to translate them into standards of right and wrong for individual human beings, but applies them directly to the "species," to mankind. The laws of Nature or History, if properly executed, are expected to produce as their end a single "Mankind," and it is this expectation that lies behind the claim to global rule of all totalitarian governments. Humanity, or, rather, the human species, is regarded as the active carrier of these laws while the rest of the universe is only passively determined by them.

At this point a fundamental difference between the totalitarian and all other conceptions of law comes to light. It is true that Nature or History, as the source of authority for positive laws, could traditionally reveal itself to man, be it as the *lumen naturale* in natural law or as the voice of conscience in historically revealed religious law. This, however, hardly made human beings walking embodiments of these laws. On the contrary, these laws remained distinct—as the authority which demanded obedience—from the actions of men. Compared to the sources of authority, the positive laws of men were considered to be changing and changeable in accordance with circumstance. Nonetheless, these laws were more permanent than the ever and rapidly changing actions of men, and they received this relative permanence from what was, in mortal terms, the timeless presence of their authoritative sources.

In the totalitarian interpretation, all laws become, instead, laws of movement. Nature and History are no longer stabilizing sources of authority for laws governing the actions of mortal men, but are themselves movements. Their laws, therefore, though one might need intelligence to perceive or understand them, have nothing to do with reason or permanence. At the base of the Nazis' belief in race laws lies Darwin's idea of man as a more or less accidental product of natural develop-ment—a development which does not necessarily stop with the species of human beings such as we know it. At the base of the Bolsheviks' belief in class lies the Marxian notion of men as the product of a gigantic historical process racing toward the end of historical time—that is, a process that tends to abolish itself. The very term "law" has changed in meaning; from denoting the framework of stability within which human actions were supposed to, and were permitted to, take place, it has become the very expression of these motions themselves.

The ideologies of racism and dialectical materialism that transformed Nature and History from the firm soil supporting human life and action into supra-gigantic forces whose movements race through humanity, dragging every individual willy-nilly with them—either riding atop their triumphant car or crushed under its wheels—may be various and com-plicated: still, it is surprising to see how, for all practical political pur-poses, these ideologies always result in the same "law" of elimination of individuals for the sake of the process or progress of the species. From the elimination of harmful or superfluous individuals, the result of nat-ural or historical movement rises like the phoenix from its own ashes; but unlike the fabulous bird, this mankind which is the end and at the same time the embodiment of the movement of either History or Nature requires permanent sacrifices, the permanent elimination of hostile or parasitic or unhealthy classes or races in order to enter upon its bloody eternity.

Just as positive laws in constitutional government are needed to trans-late and realize the immutable *ius naturale* or the eternal Commandments of God or sempiternal customs and traditions of history, so terror is needed to realize, to translate into living reality, the laws of movement of History or Nature. And just as positive laws that define transgressions in any given society are independent of them, such that their absence does not render the laws superfluous but on the contrary constitutes their most perfect rule, so, too, terror in totalitarian government, ceasing to be a means for the suppression of political opposition, becomes in-dependent of it and rules supreme when opposition no longer stands in its way.

If law, therefore, is the essence of constitutional or republican gov-ernment, then terror is the essence of totalitarian government. Laws were established to be boundaries (to follow one of the oldest images,

Plato's invocation of Zeus as the God of boundaries, at *Laws*, 843a) and to remain static, enabling men to move within them; under totalitarian conditions, on the contrary, every means is taken to "stabilize" men, to make *them* static, in order to prevent any unforeseen, free, or spontaneous acts that might hinder freely racing terror. The law of movement itself, Nature or History, singles out the foes of mankind and no free action of mere men is permitted to interfere with it. Guilt and innocence become meaningless categories; "guilty" is he who stands in the path of terror, that is, who willingly or unwillingly hinders the movement of Nature or History. The rulers, consequently, do not apply laws, but execute such movement in accordance with its inherent law; they claim to be neither just nor wise, but to know "scientifically."

Terror freezes men in order to clear the way for the movement of Nature or History. It eliminates individuals for the sake of the species; it sacrifices men for the sake of mankind—not only those who eventually become the victims of terror, but in fact all men insofar as this movement, with its own beginning and its own end, can only be hindered by the new beginning and the individual end which the life of each man actually is. With each new birth, a new beginning is born into the world, and a new world has potentially come into being. The stability of laws, erecting the boundaries and the channels of communication between men who live together and act in concert, hedges in this new beginning and assures, at the same time, its freedom; laws assure the potentiality of something entirely new *and* the pre-existence of a common world, the reality of some transcending continuity which absorbs all origins and is nourished by them. Terror first razes these boundaries of man-made law, but not for the sake of some arbitrary tyrannical will, nor for the sake of the despotic power of one man against all, nor, least of all, for the sake of a war of all against all. Terror substitutes for the boundaries and channels of communication between individual men an iron band which presses them all so tightly together that it is as though they were melded into each other, as though they were only one man. Terror, the obedient servant of Nature or History and the omnipresent executor of their predestined movement, fabricates the oneness of all men by abolishing the boundaries of law which provide the living space for the freedom of each individual. Totalitarian terror does not curtail all liberties or abolish certain essential freedoms, nor does it, at least to our limited knowledge, succeed in eradicating the love of freedom from the hearts of men; it simply and mercilessly presses men, such as they are, against each other so that the very space of free action—and this is the reality of freedom—disappears.

Terror exists neither for nor against men; it exists to provide the movement of Nature or History with an incomparable instrument of acceleration. If the undeniable automatism of historical or natural happenings is understood as the stream of necessity, whose meaning is identical to its law of movement and therefore quite independent of any event—which, on the contrary, can only be considered as a superficial and transitory outburst of the deep, permanent law—then the equally undeniable freedom of men, which is identical with the fact that each man *is* a new beginning and in that sense begins the world anew, can only be regarded as an irrelevant and arbitrary interference with higher forces. These forces, to be sure, could not be definitively deflected by such ridiculous powerlessness, yet they might still be hindered and prevented from reaching full realization. Mankind, when organized in such a way that it marches with the movement of Nature or History, as if all men were only one man, accelerates the automatic movement of Nature or History to a speed which it could never reach alone. Practically speaking, this means that terror in all cases executes on the spot the death sentences which Nature has already pronounced on unfit races and individuals or which History has declared for dying classes and institutions, without waiting for the slower and less efficient elimination which would presumably be brought about anyhow.

In a perfect totalitarian government, where all individuals have become exemplars of the species, where all action has been transformed into acceleration, and every deed into the execution of death sentences—that is, under conditions in which terror as the essence of government is perfectly sheltered from the disturbing and irrelevant interference of human wishes and needs—no principle of action in Montesquieu's sense is necessary. Montesquieu needed principles of action because for him the essence of constitutional government, lawfulness and distribution of power, was basically stable: It could only negatively set up limitations on actions, not positively establish their principles. Since the greatness, but also the perplexity, of all laws in free societies is that they only indicate what one should not do, and never what one should do, political action and historical movement in constitutional government remain free and unpredictable, conforming to, but never inspired by, its essence.

Under totalitarian conditions, this essence has itself become movement—totalitarian government *is* only insofar as it is kept in constant motion. As long as totalitarian rule has not conquered the whole earth and, with the iron band of terror, melded all individual men into one mankind, terror in its double function as the essence of the government and the principle—not of action, but of motion—cannot be fully realized. To add to this a principle of action, such as fear, would be contradictory. For even fear is still (according to Montesquieu) a principle of action and as such unpredictable in its consequences. Fear is always connected with isolation—which can be either its result or its origin—and the concomitant experiences of impotence and helplessness. The space freedom needs for its realization is transformed into a desert when the arbitrariness of tyrants destroys the boundaries of laws that hedge in and guarantee to each the realm of freedom. Fear is the principle of human movements in this desert of neighborlessness and loneliness; as such, however, it is still a principle which guides the actions of individual men, who therefore retain a minimal, fearful contact with other men. The desert in which these individual, fearfully atomized men move retains an image, though a distorted one, of that space which human freedom needs.

The close relationship of totalitarian governments to despotic rule is very obvious indeed and extends to almost all areas of government. The totalitarian abolition of classes and of those groups in the population out of which true distinction, as opposed to the arbitrarily created distinctions of orders and stripes, could emerge cannot but remind us of the ancient tale of the Greek tyrant who, in order to introduce a fellow-tyrant to the arts of tyranny, led him out of town to a wheat field and there cut all halms down to equal size. The fact, indeed, that a travesty of equality prevails under all despotic governments has led many good people into the error of believing that from equality springs tyranny or dictatorship, just as the neo-conservativism of our time stems from the radical abolition of all hierarchical and traditional authoritarian factors occurring in all forms of despotism. If we read about the economic despoliation policies so characteristic of short-term efficiency and long-term inefficiency in totalitarian economics, we cannot but remember the old anecdote with which Montesquieu characterized despotic government: The savages of Louisiana, wanting to harvest ripe fruits, simply cut the fruit trees down, because that was quicker and easier (*L'Esprit des Lois*, Book I, ch. 13). Moreover, terror, torture, and the spy system which hunts for secret and dangerous thoughts have always been mainstays of tyrannies; and it is not surprising that some tyrants even knew the terrifying use that can be made of the human inclination to forget and the human horror of being forgotten. Prisons under despotic rulers, in Asia as well as in Europe, were frequently called places of oblivion, and frequently the family and friends of the man condemned to a living death in oblivion were warned that they would be punished for even mentioning his name.

The twentieth century has made us forget many horrors of the past, but there is no doubt that totalitarian dictators could attend, if they needed instruction, a long-established school where all means of violence and slyness for the purpose of the domination of man by man have been taught and evaluated. Totalitarian use of violence and especially of terror, however, is distinct from this, not because it so far transcends past limits, and not merely because one cannot very well call the organized and mechanized regular extermination of whole groups or whole peoples "murder" or even "mass murder," but because its chief characteristic is the very opposite of all police and spy terror of the past. All the similarities between totalitarian and traditional forms of tyranny, however striking they may be, are similarities of technique, and apply only to the initial stages of totalitarian rule. Regimes become truly totalitarian only when they have left behind their revolutionary phase and the techniques needed for the seizure and the consolidation of power—without of course ever abandoning them, should the need arise again.

A much more tempting reason for the student of totalitarianism to equate this form of government with tyranny pure and simple—and the only similarity which has a direct bearing on the specific content of each—is that totalitarian and tyrannical rule both concentrate all power in the hands of one man, who uses this power in such a way that he makes all other men absolutely and radically impotent. If, moreover, we remember the insane desire of the Roman emperor Nero, who is reported by ancient legend to have wished that the whole of mankind might have only one head, we cannot help being reminded of our present-day experiences with the so-called Führer principle, which is used by Stalin to the same, or perhaps even greater, extent as by Hitler, and which operates on the assumption not just that only one will survives among a dominated population but also that only one mind suffices to take care of all human activities in general. Yet it is also at this point of closest resemblance between totalitarian and tyrannical rule that the decisive difference emerges most clearly. In his insanity, Nero wished to be confronted with only one head so that the tranquillity of his rule would never be threatened again by any new opposition: he wanted to behead mankind, as it were, once and for all, though he knew that this was impossible. The totalitarian dictator, on the contrary, feels himself the one and only head of the whole human race; he is concerned with opposition only insofar as it must be wiped out before he can even begin his rule of total domination. His ultimate purpose is not the tranquillity of his own rule, but the imitation—in the case of Hitler—or the interpretation—in the case of Stalin—of the laws of Nature or of History. But these are laws of movement, as we have seen, which require constant motion, making the mere leisurely enjoyment of the fruits of domination, the time-honored joys of tyrannical rule (which at the same time were the limits beyond which the tyrant had no interest in exerting his power), impossible by definition. The totalitarian dictator, in sharp distinction from the tyrant, does not believe that he is a free agent with the power to execute his arbitrary will, but, instead, the executioner of laws higher than himself. The Hegelian definition of Freedom as insight into and conforming to "necessity" has here found a new and terrifying realization. For the imitation or interpretation of these laws, the totalitarian ruler feels that only one man is required and that all other persons, all other minds as well as wills, are strictly superfluous. This conviction would be utterly absurd if we were to assume that in some fit of megalomania totalitarian rulers believed they had accumulated and monopolized all possible capacities of the human mind and the human will, i.e., if we were to believe that they actually think themselves infallible. The totalitarian ruler, in short, is not a tyrant and can be understood only by first understanding the nature of totalitarianism.

Still, if totalitarian rule has little in common with the tyrannies of the past, it has even less to do with certain modern forms of dictatorship out of which it developed and with which it has been frequently confused. One-party dictatorships, of either the fascist or communist type, are not totalitarian. Neither Lenin nor Mussolini was a totalitarian dictator, nor even knew what totalitarianism really meant. Lenin's was a revolutionary one-party dictatorship whose power lay chiefly in the party bureaucracy, which Tito tries to replicate today. Mussolini was chiefly a nationalist and, in contrast to the Nazis, a true worshiper of the State, with strong imperialist inclinations; if the Italian army had been better, he probably would have ended as an ordinary military dictator, just as Franco, who emerged from the military hierarchy, tries to be in Spain, with the help given and the constraint imposed by the Catholic Church. In totalitarian states, neither army nor church nor bureaucracy was ever in a position to wield or to restrain power; all executive power is in the hands of the secret police (or the élite formations which, as the instance of Nazi Germany and the history of the Bolshevik party show, are sooner or later incorporated into the police). No group or institution in the country is left intact, not just because they have to "co-ordinate" with the regime in power and outwardly support it—which of course is bad enough— but because in the long run they are literally not supposed to survive. The chess players in the Soviet Union who one beautiful day were informed that chess for chess's sake was a thing of the past are a case in point. It was in the same spirit that Himmler emphasized to the SS that no task existed which a real Nazi could perform for its own sake.

In addition to equating totalitarian rule with tyranny, and confusing it with other modern forms of dictatorship and, particularly, of one-party dictatorship, there remains a third way to try to make totalitarianism seem more harmless and less unprecedented or less relevant for modern political problems: the explanation of totalitarian rule in either Germany or Russia by historical or other causes relevant only to that specific country. Against this kind of argumentation stands, of course, the truly terrifying propaganda success both movements have had outside their home countries in spite of very powerful and very informative counter-propaganda from the most respectable and respected sources. No information on concentration camps in Soviet Russia or death factories in Auschwitz deterred the numerous fellow-travelers which both regimes knew how to attract. Yet even if we leave this aspect of attraction undiscussed, there is a more serious argument against this explanation: the curious fact that Nazi Germany and Soviet Russia started from historical, economic, ideological, and cultural circumstances in many respects almost diametrically opposed, yet still arrived at certain results which are structurally identical. This is easily overlooked because these identical structures reveal themselves only in fully developed totalitarian rule. Not only was this point reached at different times in Germany and in Russia, but different fields of political and other activity were seized at different moments as well. To this difficulty must be added another historical circumstance. Soviet Russia embarked upon the road to totalitarianism only around 1930 and Germany only after 1938. Up to those points, both countries, though already containing a great number of totalitarian elements, could still be regarded as one-party dictatorships. Russia became fully totalitarian only after the Moscow Trials, i.e., shortly before the war, and Germany only during the first years of the war. Nazi Germany in particular never had time to realize completely its evil potential, which can nevertheless be inferred by studying minutes from Hitler's headquarters and other such documents. The picture is further confused by the fact that very few people in the Nazi hierarchy were entirely aware of Hitler's and Bormann's plans. Soviet Russia, though much more advanced in its totalitarian rule, offers very little documentary source material, so that each concrete point always and necessarily remains disputable even though we know enough to arrive at correct over-all estimates and conclusions.

Totalitarianism as we know it today in its Bolshevik and Nazi versions developed out of one-party dictatorships which, like other tyrannies, used terror as a means to establish a desert of neighborlessness and loneliness. Yet when the well-known tranquillity of the cemetery had been obtained, totalitarianism was not satisfied, but turned the instrument of terror at once and with increased vigor into an objective law of movement. Fear, moreover, becomes pointless when the selection of victims is completely free from all reference to an individual's actions or thoughts. Fear, though certainly the all-pervasive mood in totalitarian countries, is no longer a principle of action and can no longer serve as a guide to specific deeds. Totalitarian tyranny is unprecedented in that it melds people together in the desert of isolation and atomization and then introduces a gigantic motion into the tranquillity of the cemetery.

No guiding principle of action taken from the realm of human action—such as virtue, honor, fear—is needed or could be used to set into motion a body politic whose essence is motion implemented by terror. In its stead, totalitarianism relies upon a new principle, which, as such, dispenses with human action as free deeds altogether and substitutes for the very desire and will to action a craving and need for insight into the laws of movement according to which the terror functions. Human beings, caught or thrown into the process of Nature or History for the sake of accelerating its movement, can become only the executioners or the victims of its inherent law. According to this law, they may today be those who eliminate the "unfit races and individuals" or the "dying classes and decadent peoples" and tomorrow be those who, for the same reasons, must themselves be sacrificed. What totalitarian rule therefore needs, instead of a principle of action, is a means to prepare individuals equally well for the role of executioner and the role of victim. This two-sided preparation, the substitute for a principle of action, is ideology.

III

Ideologies by themselves are as little totalitarian and their use as little restricted to totalitarian propaganda as terror by itself is restricted to totalitarian rule. As we have all learned to our sorrow, it does not matter whether this ideology is as stupid and barren of authentic spiritual content as racism or whether it is as saturated with the best of our tradition as socialism. Only in the hands of the new type of totalitarian governments do ideologies become the driving motor of political action, and this in the double sense that ideologies determine the political actions of the ruler and make these actions tolerable to the ruled population. I call all ideologies in this context *isms* that pretend to have found the key explanation for all the mysteries of life and the world. Thus racism or anti-Semitism is not an ideology, but merely an irresponsible opinion, as long as it restricts itself to praising Aryans and hating Jews; it becomes an ideology only when it pretends to explain the whole course of history as being secretly maneuvered by the Jews, or covertly subject to an eternal race struggle, race mixture, or whatnot. Socialism, similarly, is not an ideology properly speaking as long as it describes class struggles, preaches justice for the underprivileged, and fights for an improvement or revolutionary change of society. Socialism—or communism—becomes an ideology only when it pretends that all history is a struggle of classes, that the proletariat is bound by eternal laws to win this struggle, that a classless society will then come about, and that the state, finally, will wither away. In other words, ideologies are systems of explanation of life and world that claim to explain everything, past and future, without further concurrence with actual experience.

This last point is crucial. This arrogant emancipation from reality and experience, more than any actual content, foreshadows the connection between ideology and terror. This connection not only makes terror an all-embracing characteristic of totalitarian rule, in the sense that it is directed equally against all members of the population, regardless of their guilt or innocence, but also is the very condition for its permanence. Insofar as ideological thinking is independent of existing reality, it looks upon all factuality as fabricated, and therefore no longer knows any reliable criterion for distinguishing truth from falsehood. If it is untrue, said *Das Schwarze Korps*, for instance, that all Jews are beggars without passports, we shall change facts in such a way as to make this statement true. That a man by the name of Trotsky was ever the head of the Red Army will cease to be true when the Bolsheviks have the global power to change all history texts—and so forth. The point here is that the ideological consistency reducing everything to one all-dominating factor is always in conflict with the inconsistency of the world, on the one hand, and the unpredictability of human actions, on the other. Terror is needed in order to make the world consistent and keep it that way; to dominate human beings to the point where they lose, with their spontaneity, the specifically human unpredictability of thought and action.

Such ideologies were fully developed before anybody ever heard the word or conceived the notion of totalitarianism. That their very claim to totality made them almost predestined to play a role in totalitarianism is easy to see. What is less easy to understand, partly because their tenets have been the subject of dreary discussions for centuries in the case of racism, and for many decades in the case of socialism, is what made them such supreme principles and motors of action. As a matter of fact, the only new device the totalitarian rulers invented or discovered in using these ideologies was translating a general outlook into a singular principle ruling over all activities. Neither Stalin nor Hitler added a single new thought, respectively, to socialism or racism; yet only in their hands did these ideologies become deadly serious.

It is at this point that the problem of the role of ideologies in totalitarianism receives its full meaning. What is novel in the ideological propaganda of totalitarian movements even before they seize power is the immediate transformation of ideological content into living reality through instruments of totalitarian organization. The Nazi movement, far from organizing people who happened to believe in racism, organized them according to objective race criteria, so that race ideology was no longer a matter of mere opinion or argument or even fanaticism, but constituted the actual living reality, first of the Nazi movement, and then of Nazi Germany, where the amount of one's food, the choice of one's profession, and the woman one married depended upon one's racial physiognomy and ancestry. The Nazis, as distinguished from other racists, did not so much believe in the truth of racism as desire to change the world into a race reality.

A similar change in the role of ideology took place when Stalin replaced the revolutionary socialist dictatorship in the Soviet Union with a full-fledged totalitarian regime. Socialist ideology shared with all other isms the claim to have found the solution to all the riddles of the universe and to be able to introduce the best system into the political affairs of mankind. The fact that new classes sprang up in Soviet Russia after the October Revolution was of course a blow to socialist theory, according to which the violent upheaval should have been followed by a gradual dying out of class structures. When Stalin embarked upon his murderous purge policies to establish a classless society through the regular extermination of all social layers that might develop into classes, he realized, albeit in an unexpected form, the ideological socialist belief about dying classes. The result is the same: Soviet Russia is as much a classless society as Nazi Germany was a racially determined society. What had been mere ideological opinion before became the lived content of reality. The connection between totalitarianism and all other isms is that totalitarianism can use any of the others as an organizational principle and try to change the whole texture of reality according to its tenets.

The two great obstacles on the road to such transformation are the unpredictability, the fundamental unreliability, of man, on the one hand, and the curious inconsistency of the human world, on the other. Precisely because ideologies by themselves are matters of opinion rather than of truth, the human freedom to change one's mind is a great and pertinent danger. No mere oppression, therefore, but the total and reliable domination of man is necessary if he is to fit into the ideologically determined, factitious world of totalitarianism. Total domination as such is quite independent of the actual content of any given ideology; no matter which ideology one may choose, no matter if one decides to transform the world and man according to the tenets of racism or socialism or any other ism, total domination will always be required. This is why two systems so different from each other in actual content, in origins and objective circumstances, could in the end build almost identical administrative and terror machineries.

For the totalitarian experiment of changing the world according to an ideology, total domination of the inhabitants of one country is not enough. The existence, and not so much the hostility, of any non-totalitarian country is a direct threat to the consistency of the ideological claim. If it is true that the socialist or communist system of the Soviet Union is superior to all other systems, then it follows that under no other system can such a fine thing as a subway really be built. For a time, therefore, Soviet schools used to teach their children that there is no other subway in the world except the subway in Moscow. The Second World War put a halt to such obvious absurdities, but this will only be temporary. For the consistency of the claim demands that in the end no other subway survive except a subway under totalitarian rule: either all others have to be destroyed or the countries where they operate have to be brought under totalitarian domination. The claim to global conquest, inherent in the Communist concept of World Revolution, as it was in the Nazi concept of a master race, is no mere threat born of lust for power or mad overestimation of one's own forces. The real danger is the fact that the factitious, topsy-turvy world of a totalitarian regime cannot survive for any length of time if the entire outside world does not adopt a similar system, allowing all of reality to become a consistent whole, threatened neither by the subjective unpredictability of man nor by the contingent quality of the human world which always leaves some space open for accident.

It is an open and sometimes hotly debated question whether the totalitarian ruler himself or his immediate subordinates believe, along with his mass of adherents and subjects, in the superstitions of the respective ideologies. Since the tenets in question are so obviously stupid and vulgar, those who tend to answer this question affirmatively are also inclined to deny the almost unquestionable qualities and gifts of men like Hitler and Stalin. On the other hand, those who tend to answer this question negatively, believing that the phenomenal deceptiveness of both men is sufficient proof of their cold and detached cynicism, are also inclined to deny the curious incalculability of totalitarian politics, which so obviously violates all rules of self-interest and common sense. In a world used to calculating actions and reactions by these yardsticks, such incalculability becomes a public danger.

Why should lust for power, which from the beginning of recorded history has been considered the political and social sin par excellence, suddenly transcend all previously known limitations of self-interest and utility and attempt not simply to dominate men as they are, but also to change their very nature; not only to kill innocent and harmless bystanders, but to do this even when such murder is an obstacle, rather than an advantage, to the accumulation of power? If we refuse to be caught by mere phrases and their associations and look behind them at the actual phenomena, it appears that total domination, as practiced every day by a totalitarian regime, is separated from all other forms of domination by an abyss which no psychological explanation such as "lust for power" is able to bridge.

This curious neglect of obvious self-interest in totalitarian rule has frequently impressed people as a kind of mistaken idealism. And this impression has some kernel of truth, if we understand by idealism only absence of selfishness and common-sense motives. The selflessness of totalitarian rulers perhaps characterizes itself best through the curious fact that none was ever particularly eager to find a successor among his own children. (It is a noteworthy experience for the student of tyrannies to come across a variation which is not plagued by the ever-present worry of the classical usurper.)

Total domination for totalitarian regimes is never an end in itself. In this respect the totalitarian ruler is more "enlightened" and closer to the wishes and desires of the masses who support him—frequently even in the face of patent disaster—than his predecessors, the power politicians who no longer played the game for the sake of national interest but as a game of power for power's sake. Total domination, despite its frightful attack on the physical existence of people as well as on the nature of man, can play the seemingly old game of tyranny with such unprecedented murderous efficiency because it is used only as a means to an end.

I think that Hitler believed as unquestioningly in race struggle and racial superiority (though not necessarily in the racial superiority of the

German people) as Stalin believes in class struggle and the classless society (though not necessarily in world revolution). However, in view of the particular qualities of totalitarian regimes, which might be established according to any arbitrary opinion enlarged into a *Weltanschauung*, it would be quite possible for totalitarian rulers or the men immediately surrounding them not to believe in the actual content of their preaching; it sometimes seems as though the new generation, educated under conditions of totalitarian rule, somehow has lost even the ability to distinguish between such believing and non-believing. If that were the case, the actual aim of totalitarian rule would have to a large extent been achieved: the abolition of convictions as a too unreliable support for the system; and the demonstration that this system, in distinction from all others, has made man, insofar as he is a being of spontaneous thought and action, superfluous.

Underlying these beliefs or non-beliefs, these "idealistic" convictions or cynical calculations, is another belief, of an entirely different quality, which, indeed, is shared by all totalitarian rulers, as well as by people thinking and acting along totalitarian lines, whether or not they know it. This is the belief in the omnipotence of *man* and at the same time of the superfluity of *men*; it is the belief that everything is permitted and, much more terrible, that everything is possible. Under this condition, the question of the original truth or falsehood of the ideologies loses its relevance. If Western philosophy has maintained that reality is truth— for this is of course the ontological basis of the *aequatio rei et intellectus*—then totalitarianism has concluded from this that we can fabricate truth insofar as we can fabricate reality; that we do not have to wait until reality unveils itself and shows us its true face, but can bring into being a reality whose structures will be known to us from the beginning because the whole thing is our product. In other words, it is the underlying conviction of any totalitarian transformation of ideology into reality that it will become true whether it is true or not. Because of this totalitarian relationship to reality, the very concept of truth has lost its meaning. The lies of totalitarian movements, invented for the moment, as well as the forgeries committed by totalitarian regimes, are secondary to this fundamental attitude that excludes the very distinction between truth and falsehood.

It is for this end, that is, for the consistency of a lying world order, rather than for the sake of power or any other humanly understandable sinfulness, that totalitarianism requires total domination and global rule and is prepared to commit crimes which are unprecedented in the long and sinful history of mankind.*

The operation Hitler and Stalin performed on their respective ideologies was simply to take them dead seriously, and that meant driving their pretentious implications to that extreme of logical consequence where they would look, to the normal eye, preposterously absurd. If you believe in earnest that the bourgeoisie is not simply antagonistic to the interests of the worker, but is dying, then evidently you are permitted to kill all bourgeois. If you take literally the dictum that the Jews, far from merely being the enemies of other people, are actually vermin, created as vermin by nature and therefore predestined to suffer the same fate as lice and bedbugs, then you have established a perfect argument for their extermination. This stringent logicality as an inspiration of action permeates the whole structure of totalitarian movements and totalitarian governments. The most persuasive argument, of which Hitler and Stalin were equally fond, is to insist that whoever says A must necessarily also say B and C and finally end with the last letter of the alphabet. Everything which stands in the way of this kind of reasoning—reality, experience, and the daily network of human relationships and interdependence—is overruled. Even the advice of common self-interest shares this fate in extreme cases, as was proved over and over again by the way Hitler conducted his war. Mere logic, which starts from one single accepted premise—what Hitler used to call his supreme gift of "ice-cold reasoning"—remains always the ultimate guiding principle.

We may say, then, that in totalitarian governments, Montesquieu's principle of action is replaced by ideology. Though up till now we have been confronted with only two types of totalitarianism, each started from an ideological belief whose appeal to large masses of people had already been demonstrated and both of which were therefore thought to be highly appropriate to inspire action, to set the masses in motion. Yet, if we look closer at what is really happening, or has been happening during the last thirty years, to these masses and their individual members, we shall discover the disconcerting ease with which so many changed from a red

---

*This and the preceding ten paragraphs are from the manuscript entitled "Ideology and Propaganda." —Ed.

shirt into a brown, and if that did not work out, into a red shirt again, only to take on the brown again after a little while. These changes— and they are more numerous than we usually admit in our eagerness and hope to see people, after one bad experience, give up shirt-wearing altogether—seem to indicate that it is not even the ideologies, with their demonstrable content, which set people into action, but the logicality of their reasoning all by itself and almost independent of content. This would mean that after ideologies have taught people to emancipate themselves from real experience and the shock of reality by luring them into a fool's paradise where everything is known *a priori*, the next step will lead them, if it has not already done so, away from the content of their paradise; not to make them any wiser, but to mislead them further into the wilderness of mere abstract logical deductions and conclusions. It is no longer race or the establishment of a society based on race that is the "ideal" which appeals, nor class or the establishment of a classless society, but the murderous network of pure logical operations in which one is caught once one accepts either of them. It is as though these shirt-changers console themselves with the thought that no matter what content they accept—no matter which kind of eternal law they decide to believe in—once they have taken this initial step, nothing can ever happen to them anymore, and they are saved.

Saved from what? Maybe we can find the answer if we look once more at the nature of totalitarianism, that is, at its essence of terror and at its principle of logicality, which in combination add up to its nature. It has been frequently said, and it is perfectly true, that the most horrible aspect of terror is that it has the power to bind together completely isolated individuals and that by so doing it isolates these individuals even further. Hitler as well as Stalin may have learned from all the historical examples of tyranny that any group of people joined together by some common interest is the supreme threat to total domination. Only isolated individuals can be dominated totally. Hitler was able to build his organization on the firm ground of an already atomized society which he then artificially atomized even further; Stalin needed the bloody extermination of the peasants, the uprooting of the workers, the repeated purges of the administrative machinery and the party bureaucracy in order to achieve the same results. By the terms "atomized society" and "isolated individuals" we mean a state of affairs where people live together without having anything in common, without sharing some visible tangible realm of the world. Just as the inhabitants of an apartment house form a group on the basis of their sharing this particular building, so we, on the strength of the political and legal institutions that provide our general living together with all the normal channels of communication, become a social group, a society, a people, a nation and so forth. And just as the apartment dwellers will become isolated from each other if for some reason their building is taken away from them, so the collapse of our institutions—the ever-increasing political and physical homelessness and spiritual and social rootlessness—is the one gigantic mass destiny of our time in which we all participate, though to very differing degrees of intensity and misery.

Terror, in the sense we were speaking of it, is not so much something which people may fear, but a way of life which takes the utter impotence of the individual for granted and provides for him either victory or death, a career or an end in a concentration camp, completely independent of his own actions or merits. Terror fits the situation of these ever-growing masses to perfection, no matter if these masses are the result of decaying societies or of calculated policies.

But terror by itself is not enough—it fits but it does not inspire. If we observe from this perspective the curious logicality of the ideologies in totalitarian movements, we understand better why this combination can be so supremely valuable. If it were true that there are eternal laws ruling supreme over all things human and demanding of each human being only total conformity, then freedom would be only a mockery, some snare luring one away from the right path; then homelessness would be only a fantasy, an imagined thing, which could be cured by the decision to conform to some recognizable universal law. And then—last not least—not the concert of human minds, but only one man would be needed to understand these laws and to build humanity in such a way as to conform to them under all changing circumstances. The "knowledge" of one alone would suffice, and the plurality of human gifts or insights or initiatives would be simply superfluous. Human contact would not matter; only the preservation of a perfect functionality within the framework established by the one initiated into the "wisdom" of the law would matter.

Logicality is what appeals to isolated human beings, for man—in complete solitude, without any contact with his fellow-men and therefore without any real possibility of experience—has nothing else he can fall back on but the most abstract rules of reasoning. The intimate connection between logicality and isolation was stressed in Martin Luther's little-known interpretation of the biblical passage that says that God created Man, male and female, because "it is not good for man to be alone." Luther says: "A lonely man always deduces one thing from another and carries everything to its worst conclusion" ("Warum die Einsamkeit zu fliehen?" in *Erbauliche Schriften*).

Logicality, mere reasoning without regard for facts and experience, is the true vice of solitude. But the vices of solitude grow only out of the despair of loneliness. Now, when human contacts have been severed—either through the collapse of our common home, or through the growing expansion of mere functionality whereby the substance, the real matter of human relationships, is slowly eaten away, or through the catastrophic developments of revolutions that themselves resulted from previous collapses—loneliness in such a world is no longer a psychological matter to be handled with such beautiful and meaningless terms as "introvert" or "extrovert." Loneliness, as the concomitant of homelessness and uprootedness, is, humanly speaking, the very disease of our time. To be sure, you may still see people—but they get to be fewer and fewer—who cling to each other as if in midair, without the help of established channels of communication provided by a commonly inhabited world, in order to escape together the curse of becoming inhuman in a society where everybody seems to be superfluous and is so perceived by their fellow-men. But what do these acrobatic performances prove against the despair growing all around us, which we ignore whenever we merely denounce or call people who fall for totalitarian propaganda stupid or wicked or ill informed? These people are nothing of the sort. They have only escaped the despair of loneliness by becoming addicted to the vices of solitude.

Solitude and loneliness are not the same. In solitude we are never alone, but are together with ourselves. In solitude we are always two-in-one; we become one whole individual, in the richness as well as the limitations of definite characteristics, through and only through the company of others. For our individuality, insofar as it is one—unchangeable and unmistakable—we depend entirely on other people. Solitude in which one has the company of oneself need not give up contact with others, and is not outside human company altogether; on the contrary, it prepares us for certain outstanding forms of human rapport, such as friendship and love, that is, for all rapport which transcends the established channels of human communication. If one can endure solitude, bear one's own company, then chances are that one can bear and be prepared for the companionship of others; whoever cannot bear any other person usually will not be able to endure his own self.

The great grace of companionship is that it redeems the two-in-one by making it individual. As individuals we need each other and become lonely if through some physical or some political accident we are robbed of company or companionship. Loneliness develops when man does not find companionship to save him from the dual nature of his solitude, or when man as an individual, in constant need of others for his individuality, is deserted or separated from others. In the latter case, he is all alone, forsaken even by the company of himself.

The great metaphysical questions—the quest for God, freedom, and immortality (as in Kant) or about man and world, being and nothingness, life and death—are always asked in solitude, when man is alone with himself and therefore potentially together with everybody. The very fact that man, for the time being, is deflected from his individuality enables him to ask timeless questions that transcend the questions asked, in different ways, by every individual. But no such questions are asked in loneliness, when man as an individual is deserted even by his own self and lost in the chaos of people. The despair of loneliness is its very dumbness, admitting no dialogue.

Solitude is not loneliness, but can easily become loneliness and can even more easily be confused with it. Nothing is more difficult and rarer than people who, out of the desperate need of loneliness, find the strength to escape into solitude, into company with themselves, thereby mending the broken ties which link them to other men. This is what happened in one happy moment to Nietzsche, when he concluded his great and desperate poem of loneliness with the words: "*Mittags war, da wurde eins zu zwei, und Zarathustra ging an mir vorbei*" ("Sils-Maria," *Die Froliche Wissenschaft*). *

The danger in solitude is of losing one's own self, so that, instead of being together with everybody, one is literally deserted by everybody. This has been the professional risk of the philosopher, who, because of

---

*"It was noon, one became two, and I was done with Zarathustra." Arendt quotes from memory. —Ed.

his quest for truth and his concern with questions we call metaphysical (which are actually the only questions of concern to everybody), needs solitude, the being together with his own self and therefore with everybody, as a kind of working condition. As the inherent risk of solitude, loneliness is, therefore, a professional danger for philosophers, which, incidentally, seems to be one of the reasons that philosophers cannot be trusted with politics or a political philosophy. Not only do they have one supreme interest which they seldom divulge—to be left alone, to have their solitude guaranteed and freed from all possible disturbances, such as the disturbance of the fulfillment of one's duty as a citizen—but this interest has naturally led them to sympathize with tyrannies where action is not expected of citizens. Their experience in solitude has given them extraordinary insight into all those relationships which cannot be realized without this being alone with one's own self, but has led them to forget the perhaps even more primary relationships between men and the realm they constitute, springing simply from the fact of human plurality.

We said at the beginning of these reflections that we shall be satisfied with having understood the essence or nature of political phenomena which determine the whole innermost structure of entire eras only if we succeed in analyzing them as signs of the danger of general trends that concern and eventually may threaten all societies—not just those countries where they have already been victorious or are on the point of becoming victorious. The danger totalitarianism lays bare before our eyes—and this danger, by definition, will not be overcome merely by victory over totalitarian governments—springs from rootlessness and homelessness and could be called the danger of loneliness and superfluity. Both loneliness and superfluity are, of course, symptoms of mass society, but their true significance is not thereby exhausted. Dehumanization is implied in both and, though reaching its most horrible consequences in concentration camps, exists prior to their establishment. Loneliness as we know it in an atomized society is indeed, as I tried to show by the quotation from the Bible and its interpretation by Luther, contrary to the basic requirements of the human condition. Even the experience of the merely materially and sensually given world depends, in the last analysis, upon the fact that not one man but men in the plural inhabit the earth. . . .

Heidegger the Fox

HEIDEGGER SAYS, WITH great pride: "People say that Heidegger is a fox." This is the true story of Heidegger the fox: Once upon a time there was a fox who was so lacking in slyness that he not only kept getting caught in traps but couldn't even tell the difference between a trap and a non-trap. This fox suffered from another failing as well. There was something wrong with his fur, so that he was completely without natural protection against the hardships of a fox's life. After he had spent his entire youth prowling around the traps of people, and now that not one intact piece of fur, so to speak, was left on him, this fox decided to withdraw from the fox world altogether and to set about making himself a burrow. In his shocking ignorance of the difference between traps and non-traps, despite his incredibly extensive experience with traps, he hit on an idea completely new and unheard of among foxes: He built a trap as his burrow. He set himself inside it, passed it off as a normal burrow—not out of cunning, but because he had always thought others' traps were their burrows—

---

*This is from Arendt's *Denktagebuch* of 1953. Her *Denktagebücher* are notebooks in which she recorded her thoughts, as well as quotations from other writers, for future reference. English translation by Robert and Rita Kimber.

and then decided to become sly in his own way and outfit for others the trap he had built himself and that suited only him. This again demonstrated great ignorance about traps: No one would go into his trap, because he was sitting inside it himself. This annoyed him. After all, everyone knows that, despite their slyness, all foxes occasionally get caught in traps. Why should a fox trap—especially one built by a fox with more experience of traps than any other—not be a match for the traps of human beings and hunters? Obviously because this trap did not reveal itself clearly enough as the trap it was! And so it occurred to our fox to decorate his trap beautifully and to hang up unequivocal signs everywhere on it that quite clearly said: "Come here, everyone; this is a trap, the most beautiful trap in the world." From this point on it was clear that no fox could stray into this trap by mistake. Nevertheless, many came. For this trap was our fox's burrow, and if you wanted to visit him where he was at home, you had to step into his trap. Everyone except our fox could, of course, step out of it again. It was cut, literally, to his own measurement. But the fox who lived in the trap said proudly: "So many are visiting me in my trap that I have become the best of all foxes." And there is some truth in that, too: Nobody knows the nature of traps better than one who sits in a trap his whole life long.

Understanding Communism

[This review of *Bolshevism: An Introduction to Soviet Communism*, by Waldemar Gurian, Notre Dame, IN, 1952, was published in *Partisan Review* XX/5, September–October 1953. While it gives important indications of Arendt's growing concern at this time with the meaning of Marx's thought, the review does not suggest the great depth of her feeling for Gurian himself. She had known this "strange man," "a stranger in the world, never quite at home in it, and at the same time a realist," since the early thirties in Germany. For Arendt his was one of the lives that illuminated the darkness of the twentieth century. See "Waldemar Gurian 1903–1954" in *Men in Dark Times*.]

THIS, TO MY knowledge, is the best analytical history of Bolshevism. In about a hundred pages, it sums up with great precision the findings of most students of the subject; and the second part consists of carefully selected source material, some of it in original translations from the Russian. The emphasis throughout is on the basic tenets and ideological implications of the Soviet system.

Brevity is not a common virtue of historians. Wherever it is achieved, it rests on qualities which come only as the reward of lifelong study, of complete mastery of the material and an unerring sense of relevance.

These qualities are manifest throughout Gurian's study. But Gurian's subject is of a kind that presents special difficulties to the historian. All studies of the Soviet system, even when prepared by the most reliable experts, suffer from a decisive lack of source material. Russian archives have never been opened, and we do not know whether the Bolshevik regime will leave behind the usual kind of documentary evidence without which no factual historiography can be written. Under the influence of the social sciences, contemporary historians have unfortunately lost much of their interest in sources as such. This becomes more and more apparent in the growing literature on the Soviet system, about which we know so little that we are forced to rely continually on secondary material. And this lack of undisputed documentary evidence has led many scholars to accept Russian government sources and to succumb to Bolshevik propaganda simply because it appears to them to be more reputable than the records of personal experience by victims of the regime or the spectacular confessions of former officials.

Gurian never falls into this trap. His own solution of the problem is to concentrate on an analysis of the ideology, avoiding factual narrative as much as possible. This approach has one major shortcoming: it does not really account for the events themselves, since even the more decisive ones, like the Kronstadt rebellion, are treated in a cursory manner.

It is in the nature of this situation that general assumptions, originally designed only as working hypotheses, soon assume the status of final judgments and conclusions. These permeate the whole literature on the subject and most authors are not even aware that this is the case. One merit of the present study is that in it the principles on which most historical and sociological research into the nature of Bolshevism rest are clearly articulated and consistently followed. These principles may be enumerated as follows:

(1) An unbroken line of thought and political attitude runs from Marx to Lenin and Stalin. Marx is the discoverer and formulator of a theory which Lenin translated into practical terms and which Stalin put into effect. Strategy (Marx) is followed by the development of tactical means (Lenin) and ends with the execution of a preconceived plan (Stalin). To be sure, Gurian adheres to this argument with great caution and many qualifications, but essentially he agrees that there is no difference in principle between Marx and Stalin.

(2) Bolshevism is understood in religious terms. "What believers of

traditional religions ascribe to God . . . Bolsheviks ascribe to the allegedly scientific laws of social development." (This *quid pro quo* of God and historical law has by now apparently convinced everybody who believes that neither the existence of God nor that of historical laws can be demonstrated scientifically.) It depends on the personal religious (or anti-religious) convictions of the author whether this new secular religion is taken as the great alibi of the regime (because of the "idealism" involved) or whether, as happens more frequently, it is taken as a perversion of true materialism. More recently, however, the secular religion of Bolshevism is understood as a substitute for the true faith, the one great modern heresy growing out of a secularized society. In this latter version, which is the thesis of the present study, the very emergence of a "secular religion" is presented as a demonstration of the inevitability of human religious needs and as a supreme political warning against the abandonment of traditional religion.

(3) The new immanentist creed is the logical product of the modern secularized world and its inherent tendencies. A political life that has lost its transcendent measure and believes that ultimate aims can be reached and realized on earth can only end in some form of totalitarianism.

This is not the place to take issue with the validity of these judgments, each of which corresponds to a true predicament of the modern political situation and none of which, being "value-judgments," can be proved or disproved by the facts and the sources themselves. They are all working hypotheses, and I suspect that one reason why they became axiomatic value-judgments is that the material out of which they emerge is so very scarce. It is interesting, however, to reflect on their origin. It happens, and this cannot be a coincidence, that all three can be traced to ideological positions of Marxism or historical self-interpretations of Bolshevism itself. As a matter of fact, only the "evaluation" and the emphasis are changed.

There is no doubt that Lenin understood himself as a mere tactician, faithfully applying the revolutionary strategy of Marx to changing and changed circumstances. It is more than probable that Stalin quoted Marx and Lenin in justification of all his actions—not merely or even primarily for propaganda purposes. Bolshevik self-interpretation, long before scholars bothered to look into it, had already elevated the unbroken line from Marx to Lenin to Stalin into dogma.

It is somewhat more difficult to perceive the origin of the theory of a secular or political religion. This is meant to explain the role of ideologies in politics. Now, it was Marx of course who first systematically "explained" all religions as ideological superstructures concealing the interests of the ruling classes. He could do this because he viewed religion as an exclusively social phenomenon in whose function he was interested, but whose substantial content he consistently neglected. The social sciences have gone one step further in the same direction and dissolved all material, intellectual, and spiritual factors in human life into social functions and relationships. They are distinguished from orthodox Marxism only in that they do not believe that thought in the interest of the proletariat could by some magic be "true" and not merely an ideology. They can, in other words, talk back to Marx and tell him that Marxism, too, is an ideology, no better and no worse than the religions whose ideological character Marx unmasked.

Seen in this social context alone, ideology and religion are the same: they seem to fulfill the same basic social need. The concept of a "secular religion" without God is possible only on the basis of Marx's devastating criticism of all religions; his central point is not so much the quoted vulgarized formula "religion is an opiate of the people" (obviously religions, like everything else, can be used and misused) as the claim that the idea of God itself originated in social conditions which led to the self-estrangement of man. Just as Marx did not take seriously the religious claim of the existence of God, so the term "secular religion" implies that one need not take seriously the ideological claim of atheism.

Gurian tries to avoid the relativism of the social sciences, where things are finally of equal value if they function equally well, by insisting on the perverted relationship between the traditional and the new secular religions: the latter have simply "secularized" originally transcendent contents, whose truth consisted precisely in their being transcendent. The argument stresses that the classless society is nothing but a secularized perversion of the Kingdom of God, etc. Whether this is historically true or not, the argument for traditional and against secular religion remains weak because it rests on the assumption that socially and psychologically we cannot do without religion, an assumption leading to the use of a terminology which calls an anti-religious attitude religious too. . . . The argument itself can be faced squarely only if one admits the gulf separating faith from atheism. Insofar as Marx can rightly be called the father of the social sciences, his victory in the modern world is perhaps nowhere shown more clearly than in the acceptance of his methodology by his very opponents.

Finally, it is a matter of record that Lenin, like Marx and all the more educated Marxists, took pride in being the true heir of secularized Western thought. The point, obviously, is not that Marxist thought is still firmly embedded in the Western tradition, as it is to a larger degree than Marx himself realized, but that the secular world is unavoidably adopting Marxist habits of thought.

The great temptation, and to a degree justification, of the view of Bolshevism presented in Gurian's study lies in the fact that Communism, as against racism, contains elements intrinsic to the great tradition of political thought. The turning point, where Bolshevik totalitarianism overtook and liquidated communism as we knew it from Marx to Lenin, is difficult to perceive and can hardly be located with precision before the development of the Soviet system comes to an end. In the meantime Gurian's statement, which applies its working hypotheses cautiously and supports them with great scholarly distinction, can well be taken as a definitive test of our present knowledge and understanding of the subject.

Religion and Politics

["Religion and Politics" was prepared as a paper for delivery at a Harvard University conference on the question "Is the Struggle Between the Free World and Communism Basically Religious?" It was published in *Confluence*, II/3, 1953. Jules Monnerot replied to Arendt's essay in a letter addressed to Henry Kissinger, the editor of *Confluence*, which was published in the following issue, II/4, 1953. In his letter Monnerot, noting that Arendt "accuses [him] of confusing *ideology* with *religion*," in turn criticizes her for failing to define either term. Arendt's reply was published in the next issue of *Confluence*, III/1, 1954.]

ONE OF THE surprising by-products of the struggle between the free and the totalitarian world has been a strong tendency to interpret the conflict in religious terms. Communism, we are told, is a new "secular religion" against which the free world defends its own transcendent "religious system." This theory has larger implications than its immediate occasion; it has brought "religion" back into the realm of public-political affairs from which it has been banished ever since the separation of Church and State. By the same token, although its defenders are often not aware of this, it has put the almost forgotten problem of the relationship between religion and politics once more on the agenda of political science.

I

The interpretation of the new political ideologies as political, or secular, religions has paradoxically, though perhaps not accidentally, followed Marx's well-known denunciation of all religions as mere ideologies. But its true origin is even older. Not Communism, but atheism, was the first ism to be denounced or praised as a new religion.[1] This sounds like, and originally was meant to be, no more than a witty paradox until Dostoevsky and many after him gave it some substance. For atheism was something more than the rather stupid claim to be able to prove the non-existence of God; it was taken to mean an actual rebellion of modern man against God himself. In Nietszche's words: "*If* there were gods, how could I bear not to be one."[2]

The justification for calling atheism a religion is closely connected with the nature of religious beliefs in an era of secularity. Ever since the rise of the natural sciences in the seventeenth century, belief no less than non-belief has had its source in doubt; Kierkegaard's famous theory of the leap into belief had its predecessor in Pascal, and like Pascal attempts to reply to Descartes's *De omnibus dubitandum est*,[3] everything is to be doubted. They hold that universal doubt is an impossible, self-contradictory, and self-destroying attitude, unfit for human reason because the doubt itself is subject to doubt. Doubt, according to Kierkegaard, "is not defeated through knowledge but through belief, just as belief has brought doubt into the world."[4] Modern belief, which has leaped from doubt into belief, and modern atheism, which has leaped from doubt into non-belief, have this in common: both are grounded in modern spiritual secularism and have evaded its inherent perplexities by a violent resolution once and for all. Indeed, it may be that the leap into belief has done more to undermine authentic faith than the usually trite arguments of professional enlighteners or the vulgar arguments of professional atheists. The leap from doubt into belief could not but carry doubt into belief, so that religious life itself began to assume that curious tension between atheistic blasphemous doubt and belief as we know it from the great psychological masterpieces of Dostoevsky.

Our world is spiritually a secular world precisely because it is a world of doubt. If we wanted to eliminate secularity in true earnest, we should

[1] The notes are at the end of the essay.

have to eliminate modern science and its transformation of the world. Modern science is based on a philosophy of doubt, as distinguished from ancient science, which was based on a philosophy of *thaumadzein*, or wonder at that which is as it is. Instead of marveling at the miracles of the universe which revealed themselves in their appearance to human senses and reason, we began to suspect that things might not be what they seemed. Only when we began to distrust our sense perceptions could we make the discovery that contrary to all daily experience the earth revolves around the sun. From this basic distrust of appearances, this doubt that appearance reveals truth, two radically different conclusions could be drawn: Pascal's despair that "les sens abusent la raison par de fausses apparences"[5] from which comes the "recognition of human misery without God,"[6] or the modern scientific pragmatic affirmation that truth itself is by no means a revelation but, rather, a process of ever-changing patterns of working hypotheses.

Against the scientific optimism which must assume that the question of the existence of God is irrelevant to the (admittedly limited) possibilities of human knowledge stands the modern religious insight that no process of doubting and no working hypotheses will ever yield satisfactory answers to the riddle of the nature of the universe and the more disturbing riddle of man himself. But this insight only reveals once more the thirst for knowledge and the same fundamental loss of faith in the truth-revealing capacity of appearance, be it in the form of divine or natural revelation, that lies at the basis of the modern world. The religious character of modern doubt is still clearly present in the Cartesian suspicion that an evil spirit, and not divine Providence, sets limits to the human thirst for knowledge, that a higher being may willfully deceive us.[7] This suspicion could only rise out of so passionate a desire for security[8] that men forgot that human freedom of thought and action is possible only under conditions of insecure and limited knowledge, as Kant demonstrated philosophically.

Modern religious belief is distinguished from pure faith because it is the "belief to know" of those who doubt that knowledge is possible at all. It is noteworthy that the great writer who presented to us in so many figures the modern religious tension between belief and doubt could show a figure of true faith only in the character of *The Idiot*. Modern religious man belongs in the same secular world as his atheistic opponent precisely because he is no "idiot" in it. The modern believer who cannot bear the tension between doubt and belief will immediately lose the integrity and the profundity of his belief. The justification of the apparent paradox of calling atheism a religion, in brief, derived from the mental familiarity of the greatest of modern religious thinkers—Pascal, Kierkegaard, Dostoevsky—with atheistic experience.

Our question, however, is not whether in calling Communism a religion we have a right to use the same term for both believers and non-believers, but whether the Communist ideology belongs in the same category and the same tradition of doubt and secularism that gave the identification of atheism as a religion a more than formalistic plausibility. And this is not the case. Atheism is a marginal feature of Communism, and if Communism pretends to know the law of history, it does not ascribe to it "what believers of traditional religions ascribe to God."[9]

Communism, as an ideology, though it denies among many other things the existence of a transcendent God, is not the same as atheism. It never tries to answer religious questions specifically, but makes sure that its ideologically trained adherents will never raise them. Nor do ideologies, which always are concerned with the explanation of the movement of history, give the same kind of explication as theology. Theology treats man as a reasonable being that asks questions and whose reason needs reconciliation even if he is expected to believe in that which is beyond reason. An ideology, and Communism in its politically effective totalitarian form more than any other, treats man as though he were a falling stone, endowed with the gift of consciousness and therefore capable of observing, while he is falling, Newton's laws of gravitation. To call this totalitarian ideology a religion is not only an entirely undeserved compliment; it also makes us overlook that Bolshevism, though it grew out of Western history, no longer belongs in the same tradition of doubt and secularity, and that its doctrine as well as its actions have opened a veritable abyss between the free world and the totalitarian parts of the globe.

Until very recently this whole matter was not much more than a dispute in terminology, and the use of the term "political religion" for avowedly anti-religious political movements not much more than a figure of speech.[10] Certain liberal sympathizers, precisely because they did not understand what was going on in the Russian "great new experiment," were especially fond of the term. Somewhat later it was used by disappointed Communists to whom Stalin's deification of Lenin's corpse or the rigidity of Bolshevik theory seemed reminiscent of "medieval scholastic" methods. But recently the term of "political or secular religion" has been adopted by two quite distinct trends of thought and approach. There is first the historical approach for which a secular religion is quite literally a religion growing out of the spiritual secularity of our present world so that Communism is only the most radical version of an "immanentist heresy."[11] And there is second the approach of the social sciences which treat ideology and religion as one and the same thing because they believe that Communism (or nationalism or imperialism, etc.) fulfills for its adherents the same "function" that our religious denominations fulfill in a free society.

II

The great advantage of the historical approach is its recognition that totalitarian domination is not merely a deplorable accident in Western history and that its ideologies must be discussed in terms of self-understanding and self-criticism. Its specific shortcomings lie in a double misunderstanding of the nature of secularism and the secular world.

Secularism, to begin with, has a political as well as a spiritual meaning and the two are not necessarily the same. Politically, secularism means no more than that religious creeds and institutions have no publicly binding authority and that, conversely, political life has no religious sanction.[12] This brings up the grave question of the source of authority of our traditional "values," of our laws and customs and standards for judgment, which for so many centuries had been sanctified by religion. But the long alliance between religion and authority does not necessarily prove that the concept of authority is itself of a religious nature. On the contrary, I think it much more likely that authority, insofar as it is based on tradition, is of Roman political origin and was monopolized by the Church only when it became the political as well as spiritual heir of the Roman Empire. No doubt one of the chief characteristics of our present crisis is the breakdown of all authority and the broken thread of our tradition, but from this it does not follow that the crisis is primarily religious or has a religious origin. It does not even necessarily imply a crisis of traditional faith, though it has endangered the authority of the churches insofar as they are, among other things, public institutions.

The second misunderstanding is, I think, more obvious and more relevant. The concept of freedom (and this is primarily a struggle between the *free* world and Totalitarianism) is certainly not of religious origin. To justify an interpretation of the struggle for freedom as basically religious it would not be enough to demonstrate that freedom is compatible with our present "religious system," but that a system based on freedom is religious. And this will indeed be difficult, Luther's "freedom of Christian man" notwithstanding. The freedom which Christianity brought into the world was a freedom *from* politics, a freedom to be and remain outside the realm of secular society altogether, something unheard of in the ancient world. A Christian slave, insofar as he was a Christian, remained a free human being if only he kept himself free from secular involvements. (This is also the reason why the Christian churches could remain so indifferent to the question of slavery while clinging fast to the doctrine of the equality of all men before God.) Therefore neither Christian equality nor Christian freedom could ever have led by themselves to the concept of "government of the people, by the people, for the people" or to any other modern definition of political freedom. The only interest Christianity has in secular government is to protect its own freedom, to see to it that the powers-that-be permit, among other freedoms, freedom from politics. The free world, however, means by freedom not "Render unto Caesar what is Caesar's and unto God what is God's," but the right of all to handle those affairs that once were Caesar's. The very fact that we, as far as our public life is concerned, care more about freedom than about anything else proves that we do not live publicly in a religious world.[13]

The fact that Communist regimes liquidate religious institutions and persecute religious convictions together with a great many other social and spiritual bodies with the most divergent attitudes towards religion is only the other side of the same matter. In a country where even the chess clubs had one day to be liquidated and resurrected in bolshevized fashion, because "to play chess for chess's sake" constituted a challenge to the official ideology, the persecution of religion cannot very well be ascribed to specifically religious motives. The evidence we have about persecutions in totalitarian countries does not bear out the frequently heard assertion that religion more than any other free spiritual activity is felt to be the primary challenge to the ruling ideology. A Trotskyite in the thirties or a Titoist in the late forties was certainly in greater danger of life and limb in Soviet-dominated territory than a priest or a minister. If religious people are on the whole persecuted more frequently than non-believers, it is simply because they are harder to "convince."

Communism, in fact, carefully avoids being mistaken for a religion. When the Catholic Church recently decided to excommunicate Communists, because of the obvious incompatibility of Communism with Christian doctrine, no corresponding move occurred from the side of the Communists. To be sure, from the point of view of a Christian this is a religious fight, just as for a philosopher it is a fight for philosophy. For Communism, however, it is nothing of the sort. It is the fight against a world in which all these things, free religion, free philosophy, free art, etc., are possible at all.

III

The approach of the social sciences, the identification of ideology and religion as *functionally* equivalent, has achieved much greater prominence in the present discussion. It is based on the fundamental assumption of the social sciences that they do not have to concern themselves with the *substance* of a historical and political phenomenon, such as religion, or ideology, or freedom, or totalitarianism, but only with the *function* it plays in society. Social scientists are not bothered by the fact that both sides in the struggle, the free world as well as the totalitarian rulers, have refused to call their struggle religious and believe they can find out "objectively," that is without paying attention to what either side has to say, whether or not Communism is a new religion or whether the free world is defending its religious system. In any previous period this refusal to take either side at its own word, as though it were a matter of course that what the sources themselves say can only prove misleading, would have seemed, to say the least, quite unscientific.

The father of the social science methods is Marx. He was the first to look systematically—and not only with the natural awareness that speech can conceal truth as well as reveal it—at history as it reveals itself in the utterances of great statesmen, or the intellectual and spiritual manifestations of a period. He refused to take any of them at face value, denouncing them as "ideological" façades behind which the true historical forces conceal themselves. Later he called it the "ideological superstructure," but he started by deciding not to take seriously "what people say," but only "the real active human being" whose thoughts are "the ideological reflexes and echoes of his life process."[14] He, therefore, of all materialists was the first to interpret religion as something more than simple superstition or the spiritualization of tangible human experiences, but as a social phenomenon in which man "is dominated by the product of his own head as he is dominated in capitalistic production by the product of his own hand."[15] Religion to him had become one of many possible ideologies.

To be sure, present-day social sciences have outgrown Marxism; they no longer share the Marxian prejudice in favor of his own "ideology." In fact, since Karl Mannheim's *Ideologie und Utopie*, they have got used to talking back and telling the Marxists that Marxism, too, is an ideology. By the same token, however, they have lost even that degree of awareness for differences of substance which for Marx and Engels was still a matter of course. Engels could still protest against those who in his time called atheism a religion by saying that this makes about as much sense as calling chemistry an alchemy without the philosopher's stone.[16] It is only in our time that one can afford to call Communism a religion without ever reflecting on its historical background and without ever asking what a religion actually is, and if it is anything at all when it is a religion without God.

Moreover, while the non-Marxist heirs of Marxism have grown wise to the ideological character of Marxism and thus, in a way, have become cleverer than Marx himself, they have forgotten the philosophical basis of Marx's own writings which continues to remain their own because their methods spring from it and make sense only in its framework.

Marx's unwillingness to take seriously "what each period says about itself and imagines it is" derived from his conviction that political action was primarily violence and that violence was the midwife of history.[17] This conviction was not due to the gratuitous ferocity of a revolutionary temperament, but has its place in Marx's philosophy of history, which holds that history, which has been enacted by men in the mode of false consciousness, i.e., in the mode of ideologies, can be *made* by men in full consciousness of what they are doing. It is precisely this humanist side of Marx's teachings which led him to his insistence on the violent character of political action: he saw the making of history in terms of fabrication; historical man was to him primarily *Homo faber*. The fabrication of all man-made things necessarily implies some violence done to the matter which becomes the basic material of the fabricated thing. Nobody can make a table without killing a tree.

Marx, like all serious philosophers since the French Revolution, was confronted with the double riddle that human action, in distinction from fabrication and production, hardly ever achieves precisely what it intends because it acts in a framework of "many wills operating in different directions,"[18] *and* the fact that the sum of recorded actions which we call history nevertheless seems to make sense. But he refused to accept the solution of his immediate predecessors who, in the "ruse of nature" (Kant) or the "cunning of reason" (Hegel), had introduced a *deus ex machina* into human affairs. Instead, he proposed to explain the riddle by interpreting the whole realm of inexplicable meaning as a "super-structure" of the more elementary productive activity, in which man *is* master of his products and knows what he is doing. The hitherto inexplicable in history was now seen as the reflection of a meaning which was as securely a human product as the technical development of the world. The whole problem of humanizing political-historical affairs was consequently how to become master of our actions as we are master of our productive capacity, or, in other words, how to "make" history as we make all other things. Once this is achieved through the victory of the proletariat we shall no longer need the ideologies—that is the justification of our violence, because this violent element will be in our hands: violence, thus controlled, will be no more dangerous than the killing of a tree for the fabrication of a table. But until that time all political actions, legal precepts, and spiritual thoughts conceal the ulterior motives of a society which only pretends to act politically but in fact "makes history," albeit in an unconscious, i.e., inhuman, way.

Marx's theory of the ideological superstructure, based on the distinction "between what somebody pretends to be and what he really is," and the concomitant disregard for the truth-revealing quality of speech is entirely based on this identification of political action with violence. For violence is indeed the only kind of human action which is mute by definition; it is neither mediated nor operated through words. In all other kinds of action, political or not, we act in speech and our speech is action. In ordinary political life this close relationship between words and acts is broken only in the violence of war; then, but only then, nothing depends any longer on words and everything on the mute ferocity of arms. War propaganda therefore usually has an unpleasant ring of insincerity: here words become "mere talk," they have no acting capacity any longer, everybody knows that action has left the realm of speech. This "mere talk," which is nothing but justification or pretext for violence, has always been open to mistrust as merely "ideological." Here the search for ulterior motives is entirely justified, as historians since Thucydides have well known. In a religious war, for instance, religion has always been in grave danger of becoming an "ideology" in Marx's sense, that is, a mere pretext and justification for violence. The same, to a degree, is true for all war causes.

But only on the assumptions that all history is essentially the conflict between classes and can be resolved only by violence and that political action is inherently "violent" and conceals its true nature hypocritically, as it were, except during wars and revolutions do we have the right to disregard self-interpretation as irrelevant. This seems to me the basis for ignoring what the free world and Communism are saying about themselves.

IV

If we look at the same problem from a purely scientific viewpoint, it seems obvious that one reason for the formalization of social science categories is the scientifically comprehensible desire to find general rules which can subsume occurrences of all times and types. If we are to trust Engels's interpretation of Marx, Marx was also the father of the social sciences in this purely scientific sense. He was the first to compare natural science with the humanities and to conceive simultaneously with Comte of a "science of society" as an all-encompassing discipline, "the sum total of the so-called historical and philosophical sciences,"[19] which would share and live up to the same scientific standards as natural science. "We live not only in nature but also in human society"[20] and society therefore should be open to the same methods and rules of investigation as nature. An insistence on the complementary character of nature and society henceforth formed the basis of the formal and unhistorical categories which began to dominate the historical and social sciences.

Such categories include not only Marx's "class struggle," conceived as the law of historical development just as Darwin's law of the survival of the fittest was the law of natural development,[21] but more recently Toynbee's "challenge and response" or Max Weber's "ideal types," as they are used today, not by Max Weber himself. It looks as though "political or secular religions" is the latest addition, inasmuch as this terminology, though originally designed to interpret totalitarian movements, has already universalized itself and is now used to cover a wide range of occurrences, disparate in time as well as in nature.[22]

Social science owes its origin to the ambition to found a "positive science of history" which could match the positive science of nature.[23] Because of this derivative origin, it is only natural that the "positive science of history" should always have remained one step behind natural science which was its great model. Thus, natural scientists know today what social scientists have not yet discovered, that almost every hypothesis with which they approach nature will somehow work out and yield positive results; so great seems the pliability of observed occurrences that they will always give man the expected answer. It is as though the moment man puts a question to nature everything hurries to rearrange itself in accordance with his question. The day will come when social scientists to their dismay will discover that this is even truer in their own field; there is nothing that cannot be proved and very little that can be disproved; history arranges itself as conveniently and consistently under the category of "challenge-and-response" or in accordance with "ideal types" as it arranged itself under the category of class struggles. There is no reason why it should not show the same obedience when approached with the terminology of secular religions.

To take a convenient example, Max Weber coined his ideal type of the "charismatic leader" after the model of Jesus of Nazareth; pupils of Karl Mannheim found no difficulty in applying the same category to Hitler.[24] From the viewpoint of the social scientist, Hitler and Jesus were identical because they fulfilled the same social function. It is obvious that such a conclusion is possible only for people who refuse to listen to what either Jesus or Hitler said. Something very similar seems now to happen to the term "religion." It is no accident, but the very essence of the trend which sees religions everywhere, that one of its prominent adherents quotes in a footnote, with approval, the astonishing discovery of one of his colleagues "that God is not only a late arrival in religion; it is not indispensable that he should come."[25] Here the danger of blasphemy, always inherent in the term "secular religion," shows itself freely. If secular religions are possible in the sense that Communism is a "religion without God," then we no longer live merely in a secular world which has banished religion from its public affairs, but in a world which has even eliminated God from religion—something which Marx and Engels still believed to be impossible.[26]

It is undeniable that this desubstantializing functionalization of our categories is no isolated phenomenon occurring in some ivory tower of scholarly thought. It is closely connected with the growing functionalization of our society, or, rather, with the fact that modern man has increasingly become a mere function of society. The totalitarian world and its ideologies do not reflect the radical aspect of secularism or atheism; they do reflect the radical aspect of the functionalization of men. Their methods of domination rest on the assumption that men can be completely conditioned because they are only functions of some higher historical or natural forces. The danger is that we may *all* be well on our way to becoming members of what Marx still enthusiastically called a *gesellschaftliche Menschheit* (a socialized humanity). It is curious to see how often the very people who are passionately opposed to all "socialization of the means of production" unwittingly help and support the far more dangerous socialization of man.

V

In this atmosphere of terminological quarrels and mutual misunderstandings the fundamental question concerning the relationship between religion and politics looms large and indistinct. To approach it, it may be well to consider secularism in its political, non-spiritual aspect only and ask, Which was the religious element in the past so politically relevant that its loss had an immediate impact on our political life? Or, to put the same question in another way, Which was the specifically political element in traditional religion? The justification of this question lies in the fact that the separation of the public and religious spheres of life which we call secularism did not simply sever politics from religion in general but very specifically from the Christian creed. And if one of the chief causes of the perplexities of our present public life is its very secularity, then the Christian religion must have contained a powerful political element whose loss has changed the very character of our public existence.

A preliminary indication is perhaps given in the unusually brutal and vulgar dictum of a badly frightened king, who in his panic at the revolutionary disturbances of 1848 exclaimed, "The people must not be permitted to lose its religion." This king showed a confidence in the secular power of the Christian creed, quite surprising if we remember that during the first centuries of its existence the Christian creed had been considered by Christians and non-Christians alike as at best irrelevant to, if not dangerous and destructive of, the public sphere of life. The phrase of Tertullian: "Nothing is more alien to us [Christians] than public affairs" only sums up the early Christian attitude to secular, political life.[27] What had happened in the meantime that now, in a time which was almost as secular, it could be called upon for the very preservation of political life?[28]

Marx's answer, as brutal as the king's statement, is well known: "Religion is the opiate of the people."[29] It is a very unsatisfactory answer, not because it is vulgar but because it is so unlikely that Christian teachings in particular, with their unrelenting stress on the individual and his own role in the salvation of his soul, and their insistence on the sinfulness of man and the concomitant elaboration of a catalogue of sins greater than in any other religion, could ever be used for anything so calming as an opiate. Surely the new political ideologies in terror-ruled totalitarian countries, explaining everything and preparing for anything in an atmosphere of unbearable insecurity, are far better fitted to immunize man's soul against the shocking impact of reality than any traditional religion we know. Compared with them, the pious resignation to God's will seems like a child's pocket-knife compared to atomic weapons.

But there is one powerful element in traditional religion whose usefulness for the support of authority is self-evident, and whose origin is probably not of a religious nature, at least not primarily—the medieval doctrine of Hell. Neither the doctrine nor its elaborate description of the place of punishment after death owes very much to the preaching of Jesus[30] or to the Jewish heritage. Indeed, it required several centuries after Jesus' death to assert itself at all. It is interesting that this assertion coincided with the downfall of Rome, i.e., the disappearance of an assured secular order whose authority and responsibility only now became a charge of the Church.[31]

In striking contrast to the scarcity of references in Hebrew and early Christian writings stands the overpowering influence on political thought of antiquity and of later Christian teaching of Plato's myth of a Hereafter, with which he concludes so many of his political dialogues. Between Plato and the secular victory of Christianity which brought with it the religious sanction of the doctrine of Hell (so that from then on this became so general a feature of the Christian world that political treatises did not need to mention it specifically), there is hardly an important discussion of political problems—except in Aristotle—which did not conclude with an imitation of the Platonic myth.[32] For it is Plato, and not the strictly Jewish-Christian religious sources, who is the most important forerunner of Dante's elaborate descriptions; in him we find already the geographical separation of Hell, Purgatory, and Paradise, and not merely the concept of final judgment about eternal life or eternal death and the hint at possible punishment after death.[33]

The purely political implications of Plato's myth in the last book of the *Republic*, as well as the concluding parts of *Phaedo* and *Gorgias*, are indisputable. In the *Republic* this myth corresponds to the story of the cave, which is the center of the whole work. An allegory, the cave story is intended for the few who are able to perform without fear or hope of a Hereafter the Platonic *periagogē*, the turning around from the shadowy life of seeming reality to confront the clear sky of "ideas." Only those few will understand the true standards of all life, including political affairs, in which last, however, they will no longer be interested per se.[34] To be sure, those who could understand the story of the cave were not supposed to believe the concluding myth about final reward and punishment, because whoever grasped the truth of the ideas as *transcendent* standards[35] no longer required any *tangible* standards such as life after death. The concept of life after death does not make much sense in their case since the story of the cave already describes life on earth as a kind of underworld. In fact, Plato's use of the words *eidōlon* and *skia* which were the key words of Homer's description of Hades in the *Odyssey* makes the whole story read like a reversal of, and a reply to, Homer; it is not the soul which is the shadow, nor is it its life after death in substantial motion, but the bodily life of ordinary mortals who do not succeed in turning away from the cave of earthly life; our life on earth is life in an underworld, our body is the shadow and our only reality is the soul. Since the truth of the ideas is self-evident, the true standards for earthly life can never be satisfactorily argued out and demonstrated.[36]

Belief therefore is necessary for the multitude which lacks the eyes for the invisible measurements of all visible things. Whatever the nature of Plato's own belief in the immortality of the soul, the myth of graduated bodily punishment after death is clearly the invention of a philosophy which deemed public affairs secondary and therefore subject to the rule of a truth which is accessible only to a few.[37] Indeed only the fear of being ruled by the majority could induce the few to fulfill their political duties.[38] The few cannot persuade the multitude of truth because the truth cannot become the object of persuasion and persuasion is the only way to deal with the multitude. But while the multitude cannot be instructed in the doctrine of truth, it can be persuaded to believe an opinion *as though this opinion were the truth*. The appropriate opinion which carries the truth of the few to the multitude is the belief in Hell; persuading the citizens of its existence will make them behave as though they knew the truth.

In other words, the doctrine of Hell in Plato is clearly a political instrument invented for political purposes.[39] Speculations about life after death and descriptions of the Hereafter are no doubt as old as the conscious life of man on earth. Still, it may be that in Plato we find for "the first time in the history of literature that any such legend (sc., of punishment and reward among the dead) has been definitely enlisted in the service of righteousness,"[40] i.e., in the service of public, political life. This seems confirmed by the fact that the Platonic myth was so eagerly used by purely secular writers in antiquity, who indicated as clearly as Plato that they did not seriously believe in it, while on the other hand the Christian creed shows no such doctrine of Hell as long as Christianity remained without secular interests and responsibilities.[41]

Whatever other historical influences may have been at work to elaborate the doctrine of Hell, it continued during antiquity to be used for political purposes. Christianity adopted it officially only *after* its purely religious development had ceased. When in the early Middle Ages the Christian Church became increasingly aware of, and willing to take over, political responsibilities, the Christian creed found itself confronted with a perplexity similar to Plato's political philosophy. Both tried to enforce absolute standards on a realm whose very essence seems to be relativity, and this under the eternal human condition that the worst that man can do to man is to kill him, that is to bring about what one day is bound to happen to him anyhow. The "improvement" on this condition proposed in the doctrine of Hell is precisely that punishment can mean more than eternal death, namely, eternal suffering in which the soul yearns for death.[42]

The outstanding political characteristic of our modern secular world seems to be that more and more people are losing the belief in reward and punishment after death, while the functioning of individual consciences or the multitude's capacity to perceive invisible truth has remained politically as unreliable as ever. In totalitarian states we see the almost deliberate attempt to build, in concentration camps and torture cellars, a kind of earthly hell whose chief difference from medieval hell-images lies in technical improvements and bureaucratic administration, but also in its lack of eternity. Moreover, Hitler-Germany demonstrated that an ideology which almost consciously reversed the command "Thou Shalt Not Kill" need meet no overwhelming resistance from a conscience trained in the Western tradition. On the contrary, Nazi ideology often was able to reverse the functioning of this conscience, as though it were nothing but a mechanism to indicate whether or not one is in conforming agreement with society and its beliefs.

The political consequence of the secularization of the modern age, in other words, seems to lie in the elimination from public life, along with religion, of the only *political* element in traditional religion, the fear of Hell. This loss is politically, though certainly not spiritually, the most significant distinction between our present period and the centuries before. Certainly, from a viewpoint of mere usefulness, nothing could compete better with the inner coercion of totalitarian ideologies in power over man's soul than fear of Hell. Yet, no matter how religious our world may turn again, or how much authentic faith still exists in it, or how deeply our moral values may be rooted in our religious systems, the fear of Hell is no longer among the motives which would prevent or stimulate the actions of the majority. This seems inevitable if secularity of the world involves separation of the religious and political realms of life; under these circumstances religion was bound to lose its primarily political element, just as public life was bound to lose the religious sanction of a transcendent authority. This separation is a fact and, moreover, has its singular advantages for religious as well as irreligious people. Modern history has shown time and again that alliances between "throne and altar" can only discredit both. But while in the past the danger chiefly consisted of using religion as a mere pretext, thus investing political action as well as religious belief with the suspicion of hypocrisy, the danger today is infinitely greater. Confronted with a full-fledged ideology, our greatest danger is to counter it with an ideology of our own. If we try to inspire public-political life once more with "religious passion" or to use religion as a means of political distinctions, the result may very well be the transformation and perversion of religion into an ideology and the corruption of our fight against totalitarianism by a fanaticism which is utterly alien to the very essence of freedom.

[Arendt's reply to Jules Monnerot's criticism:]

Crucial in M. Monnerot's argument is that he overlooks the difference between Marx's statement that religions are ideologies and his own theory that ideologies are religions. To Marx, religion, among many other matters, lay in the realm of ideological superstructures, not all things in this realm were the same; a religious ideology was not the same as a nonreligious one. The distinction in content between religion and nonreligion was preserved. M. Monnerot and the other defenders of "secular religions" say that no matter what the content of an ideology, all ideologies are religions. In this theory, but not in the doctrine of Marx, religion and ideology have become identical.

The reason given for this identification is that ideologies play the same role as religions. With the same justice, one could identify ideology with science, which M. Monnerot almost does when he states that the communist ideology "usurps the prestige which science has in the eyes of the masses." It would, of course, be an error to identify science with the communist ideology for this reason, but this error, in fact, would contain more truth than the logically similar identification with religion insofar as communism pretends to be "scientific," but not to be "religious," and argues in scientific style; in other words, it answers scientific rather than religious questions. As far as M. Monnerot's argument is concerned, only the respect he has for science (as distinguished from religion) could prevent his seeing that according to his argument there is no reason why he should not identify the communist ideology with science rather than with religion.

The underlying confusion is simple and appears very neatly in M. Monnerot's statement that "the communists have an answer to everything. This is characteristic of all orthodoxies," implying that therefore communism is orthodoxy. The fallacy in this reasoning has been familiar ever since the Greeks amused themselves with paralogisms and following a similar logical process arrived to their delight at the definition of man as a plucked chicken. At present, unfortunately, this kind of thing is not just funny.

M. Monnerot complains that I do not follow the current equation methods and do not "define" religion and ideology. (The question of what an ideology is can only be answered historically, since ideologies appeared for the first time in the beginning of the nineteenth century. I tried to give such an answer, though not a definition, in an article, "Ideology and Terror: A Novel Form of Government" in *The Review of Politics*, July 1953.)[43] I cannot go into the question here of what a definition is and to what an extent we may, by inquiring into the nature of things, arrive at definitions. One thing is obvious: I can define only what is distinct and arrive at definitions, if at all, only through making distinctions. To say ideologies are religions does not define either of them, but, on the contrary, destroys even that amount of vaguely felt distinctness which is inherent in our everyday language and which scientific inquiries are supposed to sharpen and enlighten.

Yet, while it may be possible to define such a relatively recent phenomenon as an ideology, how arrogant would I have been if I had dared to define religion! Not because so many scholars have tried and failed before me but because the wealth and treasure of historical material must properly overawe everybody who still has any respect for sources, history, and the thought of the past. Suppose I defined religion and some great religious thinker—not of course the worshiper of the kangaroo, whom I could easily take into account—had escaped my notice! In historical inquiries, it is not important to arrive at ready-made definitions, but constantly to make distinctions, and these distinctions must follow the language we speak and the subject matter we deal with. Otherwise, we shall soon land in a state of affairs where everybody speaks his own language and proudly announces before he starts: *I* mean by . . . whatever helps me and strikes my fancy at the moment.

The confusion arises partly from the particular viewpoint of sociologists who—methodically ignoring chronological order, location of facts, impact and uniqueness of events, substantial content of sources, and historical reality in general—concentrate on "functional roles" in and by themselves, thereby making society the Absolute to which everything is related. Their underlying assumption can be summed up in one sentence: Every matter has a function and its essence is the same as the functional role it happens to play.

Today in some circles this assumption has achieved the doubtful dignity of a commonplace and some sociologists, like M. Monnerot, simply cannot trust their eyes or ears if they meet someone who does not share it. I, of course, do not think that every matter has a function, nor that function and essence are the same, nor that two altogether different things—as for instance the belief in a Law of History and the belief in God—fulfill the same function. And even if under certain queer circumstances, it should occur that two different things play the same "functional role," I would no more think them identical than I would think the heel of my shoe is a hammer when I use it to drive a nail into the wall.

NOTES

1. Engels reports that in Paris in the forties one used to say, *"Donc, l'athéisme c'est votre religion,"* he thinks because one "could conceive of a man without religion only as a monster." See "Feuerbach and the End of Classical German Philosophy" in *Karl Marx and Frederick Engels, Selected Works*, London, 1950, II, 343.

2. *Thus Spoke Zarathustra*, II, "Upon the Blessed Isles." —Ed.

3. Pascal's negative dependence upon Descartes is too well known to need further documentation. *Johannes Climacus or De omnibus dubitandum est* belongs to the earliest philosophical manuscripts of Kierkegaard (winter 1842/3); writing in the form of a spiritual autobiography, Kierkegaard tells us how this one sentence played a decisive role in his entire life, and that he was sorry, after learning from Hegel about Descartes, not to have started his philosophical studies with Descartes (p. 75). Following Hegel's interpretation of Descartes, he saw in it the quintessence of modern philosophy, its principle and beginning. The little treatise is contained in the Danish edition of Kierkegaard's *Collected Works*, 1909, vol. IV. I used the German translation by Wolfgang Struve, Darmstadt, 1948.

4. *Ibid.*, p. 76.

5. *Pensées*, ed. Jacques Chevalier, La Pléiade, Paris, 1950, No. 92, p. 370. The whole paragraph shows even more clearly how deeply Pascal's belief was rooted in his despair about the possibilities of secure knowledge: *"L'homme n'est qu'un sujet plein d'erreur, naturelle et ineffaçable sans la grâce. Rien ne lui montre la vérité. Tout l'abuse. Ces deux principes de vérité, la raison et les sens, outre qu'ils manquent chacun de sincérité, s'abusent réciproquement l'un l'autre. Les sens abusent la raison par de fausses apparences; et cette même piperie qu'ils apportent à la raison, ils la reçoivent d'elle à leur tour: elle s'en revanche. Les passions de l'âme troublent les sens, et leur font des impressions fausses. Ils mentent et se trompent à l'envie."* Although Pascal tells us here, as elsewhere, that reason, too, is only a source of error, it is obvious that the chief source of error is the senses (reason only "takes its revenge") in the double sense of sense-perception and sensual passion.

6. *Ibid.*, No. 75, p. 416.

7. Descartes, *Principes*, No. 5: We must doubt everything *"principalement parce que nous avons ouï dire que Dieu, qui nous a crée, peut faire tout ce qui lui plaît, et que nous ne savons pas encore si peut-être il n'a point voulu nous faire tels que nous soyons toujours trompés . . . car, puisqu'il a bien permis que nous nous soyons trompés quelquefois . . . pourquoi ne pourrait-il pas permettre que nous nous trompions toujours?"*

8. Descartes, *Discours de la Méthode*, Première Partie: *"Et j'avais toujours un extrême désir d'apprendre à distinguer le vrai d'avec le faux, pour voir clair en mes actions et marcher avec assurance en cette vie"* (my emphasis).

9. Waldemar Gurian, in his excellent brief history of *Bolshevism*, Notre Dame, 1952, gives for his understanding of the Bolshevik-Communist movement "as a social and political secular religion" chiefly the following reason: What believers of traditional religions ascribe to God and what Christians ascribe to Jesus Christ and the Church, the Bolsheviks ascribe to the allegedly scientific laws of social, political and historical development, which . . . they have formulated in the doctrine established by Marx and Engels, Lenin and Stalin. Therefore, their acceptance of these doctrinal laws . . . can be characterized as a secular religion," p. 5.

Only deists, who use God as an "idea" with which to explain the course of the world, or atheists, who believe that the riddles of the world are solved by assuming that God does not exist, are guilty of this kind of secularization of traditional concepts.

10. As far as I can see, the term occurred first in a definite terminological meaning and with respect to modern totalitarian movements in a small book by Eric Vögelin, *Die Politischen Religionem*, in 1938, in which he himself quotes as his only predecessor Alexander Ular, *Die Politik* (in the series *Die Gesellschaft*, ed. M. Buber, 1906, vol. III). The latter maintains that all political authority has a religious origin and a religious nature, and that politics itself is necessarily religious. His demonstrations he derives primarily from primitive tribal religions; his whole argument can be summed up in the following sentence: "The medieval god of the Christians is in fact nothing but a totem of monstrous dimensions. . . . The Christian is his child as the Australian native is the child of the kangaroo." In his early book, Vögelin himself still uses primarily examples from Tibetan religions as justification for his argument. Although he later abandoned this line of reasoning entirely, it is noteworthy that the term originally derived from anthropological studies and not from an interpretation of Western tradition *per se*. Anthropological and tribal psychological implications of the term are still quite manifest in its use by the social sciences.

11. By far the most brilliant and most thoughtful exposition is to be found in Eric Vögelin, *The New Science of Politics*, Chicago, 1952.

12. I quite agree with Romano Guardini's recent statement that secularity of the world, the fact that our daily public existence is "without consciousness of a divine Power," does not "imply that individuals are becoming increasingly irreligious; but public consciousness is moving increasingly away from religious categories," although I do not follow him to his conclusion that religion where it exists "is retiring to the

'inner world.' " I quote from *Commonweal*, vol. LVIII, no. 13, July 3, 1953, which prints extensive excerpts from an article in the current *Dublin Review*, London.

13. To say that this struggle is basically religious may very well mean that we want to assert *more than* freedom. This, however, would be very dangerous, no matter how tolerant the definition of the more-than-freedom would turn out to be; it could very well involve us in a kind of spiritual civil war in which we would exclude from our common fight everything that is contrary to "religion." And since in this, as in all other fields, no binding authority exists to define once and for all what is compatible and what is not, we would be at the mercy of ever-changing interpretations.

14. *Die deutsche Ideologie*, MEGA, Feuerbach, I, v, 15.

15. *Das Kapital*, I, chap. xxiii, 1.

16. Engels, *op. cit.*, "If religion can exist without its god, alchemy can exist without its philosopher's stone."

17. In Marx's own words: "Die Gewalt ist der Geburtshelfer jeder alten Gesellschaft, die mit einer neuen schwanger geht. Sie selbst ist eine ökonomische Potenz." *Das Kapital*, chap. xxiv, §6. Also: "In der wirklichen Geschichte spielen bekanntlich Eroberung, Unterjochung, Raubmord, kurz Gewalt die grosse Rolle." *Ibid.*, §1.

18. Engels, *Selected Works*, 354.

19. *Ibid.*, p. 340.

20. *Ibid.*

21. Engels frequently compared Marx to Darwin, most eloquently in his "Speech at the Graveside of Karl Marx": "Just as Darwin discovered the law of development of organic nature, so Marx discovered the law of development of human history," *ibid.*, p. 153.

22. A good example of this thoroughly confusing method is Jules Monnerot, *Sociology and Psychology of Communism*, Boston, 1953.

23. These two positive sciences together were supposed to comprehend not only the knowledge of all data, but also all possible substantial thought: "That which still survives of all earlier philosophy is the science of thought and its laws—formal logic and dialectics. Everything else is subsumed in the positive science of nature and history." Engels, "Socialism: Utopian and Scientific," in *Selected Works*, II, 123. It would be worth while to show to what extent our new disciplines of formal logic and semantics owe their origin to the social sciences.

24. So for instance in Hans Gerth, "The Nazi Party," *American Journal of Sociology*, vol. 45, 1940. By taking this example, I do not mean to imply that Max Weber himself could ever have been guilty of such monstrous identifications.

25. Monnerot, *op. cit.*, p. 124, quoting Van der Leeuw, *Phénoménologie de la religion*, Paris, 1948, and Durkheim, *De la Définition des phénomènes religieux*.

26. Marx and Engels believed that religions are ideologies, they did not think that ideologies could simply become religions. According to Engels, "it never occurred to [the bourgeoisie] to put a new religion [sc., its own new ideology] in place of the

old. Everyone knows how Robespierre failed in his attempt." "Feuerbach and the End of Classical German Philosophy," *Selected Works*, II, 344.

27. Apol. 38: *nobis nulla magis res aliena quam publica.*

28. The possible usefulness of religion for secular authority could be noticed only under conditions of complete secularity of public-political life, i.e., at the beginning of our era and in the modern age. During the Middle Ages the secular life itself had become religious and religion therefore could not become a political instrument.

29. The frequently misquoted phrase does not imply that religion was *invented* as an opiate for the people, but that it was *used* for such purposes.

30. St. Luke, 16, 23–31, is, as far as I know, the most explicit passage.

31. See Marcus Dods, *Forerunners of Dante* (Edinburgh, 1903), and Fredric Huidekoper, *Belief of the First Three Centuries Concerning Christ's Mission to the Underworld*, New York, 1887.

32. Outstanding among these are Scipio's dream which concludes Cicero's *De Re Publica* and the concluding vision in Plutarch's *Delays of Divine Justice*. Compare also the sixth book of the *Aeneid*, which is so different from the eleventh book in the *Odyssey*.

33. This viewpoint is especially stressed in Marcus Dods, *op. cit.*

34. See especially *Republic*, Book 7, 516d.

35. "The idea that there is a supreme art of measurement and that the philosopher's knowledge of values is the ability to measure, runs through all Plato's work right down to the end." Werner Jaeger, *Paideia*, II, 416, note 45.

36. It is characteristic of all of Plato's dialogues on justice that a break occurs somewhere and the strictly argumentative process has to be abandoned. In the *Republic*, Socrates eludes his questioners several times; the baffling question is whether justice is still possible if it is hidden from men and gods. See especially the break at 372a which is taken up again at 427d where he defines wisdom and *euboulia*; he comes back to the main question in 430d and discusses *sōphrosynē*. He then starts again at 433b and comes almost immediately to a discussion of the forms of government, 445d ff., until the seventh book with the cave story puts the whole argument on an entirely different, non-political level. Here it becomes clear why Glaukōn cannot receive a satisfactory answer: justice is an idea and must be perceived; that is the only possible demonstration.

37. The clearest proof for the political character of Plato's myths of a Hereafter is that they, insofar as they imply bodily punishment, are in flagrant contradiction to his theory of the mortality of the body and the immortality of the soul. Plato, moreover, was quite aware of this inconsistency. See *Gorgias*, 524.

38. *Republic*, 374c.

39. This is also obvious from the concluding myths in *Phaedo* and *Gorgias*, which do not contain allegories, like the cave story, in which the philosopher tells the truth. *Phaedo* deals primarily not with the soul's immortality, but is a "revised Apology 'more persuasive than the speech (Socrates) made in (his) defense before the

judges.' " (F. M. Cornford, *Principium Sapientiae: The Origins of Greek Philosophical Thought*, Cambridge, 1952, 69). *Gorgias*, which shows the impossibility to "prove" that it is better to suffer wrong than to do wrong, tells the myth at the end as a kind of *ultima ratio*, with great diffidence and clearly indicating that Socrates himself does not take it too seriously.

40. Marcus Dods, *op. cit.*, p. 41.

41. Christian writers during the first centuries unanimously believed in a mission of Christ to the Underworld whose main purpose had been to liquidate Hell, defeat Satan, and liberate the souls of dead sinners as he had liberated the souls of Christians, from death as well as punishment. The only exception was Tertullian. See Huidekoper, *op. cit.*

42. The longing for death was a frequent motive in Hebrew visions of Hell. See Dods, *op. cit.*, p. 107ff.

43. This essay is included in the 1958 and all subsequent editions of *The Origins of Totalitarianism*. —Ed.

The Ex-Communists

T HIS IS ABOUT the role of ex-Communists, not former Communists. The line between them can theoretically be easily drawn and grasped. There are not only in the United States but everywhere in the world many people who at one time or another, and for the most varied reasons, belonged to a totalitarian movement, as party members, as fellow-travelers, as sympathizers. Among them are people whose prominence in these parties was never due to their political importance, but who, because they had achieved prominence in some other field, lent prestige to the parties to which they belonged.

Picasso is not a prominent Communist; he is a great painter who happens to have fallen for Communism. His responsibility is in art; he loses his artistic integrity if he starts painting bad pictures for the sake of Communism, not if he begins to utter political opinions. If Picasso were to leave the Party tomorrow, he would become a former Communist, not an ex-Communist.

To this same category of former Communists belongs an altogether different group of people, whose chief interest always was political. Communism played a decisive role in their lives. Their chief responsi-

The Commonweal, March 20, 1953.

bility was engaged there and their prominence, as long as it lasted, was the result of political activities. Among their common characteristics is that they left the Party early; they were sufficiently informed to sense, if not to know articulately, the stages by which a revolutionary party developed into a full-fledged totalitarian movement, and they had their own criteria to judge this. These criteria may not appear sufficient in the light of what we know today; they were enough then. Important among them were the abolition of inner-party democracy, the liquidation of independence for the various national Communist parties and their total submission under the orders of Moscow. The Moscow Trials, which in many respects are the turning point in this whole history, concluded the process.

We are not interested here in the destinies of these people, and it would be hard, indeed, to find a common denominator for them after they left the Party. They disappeared into public and private life, as writers or journalists, or businessmen, and as members of all existing parties, from the so-called Right to the so-called Left. Many of them lost their interest in politics altogether. Decisive is that their Communist past remained an important biographical fact, but did not become the nucleus of their new opinions, viewpoints, *Weltanschauungen*. They neither looked for a substitute for a lost faith nor concentrated all their efforts and talents on the fight against Communism.

It is easy, perhaps all too easy, to construct a type of ex-Communist. In order to avoid all misunderstandings, I shall choose in my considerations no product of my own imagination, but take as my model Whittaker Chambers, whom society at large, for the good reason of his articulateness and gifts as a writer, has accepted as the spokesman for the ex-Communists, and whom they themselves, it seems, have more or less recognized as their voice.

It is easy to draw a theoretical line between ex-Communists and former Communists. In practice it has become complicated. The ex-Communists, though of course much smaller in number than former Communists, have become prominent on the strength of their past alone. Communism has remained the chief issue in their lives. They feel that their potential strength is much greater than their small number actually indicates because their past, on which they base present careers and ambitions, is shared by a much larger section of society. They work to persuade their former friends to join them: to make a confession, own up to a conversion, and form a solid political group.

This puts former Communists at an obvious disadvantage: it looks as though they are less decent, less honest, less convinced of the dangers of Communism. Moreover, to have been a Communist, even at the age of seventeen, has become a great handicap under present circumstances. The temptation to join the ex-Communists is all the greater as the public humiliation of a spectacular confession is compensated by the advantage of an unbroken public career.

Against the gesture of a conversion stands the fact that one can smoothly develop from a Communist politician into an expert in Communist politics. The admission of a broken personal life is compensated for by unbroken public prominence; the public humiliation spares one the private humiliations implied in having to change one's profession and being demoted from prominence to the average life of an average citizen.

At this moment, the ex-Communists still play their role chiefly as experts, called in by free society to help in the fight against totalitarianism because they are supposed to know best the means of the enemy and therefore are best qualified to design the means with which to counteract the enemy.

In what does this knowledge, in their own opinion, consist? Chambers sums it up in the following sentence: "No one knows so well as the ex-Communists the character of the conflict, and of the enemy, or shares so deeply the same power of faith and willingness to stake his life on his beliefs . . . for that struggle cannot be fought, much less won, or even understood, except in terms of total sacrifice. . . ." Therefore—quoting Silone: "The final conflict will be between the Communists and the ex-Communists" . . . who have understood that "in our time, informing is a duty."

Let me briefly interpret this passage: Like the Communists, the ex-Communists see the whole texture of our time in terms of one great dichotomy ending in a final battle. There is no plurality of forces in the world; there are only two. These two are not the opposition of freedom against tyranny (or however else one may want to formulate it in traditional terms), but of one faith against another. These two faiths, moreover, spring from the same source. The ex-Communists are not former Communists, they are Communists "turned upside down";

without their former Communism, they insist, nobody can understand what they are doing now. What they are doing concerns the central crisis of our time; this is really known only by two groups: the Communists themselves and the ex-Communists. Ultimately, others don't count; we are only bystanders in the great battle of history being fought out by these two protagonists. Surely, they need allies; but as the allies of the Communists are always led, in accordance with Communist theory and practice, by the superior knowledge of the Communist Party, so the ex-Communists offer to lead their anti-Communist allies by means of their superior wisdom. The same contempt which the Communists used to have for their supporters and allies, the ex-Communists announce for theirs.

Just as the Communists respect only their real opponents, so the ex-Communists show respect only for people who either have become ex-Communists or are still Communists. Since they have divided the world into two, they can account for the disturbing variety and plurality of the world we all live in only by either discounting it as irrelevant altogether or by stating that it is due to lack of consistency and character.

American liberalism, to take the outstanding example, has for decades been denounced by Communism as an inconsistent, inconsequential attitude in the service of the bourgeoisie (or capitalism or whatnot) and is now denounced by ex-Communists as the inconsistent, inconsequential ally of Communism. Anti-liberalism as attitude and chief idiosyncrasy has remained the same. The liberals were the (unconscious and therefore stupid or cowardly) helpers of capitalism; they now have become those who are too stupid or too cowardly to think their own tenets through and find that the result naturally leads them into Communism.

Informing, which plays such a great role in Chambers's book,* is a duty in a police state where people have been organized and split into two ever-changing categories: those who have the privilege to be the informers and those who are dominated by the fear of being informed upon. It is the old story: one cannot fight a dragon, we are told, without becoming a dragon; we can fight a society of informers only by becoming informers ourselves.

However, up to now this has always been regarded as the danger

---

*Witness, New York, 1952, is Chambers's own account of his life. —Ed.

inherent in political life; we were warned lest we become dragons when we started to fight them; we were not told that we first had to be trained as dragons. The reason why the wisdom of the past never tried to solve one of the basic perplexities of politics in so plausible a manner as our ex-Communists propose is simple: If we became dragons ourselves, it would be of small interest which of the two dragons should eventually survive. The meaning of the fight would be lost.

The advice to use totalitarian means in order to fight totalitarianism is justified by the ex-Communists by pointing to the special historical circumstances. The end, we are told, justifies the means. You cannot make an omelet without breaking eggs. It is the end which commands the means.

Despite its obvious fallacy, the doctrine that the end justifies the means has a dangerous attraction for all of us because it is so deeply embedded in our whole tradition of political thought.

The *summum bonum*, the commonweal, the happiness of the greatest number, etc., have all been thought to be ends to be achieved by the appropriate political means. I personally hold no brief for these various political and theological doctrines; however, in one decisive respect they all differed from the new ideological ends of our new totalitarian politicians: they were not ends which men could immediately achieve and prove to exist in any tangible form.

The *summum bonum* which, according to St. Augustine, was the only good which I was permitted to enjoy for its own sake, while all the other goods I was asked to use only as means to an end, was not of this world; it could organize all other *bona*, put them into a certain hierarchy, become, in other words, the chief criterion, the standard of all actions and judgments; it could not be fabricated because it transcended all fabrication and all actions the way the yardstick "transcends" and, therefore, can measure all other concrete lengths. This is true for all the traditional concepts of the end of politics: the commonweal, the happiness of the greater number, the good life, etc.—none of which are transcendent in the absolute sense of a *summum bonum*. Strictly speaking, they are not *political* ends. The categories of means and end are not applied within the field of human action, but human action itself is seen as a means to an end which transcends it.

The dangers which were always inherent in these theories became real only when the end of political action was conceived as political itself, as in the concept of a classless society or a race society or whatever else the ideal or the cause might be.

If we insist on applying the category of means and end to action and human relationships, we shall see that everything comes to stand on its head. It is perfectly true that the end of making a table justifies the instruments and means, including killing the tree. But it is no less true that between men a good deed done for the sake of a bad cause eventually will make this world of human relationship somewhat better, improve it, while a bad deed for a good cause instantly makes our common world a little worse. If for the bad cause of making Communism more respectable a Communist would behave like a decent human being, the net effect would not be propaganda for Communism but a little decency. The reason why Communists so seldom indulge in good deeds for their bad cause is that they know this; they know that decency spread for a bad cause will ultimately only result in a more decent, and therefore stronger, society.

Plato stated that it is not action (*pragma*) but contemplation (*theoria*) that adheres to truth. The main shortcoming of action, it has been repeated time and again since, lies in the fact that I never quite know what I am doing. Thinking or making things, I know, or am supposed to know, exactly what I am doing. Whatever the result, nobody else can be held responsible for it. This is not true for action. Since I act in a web of relationships which consists of the actions and the desires of others, I never can foretell what ultimately will come out of what I am doing now. This is the reason why we can act politically but cannot "make history." The reason, on the other hand, that Communists and ex-Communists alike are so unsqueamish in their means is that they are quite convinced that they know what they are doing. They think of themselves as being the makers of history.

The confusion of political action with the making of history goes back to Marx. Marx hoped, after Hegel had interpreted the history of mankind, that he would be able to "change the world," that is to *make* mankind's future. Marxism could be developed into a totalitarian ideology because of its perversion, or misunderstanding, of political action as the making of history.

The totalitarian element in Marxism is as little the concept of class or classless society as the concept of race or race society, as such, is what made Nazism totalitarian. In both instances, the decisive element is the belief that history can be made, which teaches certain procedures by which one can bring about its end—and of course never does. The breaking of eggs in action never leads to anything more interesting than the breaking of eggs. The result is identical with the activity itself: it is a breaking, not an omelet.

A friend of mine, with whom I was discussing Chambers's book, observed that it was obvious that this fellow never was interested in politics. And indeed, the book tells us how little Chambers relished the political life of his party, how he looked down on it and escaped from it into the inner apparatus where commands were given and obeyed, where history was made, behind the scenes of official Communist politics. And in this respect, Chambers has not changed.

When, in September 1939, he first went to Washington to warn the government of Soviet espionage, he felt that he had a historic mission, and was acting in a historic moment; it never occurred to him, what to the reader is obvious from his own report, that it was a mere coincidence that his interview took place at this particular moment. The appointment had been made several months earlier. So much does he feel himself to be an actor in the historical drama that he actually persuaded himself that it was the Hitler-Stalin pact which inspired his act. He makes history, he does not simply act politically.

It is against these makers of history that a free society has to defend itself, regardless of the vision they harbor. And this involves more than the natural reaction which we instinctively feel against the arrogance of people who are engaged in so "sublime" a task. The idea that I can do more than act for, and in, the present (i.e., that I can make the future) implies two fundamental errors. It implies that I know the end and therefore can decide freely about the means, and that I know what I am doing in action the way I know what I am doing in making things.

The first is impossible because I am mortal; I never shall know the end of history because I never shall see the end of it. The second is wrong because human action in its ultimate consequences is unpredictable by definition. The great tradition of Western political thought has always known this and interpreted it as a predicament. It is the reason why politics as a human activity was deemed (since Plato and Aristotle) to be inferior in quality to other forms of human activity. Politics was justified by the tradition, not in political terms, but as necessary for some higher form of life: the *bios theōrētikos*, or undisturbed occupation with the salvation of one's soul.

No matter how doubtful these interpretations of the whole political realm of human life may appear to us today, one thing is certain: They preserved, together with a depreciation of political action, the awareness of its basic uncertainties.

It is unfortunate, and perhaps symptomatic of the general situation of our present political thinking, that all proverbs and imagery that are plausible enough to strike home and appeal directly to common sense are on the side of our history-makers, not on the side of free society. Propaganda successes of totalitarian-minded people are largely due to their use of such sayings as "you can't make an omelet without breaking eggs," "who said A must say B," "we must be united like one man against the common danger," etc. Against these stand only a few lonely utterances of great statesmen, out of the depth of their political experience and sometimes expressing its quintessential truth. None of them has as yet achieved the plausibility of the false banalities in which we all were raised and which only now show that they are even more dangerous than they are trite. One of these statements which to me always seemed to express succinctly at least one essential part of all political life and public concern is the statement which Clemenceau uttered during the Dreyfus Affair, when the very existence of the Third Republic was at stake and which was perhaps saved by Clemenceau. He said: *"L'affaire d'un seul est l'affaire de tous"* ("The case of one single man is the concern of all"). What does that mean?

Dreyfus was personally a man who never could have become Clemenceau's friend. He was, for all practical purposes, what might be called a "bad man." I mention this because I recently overheard a remark which is very characteristic of our present confusion. One man said to another: "But what are you complaining about? Up to now, no good man has been slandered or hurt." The point, of course, is not whether this is true or false, but that the law looks on good and bad men with an equal eye and that the reputation of a "bad man" is as important politically as that of any other. The General Staff of the French Army was sure that it could undermine the Republic by picking out a man with whom no one sympathized. And it might have succeeded if Clemenceau had not understood that the law is impartial toward both good and bad, and that the breach of the law (or, for that matter, the risking of civil liberties in order to trap a bad man) is necessarily the beginning of the end of civil liberties for all.

The final conflict will not be between Communists and ex-Communists. That conflict still belongs to the history of the factional strife within the Communist party that preceded its Bolshevization. It either is simply another stage of the disintegration of the so-called Left, or it is an ideological struggle among the makers of history who naturally have different ideas about the end which justifies their means.

As far as free society is concerned, there will be no final conflict with totalitarianism, because neither defeat nor victory will ever be conclusive. Victory by itself solves no problems; it only makes their solution possible. Moreover, totalitarianism has brought with it an entirely new form of government which as a potentiality and an ever-present danger is only too likely to stay with us from now on—just as other forms of government which came about in different historical moments have stayed with mankind regardless of temporary defeats: monarchies and republics, tyrannies, dictatorships and despotisms. It belongs to totalitarian thinking to conceive of a final conflict at all. There is no finality in history—the story told by it is a story with many beginnings but no end.

Meanwhile, the dangers of the ex-Communists' role in social and public life are clear and present. They have told us quite frankly on what their claim to prominence is based, what their aim is, and what methods they want to introduce. Their claim is based on the fact that they once have been Communists and therefore are trained in totalitarian thinking. Their aim is to apply this training to a new cause after the old cause has disappointed them. Their methods have, in some instances, consisted in arrogating to themselves the role of the police and almost always result in sowing mistrust among citizens whose "friendship," *philia*, according to Aristotle, is the surest foundation of political life.

To this, we reply: We know that this century is full of dangers and perplexities; we ourselves do not always, and never fully, know what we are doing. We know that some of the best of us at one time or another have been driven into the totalitarian predicament. Those who have turned their back on it are welcome; everyone is welcome who has not become a murderer or a professional spy in the process. We are anxious to establish friendship wherever we can, and this goes for former Fascists or Nazis as well as it goes for former Communists and Bolshevists. The fact that one was formerly wrong should carry with it no permanent stigma.

But we cannot accept your claim, your aim, and least of all your methods. Your claim that one can fight the dragon only if one has become a dragon contradicts all our experiences and is hostile to our ultimate concern, which is to assert the humanity of man. Your aim, to make of democracy a "cause" in the strict ideological sense, contradicts the rules and laws by which we live and let live.

America, this republic, the democracy in which we live, is a living thing which cannot be contemplated and categorized, like the image of a thing which I can make; it cannot be fabricated. It is not and never will be perfect because the standard of perfection does not apply here. Dissent belongs to this living matter as much as consent does. The limitations of dissent lie in the Constitution and the Bill of Rights and nowhere else. If you try to "make America more American" or a model of democracy according to any preconceived idea, you can only destroy it. Your methods, finally, are the justified methods of the police, and only of the police.

We know that it is dangerous and risky to live in freedom; we therefore are happy to pay taxes and train a special force among our citizens who are qualified to watch and who use their own methods, which, however, we control. No private citizen has any right to arrogate to himself these highly specialized and limited functions.

Much as we desire to establish friendship with you, much as we are in sympathy with your experiences and frequently with your personalities, as long as you insist on your role as ex-Communists, we must warn against you. In this role, you can only strengthen those dangerous elements which are present in all free societies today and which we do not want to crystallize into a totalitarian movement or a totalitarian form of domination, no matter what its cause and ideological content.

A Reply to Eric Voegelin

[This "Reply" is to a review of *The Origins of Totalitarianism* by the
political philosopher Eric Voegelin, who was, like Arendt, a German
émigré. The review, the "Reply," and a "Concluding Remark" by Voegelin were published in the January 1953 issue of *The Review of Politics*.
The principal contention between Voegelin and Arendt centered on the
question of "human nature." Voegelin argued that human nature as
such is unchangeable and that the origins of totalitarianism lie in "the
spiritual disease of agnosticism." In her "Reply," Arendt explains more
fully than elsewhere the method she followed in attempting to deal with
the phenomenon of totalitarianism and its "liquidation" of human
freedom.]

MUCH AS I appreciate the unusual kindness of the editors
of *The Review of Politics* who asked me to answer Professor
Eric Voegelin's criticism of my book, I am not quite sure that
I decided wisely when I accepted their offer. I certainly would not, and
should not, have accepted if his review were of the usual friendly or
unfriendly kind. Such replies, by their very nature, all too easily tempt
the author either to review his own book or to write a review of the review.
In order to avoid such temptations, I have refrained as much as I could,

even on the level of personal conversation, to take issue with any reviewer of my book, no matter how much I agreed or disagreed with him.

Professor Voegelin's criticism, however, is of a kind that can be answered in all propriety. He raises certain very general questions of method, on one side, and of general philosophical implications on the other. Both of course belong together; but while I feel that within the necessary limitations of a historical study and political analysis I made myself sufficiently clear on certain general perplexities which have come to light through the full development of totalitarianism, I also know that I failed to explain the particular method which I came to use, and to account for a rather unusual approach—not to the different historical and political issues where account or justification would only distract—to the whole field of political and historical sciences as such. One of the difficulties of the book is that it does not belong to any school and hardly uses any of the officially recognized or officially controversial instruments.

The problem originally confronting me was simple and baffling at the same time: all historiography is necessarily salvation and frequently justification; it is due to man's fear that he may forget and to his striving for something which is even more than remembrance. These impulses are already implicit in the mere observation of chronological order and they are not likely to be overcome through the interference of value-judgments which usually interrupt the narrative and make the account appear biased and "unscientific." I think the history of anti-Semitism is a good example of this kind of history-writing. The reason why this whole literature is so extraordinarily poor in terms of scholarship is that the historians—if they were not conscious anti-Semites, which of course they never were—had to write the history of a subject which they did not want to conserve; they had to write in a destructive way and to write history for purposes of destruction is somehow a contradiction in terms. The way out has been to hold on, so to speak, to the Jews, to make them the subject of conservation. But this was no solution, for to look at the events only from the side of the victim resulted in apologetics—which of course is no history at all.

Thus my first problem was how to write historically about something—totalitarianism—which I did not want to conserve but, on the contrary, felt engaged to destroy. My way of solving this problem has given rise to the reproach that the book was lacking in unity. What I did—and what I might have done anyway because of my previous training and the way of my thinking—was to discover the chief elements of totalitarianism and to analyze them in historical terms, tracing these elements back in history as far as I deemed proper and necessary. That is, I did not write a history of totalitarianism but an analysis in terms of history; I did not write a history of anti-Semitism or of imperialism, but analyzed the element of Jew-hatred and the element of expansion insofar as these elements were still clearly visible and played a decisive role in the totalitarian phenomenon itself. The book, therefore, does not really deal with the "origins" of totalitarianism—as its title unfortunately claims—but gives a historical account of the elements which crystallized into totalitarianism; this account is followed by an analysis of the elemental structure of totalitarian movements and domination itself. The elementary structure of totalitarianism is the hidden structure of the book, while its more apparent unity is provided by certain fundamental concepts which run like red threads through the whole.

The same problem of method can be approached from another side and then presents itself as a problem of "style." This has been praised as passionate and criticized as sentimental. Both judgments seem to me a little beside the point. I parted quite consciously with the tradition of *sine ira et studio* of whose greatness I was fully aware, and to me this was a methodological necessity closely connected with my particular subject matter.

Let us suppose—to take one among many possible examples—that the historian is confronted with excessive poverty in a society of great wealth, such as the poverty of the British working classes during the early stages of the Industrial Revolution. The natural human reaction to such conditions is one of anger and indignation because these conditions are against the dignity of man. If I describe these conditions without permitting my indignation to interfere, I have lifted this particular phenomenon out of its context in human society and have thereby robbed it of part of its nature, deprived it of one of its important inherent qualities. For to arouse indignation is one of the qualities of excessive poverty insofar as poverty occurs among human beings. I therefore cannot agree with Professor Voegelin that the "morally abhorrent and the emotionally existing will overshadow the essential," because I believe them to form an integral part of it. This has nothing to do with sentimentality or moralizing, although, of course, either can become a pitfall for the author. If I moralized or became sentimental, I simply did not do well

what I was supposed to do, namely, to describe the totalitarian phenomenon as occurring, not on the moon, but in the midst of human society.
To describe the concentration camps *sine ira* is not to be "objective," but
to condone them; and such condoning cannot be changed by a condemnation which the author may feel duty bound to add but which remains
unrelated to the description itself. When I used the image of Hell, I did
not mean this allegorically but literally: it seems rather obvious that men
who have lost their faith in Paradise will not be able to establish it on
earth; but it is not so certain that those who have lost their belief in
Hell as a place of the hereafter may not be willing and able to establish
on earth exact imitations of what people used to believe about Hell. In
this sense I think that a description of the camps as Hell on earth is
more "objective," that is, more adequate to their essence than statements
of a purely sociological or psychological nature.

The problem of style is a problem of adequacy and of response. If I
write in the same "objective" manner about the Elizabethan age and the
twentieth century, it may well be that my dealing with both periods is
inadequate because I have renounced the human faculty to respond to
either. Thus the question of style is bound up with the problem of
understanding, which has plagued the historical sciences almost from
their beginnings. I do not wish to go into this matter here, but I may
add that I am convinced that understanding is closely related to that
faculty of imagination which Kant called *Einbildungskraft* and which has
nothing in common with fictional ability. The *Spiritual Exercises* are
exercises of imagination and they may be more relevant to method in
the historical sciences than academic training realizes.

Reflections of this kind, originally caused by the special nature of
my subject, and the personal experience which is necessarily involved
in a historical investigation that employs imagination consciously as an
important tool of cognition resulted in a critical approach toward almost
all interpretation of contemporary history. I hinted at this in two short
paragraphs of the Preface, where I warned the reader against the concepts of Progress and of Doom as "two sides of the same medal" as well
as against any attempt at "deducing the unprecedented from precedents."
These two approaches are closely interconnected. The reason why Professor Voegelin can speak of "the putrefaction of Western civilization"
and the "earthwide expansion of Western foulness" is that he treats
"phenomenal differences"—which to me as differences of factuality are

all-important—as minor outgrowths of some "essential sameness" of a doctrinal nature. Numerous affinities between totalitarianism and some other trends in Occidental political or intellectual history have been described with this result, in my opinion: they all failed to point out the distinct quality of what was actually happening. The "phenomenal differences," far from "obscuring" some essential sameness, are those phenomena which make totalitarianism "totalitarian," which distinguish this one form of government and movement from all others and therefore can alone help us in finding its essence. What is unprecedented in totalitarianism is not primarily its ideological content, but the *event* of totalitarian domination itself. This can be seen clearly if we have to admit that the deeds of its considered policies have exploded our traditional categories of political thought (totalitarian domination is unlike all forms of tyranny and despotism we know of) and the standards of our moral judgment (totalitarian crimes are very inadequately described as "murder" and totalitarian criminals can hardly be punished as "murderers").

Professor Voegelin seems to think that totalitarianism is only the other side of liberalism, positivism, and pragmatism. But whether one agrees with liberalism or not (and I may say here that I am rather certain that I am neither a liberal nor a positivist nor a pragmatist), the point is that liberals are clearly not totalitarians. This, of course, does not exclude the fact that liberal or positivistic elements also lend themselves to totalitarian thinking; but such affinities would only mean that one has to draw even sharper distinctions because of the *fact* that liberals are not totalitarians.

I hope that I do not belabor this point unduly. It is important to me because I think that what separates my approach from Professor Voegelin's is that I proceed from facts and events instead of intellectual affinities and influences. This is perhaps a bit difficult to perceive because I am of course much concerned with philosophical implications and changes in spiritual self-interpretation. But this certainly does not mean that I described "a gradual revelation of the essence of totalitarianism from its inchoate forms in the eighteenth century to the fully developed," because this essence, in my opinion, did not exist before it had come into being. I therefore talk only of "elements," which eventually crystallize into totalitarianism, some of which are traceable to the eighteenth century, some perhaps even farther back (although I would doubt Voegelin's own theory that the "rise of immanentist sectarianism" since the late Middle Ages eventually ended in totalitarianism). Under no circumstances would I call any of them totalitarian.

For similar reasons and for the sake of distinguishing between ideas and actual events in history, I cannot agree with Professor Voegelin's remark that "the spiritual disease is the decisive feature that distinguishes modern masses from those of earlier centuries." To me, modern masses are distinguished by the fact that they are "masses" in a strict sense of the word. They are distinguished from the multitudes of former centuries in that they do not have common interests to bind them together or any kind of common "consent" which, according to Cicero, constitutes *inter-est*, that which is between men, ranging all the way from material to spiritual and other matters. This "between" can be a common ground and it can be a common purpose; it always fulfills the double function of binding men together *and* separating them in an articulate way. The lack of common interest so characteristic of modern masses is therefore only another sign of their homelessness and rootlessness. But it alone accounts for the curious fact that these modern masses are formed by the atomization of society, that the mass-men who lack all communal relationships nevertheless offer the best possible "material" for movements in which peoples are so closely pressed together that they seem to have become one. The loss of interests is identical with the loss of "self," and modern masses are distinguished in my view by their selflessness, that is, their lack of "selfish interests."

I know that problems of this sort can be avoided if one interprets totalitarian movements as a new—and perverted—religion, a substitute for the lost creed of traditional beliefs. From this, it would follow that some "need for religion" is a cause of the rise of totalitarianism. I feel unable to follow even the very qualified form in which Professor Voegelin uses the concept of a secular religion. There is no substitute for God in the totalitarian ideologies—Hitler's use of the "Almighty" was a concession to what he himself believed to be a superstition. More than that, the metaphysical place for God has remained empty. The introduction of these semi-theological arguments in the discussion of totalitarianism, on the other hand, is only too likely to further the wide-spread and strictly blasphemous modern "ideas" about a God who is "good for you"—for your mental or other health, for the integration of your personality, and God knows what—that is, "ideas" which make of God a function of man or society. This functionalization seems to me in many respects the last and perhaps the most dangerous stage of atheism.

By this, I do not mean to say that Professor Voegelin could ever become guilty of such functionalization. Nor do I deny that there is some connection between atheism and totalitarianism. But this connection seems to me purely negative and not at all peculiar to the rise of totalitarianism. It is true that a Christian cannot become a follower of either Hitler or Stalin; and it is true that morality as such is in jeopardy whenever the faith in God who gave the Ten Commandments is no longer secure. But this is at most a condition *sine qua non*, nothing which could positively explain whatever happened afterward. Those who conclude from the frightening events of our times that we have got to go back to religion and faith for political reasons seem to me to show just as much lack of faith in God as their opponents.

Professor Voegelin deplores, as I do, the "insufficiency of theoretical instruments" in the political sciences (and with what to me appeared as inconsistency accuses me a few pages later of not having availed myself more readily of them). Apart from the present trends of psychologism and sociologism, about which I think Professor Voegelin and I are in agreement, my chief quarrel with the present state of the historical and political sciences is their growing incapacity for making distinctions. Terms like nationalism, imperialism, totalitarianism, etc., are used indiscriminately for all kinds of political phenomena (usually just as "highbrow" words for aggression), and none of them is any longer understood with its particular historical background. The result is a generalization in which the words themselves lose all meaning. Imperialism does not mean a thing if it is used indiscriminately for Assyrian and Roman and British and Bolshevik history; nationalism is discussed in times and countries which never experienced the nation-state; totalitarianism is discovered in all kinds of tyrannies or forms of collective communities, etc. This kind of confusion—where everything distinct disappears and everything that is new and shocking is (not explained but) explained away either through drawing some analogies or reducing it to a previously known chain of causes and influences—seems to me to be the hallmark of the modern historical and political sciences.

In conclusion, I may be permitted to clarify my statement that in our modern predicament "human nature as such is at stake," a statement which provoked Professor Voegelin's sharpest criticism because he sees in the very idea of "changing the nature of man or of anything" and in the very fact that I took this claim of totalitarianism at all seriously a "symptom of the intellectual breakdown of Western civilization." The problem of the relationship between essence and existence in Occidental thought seems to me to be a bit more complicated and controversial than Voegelin's statement on "nature" (identifying "a thing as a thing" and therefore incapable of change by definition) implies, but this I can hardly discuss here. It may be enough to say that, terminological differences apart, I hardly proposed more change of nature than Professor Voegelin himself in his book on *The New Science of Politics*; discussing the Platonic-Aristotelian theory of soul, he states: "one might almost say that before the discovery of psyche man had no soul" (p. 67). In Voegelin's terms, I could have said that after the discoveries of totalitarian domination and its experiments we have reason to fear that man may lose his soul.

In other words, the success of totalitarianism is identical with a much more radical liquidation of freedom as a political and as a human reality than anything we have ever witnessed before. Under these conditions, it will be hardly consoling to cling to an unchangeable nature of man and conclude that either man himself is being destroyed or that freedom does not belong to man's essential capabilities. Historically we know of man's nature only insofar as it has existence, and no realm of eternal essences will ever console us if man loses his essential capabilities.

My fear, when I wrote the concluding chapter of my book, was not unlike the fear which Montesquieu already expressed when he saw that Western civilization was no longer guaranteed by laws, although its peoples were still ruled by customs which he did not deem sufficient to resist an onslaught of despotism. He says in the Preface to *L'Esprit des Lois*, "L'homme, cet être flexible, se pliant dans la société aux pensées et aux impressions des autres, est également capable de connaître sa propre nature lorsqu'on la lui montre, et d'en perdre jusqu'au sentiment lorsqu'on la lui dérobe." (Man, this flexible being, who submits himself in society to the thoughts and impressions of his fellow-men, is equally capable of knowing his own nature when it is shown to him and of losing it to the point where he has no realization that he is robbed of it.)

Dream and Nightmare

W HAT IMAGE DOES Europe have of America? Whatever it may be, it is a reflection of actual conditions in this country, it contains an evaluation of America's role in international politics, and it expresses the attitude of the nation concerned with respect to both. The faithfulness of such images to the original is always open to question; they cannot, and are not meant to, conform to standards of photographic objectivity or even journalistic reportage. The present image of America abroad is no exception to this rule, and it is neither less nor more distorted than the images nations used to form of each other in the course of their history and mutual relationships. If there were nothing more involved than misunderstandings, misinterpretations, and occasionally violent outbursts of resentment or dislike, the matter would be hardly of more than historical, limited interest.

There are, however, several respects in which the image of America abroad does not conform to the general rule. The first, and perhaps most relevant, exception is the fact that the European image, in distinction

The Commonweal, September 10, 1954. This and the next two essays were based on a lecture the author gave at Princeton University at a conference on "The Image of America Abroad."

from others, cannot be considered a mere reflection and interpretation of actual conditions, for it predates not only the birth of the United States, but the colonization and to some extent even the discovery of the American continent.

Without an image of America, no European colonist would ever have crossed the ocean. The dream and purpose carried by the colonists eventually led to the establishment of one part of European mankind on this side of the Atlantic; it was both the first European image of America and the guiding idea that inspired this country's colonization and political institutions. This image of America was the image of a New World—a name given to no other of the many new lands discovered at the beginning of the modern age. Its content was a new ideal of equality and a new idea of freedom. Both of these, as Tocqueville said, were "exported" from Europe, and neither was fully comprehensible except in the context of European history. Only in the United States did this image find a political realization, through the establishment of the American Republic. Yet even this realization was partly an import from Europe, since the founders of the Republic sought counsel in Locke and Montesquieu, who more clearly and more elaborately than Rousseau and the French ideologues (who influenced the history of European revolutions) had laid down the legal and political principles for the foundation of a new body politic.

Through the American Revolution, Europe's image of America came true. A new world was being born because a new body politic had come into existence. By the same token and at the same moment, Europe and the United States (i.e., that part of the new continent which, indeed, had become a new world) parted company. Whatever image Europe had of America, this image could never again become a model or guiding idea for whatever was done or happened in the United States.

Ever since this part of European mankind ceased to be a colony, framed its Constitution, and declared itself an independent republic, America has been both the dream and the nightmare of Europe. Up until the last third of the nineteenth century, the content of the dream was freedom from both want and oppression plus the assertion of human autonomy and power against the weight of the past, a past which through the authority of political institutions and the tradition of spiritual heritages seemed to hinder the full development of the new forces of the sixteenth and seventeenth centuries. At the same time, the very dream was a nightmare to those who were apprehensive of this modern development, and the decision as to whether America was a dream or a nightmare depended primarily not upon concrete experiences in this country but upon the political views of the writer, as seen in the attitude he had taken toward the conflicts and discussions of his native land.

Thus America and Europe had parted company. But the image of America as it shines through travelers' reports and novels, poems and political treatises was never alien or exotic, like the images of Africa or Asia or the South Sea Islands. Instead, it remained the sometimes fantastically exaggerated and distorted picture of a reality where the most recent traits of European civilization had developed in an almost undiluted purity.

This attitude toward America, first of all, was of course Tocqueville's own, as was indicated quite openly in the very title of his work—*Democracy in America*. The whole book bears witness to the fact that his interest in the workings of democracy as a European possibility—or even a necessity—was greater than his interest in descriptions of a foreign country. He came to America to learn the true lesson of the French Revolution, to find out what happened to men and society under the unprecedented conditions of equality. He regarded the United States as a large and wonderfully equipped laboratory where the most recent implications of European history were tried out. Europe, he was sure, if not the whole world, was about to be Americanized; but he would never have thought this process could be somehow in opposition to the European development, as though America and Europe were different in origin and historical destiny.

To Tocqueville, Americans were not a young people against whom Europeans could summon up either pride of ancestry and civilization or, as the case might be, to whom they would feel inferior in vitality. The Americans, he said, "are a very old and a very enlightened people who have fallen upon a new and unbounded country." Had Americans told him, and they were in fact even then quite likely to, that "the American nation, as it is today, was hewn from the forests in comparatively recent times, when brilliant and complex civilizations had already existed . . . for many centuries" (as Robert Trumbull said early this year in the *New York Times Magazine*), he might have replied that the origin of this delusion of youth was in eighteenth-century ideas about "noble savages" and the purifying influence of uncivilized nature, rather than in actual experiences of pioneerdom and colonization. Or, to put it another way, only because the new history-consciousness of the West used the metaphor of individual biological life for the existence of nations could Europeans as well as Americans delude themselves with the fantastic notion of a second youth in a new country.

However that may be, Tocqueville came to America to look at "the image of democracy itself, with its inclinations, its character, its prejudices and its passions, in order to learn what we have to fear or to hope from its progress." The principle of equality, far from having its roots in the new continent, had been, politically, the most relevant and most striking result of all great events "of the last seven hundred years" of European history. From the viewpoint of modern Europe and the development of the modern age, the United States was an older and more experienced country than Europe herself. So confident was Tocqueville in this view of America as the product of a European development, that he saw even strictly intra-American developments, such as the migration to the West, as a stream that began "in the middle of Europe, [crossed] the Atlantic Ocean, and [advanced] over the solitudes of the New World."

In its details, Tocqueville's view can be debated and stands in need of correction. But by and large it is corroborated by the historical fact. The American Republic owes its origin to the greatest adventure of European mankind, which, for the first time since the Crusades and at the height of the European nation-state system, embarked upon a common enterprise whose spirit proved to be stronger than all national differences.

Tocqueville is the greatest but not the only author of the last century who saw the New World as the outcome of an old history and civilization. Today this view is the element conspicuously missing in Europe's image of America. All other opinions of nineteenth-century writers, insights and errors, dreams and nightmares alike, have somehow survived, although they have degenerated into clichés whose triviality makes it almost impossible to consider seriously the constantly increasing literature on the subject. But today the U.S. is considered to have no more relationship with Europe than any other country, and frequently considerably less than Russia or even Asia, both of which are being Europeanized through Marxism for a considerable segment of European opinion—by no means including only Communists or fellow-travelers.

There are many reasons for this recent estrangement. Among them is American isolation, which before it became a political slogan had been a political reality for more than a hundred years. In this respect, the European image of America as outside and unconnected with her own development has its origin in America. There is a much more cogent reason, however, which also goes a long way toward explaining why Europe will so often pretend to find herself in closer kinship with non-European nations than with America; this is the stupendous wealth of the United States.

America, it is true, has been the "land of plenty" almost since the beginning of its history, and the relative well-being of all her inhabitants deeply impressed even early travelers. The general high standard of living (which was not hindered by and did not prevent the formation of gigantic fortunes) was early observed and rightly seen in connection with the political principles of democracy and the concomitant economic principle that nothing ought to be so expensive as personal services and nothing so rewarding as human labor. It is also true that the feeling was always present that the difference between the two continents was greater than national differences in Europe itself even if the actual figures did not bear this out. Still, at some moment—presumably after America emerged from her long isolation and became once more a central preoccupation of Europe after the First World War—this difference between Europe and America changed its meaning and became qualitative instead of quantitative. It was no longer a question of better, but of altogether different conditions, of a nature which makes understanding well nigh impossible. Like an invisible but very real Chinese wall, the wealth of the United States separates it from all other countries of the globe, just as it separates the individual American tourist from the inhabitants of the countries he visits.

We all know from personal experience that friendship involves equality. Although friendship can be an equalizer of existing natural or economic inequalities, there is a limit beyond which such equalization is utterly impossible. In the words of Aristotle, no friendship could ever exist between a man and a god. The same holds true for the relationships between nations where the equalizing force of friendship does not operate.

Between nations, a certain equality of condition, though not an identity, is necessary for understanding and frankness. The problem with

American wealth is that, at some moment, it progressed beyond the point where understanding from other peoples, and more specifically from those who inhabit the mother-countries of many American citizens, no longer seems possible and where even personal friendships across the ocean are put in jeopardy.

Those who believe that this situation can be easily corrected by Marshall plans or Point Four programs are, I am afraid, mistaken. To the extent that material aid is motivated by authentic generosity and a feeling of responsibility beyond the more obvious political and economic interests and necessities of American foreign policy, it will earn us no more than the very doubtful gratitude which the benefactor expects—but generally does not receive—from the object of his beneficence.

Mistrust of American intentions, the fear of being pressured into unwanted political actions, suspicion of sinister motives when help is given without political strings attached—these things are natural enough and need no hostile propaganda to arouse them. But even more is involved. In this case, as in all beneficence, the prerogative of action and the sovereignty of decision rest with the benefactor, and therefore, to cite Aristotle once more, it is only natural that the benefactor should love his beneficiaries more than he is loved by them. Where they have suffered passively, he has done something; they have become, as it were, his work.

To these real problems in America's international relationships, Communist propaganda abroad adds the palpably false accusation that the United States became rich from imperialist exploitation, and the even more obvious fantasy of a class-ridden economy where masses toil in misery. These lies are easily contradicted by reality, and they will not live as long as the recent and more dangerous attempt to translate the Marxian division between capitalist and proletariat into terms of foreign policy. This interpretation divides the nations of the world into have- and have-not countries, and according to this interpretation the only country to fall into the first category is, of course, the United States. Unfortunately, this image of America can draw upon a certain store of experience, and it is now in turn dangerously reinforced by certain current "Americanistic" attitudes and ideologies in the United States. These, I am afraid, are much more widespread and express a more general mood than traditional isolationism or the limited appeal of America First movements. Abroad, the anti-Americanism which is the other side of this coin is actually much more dangerous than all the tirades against an imperialist, capitalistic land which have become the stock-in-trade of Communist propaganda, precisely because it corresponds to a growing "Americanism" at home.

The question of the wealth of the United States is no trivial matter, and on the international scene it probably constitutes one of this nation's gravest long-range political problems. It almost seems that the consistent development of the principle of equality under circumstances of great natural abundance has so changed the conditions of human life that U.S. citizens appear to belong to a *species sui generis*. Nor does this situation improve when the average American tourist naively assumes that a similar miracle could occur in other countries if only their people had the wisdom to adopt American institutions and the American way of life.

Perhaps the average American cannot be expected to understand that although equality of condition is spreading throughout the whole world, this equalization will take a different course and require different measures in countries lacking the natural abundance of the American continent. More serious is the fact that the inability to understand each other's circumstances has begun to rear its head in our foreign policy. Much of the unpleasantness in recent British-American relationships, for example, can be explained on these grounds. It is the old story; nothing seems so difficult to understand and stands so squarely in the way of friendship as a radical difference in exterior circumstances.

It has always been the misfortune of rich people to be alternately flattered and abused—and still remain unpopular, no matter how generous they are. That Americans abroad should get a little of this age-old treatment is neither surprising nor unduly disturbing. But it is an altogether different matter that a radical shift has taken place recently in the class structure of those Europeans who are in sympathy with America and those who are not.

For centuries, this country has been the dream of Europe's lower classes and freedom-loving people. At the same time it remained a nightmare for the rich bourgeoisie, the aristocracy, and a certain type of intellectual, who saw in equality a threat to culture rather than a promise of freedom. To many of the lower classes in Europe, the restrictions on immigration after the First World War put an end to their hopes of solving their problems through emigration to America. To them, for the first time, America became a bourgeois country, her wealth having become as inaccessible as the wealth of their own bourgeoisie.

After the Second World War this situation became more acute, as United States policies first supported the re-establishment or the continuation of the status quo everywhere, and then adopted an unfriendly attitude toward Great Britain's peaceful and, on the whole, moderate and controlled change of her own social conditions under the Labour government. Since then, America has seemed not only rich beyond the wildest fantasy, but determined to support the interests of the rich all over the world. Certainly this was neither the intention nor the outcome of American policy abroad, least of all in Europe, where the Marshall Plan benefited every class of the population and American officials frequently went out of their way to find some remedy for the worst social injustices. Nevertheless that is the way things have *seemed* to be. As a result, sympathy for America today can be found, generally speaking, among those people whom Europeans call "reactionary," whereas an anti-American posture is one of the best ways to prove oneself a liberal.

Anti-American feeling is, of course, exploited by Communist propaganda, like all other troublesome issues. But to consider it a propaganda product is a serious underestimation of its popular roots. In Europe, it is well on the way to becoming a new *ism*. Anti-Americanism, its negative emptiness notwithstanding, threatens to become the content of a European movement.

If it is true that each nationalism (though, of course, not the birth of every nation) begins with a real or fabricated common enemy, then the current image of America in Europe may well become the beginning of a new pan-European nationalism. Our hope that the emergence of a federated Europe and the dissolution of the present nation-state system will make nationalism itself a thing of the past may be unwarrantedly optimistic. On its more popular levels—not, to be sure, in the deliberations of statesmen in Strasbourg—the movement for a united Europe has recently shown decidedly nationalistic traits. The line between this anti-American Europeanism and the very healthy and necessary efforts to federate the European nations is further confused by the fact that the remnants of European fascism have joined the fight. Their presence reminds everybody that after Briand's futile gestures at the League of

Nations it was Hitler who started the war with the promise that he would liquidate Europe's obsolete nation-state system and build a united Europe. The widespread and inarticulate anti-American sentiments find their political crystallization point precisely here. Since Europe is apparently no longer willing to see in America whatever it has to hope or to fear from her own future development, it has a tendency to consider the establishment of a European government an act of emancipation from America.

Americanism on one side and Europeanism on the other side of the Atlantic, two ideologies facing, fighting and, above all, resembling each other as all seemingly opposed ideologies do—this may be one of the dangers we face.

Europe and the Atom Bomb

I N E U R O P E T O D A Y , the development, possession, and threatened use of atomic weapons by the United States is a primary fact of political life. Europeans have, of course, engaged in the now-familiar debates about the soullessness of a country dominated by modern technology, the monotony of the machine, the uniformity of a society based upon mass-production, and the like for many years. But today the matter has gone much beyond that. The intimate connection between modern warfare and a technicalized society has become obvious to everybody, and as a result large segments of the population—and not only the intellectuals—are passionately opposed to, and afraid of, technological progress and the growing technicalization of our world.

Technology and its transformation of the world are so clearly part and parcel of European history since the beginning of the modern age that it is obviously absurd to blame its consequences on America. Europeans used to see technical progress in America as Tocqueville saw the progress of American democracy, that is, as something which fundamentally concerned Western civilization as a whole, though for certain specific reasons it had found its first and clearest expression in the United

The Commonweal, September 17, 1954.

States. This attitude changed after the atomic bomb was dropped on Hiroshima; since then, there has been a growing tendency both to look upon all technical achievements as inherently evil and destructive and to see in America chiefly, and in Russia sometimes, the epitome of destructive technicalization which is hostile and alien to Europe.

This trend toward viewing recent technical developments as essentially non-European is all the more surprising since Europeans know perfectly well that the discovery of atomic energy largely resulted from the efforts of European scientists forced to come to America by political events in their homelands. Objectively speaking, there is little reason to cite the production of atomic weapons as an indication that technicalization is a non-European, American phenomenon. But, reasonable or not, this is the way Europeans feel.

One change in the present discussions of technology is obvious. The destructive potentialities of the new weapons are so great, and the possibility of physical destruction of European countries is felt to be so imminent, that the process of technicalization is no longer primarily seen as anti-spiritual or soul-killing, but as fraught with the danger of sheer physical destruction. As a result, the anti-technical mood is no longer a specialty of intellectuals; the masses no longer look upon technical development as a source of material improvement.

The political relevance of the general hostility to technology—and by implication, to America—lies in this fact that *everybody* has become frightened. All are inclined to think with Goethe's Mephisto in *Faust*: *"Die Elemente sind mit uns verschworen und auf Zerstörung läuft's hinaus"* ("The elements conspire with us and destruction is the aim").*

There seems to be this much to be said for the argument: the release of natural forces is more characteristic of recent developments in technology than the constant improvement of methods of production. The chain reaction of the atom bomb, therefore, can easily become the symbol for a conspiracy between man and the elementary forces of nature, which, when touched off by human know-how, may one day take their revenge and destroy all life on the surface of the earth and perhaps even the earth itself. Rightly or wrongly, when Europeans think of technology they see, not a television set in every home, but the mushroom-cloud

---

Faust, II, 11549–50. Once again Arendt quotes from memory: Goethe wrote *Vernichtung*, not *Zerstörung*. —Ed.

over Hiroshima. That A-bomb was dropped by the United States, and the U.S. has been in the forefront of the development of atomic weapons ever since. As a result, American political power is increasingly identified with the terrifying force of modern technology, with a supreme, irresistible power of destruction.

The standard reply to this fearful image of America is that atomic energy in the hands of the American Republic is sure to be used only for purposes of defense or retaliation. As long as this instrument is in the hands of a free country, the argument goes, it is sure to serve the cause of freedom all over the world.

This argument has many weaknesses, not the least of which is the unpredictability inherent in the very concept of freedom. Freedom can be guaranteed by laws even less than justice; a legal framework that would attempt to insure permanence of freedom would not only kill all political life, but would abolish even that margin of unpredictability without which freedom cannot exist.

However, there are worse troubles with the standard argument that the preservation of freedom justifies the use of the means of violence, and that violence used for the sake of freedom will always respect certain limitations.

Ultimately, this argument rests on the conviction that it is better to be dead than to be a slave. It is based on a political philosophy that, since the ancients, has considered courage to be the political virtue *par excellence*, the one virtue without which political freedom is wholly impossible.

Originally, the time-honored conviction that courage is the highest political virtue was based on a pre-Christian philosophy which deemed that life is not the most sacred good and that there are conditions on which it is not worth having. For the ancients such conditions existed whenever the individual man was utterly delivered to the necessities of preserving sheer animal life, and therefore was judged incapable of freedom. This could happen in the case of slavery, say, or in the case of incurable illness; in both instances, suicide was considered to be the appropriate solution demanded by courage as well as by human dignity.

With the victory of Christianity in the Western world and especially of the originally Hebrew conviction of the sacredness of life as such, this code of individual morality as it had been known throughout the ancient world lost its absolute validity. Wars could be justified on religious grounds, but not on the ground of secular political freedom as such. By the same token wholesale slaughter, so well known in the ancient world, might happen, but it could no longer be justified. By and large, Western civilization was agreed that, in the words of Kant, nothing should happen during a war that would make a future peace impossible. This agreement is no longer universal.

With the appearance of atomic weapons, both the Hebrew-Christian limitation on violence and the ancient appeal to courage have for all practical purposes become meaningless, and, with them, the whole political and moral vocabulary in which we are accustomed to discuss these matters. Limitations can be applied in reality only to foreseeable developments; they cannot reckon with that "surprise technique" which Raymond Aron recently analyzed as the central event of the First World War, and which, as long as we are caught in the process of progressing technicalization, will inevitably produce new "miracle" weapons. Under existing circumstances, as a matter of fact, nothing is more probable than these "miracles."

In fact, of course, even our present potentialities for destruction have already far outstripped the matter-of-course limitations of previous wars. And this situation has placed in jeopardy the very value of courage itself. The fundamental human condition of courage is that man is not immortal, that he sacrifices a life that one day will be taken from him in any case. No human courage would be conceivable if the condition of individual life were the same as that of the species. Greece's immortal gods had to leave this one virtue, courage, to mortal men; all other human virtues could appear in divine shape, could be deified and worshipped as divine gifts. Courage alone is denied to the immortals; because of the everlasting presence of their existence, the stakes are never high enough. If life were not normally taken from mortal man one day anyhow, he could never risk it. The stakes would be too high, the courage required would be literally inhuman, and life would not only appear to be the highest good, it would become the central human concern, overruling all other considerations.

Closely connected with this fact is another limitation of human courage—the conviction that posterity will understand, remember, and respect the individual mortal's sacrifice. Man can be courageous only as long as he knows he is survived by those who are like him, that he fulfills a role in something more permanent than himself, "the enduring chronicle of mankind," as Faulkner once put it. Thus in antiquity, when wars were likely to end with the extermination or enslavement of whole peoples, the victor felt obliged to preserve for posterity the deeds and the greatness of the enemy. So Homer sang the praise of Hector, and Herodotus reported the history of the Persians.

Courage, under the circumstances of modern warfare, has lost much of its old meaning. By putting in jeopardy the survival of mankind and not only individual life or at the most the life of a whole people, modern warfare is about to transform the individual mortal man into a conscious member of the human race, of whose immortality he needs to be sure in order to be courageous at all and for whose survival he must care more than for anything else. Or, to put it another way, while there certainly are conditions under which individual life is not worth having, the same cannot be true for mankind. The moment a war can even conceivably threaten the continued existence of man on earth, the alternative between liberty and death has lost its old plausibility.

As long as Europe remains divided, she can afford the luxury of dodging these very disturbing problems of the modern world. She can continue to pretend that the threat to our civilization comes to her from without, and that she herself is in danger from two outside powers, America and Russia, which are equally alien. Both anti-Americanism and neutralism are, in a sense, clear signs that Europe is not prepared at this moment to face the consequences and problems of her own development.

If Europe were united, pooling great industrial resources in material and manpower, and strong enough to build her own atomic plants and fabricate her own atomic weapons, this escape route would automatically be closed. Then the discussion presently in disguise as a discussion of foreign policy would quickly show its true face. The present estrangement of Europe from America would come to an end, because it would become obvious that technological development has its origin in the whole of Western history and instead of being just an American affair, has only come to a climax in America first.

The Threat of Conformism

F EW AMERICANS RETURNING from Europe in recent years have failed to report with a certain bitterness the great prominence given in Europe to everything we have come to include under the name of McCarthyism. Americans are usually inclined to consider this emphasis altogether misplaced and are very likely, no matter where their sympathies lie, to look upon such experiences as demonstrations of the distorted image of America abroad.

One point here is often overlooked in this country. Experiences with totalitarianism, either in the form of totalitarian movements or outright totalitarian domination, are familiar to all European countries except Sweden and Switzerland. To Americans, these experiences appeared strange and "un-American," just as foreign as specifically modern American experiences frequently appear to Europeans. The standard reply to victims of Nazism and Bolshevism used to be, and to an extent still is, "It can't happen here." To Europeans, McCarthyism appears to be conclusive proof that it can.

There are two possibilities. You can take the assumptions of the investigators at face value. You can believe with them, not that Soviet

The Commonweal, September 24, 1954.

Russia constitutes the gravest problem of American foreign policy (which it obviously does), but that Bolshevism in the form of a domestic conspiracy permeates all levels of the population right up to the highest places in American government. In that case the conclusion is inevitable that it can very well happen here and that it does not thanks only to the activities of investigating Senators. On the other hand, if you do not believe in this myth of a top-to-bottom domestic conspiracy, it is very easy to detect in the methods of these committees ominously familiar traits, up to and including the traditional fabrication of a conspiracy myth. This line of reasoning is rather obvious, especially for Europeans. This reaction may be annoying and occasionally even offensive; it may hurt some feelings, but it will do no serious harm in the long run.

Much more relevant is another aspect of the same matter. In view of the prominence given the issue itself, it is curious to observe in Europe how little reported is the opposition to McCarthyism, which is voiced in entire freedom in the United States. Even well-informed Europeans expect every American to have the same opinion on this matter, and the way in which they view this position, not as an opinion of individual American citizens, but as American opinion in general, is highly distressing. What comes to light here is a characteristically European expectation of encountering a kind of conformism which needs no threats or violence, but arises spontaneously in a society that conditions each of its members so perfectly to its exigencies that no one knows that he is conditioned. The conditioning of the individual to the demands of society was early considered a characteristic trait of American democracy. Indeed, it became perhaps the chief reason America could develop into the nightmare of Europe, even of a freedom-loving Europe, something Americans find hard to understand.

Historically, the European conflict between the State and the individual frequently was solved at the expense of individual freedom. This fact was taken by Americans as proof of the sacrifice of human liberties to the State. By Europeans, on the other hand, the situation was viewed in terms of a conflict between State and society, so that the individual, even if his liberties were violated by the government, could always find a relatively safe refuge in his social and private life. Totalitarian domination, but no other government, not even absolute despotism or modern dictatorships, has succeeded in destroying this private social sphere, this refuge of individual liberty. Europe's fear with respect to American circumstances has always been that such a refuge in society could not exist here, precisely because they felt the distinction between government and society did not exist. The European nightmare was that under conditions of majority rule society itself would be the oppressor, with no room left for individual freedom.

In Tocqueville's words, "whenever social conditions are equal, public opinion presses with [such] enormous weight upon the mind of each individual" that "the majority do not need to force him, they convince him"; the non-violent coercion of public disapproval is so strong that the dissenter has nowhere to turn in his loneliness and impotence, and in the end will be driven either to conformity or to despair. If we apply Tocqueville's insight to modern conditions, if we try to visualize present European thought in his terms, then we may say that Europeans fear that terror and violence may not be necessary in order for freedom to disappear in America. Europe's disquiet may be traced to the conviction that freedom can dwindle away through some sort of general agreement, in some almost intangible process of mutual adjustment. And this is something which up to now has not yet happened in any part of the Western world.

The danger of conformism and its threat to freedom is inherent in all mass societies. But its importance has more recently been overshadowed by the horrors of terror when combined with ideological propaganda—the specifically totalitarian form of organizing great and unstructured masses of people. This method served as the instrument both to destroy the remnants of older class or caste systems, and to prevent the coming into being of new classes or new groups, which is the usual outcome of successful revolutions. Under conditions of an already existing mass society—as distinguished from the class disintegration whose processes are accelerated by totalitarian movements—it is not inconceivable that totalitarian elements could for a limited time rely on conformism, or rather on the activization of a dormant conformism, for its own ends. In the initial stages, conformism could conceivably be used to make terror less violent and ideology less insistent; thereby it would serve to make the transition from a free climate into the stage of a pre-totalitarian atmosphere less noticeable.

In America, the potentially dangerous consequences or by-products of equality of condition (i.e., of the absence of a class system which, much more than sheer numbers, is the outstanding trait of a mass society) have been remote, but will remain so only as long as the Constitution remains intact and the "institutions of liberty" function. In Europe, however, the old class system is disintegrating beyond repair, and even in a non-totalitarian atmosphere it is rapidly developing into a mass society. There the safeguards against the worst dangers of conformism which have protected America do not for the most part exist. Where they do exist, they have in part been imported from America, and on the whole they have not yet had the time to prove themselves, nor have the people become educated in their use. Specifically European safeguards, on the other hand, such as customs and traditions, have already proved once to be almost useless in modern emergencies and predicaments. When Europeans see conformism in America, therefore, they are rightly alarmed; the specifically American safeguards against the dangers inherent in conformism are naturally less visible to them from the outside, and the European is quite correct in his judgment that without such safeguards conformism could very well be as deadly as other, more bloody forms of modern mass organization.

America has, of course, a much longer experience with conformism than Europe. In discussing the subject, Europeans will naturally adopt the attitude of "It can't happen here," just as Americans did when they first learned about totalitarianism. But in reality, whatever can happen in Europe can happen in America, and vice versa, because, all differences notwithstanding, the history of the two continents is fundamentally the same. Indeed, since Western civilization has spread its influence all over the globe, the moment is rapidly approaching when we shall be able to say that hardly anything can happen in any country that could not happen in any other. In this matter, however, as in the matter of atomic warfare, the point is that Europe feels herself much more exposed to the dangers of such a development than America. Just as she feels that her cities are more open to attack and more easily destroyed, so she also feels that her political institutions are less stable, less firmly rooted, and her liberties even more exposed to crises from within.

In reality, the process which Europeans dread as "Americanization" is the emergence of the modern world with all its perplexities and implications. It is probable that this process will be accelerated rather than hindered through the federation of Europe, which is also very likely a condition *sine qua non* for European survival. Whether or not European federation will be accompanied by the rise of anti-American, pan-

European nationalism, as one may sometimes fear today, unification of economic and demographic conditions is almost sure to create a state of affairs which will be very similar to that existing in the United States.

One hundred and twenty years ago the European image of America was the image of democracy. Though not all Europeans could love it, they had to come to terms with it because they knew quite well that it presented part and parcel of the history of the West. Today the image of America is modernity. It is the image of the world as it rose from the modern age which gave birth to both present-day Europe and America.

The world's central problems today are the political organization of mass societies and the political integration of technical power. Because of the destructive potentialities inherent in these problems, Europe is no longer sure whether she can come to terms with the modern world at all. As a result, she tries to escape the consequences of her own history under the pretext of separating herself from America.

The image of America which exists in Europe may not tell us much about American realities or the daily lives of United States citizens, but if we are willing to learn, it may tell us something about the justified fears of Europe for her spiritual identity and her even deeper apprehensions about her physical survival. And these fears and apprehensions are not specifically European, no matter what Europeans may tell us. They are the fears of the whole Western world, and ultimately of all mankind.

Concern with Politics
in Recent European
Philosophical Thought

[The Arendt collection in the Library of Congress contains various drafts of this unpublished lecture, originally delivered to the American Political Science Association in 1954. The present version is primarily based on what appears to be the last draft, incorporating additions and corrections.]

C ONCERN WITH POLITICS is not a matter of course for the philosopher. What we political scientists tend to overlook is that most political philosophies have their origin in the philosopher's negative and sometimes even hostile attitude toward the *polis* and the whole realm of human affairs. Historically, those centuries prove to be richest in political philosophies which were least propitious for philosophizing, so that self-protection as well as outright defense of professional interests have more often than not prompted the philosopher's concern with politics. The event which started our tradition of political thought was the trial and death of Socrates, the condemnation of the philosopher by the *polis*. The questions, which had haunted Plato and to which almost as many answers have since been given as there are original political philosophies, have been: How can philosophy protect and liberate itself from the realm of human affairs? What are the best conditions (the "best form of government") for philosophical activity? The answers, despite their diversity, tend to agree on the following points: Peace is the highest good of the commonwealth, civil war is the greatest of all evils, and permanence is the best criterion for judging forms of government. In other words, what the philosophers almost unanimously have demanded of the political realm was a state of affairs where action, properly speaking (i.e., not execution of laws or application of rules or any other managing activity, but the beginning of something new whose outcome is unpredictable), would be either altogether superfluous or remain the privilege of the few. Traditional political philosophy, therefore, tends to derive the political side of human life from the necessity which compels the human animal to live together with others, rather than from the human capacity to act, and it tends to conclude with a theory about the conditions that would best suit the needs of the unfortunate human condition of plurality and best enable the philosopher, at least, to live undisturbed by it. In modern times, we hardly hear anything of this age-old quest. One is tempted to think that it died when Nietzsche admitted too frankly what most philosophers before him had carefully hidden from the multitude, namely, that "politics should be arranged in such a way that mediocre minds are sufficient for it and not everybody needs to be aware of it every day."[1]

In other words, we political scientists, because of our special interest, tend to overlook the large measure of truth in Pascal's remark: "We can only think of Plato and Aristotle in grand academic robes. They were honest men, like others, laughing with their friends, and when they diverted themselves with writing their *Laws* and *Politics*, they did it for amusement. That part of their life was the least philosophic and the least serious. . . . If they wrote on politics, it was as if laying down rules for a lunatic asylum; if they presented the appearance of speaking of a great matter, it was because they knew that the madmen, to whom they spoke, thought they were kings and emperors. They entered into their principles in order to make their madness as little harmful as possible."[2] Many passages in Plato and Aristotle warning their pupils not to take human affairs too seriously could support this statement, and it may be even more valid for those who came after them.

Contemporary political thought, though it cannot compete in artic-

[1] The notes are at the end of the essay.

ulateness with the past, distinguishes itself from this traditional background in that it recognizes that human affairs pose authentic philosophic
problems and that politics is a domain in which genuine philosophic questions arise, and not merely a sphere of life which ought to be
ruled by precepts that owe their origin to altogether different experiences.
Nobody, as a matter of fact, any longer sincerely believes that all we
need is "wise men" and that all they can learn from political events is
the "foolishness of the world." This changed attitude may give hope for
a "new science of politics."[3] This will be all the more welcome because
philosophy in the past—though it became (Pascal's remark notwithstanding) the mother of political science as of all other sciences—has
frequently shown an unhappy inclination to treat this one of her many
children as though it were a stepchild.

Like all political philosophies, the present concern with politics in
Europe can be traced back to disturbing political experiences, notably
the experiences of two world wars, totalitarian regimes, and the dreaded
prospect of atomic war. In one respect these events found philosophy
better prepared for and the philosophers more willing to acknowledge
the relevance of political happenings than they had been in the past.
The modern concept of history, especially in its Hegelian version, has
given the realm of human affairs a dignity it never enjoyed in philosophy
before. The great fascination Hegel exerted on the first post-war generation (and which came after an almost total eclipse of more than fifty
years) was due to his philosophy of history, which enabled the philosopher
to discover meaning in the political realm, and yet to understand this
meaning as an absolute truth which transcended all willed intentions
and worked behind the back of the political actor. For this generation,
Hegel seemed to have solved once and for all the decisive problem of
political philosophy: how to deal philosophically with that realm of Being
that owes its origin exclusively to man and which therefore could not
reveal truth as long as truth was understood as not man-made but given
to man's senses or reason. The ancient and the Christian solution had
been to consider this whole realm as essentially instrumental, as existing
only for the sake of something else. This solution had been felt to be
unsatisfactory for the entire modern age, whose central philosophical
tenet—that we can know only what we have made ourselves—clashed
with the whole body of past philosophy. In Hegel's solution, individual
actions remain as meaningless as before, while their process in its entirety

reveals a truth that transcends the realm of human affairs. This was so very ingenious because it opened a way to take historical-political happenings seriously, without abandoning the traditional concept of truth.

Seen from this viewpoint, the modern philosophers' tendency to talk about history when they are confronted with the task of a political philosophy may well appear as the last in a long series of attempts to dodge the question—attempts which Pascal mentioned so sarcastically and with so much sincere approval and admiration. While this may help to explain Hegel's influence in Germany after the first war and in France after the second war, it discloses only part of a much more complex situation. According to a widespread sentiment in Europe, twentieth-century political events have brought out and made public a deep-rooted crisis of Western civilization of which the non-academic philosophers had been aware long before it assumed a political reality. The nihilistic aspects of political movements, particularly conspicuous in totalitarian ideologies (which rest on the assumption that everything is possible, thus establishing a pseudo-ontological basis for the earlier nihilistic claim that everything is permitted), were indeed so familiar to the philosopher that he could easily detect in them his own predicaments. What attracts modern philosophy to the political realm is that its theoretical predicaments have assumed a tangible reality in the modern world. This curious coincidence leads to a decisive step beyond Hegel's pre-established harmony, in which philosophy and politics, thought and action, become reconciled in history without, for that matter, touching upon the philosopher's most cherished privilege of being the only one to whom truth is revealed. This intimate connection of thoughts and events, where thoughts seemed to have grasped the meaning of events before and not after they had come to pass, and where events seemed to substantiate and illuminate thoughts, has most effectively thrown the philosopher out of his ivory tower—at least to the extent that he was willing to recognize that this connection was not one of causality. The question of whether events caused the philosophers to think or whether philosophic thoughts were responsible for certain actions (as if Nietzsche had submitted meekly to the nihilistic trends of his time or, on the contrary, was to blame for the rise of Nazism) was seen as inadequate and essentially futile. The connection of thought and event seemed, instead, to indicate that thought itself is historic and that neither the philosopher (e.g., Hegel's backward-looking thinker) nor *what* he thinks (e.g., Hegel's modes of the Absolute) stands outside history or reveals something which transcends it.

It is because of such considerations that the term "historicity" (*Geschichtlichkeit*) began to play its role in post-war German philosophy. From there it was introduced into French existentialism, where it received a much stronger Hegelian flavor. The true representative of this philosophy remains Heidegger, who already, in *Sein und Zeit* (1927), had formulated "historicity" in ontological, as distinguished from anthropological, terms and more recently has arrived at an understanding according to which "historicity" means to be sent on one's way (*Geschichlichkeit* and *Geschicklichkeit* are thought together in the sense of being sent on one's way and being willing to take this "sending" upon oneself), so that for him human history would coincide with a history of Being which is revealed in it. The point against Hegel is that no transcendent spirit and no absolute is revealed in this ontological history (*Seinsgeschichte*); in Heidegger's own words: "We left the arrogance of all Absolutes behind us" ("*Wir haben die Anmassung alles Unbedingten hinter uns gelassen*").[4] In our context, this means that the philosopher has left behind him the claim to being "wise" and knowing eternal standards for the perishable affairs of the City of men, for such "wisdom" could be justified only from a position outside the realm of human affairs and be thought legitimate only by virtue of the philosopher's proximity to the Absolute. In the context of the spiritual and political crisis of the time, it means that the philosopher, together with all others, after having lost the traditional framework of so-called values will not seek either the re-establishment of the old or the discovery of new values.

The abandonment of the position of "wise man" by the philosopher himself is politically perhaps the most important and the most fruitful result of the new philosophical concern with politics. The rejection of the claim to wisdom opens the way to a re-examination of the whole realm of politics in the light of elementary human experiences within this realm itself, and implicitly discards traditional concepts and judgments, which have their roots in altogether different kinds of experience. Such a development naturally does not proceed unequivocally. Thus we find the old hostility of the philosopher toward the *polis* in Heidegger's analyses of average everyday life in terms of *das Man* (the "they" or the rule of public opinion, as opposed to the "self") in which the public realm has the function of hiding reality and preventing even the appearance of truth.[5] Still, these phenomenological descriptions offer most penetrating insights into one of the basic aspects of society and, moreover, insist that these structures of human life are inherent in the human condition as such, from which there is no escape into an "authenticity" which would be the philosopher's prerogative. Their limitations appear only if they are taken to cover the whole of public life. More important, therefore, are the limitations inherent in the concept which is meant to cover the public realm outside of *das Man*, outside of society and public opinion. It is here that the concept of historicity appears, and this concept, despite its new guise and greater articulateness, shares with the older concept of history the fact that, despite its obvious closeness to the political realm, it never reaches but always misses the center of politics—man as an acting being. The transformation of the concept of history into historicity came about through the modern conception of the connectedness of thought and event, and as such it is by no means a monopoly of Heidegger's thought; although it is in Heidegger—in whose later philosophy the "event" (*das Ereignis*) plays an ever increasing role— that the coincidence of thought and event comes out most clearly. Yet, even so, it is obvious that this conceptual framework is better prepared to understand history than to lay the groundwork of a new political philosophy. This seems to be the reason why it is highly sensitive to general trends of the time, to all the modern problems that can be best understood in historical terms, such as the technicalization of the world, the emergence of one world on a planetary scale, the increasing pressure of society upon the individual, and the concomitant atomization of society. Meanwhile, the more permanent questions of political science which, in a sense, are more specifically philosophic—such as, What is politics? Who is man as a political being? What is freedom?—seem to have been forgotten altogether.

It is obvious that the same problems can be looked upon from the opposite point of view. Nihilism in terms of historicity is considered to be the innermost fate of the modern age, that which sent modern man along its road and therefore can be overcome only on its own terms. But nihilism can also be viewed as that which happened to man when the modern age wandered in error from the "right path," strayed from the road of ancient and Christian tradition. The latter is not only the position of modern Catholic philosophy, but also, and more generally, of all those—and they are very numerous in Europe today and write on a very high level—who see in the secularization of the modern age the roots of the modern world's perplexities. Against "the worst philosophic chaos the world has ever seen,"[6] a "science of order" is summoned up whose essence is the re-subordination of the temporal-political realm to the spiritual, in which the spiritual can be represented by the Catholic Church or the Christian faith in general or by all sorts of revived Platonism.[7] In any event, the subordination is justified in traditional terms—as the inherent superiority of ends over means, the eternal over the temporal. The main impulse is always to bring order into the things of this world, which cannot be grasped and judged without being submitted to the rule of some transcending principle. This impulse is especially strong among those who best know the problems of modern nihilism from their experiences with continental, particularly Central European, historicism and who no longer believe with Meinecke that historicism will be able "to heal the wounds it inflicted [on modern man] through the relativization of values."[8] Yet it is precisely because the revival of tradition owes its impetus to historicism, which taught man to read "as he never read before,"[9] that such a large amount of authentic modern philosophy is contained in interpretations of the great texts of the past. Quite apart from all commitments as to whether or not the breakdown of the authority of tradition is an irreversible event, these interpretations breathe a directness and vitality that is conspicuously absent from the many boring histories of philosophy produced fifty to seventy-five years ago. Those who argue for a return to tradition cannot and do not want to escape the modern climate, and their interpretations therefore frequently bear the marks of Heidegger's influence—he was among the first to read the old texts with new eyes—although they may reject Heidegger's own philosophic tenets altogether. In any event, this contemporary view of the whole extant body of past thought is no less startlingly new, is no less "deforming," and does no less "violence" to reality if judged by Alexandrine standards than is modern art's view of nature.

It is of course no accident that it is the Catholic philosophers who have contributed more significant work to problems of political thought than almost any other modern school. Men like Maritain and Gilson in France, and Guardini and Josef Pieper in Germany exert an influence far beyond the Catholic milieu because they can awaken an almost lost awareness of the relevance of the classical and permanent problems of political philosophy. This, to some extent, they can do because of their blindness to the problem of history and their immunity to Hegelianism. Their shortcomings lie, as it were, in the opposite direction from that of the approach mentioned above. The answers they give to these problems can hardly contain more than restatements of "old truths" and this, i.e., the specifically positive side of their work, is inadequate and even in a way begs the question. For the whole enterprise of restatement had been made necessary by problems whose very perplexity lies in their not being foreseen by the tradition. The return to tradition, therefore, seems to imply much more than the re-ordering of a world that is "out of joint"; it implies the re-establishment of a world that is past. And even if such an enterprise were possible, the question of which of the many worlds covered by one tradition should be re-established could be answered only in terms of arbitrary choice.

In order to avoid this difficulty, the advocates of tradition have shown a definite inclination to minimize the experiences that, among other things, aroused their own concern with politics. The following examples were selected because there exists a certain vague agreement on them.

• The reality of totalitarian domination is depicted almost exclusively under its ideological aspect, with ideologies understood as "secular religions" which either grow out of the "heresy" of secularization and immanentism or are supposed to answer men's assumed eternal need for religion. In both cases, a simple return to right religion appears to be the adequate cure. This interpretation minimizes the shock of the crimes actually committed and dodges the question posed by that aspect of modern society most conspicuous in, but not confined to, totalitarianism—the tendency to deny the relevance of religion and profess an atheism of utter indifference.

• It is true that Catholic thinkers are almost the only ones who consider the problem of labor in other than mere terms of social justice. Yet, by applying to the problem the old terms *vita activa* and *vita contemplativa*, or work and leisure, they overlook the fact that this hierarchical order does not reckon with the entirely novel condition of universal equality, which lies at the source of our present difficulties because it involves not merely the equality of workers as persons, but also the equality of the laboring activity with, and even its precedence over, all others. This is essentially what we mean when we say that we live in a society of jobholders.

• Finally, the global character of contemporary events—which, according to Gilson and others, "distinguishes them from everything earlier, since the beginning of history"[10]—seems to make the establishment of a "universal society" almost a necessity. A universal society, in turn, is possible only if everybody adheres to one principle that can unite all nations because it equally transcends them all. The alternatives seem to be totalitarianism, with its claim to global rule, and Christianity, in whose history the notion of a universal society (in the varied forms of a *civitas Dei*) arose for the first time. Yet again the dangers of the factual situation are minimized and the problem rendered harmless, as it were. Our problem is that our concept of freedom, at least in its political aspects, is inconceivable outside of plurality, and this plurality includes not only different ways but different principles of life and thought. A universal society can only signify a threat to freedom. On the other hand, it is undeniable that under conditions of non-unity every nation feels the consequences and must bear the responsibility (not morally, but in plain political factuality) for every crime and blunder that may be committed at the other end of the world.

These remarks may sound more critical than they are intended to be. As matters stand in the political and social sciences today, we are deeply indebted to the traditional trend in political philosophy for its constant awareness of the crucial questions and its remarkable freedom from all kinds of modern nonsense. In the midst of controversies where it seems so difficult to remember what one is talking about, it would have been enough if they had merely revived and reformulated the old question, What is politics all about? But they have done much more. They have thrown the old answers into the new confusion, and while these may not be wholly adequate to the perplexities that caused the confusion, they are certainly the greatest single help in clarification, and constantly force upon us a sense of relevance and depth.

The French existentialists—Malraux and Camus on one side, Sartre and Merleau-Ponty on the other—with their open rejection of all philosophy antedating the French Revolution and their emphatic atheism, constitute the opposite pole from the modern revival of Thomism. Their dependence upon the work of German contemporary philosophers, notably Jaspers and Heidegger, has been somewhat exaggerated. It is true that they appeal to certain modern experiences that became urgent in France only during and after the Second World War, and these had already been formulated in Germany by the older generation during the twenties. The break with academic philosophy, prepared for even before the first war by Simmel in Germany and Bergson in France, happened in France twenty years later than in Germany. Today, however, this break is much more radical in Paris, where the greater part of significant philosophic work is done and published outside the universities. Moreover, the influence of Pascal, Kierkegaard, and Nietzsche is less marked in France and is supplemented by a strong injection of Dostoevsky and the Marquis de Sade. But all are overshadowed by the influence of Hegel and Marx in France, as distinguished from Germany. Yet what is striking, even at first glance, is that the style and form of expression remain in the line of the French *moralistes* and that the extreme subjectivism of Cartesian philosophy has found here its last and most radical expression.

In our context, the French existentialists stand apart from other trends in modern philosophy in that they are the only ones whose concern with politics is at the very center of their work. For them, it is not a question of finding appropriate philosophic answers to political perplexities; nor are they much interested or particularly skillful in analyzing historical trends and discovering their philosophic relevance. They look, on the contrary, to politics for the solution of philosophic perplexities that in their opinion resist solution or even adequate formulation in purely philosophic terms. This is why Sartre never fulfilled (or mentioned again) his promise at the end of L'Etre et le Néant to write a moral philosophy,[11] but, instead, wrote plays and novels and founded a quasi-political magazine. It is as though that whole generation tried to escape from philosophy into politics; and in this they were preceded by Malraux, who had stated in the twenties: "One always finds the horror in oneself. . . . Fortunately, one can act." Under present circumstances, true action, namely, the beginning of something new, seems possible only in revolutions. Therefore, "the revolution plays . . . the role once played by eternal life"; it "saves those who make it."[12]

In this sense and for these primarily philosophical, rather than social, reasons, the existentialists all became revolutionaries and entered active political life. Sartre and Merleau-Ponty adopted a modified Hegelian Marxism as a kind of *logique* of the revolution, while Malraux and especially Camus continue to insist on rebellion without a historical system or an elaborate definition of ends and means, on *l'homme revolté*, on man in rebellion, in Camus's telling phrase.[13] This difference is important enough, but the original impulse, which the former diluted for the sake of Hegelian metaphysics and the latter kept in great purity, is the same: the point is not that the present world has reached a crisis and is "out of joint," but that human existence as such is "absurd" because it presents insoluble questions to a being endowed with reason.[14] Sartre's nausea before senseless existence, i.e., man's reaction before the sheer density and givenness of the world, coincides with his hatred of the *salauds*, the bourgeois philistines, who in their complacency believe that they live in the best of all possible worlds. The image of the bourgeois is not that of the exploiter, but of this complacent *salaud* who assumes an almost metaphysical significance.[15] The way out of this situation opens when man becomes aware that he is "condemned to be free" (in Sartre's phrase) and "jumps" into action—just as Kierkegaard jumped into belief out of universal doubt. (The Cartesian origin of the existentialist leap is just as manifest in the leap into action as into belief: the springboard being the certitude of individual existence in the midst of an uncertain, incoherent, and incomprehensible universe, which only belief, as in Kierkegaard, can illuminate, or only action can endow with humanly comprehensible meaning.) The disgust with an absurd existence disappears when man discovers that he himself is not given to himself, but through commitment (*engagement*) can become whoever he chooses to be. Human freedom means that man creates himself in an ocean of chaotic possibilities.

It would be a contradiction in terms if this political salvation in a nihilistic situation, or this salvation from thought through action, developed a political philosophy. It cannot even be expected to formulate political principles in the most formal sense, let alone give direction to political choice. As philosophers, the French existentialists can lead to the point where only revolutionary action, the conscious change of a meaningless world, can dissolve the meaninglessness inherent in the absurd relationship between man and world; but they cannot indicate any orientation in terms of their own original problems. From the angle of pure thought, all their solutions bear the hallmark of a heroic futility most noticeable in Camus and Malraux, who hail the old virtues in the spirit of a desperate defiance of their senselessness. Thus Malraux insists that man saves himself from death through the defiance of death in courage. It is because of the illusionary character of all the solutions that originate in their own philosophy that Sartre and Merleau-Ponty simply adopted, superimposed, as it were, Marxism as their frame of reference for action, although their original impulses owed hardly anything to Marxism. It is not surprising that, once they argued themselves out of the impasse of nihilism with essentially identical arguments, they parted company and adopted altogether different positions on the political scene: within the field of action, everything becomes entirely arbitrary as long as it promises revolutionary change.

All this, one may object, holds little hope for political philosophy and more often than not looks like a very complicated game of rather desperate children. The fact is, however, that each of these men has a definite influence on the French political scene and that they, more than any other group, feel obliged to take a stand on everyday questions, to become editors of dailies and address political meetings. Whatever one may hold against them, they have taken seriously the rejection of academic philosophy and the abandonment of the contemplative position. What separates them from Marxism or Gaullism or any other movement they join is, first, in the words of an excellently informed English writer, that they never "seek to validate their reasoning by reference to fixed principles,"[16] and, second, that their revolution is never primarily directed against social or political conditions, but against the human condition as such. Courage, according to Malraux, challenges the human condition of mortality; freedom, according to Sartre, challenges the human condition of "being thrown into the world" (a notion he took over from Heidegger); and reason, according to Camus, challenges the human condition of having to live in the midst of absurdity.

Their common political denominator may be best described as a kind of activist or radical humanism that does not compromise on the old claim that Man is the highest being for man, that Man is his own God. In this activist humanism, politics appears as the sphere where, through the concerted efforts of many, a world may be built that constantly defies and gives the lie to the human condition; this, in turn, will permit human nature, conceived as that of the *animal rationale*, to develop to the point where it builds a reality, creates conditions of its own. Men, then, will move in an entirely humanized, man-made reality, so that the absurdity of human life will cease to exist—not, of course, for the individual, but for mankind in the midst of the human artifice. At least while he is alive, man will live in a world of his own, coherent and ordered and understandable in the light of his own reason. He will defy God or the gods by living as though the limitations of his condition did not exist, even though he as an individual may never hope to escape them. Man can create himself and become his own God if he decides to live as though he were a god. From the paradox that man, though he did not make himself, is held responsible for what he is, Sartre concludes that he therefore must be held to be his own Maker.[17]

The utopian elements in this approach to politics, or, rather, this attempt to save one's soul through political action, are too obvious to be pointed out. It is interesting that the attempt to save human nature at the expense of the human condition comes at a time when we are all too familiar—in totalitarian regimes and, unfortunately, not only there—with attempts to change human nature by radically changing traditional conditions. All the manifold experiments in modern science and politics to "condition" man have no other aim than the transformation of human nature for the sake of society. I am afraid that it would be overly optimistic to claim that these two opposite attempts are equally doomed to failure. With its inherent unpredictability (the "darkness of the human heart," in biblical language)—which philosophically means that it cannot be defined like other things—human nature may be more likely to yield to "conditioning" and transformation (though perhaps only for a limited time) than the human condition itself, which in all circumstances seems to remain the condition under which life on earth is given to man at all.

Compared with French existentialism, the concern with politics in modern German philosophy, where Jaspers and Heidegger have been in the foreground for more than thirty years, is less direct and more elusive. Political convictions hardly play any role there, and even specific philosophic tenets about politics are conspicuously absent. Whatever contributions Jaspers and Heidegger may have made to a political philosophy must be looked for in their philosophies themselves, rather than in books or articles in which they explicitly take positions with respect to contemporary events or implicitly (and then always somewhat equivocally) in critical analyses of the "spiritual situation of the time."[18]

Among all the philosophers we have considered here, Jaspers occupies a unique position in that he alone is a convinced disciple of Kant, which, in our context, carries a special weight. Kant is among the few philosophers to whom the remark of Pascal I quoted above does not apply. Of the three famous Kantian questions—What can I know? What ought I to do? What may I hope?—the second occupies a key position in Kant's own work. Kant's so-called moral philosophy is in essence political, insofar as he attributes to all men those capacities of legislating and judging that, according to tradition, had been the prerogative of the statesman. Moral activity, according to Kant, is legislation—acting in such a way that the principle of my action could become a general law—and to be a "man of good will" (his definition of a good man) means to be constantly concerned, not with obedience to existing laws, but with legislating. The guiding political principle of this legislative moral activity is the idea of mankind.

For Jaspers, not unlike Gilson, the decisive political event of our time is the emergence of mankind from its purely spiritual existence as a utopian dream, or a guiding principle, into an ever present urgent political reality. What Kant therefore once called the philosophic task of future historians, namely, to write a history *"in weltbürgerlicher Absicht"* ("with a cosmopolitan intent"),[19] Jaspers in a way has recently been trying to do as a philosopher, that is, to present a world history of philosophy as the proper foundation for a world-wide political body.[20] This, in turn, has been possible only because in Jaspers' philosophy communication constitutes the "existential" center and becomes actually identical with truth. The adequate attitude of philosophic man in the new global situation is that of "limitless communication," which implies faith in the comprehensibility of all truths along with the good will to reveal and to listen as primary conditions of authentic human being-together. Communication is not an "expression" of thoughts or feelings, which then could be only secondary to them; truth itself is communicative and disappears outside of communication. Thinking, insofar as it must necessarily end in communication if it is to attain to truth at all, becomes practical, though not pragmatic. It is a practice carried out between men rather than the performance of one individual in his self-chosen solitude.

Jaspers, as far as I know, is the only philosopher who ever protested against solitude, to whom solitude appears "pernicious," and who even wants to examine "every thought, every experience, every subject" as to "what they signify for communication. Are they of a kind that may help or of a kind that will prevent communication? Do they seduce one to solitude or excite communication?"[21] Philosophy here becomes the mediator between many truths, not because it holds the one truth valid for all men, but because only in reasoned communication can what each man believes in his isolation from all others become humanly and actually *true*. Here too—albeit in a different way—philosophy has lost its arrogance toward the common life of men; it tends to become *ancilla vitae* for everybody in the sense in which Kant once conceived it, namely, by "carrying the torch in front of her gracious lady rather than the train of her dress behind."[22]

It can easily be seen that Jaspers' cosmopolitan philosophy, though it starts from the same problem of the actuality of mankind, takes an opposite position from that of Gilson and other Catholic thinkers. Gilson maintains: "Reason is what divides us; faith is what unites us,"[23] which, of course, is true if we consider reason to be a solitary capacity, inherent in each of us—who, when we begin to think outside the beaten path of public opinion, will necessarily arrive at strictly individual results. (The notion that innate reason will automatically relate the same thing to all men either perverts the faculty of reason into a purely formal mechanism, a "thinking machine," or presupposes a kind of miracle, which never actually happens.) Faith understood as the opposite of this subjectivistic reason, whose subjectivity is not unlike that of the senses, is bound to some "objective" reality capable of uniting men from the outside, through "revelation," in the recognition of one truth. The trouble with this uniting factor in a future universal society would be that it never exists *between*, but above, men; politically speaking, it would force all men with equal authority under one principle. The advantage of Jaspers' position is that reason can become a universal bond, because it is neither entirely within nor necessarily above men, but, at least in its practical reality, between them. Reason that does not want to communicate is already "unreasonable." We have only to remind ourselves of the twofold definition of man in Aristotle—that man is *dzōon politikon* and *logon echon*, that insofar as he is political he has the faculty of speech, the power to understand, to make himself understood, and to persuade—in order to realize that Jaspers' definitions of reason hark back to very old and authentic political experiences. On the other hand, it seems rather obvious that "communication"—the term as well as the underlying experience—has its roots not in the public political sphere, but in the personal encounter of I and Thou. This relationship of pure dialogue is closer to the original experience of thinking—the dialogue of one with oneself in solitude—than to any other. By the same token, it contains less specifically political experience than almost any relationship in our average everyday lives.

The limitations of Jaspers' philosophy in terms of politics are essentially due to the problem that has plagued political philosophy almost throughout its history. It lies in the nature of philosophy to deal with man in the singular, whereas politics could not even be conceived of if men did not exist in the plural. Or to put it another way: the experiences of the philosopher—insofar as he is a philosopher—are with solitude, while for man—insofar as he is political—solitude is an essential but nevertheless marginal experience. It may be—but I shall only hint at this—that Heidegger's concept of "world," which in many respects stands at the center of his philosophy, constitutes a step out of this difficulty. At any rate, because Heidegger defines human existence as being-in-the-world, he insists on giving philosophic significance to structures of everyday life that are completely incomprehensible if man is not primarily understood as being together with others. And Heidegger himself has been very much aware of the fact that traditional philosophy "has always passed beyond and neglected"[24] what was most immediately apparent. For the same reason Heidegger in his earlier writings studiously avoided the term "man," while in his later essays he is inclined to borrow from the Greeks the term "mortals." What is important here is not the emphasis on mortality, but the use of the plural.[25] However, since Heidegger has never articulated the implications of his position on this point, it may be presumptuous to read too much significance into his use of the plural.

Among the more disturbing aspects of contemporary philosophy may well be the fact that the differences between the various schools and individuals are so much more striking than what they have in common. Whenever discussions between them take place, philosophic chaos is likely to dominate the scene to such an extent that not even significant opposition is possible. To the outsider, however, it frequently appears as though all these considerations and new attempts have developed in and created an identical climate, and this observation contains a certain amount of truth. What they have in common is a conviction of the relevance of philosophy, unlike all those who try to trivialize the urgency of philosophic questions and substitute for them some kind of science or pseudo-science, such as Marxian materialism, or psychoanalysis, or logistics, or semantics, or whatnot. And this negative solidarity against current fashions draws its strength from the common fear that such a thing as philosophy and philosophizing may not be possible and meaningful at all under the circumstances of the modern world. I said above that philosophy has left its proverbial ivory tower and the philosopher has abandoned his claim to the position of the "wise man" within society. Inherent in this abandonment of the traditional position is also a self-doubt about the viability of philosophy, and in this sense concern with politics has become a life-or-death matter for philosophy itself.

The point seems to be that the Hegelian escape from concern with politics into an interpretation of history is no longer open. Its tacit assumption was that historical events and the entire stream of past happenings could make sense and, despite all evil and negative aspects, disclose positive meaning to the backward-directed glance of the philosopher. Hegel could interpret the past course of history in terms of a dialectical movement toward freedom and understand the French Revolution and Napoleon Bonaparte accordingly. Today, nothing appears more questionable than that the course of history in and by itself is directed toward the realization of more and more freedom. If we think in terms of trends and tendencies, the opposite seems far more plausible. Moreover, Hegel's grandiose effort to reconcile spirit with reality depended entirely on the ability to harmonize and see something good in every evil. It remained valid only as long as "radical evil" (of which, among the philosophers, only Kant had the conception, if hardly the concrete experience) had not happened. Who would dare to reconcile himself with the reality of extermination camps or play the game of thesis-antithesis-synthesis until his dialectics have discovered "meaning" in slave labor? Wherever we find similar arguments in present-day philosophy, we remain either unconvinced because of the inherent lack of a sense of reality or we begin to suspect bad faith.

In other words, the sheer horror of contemporary political events, together with the even more horrible eventualities of the future, are behind all the philosophies we have alluded to. It seems to me characteristic that not one of the philosophers has mentioned or analyzed in philosophical terms this background in experience. It is as though in this refusal to own up to the experience of horror and take it seriously the philosophers have inherited the traditional refusal to grant the realm of human affairs that *thaumadzein*, that wonder at what is as it is, which, according to Plato and Aristotle, is at the beginning of all philosophy, yet which even they had refused to accept as the preliminary condition for political philosophy. For the speechless horror at what man may do and what the world may become is in many ways related to the speechless wonder of gratitude from which the questions of philosophy spring.

Many of the prerequisites for a new political philosophy—which in all likelihood will consist in the reformulation of the philosopher's attitude toward the political realm, or of the connection between man as a philosophical and as a political being, or of the relationship between thought and action—already exist, although they may appear at first glance to be concerned with the elimination of traditional obstacles rather than with the erection of a new fundament. Among them are Jaspers' reformulation of truth and Heidegger's analysis of average everyday life, as well as the French existentialists' insistence on action against the old philosophic suspicions of it—"its origin is unknown, its consequences are unknown: therefore has action any value at all?"[26] Crucial for a new political philosophy will be an inquiry into the political significance of thought; that is, into the meaningfulness and the conditions of thinking for a being that never exists in the singular and whose essential plurality is far from explored when an I-Thou relationship is added to the traditional understanding of human nature. Such re-examinations need to remain in contact with the classical questions of political thought as presented to us in many variations in contemporary Catholic philosophy.

But all these are only prerequisites. An authentic political philosophy cannot ultimately arise out of analyses of trends, partial compromises, and reinterpretations; nor can it arise out of rebellion against philosophy itself. Like all other branches of philosophy, it can spring only from an original act of *thaumadzein* whose wondering and hence questioning impulse must now (i.e., contrary to the teaching of the ancients) directly grasp the realm of human affairs and human deeds. To be sure, for the performance of this act the philosophers, with their vested interest in being undisturbed and their professional experience with solitude, are not particularly well equipped. But who else is likely to succeed if they should fail us?

NOTES

1. Vol. 5, the Kröner pocketbook edition, "Blicke in die Gegenwart und Zukunft der Völker," No. 17. Cf. also *Morgenröte*, No. 179.

2. *Pensées*, No. 331, translated by W. F. Trother, Harvard Classics, 1910.

3. This is the title of Eric Voegelin's new book, *A New Science of Politics*, 1952, which aims at a "restoration" of political science in the Platonic spirit.

4. "Das Ding," in *Gestalt und Gedanke*, Jahrbuch der Bayerischen Akademie der Schönen Künste, 1951, 146.

5. *Sein und Zeit*, ¶26 and ¶27. [In what appears to be the first draft of this essay, Arendt offers a somewhat different view:] It is almost impossible to render a clear account of Heidegger's thoughts that may be of political relevance without an elaborate report on his concept and analysis of "world." This is all the more difficult because Heidegger himself has never articulated the implications of his philosophy in this regard, and in some instances has even used terms with connotations that are quite apt to mislead the reader into believing he is dealing with the old prejudice of the philosopher against politics as such, or with the modern rashness of escaping from philosophy into politics. The former finds evidence in Heidegger's much exploited analyses of *das Man*, of public opinion or the "others," as opposed to the "self" and its authentic being, according to which public reality functions to hide true reality and prevent the appearance of truth. The latter finds its support in the interpretation of *Entschlossenheit* (resoluteness), which, since it is understood as a state of being, seems to lack an object. For our purposes what is much more important than these concepts is Heidegger's definition of human being as being-in-the-world.

6. Etienne Gilson, *Les Métamorphoses de la Cité de Dieu*, 1952, 151.

7. Voegelin is a good example of a combination which is not committed to any particular church or school. To him, Plato's ideas, as the invisible measures of the visible world, are later "confirmed through the revelation of the measure itself." Cf. *A New Science of Politics*, 68–78.

8. *Die Entstehung des Historismus*, 1936, I, 5.

9. *Ibid.*, II, 394, in the discussion of Herder: "So hatte noch niemand vor ihm gelesen."

10. Gilson, *op. cit.*, 1ff.

11. Cf. the last sentence of *L'Etre et le Néant*, 1943: "*Toutes ces questions, qui nous renvoient à la réflexion pure et non complice, ne peuvent trouver leur réponse que sur le terrain moral. Nous y consacrerons un prochain ouvrage.*"

12. *La Condition Humaine*, 1933; in English, *Man's Fate*, 1934.

13. This is the title of Camus's last book, *L'Homme Revolté*, 1951.

14. For the absurdity of human existence, see especially Camus's earlier book *Le Mythe de Sisyphe, Essai sur L'Absurde*, 1942.

15. Sartre's pre-war novel *La Nausée*, 1938, is perhaps the most impressive presentation of this attitude.

16. Everett W. Knight, "The Politics of Existentialism," in *Twentieth Century*, August 1954.

17. For this activist humanism, see Sartre's *L'Existentialisme est un humanisme*, 1946, and M. Merleau-Ponty's *Humanisme et Terreur*, 1947.

18. The quotation is the title under which Jaspers published an analysis of trends in modern society, *Die geistige Situation der Zeit*, 1931. In his *Vom Ursprung und Zeil der Geschichte*, 1949, he devotes the second part to an interpretation of the modern world. Both works appeared in English [*Man in the Modern Age*, 1951, and *The Origin and Goal of History*, 1953]. Similar concern with the modern world, though altogether different in content, is found in Heidegger's *Holzwege*, 1950, especially in the essay "Die Zeit des Weltbildes," which in many respects is added to and revised in his recent lecture "Die Frage nach der Technik," in *Die Künste im Technischen Zeitalter*, Jahrbuch der Bayerischen Akademie der Schönen Künste, 1954.

19. In his *Idee zu einer allgemeinen Geschichte in weltbürgerlicher Absicht*, 1784.

20. This is the central intention of his philosophy of history and its thesis of an "axial time of world history" (passing through the fifth century B.C. and becoming the origin of all great world civilizations) as presented in the work cited above [*Vom Ursprung und Ziel der Geschichte*]. Since then, Jaspers has been working on a "world history of philosophy."

21. "Uber meine Philosophie" in *Rechenschaft und Ausblick*, 1951, 350ff.

22. The translation is borrowed from Carl J. Friedrich's *Eternal Peace*, 1948.

23. Gilson, *op. cit.*, 284.

24. "*Ein Blick auf die bisherige Ontologie zeigt, dass mit dem Verfehlen der Daseins-verfassung des In-der-Welt-seins ein Uberspringen des Phänomens der Weltlichkeit zusammengeht.*" *Sein und Zeit*, 65.

25. [The earlier version continues:] One of the decisive handicaps of philosophy in its dealings with politics has always been to speak of man in the singular, as if there were such a thing as one human nature, or as if originally one man inhabited the earth. The trouble has always been that the whole political sphere of human life exists only because of the plurality of men, because of the fact that one man would not be human at all. In other words, all problems of political philosophy begin where traditional philosophy, with its concept of man in the singular, stops.

26. Thus Nietzsche in *Wille zur Macht*, No. 291.

Index

Second World War. *See* World War II

Secularism, 46–47, 369, 372, 379–80, 383–84, 387–88n12, 433–34

Sein und Zeit (Heidegger). *See Being and Time*

Serb National Defense Council, 92–93

Sforza, Count, 86, 87

Shame, 131

Silone, Ignazio, 279

Simmel, Georg, 45, 437

Simms, William Philip, 92

Singing Circle, 62–63

Slavery, 359, 373

Sleepwalkers, The (Broch), 160

Slovak League, 90

Slovak V Amerike, 92

Social class. *See* Class

Social Democratic movement, 7

Socialism, 339. *See also* Communism; Marxism

Sociology: destructuring in, 29, 30, 33–34, 42n3; and human existence, 31–32, 37, 38; vs. philosophy, 29, 31; vs. psychoanalysis, 33–34; and reality, 36–37; and religion, 385–86

Socrates, 173, 183

Solomon, King, 312

Soviet Union, 100, 156–57. *See also* Anti-Stalinism; Communism; Ex-Communists; Stalinism; Totalitarianism; Totalitarian terror

Sozialistische Monatshefte, 7

Spain, 141, 337

Stalin, Josef, 119, 203–4, 344

Stalinism, 275–77, 336–37; and ideology, 203–4, 341, 342, 344; and Marxism, 275–76, 364, 365. *See also* Anti-Stalinism; Totalitarianism

State: and nationalism, 208–9, 210–11; restoration of, 117–20; and truth, 19. *See also* Government; Nationalism

Stein, Alexander, 141

Stein, Heinrich von, 53

Strasser, Gregor, 218

Strasser, Otto, 272

Streicher, Julius, 128

Sturzo, Don Luigi, 86

Suicide, 180, 242, 420

Surrealism, 76

Terror. *See* Totalitarian terror

Tertullian, 380, 390n41

Thought: and class, 29, 43n44; and history, 37, 38; mistrust of, 39; and reality, 33–34; self-conception of, 40; situation-boundness of, 28–30, 33

Tito, Josip Broz, 219, 337

Tocqueville, Alexis de, 22, 410, 411–12, 418, 425

Totalitarianism, 270–71, 281–84, 318–50; and atomization, 346–47; and breakdown of morality, 304–6, 318–19; citizen vs. individual in, 323–24; and conformism, 425; as country-specific, 337–38; and dictatorships, 336–37; and equality, 334–35; and human nature, 407–8; and ideology, 339–46; and law of movement, 330–34, 338–39; and logicality, 294–95, 307–8, 329–30, 345, 346, 347–48; and loneliness, 348–50; and Montesquieu's theories, 304–6, 315n9, 319–28, 333; nihilism of, 431; and political philosophy, 444–45; vs. pragmatism, 307; and religion, 406–7, 435; vs. tyranny, 335–36, 343, 354–55, 358; unprecedented nature of, 299–300, 308–9, 329–30, 335, 338, 358, 405. *See also* Communism; Fascism; Nazi Germany; Nazi terror; Stalinism; Totalitarian terror; Totalitarianism, understanding of

Totalitarianism, understanding of, 297–313; and action, 311–12, 316n19; and forgiving, 298; and history, 299–300, 308–10, 314n3, 315nn12,13, 316nn14–18, 405–6; and imagination, 312–13, 317nn21,22; importance of, 300, 314n4; and indoctrination, 298–99, 313n2; and knowledge, 300–301, 314nn5,6; and logicality, 307–8; and meaninglessness, 303–5, 306–7, 315n10; and philosophy, 312, 317n20; and popular language, 301–3, 314n7, 315n8, 407; and science, 301, 303, 313n1, 314n5, 329; and self-interpretation, 328–29. *See also* Totalitarianism